INTRODUCTION TO THE

TANTRĀLOKA

INTRODUCTION TO THE

TANTRĀLOKA

A Study in Structure

NAVJIVAN RASTOGI

MOTILAL BANARSIDASS
Delhi Varanasi Patna Madras

First Edition: Delhi, 1987

Bungalow Road, Jawahar Nagar, Delhi 110 007

Branches

Chowk, Varanasi 221 001

Ashok Rajpath, Patna 800 004

120 Royapettah High Road, Mylapore, Madras 600 004

ISBN: 81-208-0180-6

PRINTED IN INDIA

BY JAINENDRA PRAKASH JAIN AT SHRI JAINENDRA PRESS, A-45 NARAINA PHASE I, NEW DELHI 110 028 AND PUBLISHED BY NARENDRA PRAKASH JAIN FOR MOTILAL BANARSIDASS, DELHI 110 007.

To the lotus feet of my parents

SHRIMATI INDRANI DEVI
SHRI BITHAL DASS

PREFATORY NOTE

When I accepted the proposal of the publishers to contribute an introduction to the *Tantrāloka* some time back, I welcomed the opportunity to reacquaint myself with the most towering personality of the medieval India. But, when face to face with the text, I could easily gather that it was a sheer case of overestimation of my capacities. In addition to other failings I was confronted with one very serious handicap. I did not know Italian into which R. Gnoli translated the *Tantrāloka.** This has remained a constant drawback. Shortage of time was another major

* I am extremely thankful to Prof. Harvey P. Alper of the Southern Methodist University, Dallas, Texas who very kindly provided an English rendering of the table of contents from Gnoli's translation. I reproduce below the relevant portion of Prof. Alper's letter of the 15th July, 1983 verbatim—

> "The most important thing to note about the introduction to the TĀ is that the vast bulk of it is drawn virtually verbatim from the earlier and longer introduction to the TS! Below I provide a table in which the left hand column lists the sub-sections of the TĀ Introduction, the middle column lists the pages in Gnoli's translation where they appear, while the third column lists the pages from the Introduction to the TS from which they have been taken. Frankly I don't think that this speaks very well of Gnoli: did he have nothing new to say? does he really think that the TĀ is identical *in all respects* to the TS—in spite of the vast difference in length?
>
> The bibliographical information on the TĀ translation is: *Luce delle Sacre Scritture* (*Tantrāloka*) *di Abhinavagupta* (Classici delle religioni, sezione prima: le religions orientali) Torino: Unione Tipografico-editrice torinese, 1972.

handicap. As the *Tantrāloka* is the *magnum opus* of Abhinavagupta, one of the greatest Indian encyclopaedic thinkers of all times, all that I have been able to do is to touch the outer fringe alone of his great contribution.

The *Tantrāloka* is both an inspiration and a challenge for the students of the tantric lore. It is an indispensable guide and no study on tantra should

1. The Śaivite Scriptures	11-14	
2. Schools and Masters	15-19	
3. Kashmiri masters and thinkers of the 9th and 10th centuries	19-20	
4. The school of recognition	20-21	
5. Buddhist and grammatical speculation	21-22	25-27
6. Light (prakāśa) and thought (vimarśa)	22-24	27, 29-33
7. Will	24-25	33-36
8. The theory of images (ābhāśa)	26-27	36-39
9. The I	27-31	29-40, 42-46
10. Language and mantra	31-33	47-49, 51-53
11. Māyā and the divine powers	33-37	53-59
12. The authority of the holy scriptures	37-40	59-63
13. The method of realization	40-42	63-67
14. The vital breath	43-44	67-70
15. The wheel (cakra)	45-46	70-71
16. Initiation (dīkṣā)	46-48	81-83
17. The 36 principles	48-53	83-86, 86-88, 89."

Similarly Goudriaan's following remark about Gnoli's translation is quite illustrative—

"Trsl. into Italian by Raniero Gnoli; Luce delle Sacre Scritturure, Torino 1972, a pioneer work of great merit, although the translator allowed himself too much freedom on some points, while in some cases he paraphrases Jayartha's comments without noticing the reader."

(Hindu Tantric and Śākta Literature, p. 162)

be deemed complete if it does not take the *Tantrāloka* into account. Written on very scientific principles it offers a most uptodate (of course till his period), extremely comprehensive and truly systematic account of the tantric material and thereby offers a model for modern research. It also constitutes the most important single source of authentic tantric information and material. It poses an enormous challenge when it comes to identify the sources cited and decide on their precise whereabouts and the issues involved. A detailed and critical study of the *Tantrāloka* is, therefore, desperately needed for which this *Introduction* cannot even be a poor substitute. However, being guided by Abhinava's own maxim[1] that each small step forward brings us nearer the goal, an humble attempt is contemplated in the following pages. At the moment, besides Gnoli, there is only one study that addresses itself to the study of the *Tantrāloka* proper.[2] Since this study is limited to first three Āhnikas and does not examine other aspects than the philosophical, most of the *Tantrāloka* remains practically unexplored. There are three other

1. ऊर्ध्वोर्ध्वमारुह्य यदर्थतत्त्वं धीः पश्यति श्रान्तिमवेदयन्ती ।
फलं तदाद्यैः परिकल्पितानां विवेकसोपानपरम्पराणाम् ।।
चित्रं निरालम्बनमेव मन्ये प्रमेयसिन्धौ प्रथमावतारम् ।
तन्मार्गलाभे सति सेतुबन्धपुरप्रतिष्ठादि न विस्मयाय ।।
तस्मात्सतामत्र न दूषितानि मतानि तान्येव तु शोधितानि ।
पूर्वप्रतिष्ठापितयोजनासु मूलप्रतिष्ठाफलमामनन्ति ।।

Abhinavabhāratī on N.S. 6.31

2. The Philosophy of the *Tantrāloka* in the First Three Āhnikas with translation into English, by Ira Bajpai, thesis submitted to the Lucknow University for Ph. D. Degree in 1971 (unpublished).

studies[1] which merit special mention here. Pandey and myself have constantly dwelt on the *Tantrāloka*, but the whole exercise becomes of secondary importance because it is Abhinavagupta or Krama system, as the case may be, that is being studied and not the *Tantrāloka* and as such, only the relevant material is being referred to. For example, Pandey's mainstay are the 1st to 5th and 29th Āhnikas, while mine are the 1st, 4th, 13th and 30th. Goudriaan's observations are important, but he takes up the *Tantrāloka* for a very brief treatment.[2] Recently a major work that has come to our notice is the *Upodghāta* (Sanskrit introduction to the *Luptāgamasaṁgraha*[3] by B.V. Dwivedi). It comes as an appendix to the first two volumes of the *Luptāgamasaṁgraha* which are the compilation of citations from the Āgamas in various sources and has assumed the form of an introduction to the 2nd Volume. The *Upodghāta* deals, inter alia, with the citations in the *Tantrāloka* and the *Tantrālokaviveka*. In the first part Dwivedi's perspective is

1. (i) K.C. Pandey — Abhinavagupta : An Historical and Philosophical Study (Abhi.), Chowkhamba, 2nd Edition, 1963.
   (ii) T. Goudriaan and S. Gupta — Hindu Tantric And Śākta Literature (HTSL), A History of Indian Literature—Vol. II-Fasc 2, Wiesbaden, 1981.
   (iii) N. Rastogi — Krama Tantricism of Kashmir (K.T.), Vol. I, Motilal Banarsidass, Delhi, 1979.
2. Cf. HTSL, pp. 5,20, 29, 37, 40 etc., 162.
3. The work was under print at the time of the writing of these lines. The proofcopy was supplied by the author. The *Upodghāta* is being published by Sampurnanand Sanskrit University, Varanasi.

primarily historical while in the 2nd he deals with the doctrinal/theoretical issues in a wider tantric framework. Although the *Tantrāloka* is not Dwivedi's immediate problem, his study throws sufficient light on many aspects particularly the historical one. We shall have occasion to refer to these works as and when necessary.

In this *Introduction* an attempt is made only to introduce the principal work. It should be treated as an elementary study of some of the material which appeared to me more important to begin with. I have taken special precaution to confine myself to the contents of the *Tantrāloka* proper and allow the conclusions emerge on their own. How far I have succeeded in my efforts, it is for the scholars to judge.

The following pages that comprise the *Introduction* actually constitute the Volume One of the ambitious eight-volume reproduction of the KSTS edition by the present publishers in a much enlarged form. During the course of printing it was felt by them that the *Introduction*, if published separately in the form of a book, might serve the needs of common readers better who otherwise would not immediately require the text or are already possessed of the original KSTS text. As the idea sounded reasonable, the Volume One is simultaneously being brought out as an independendent work. I had a keen desire to add one more chapter on the basic/agamic sources of the *Tantrāloka* in the present volume, but the idea had to be abandoned for reasons of time and space. A monograph, to be published shortly, will take care of this desire. The present volume, nevertheless, incorporates a detailed Kārika-wise table of contents in Sanskrit as Appendix 17 which has been divided volume-wise in the reprinted edition of the *Tantrāloka* text.

Before proceeding further I must seek the reader's indulgence for certain inconveniences he is likely to be put to while wading through the pages of the present work. In between the appendices on texts, persons and systems certain words/references may be found common or overlapping leading to some sort of confusion. This has been unavoidable due to one of the following factors—(a) uncertainty about the precise status owing to incomplete data, (b) a word denoting not only a text but also a system or school, (c) a word standing for a person as well as a school. The reader is requested to kindly to bear this in mind.

As the new edition (text reprinted by MLBD) was not available when the printing of the *Introduction* began, all the reference to the text appearing here were made to the volumes of the KSTS edition. This however, would have turned vexatious for the reader of the new edition. It was, therefore, thought desirable and expedient to have references to both the editions e.g., KSTS as well as MLBD, so that the entire community of readers—those who possess the KSTS edition and those who own the MLBD one—may be equally benefitted. All the relevant appendices, accordingly, have been re-done. Moveover, since this decision came when almost the entire *Introduction* (excluding the appendices) had already been printed, a table of conversion comprising Appendix-20 has been appended in order to facilitate the reader. This development has put the publication somewhat behind the original time-schedute.

In the absence of a critically edited text (the editors of the enlarged reprinted edition have not attempted a critical edition of the text for various reasons) some other problems have also surfaced. Under the "Detailed Table of Contents" (Appendix 17), marking of numbers has been a difficult affair. Abhinava has scrupulously adhered to what Jayaratha calls Sañcaya-nyāya (see pp. 76, 164 inside) even in between the individual Kārikās. He usually introduces the next idea in the second half-verse. I have, therefore, followed the practice of the editors of the KSTS edition (retained by the editors of the reprinted edition as well) and have alluded to the subject-matter as being denoted by the existing printed numbering even if the idea has continued upto the first half of the next verse or has already exhausted itself in the second half of the preceding verse. The reader will kindly bear with the occasional over- or under-lapping of certain ideas which has been unavoidable under the circumstances. Exceptions have been made only when I was sure of the completion of an idea in the particular Kārikā/s. In this context a further observation regarding the Detailed Table of Contents may be of some help. Here the basic thrust has been marked by twin objectives—one, it should give a precise idea of the content of the Kārikā/s concerned and two, even a cursory peep into the Table should unravel the underlying thematic progression of the concepts independently of the text. An earnest effort has been made to secure both these ends but, in all fairness, it must be acknowledged that even the limited success has been far from easy to achieve. It is particularly true of the thirty-first Āhnika which has proved most enigmatic.

I have been increasingly conscious of the fact that this *Introduction* has turned out to be an introduction to the study of the *Tantrāloka*, instead of being an introduction to the text itself. In sum, the present endeavour has crystalized into a sort of more or less structural analysis and a groundwork, as it were, for more intensive future investigation in this area.

Before I wind up I must take this opportunity to thank Jain brothers (M/s. N.P. & J.P.), directors of M/s Motilal Banarsidass, for affording me an opportunity to pay once again my tribute to the all-time genius called Abhinavagupta and study a little bit of his *magnum opus*. I am deeply indebted to Prof. Braj Vallabha Dwivedi, the retired Head, Yoga & Tantra Department, Sampurnanand Sanskrit University, who was extremely generous in sending the proof-copy of his Upodghāta to the *Luptāgama-saṁgraha*. I am also thankful to him for discussing the proposed format and scope of the *Introduction*, although I am guilty of not using some of his suggestions with regard to the discussion on philosophical/doctrinal matters. My reasons for eschewing philosophical issues are simple. Something must be said over and above what has already been said by Pandey and other learned scholars. With the limited amount of time at my command it was not possible to make such a deep study as is demanded by philosophical and theoretical issues. I am indeed beholden to Thakur Jaidev Singh, a great authority of our times on Kashmir Śaivism, for offering his valuable suggestions about the proposed direction and contents of the *Introduction*. Prof. H. P. Alper of the Southern Methodist University, USA has put me under a dept by discussing the proposed format and agenda of the *Introduction* and for finding time to translate 'contents' of Gnoli's *Introduction* to his celebrated translation. In this context I am happy to record my appreciation of the kind gesture of Dr. Andre Padoux (Direetor, Centre National De La Recherche Scientifique, Paris) in presenting a copy of Naudou's valuable book to me. I must remember two more scholars with gratitude. It was Dr. Ashok Kumar Kalia's (my esteemed colleague in the Department of Sanskrit, Lucknow University) idea to furnish all available information in respect of the texts cited by Abhinava and Jayaratha. Dr. Mark Dyczkowski, then camping in India, made this work easier by allowing me to have a photostat copy of the relevant extracts from some of the MSS - catalogues, so assiduously compiled by him. As a result the Appendix One was completely revised for which I once again thank these two friends. Dr. Kalia has also earned my gratitude for going through the entire Table of Contents (Viṣayānukramaṇikā in Sanskrit) and suggesting various improvements. The list will remain incomplete without mention of my esteemed friends, Professors Harsh Narain (of late Visiting Professor of Philosophy, Aligarh University) and Kameshwar Nath Misra (Central Institute of Higher Tibetan Studies, Sarnath) and Dr. J. P. Sinha (my senior colleague in the Department of Sanskrit, Lucknow University) for maintaining sustained and constructive interest in the progress of the work. I also sincerely thank Drs. K.S. Pandey, H.S.B. Sinha and Sri K.M. Vishnoi for valuable secretarial assistance. Besides, I remember Dr. M. R. Yadav with affectionate gratitude for his manifold selfless cooperation.

This *Introduction* is now being humbly placed

before the discerning judgement of the scholars for what it is worth with a citation from the *Tantrāloka* itself :

अध्युष्टसंततिस्रोतःसारभूतसाहृतिम् ।
विधाय तन्त्रालोकोऽयं स्यन्दते सकलान् रसान् ॥

(T.A. 36.45)

Lucknow,
Mahāśivarātri, '86. Navjivan Rastogi

CONTENTS

ABBREVIATIONS

Abhi.	Abhinavagupta: An Historical and Philosophical Study
A. Bh.	Abhinava-bhāratī
Āh.	Āhnika
Comm.	Commentary
Dh. L.	Dhvanyāloka-locana
H.T.S.L.	Hindu Tantric and Śākta Literature
I.P.K.	Īśvara-pratyabhijñā-kārikā
I.P.K.V.	Īśvara-pratyabhijñā-kārikā-vivṛti
I.P.V.	Īśvara-pratyābhijñā-vimarśinī
I.P.V. (Bh.)	Bhāskarī on Īśvara-pratyabhijñā-vimarśinī
I.P.V.V.	Īśvara-pratyābhijñā-vivṛti-vimarśinī
J.M.V.	Janma-maraṇa-vicāra
K.M.	Kāvyamālā
K.S.	Kashmir Śaivism
K.S.S./K.S.T.S.	Kashmir Series of Texts & Studies
K.T.	Krama Tantricism of Kashmir: Vol. I
M.M.P.	Mahārtha-mañjarī-parimala
M.P. (T)	Mahānaya-prakāśa (Trivendrum Sanskrit Series)
M.S./MSS	Manuscript/s
M.V.T.	Mālinī-vijayottara-tantra
M.V.V.	Mālinī-vijaya-vārtika
Nagarajan	Contribution of Kashmir to Sanskrit Literature (by K.S. Nagarajan)
N.S.	Nāṭya Śāstra
N.S.T.	Nityā-ṣoḍaśikārṇava (-tantra)
Philosophy	The Philosophy of the Tantrāloka in the First Three Āhnikas with Translation into English
P.T.	Parā-triṁśikā or Parā-triśikā
P.T.V.	Parā-triṁśikā-vivaraṇa
Sp.K.	Spanda-kārikā
S.T.	Śāradā-tilaka (-tantra)
SV.T/Sv.T	Svaccanda-tantra

SV.T.U. /S.T.U.	Svaccanda-tantra-uddyota
T.A.	Tantrāloka
T.A.V.	Tantrāloka-viveka
T.S.	Tantra-sāra
Tā.Sā.	Tāntrika Sāhitya
T.V.D.	Tantra-vaṭa-dhānikā
Upodghāta	Upodghāta to the Luptāgamasaṁgraha
V.M.V.	Vāmakeśvarī-mata-vivaraṇa

SELECT BIBLIOGRAPHY

Abhinavagupta

(i) Abhinavabhāratī (A. Bh.), a commentary on the Nāṭya Śāstra, Vol. I, ed. Ramkrishna Kavi, 2nd edition, Baroda, 1956.

(ii) Mālinī-vijayottara-vārtika, ed. M. S. Kaul, KSTS No. XXXI, 1921.

(iii) Paramārthasāra, with Vivṛti by Yogarāja, ed. J. C. Chatterji, KSTS No. VII, 1916.

(iv) Parātriṁśikā-vivaraṇa (P.T.V.), ed. M. R. Shastri, KSTS No. XVIII, 1918.

(v) Tantrasāra (T.S.), ed. M.R. Shastri, KSTS No. XVII, 1918.

(vi) Tantrāloka, with 'Viveka' by Jayaratha, 12 volumes (Part I ed.by M.R. Shastri and Parts II-XII ed. by M. S. Kaul), KSTS, 1918-1938.

(vii) Tantravaṭadhānikā, ed. M. R. Shastri, KSTS No. XXIV, 1918.

Bajpai, Ira

The Philosophy of the Tantrāloka in the First Three Āhnikas with Translation into English, doctoral thesis submitted to the Lucknow University, 1971 (unpublished).

Dwivedi, B. V.

(i) Upodghāta (Upodghāta) to the Luptāgama-saṁgraha, Vol. II, S. Sanskrit University, Varanasi, 1984.

(ii) Upodghāta to the Nityāṣoḍaśikārṇava with two commentaries—Ṛjuvimarśinī and Artharatnāvalī, S. Sanskrit University, Varanasi, 1968.

Gnoli, R.

(i) Luce delle Sacre Scritture (Tantrāloka) di Abhinavagupta, translated into Italian with Introduction, Torino, 1972.

(ii) Essenza dei Tantra, translation of the Tantrāsāra with notes in Italian, with a long introduction by R. Gnoli, Torino, 1960.

Gonda, Jan

Medieval Religious Literature in Sanskrit (A History of Indian Literature Vol. II), Wiesbaden, 1977.

Goudriaan, T. and gupta, S. Hindu Tantric and Śākta Literature [HTSL] (A History of Indian Literature Vol. II-*Fasc* 2), Wiesbaden, 1981.

Jayaratha Vāmakeśvarīmata-vivaraṇa, ed. M.K. Shastri, KSTS No. LXVI, 1945.

Kane, P. V. The History of Sanskrit Poetics (published together with the Sāhityadarpaṇa of Viśvanātha), 3rd edition, Bombay, 1951.

Kaviraj, G. N. Tāntrika Sāhitya (Tā. Sā.), Hindi Samiti, Lucknow, 1972.

Misra, K. K. Significance of the Tantric Tradition, Varanasi, 1981.

— Mālinīvijayottara Tantra, ed. M. S. Kaula, KSTS No. XXXVII, 1922.

Nagarajan, K. S. Contribution of Kashmir to Sanskrit Literature (contribution), doctoral thesis submitted to the University of Poona, 1961 (unpublished).*

Naudou, Jean Buddhists of Kashmir, translated from French into English by Brereton & Picron, Delhi, 1980.

Pandey, K. C. Abhinavagupta : An Historical and Philosophical Study (Abhi.), 2nd revised edition, Varanasi, 1963.

Pathak, V. S. History of Śaiva Cults in Northern India (From Inscriptions 700 A.D. to 1200 A.D.), ed. G. C. Pandey, Allahabad, 1980.

— Pratiṣṭhālakṣaṇasārasamuccaya, ed. Damodar Sharma, two volumes, Nepal, Saṁ-2023.

Raghavan, V. (i) Abhinavagupta and His Works, Varanasi-Delhi, 1981.

(ii) New Catalogus Catalogorum, Vols. I-XI, University of Madras, 1935-82.

Rastogi, N. (i) The Krama Tantricism of Kashmir (K.T.),

*While these lines were under print we came to learn from Dr. Kosellya Walli, University of Jammu, that the work has since been published by the author.

Vol. I (Historical and General Sources), Delhi, 1979.

(ii) Abhinavagupta Ke Stotra: Eka Adhyayana, dissertation submitted to the Lucknow University for partial completion of postgraduate course, 1959 (unpublished).

Silburn, L. Le Paramārthasāra de Abhinavagupta, Translation into French with Introduction, Paris, 1979.

— Svacchanda Tantra (SV.T), with Uddyota by Kṣemarāja (SV.T.U.), 6 volumes (Vol. 5 in two parts), KSTS, 1921-35.

Yogin, Madhurāja Gurunātha-Parāmarśa,

(i) ed. P. N. Pushp, published in Kashmir Research Bi-annual, Vol. I, Srinagar, 1960 (later published as KSTS No. 85);

(ii) ed. V. Raghavan, included in his "Abhinavagupta and His works".

CATALOGUES

An Alphabetical List of Manuscripts in the Oriental Institute, Baroda, ed. R.N. Shiromani, two vols., GOS XCVII & CXIV, Baroda, 1942/1950.

Āryabhāṣā Pustakālaya Nāgarī Pracāriṇī Sabhā Kāśī Meṃ Upalabdha Hastalikhita Saṁskṛta-granthasūcī, ed. S. Pandey, K. Tripathi and M Tewari, IInd Vol., Varanasi, 1967.

Bhāratīya Itihāsa Saṁśodhaka-Maṇḍalasthā Hastalikhitagranthānukramaṇikā, ed. Khare K.H. Ganesh, Shivajinagar, 1960.

Catalogue of Sanskrit Manuscripts in the Raghunath Temple Library of His Highness the Maharaja of Jammu and Kashmir, ed. M.A. Stein, Bombay, 1894.

A Catalogue of Palm Leaf and Selected Paper Manuscripts belonging to the Darbar Library, Nepal, ed. H.P. Sastri and C. Bendall, two volumes, Calcutta 1905, 1908.

Catalogue of the Sanskrit MSS in the Sanskrit College Library, Benaras, 1911 antra Section).

Catalogue of VVRI Manuscript Collection, two parts, ed. Viśvabandhu and others, Hoshiarpur, 1960.

A Catalogue of Sanskrit and Prakrit Manuscripts in the Rajasthan Oriental Research Institute (Jodhpur Collection), ed. Muni Jina Vijaya, Jodhpur, 1963.

Catalogue of Sanskrit Manuscripts in the Punjab University Library, Vol. I, (Sections VIII-IX), 1932.

A Descriptive Catalogue of the Sanskrit Manuscripts in the Collections of the Royal Asiatic Society of Bengal, Vol. VIII, Pts. I & II, ed. Chintaharaṇa Chakravarti, Calcutta, 1938, 1940.

Descriptive Catalogue of Raj Manuscripts preserved in the Kameshwar Singh Sanskrit University Library, Darbhanga, ed. B.R. Sarma, Darbhanga, 1969.

A Descriptive Catalogue of the Sanskrit Manuscripts in the Private Library of His Highness Srīrājarājeśvara Mahārājādhirāja Mahārājā Sri Harisinghjī Bahādur of Jammu and Kashmir, ed. Ramcanda Kāk and Nowabhatta Shastri, Poona, 1927.

Descriptive Catalogue of the Sanskrit Manuscripts in the Government Oriental Manuscripts Library, Madras, Vols. X & XII-XV, Madras, 1910-1913.

A Descriptive Catalogue of the Government Collection of Manuscripts deposited at the Bhandarkar Oriental Research Institute, ed. H.D. Sharma, Vol. XVI, Pt. II, Poona, 1976.

A Descriptive Catalogue of the Sanskrit Manuscripts in the Tanjore Maharaja's Sarfoji's Saraswati Mahal Library, ed. P.P.S. Sastri, Srirañgam, Vols. XVIII-XIX.

A Descriptive Catalogue of Sanskrit Manuscripts in the Curator's Office Library, Trivendrum, Vol. V, ed. by K. Mahadeva Sastri; Vol. VI, ed. by P.K. Narain Pillai, Trivendrum, 1939-40.

Descriptive Catalogue of Sanskrit Manuscripts in the Gaekwad Library, Bhārata Kalā Bhavan and Sanskrit Mahāvidyālaya Library, Banaras Hindu University, Vol. VI, ed. R.S. Tripathi, Varanasi, 1971.

Śrīnepālarāṣṭrīyābhilekhālayasthā Hastalikhitapustakānām Bṛhacchūcīpatram, ed. Buddhisagar Sharma, Vol. IV (in two parts), Kathmandu, 1964-1969.

CHAPTER ONE

EXPLORING THE TANTRĀLOKA

Strange as it may appear, the *Tantrāloka* happens to be the only major 'original' work of Abhinava while his all other important works[1] come to us in the form of a commentary on some earlier valuable text notwithstanding his own description of the *Tantrāloka* as a gloss, as we shall see in the sequel.

(i) *Traditional Approach to the Tantrāloka*

A peep into and a look around the *Tantrāloka* offers many illuminating insights. Towards twelfth century Śivānanda, the author of the *Ṛjuvimarśinī*, refers to it as the *Trika-śāstra*[2] or *Trika-sāraśāstra*[3] and the verses cited are traceable to the published edition of the *Tantrāloka*. It, therefore, appears that by that time it came to be regarded as the most representative text of Trika system. Kṣemarāja, the illustrious pupil of Abhinavagupta, talks of two characteristics of the text. One, it was composed in the state of Absolutic trance[4] and other, it is a key to the secrets of entire

1. Abhinava's other major works include A.Bh. (Comm. on the N.S.), I.P.V (Comm. on I.P.K.), I.P.V.V. (Comm. on the I.P.K.V.) and Locana (Comm. on the Dh. L.).

2. तदुक्तं श्रीत्रिकशास्त्रे । NST with Ṛjuvimarśinī and Artharatnāvalī, ed. B.V. Dvivedi, Varanasi, p. 19. The verses quoted are traceable to T.A. 3.94-95.

3. तदुक्तं श्रीत्रिकसारशास्त्रे । Ibid., pp. 138-139. The verses are traceable to T.A. 15.285-287.

4. परभैरवस्फारमयैरस्मद्गुरुभिरपि तन्त्रालोके । S.T.U., I, pp. 39-40

agamic literature.[1] In the *Tantrasāra*, Abhinavagupta invariably describes the *Tantrāloka* as a detailed treatise and asks the author to turn for detailed discussion of the problem to the latter which incorporates all the prescriptive and negative injunctions emanating not only from Vedic but from Śaiva, Tantra and Trika sources also.[2] The view has been consistently hammered again and again.[3] According to the *Tantrasāra*, the *Tantrāloka* was not only a repository of agamic lore but a critical text which minutely recorded even internal and mutual divergences.[4] Thus the image of the *Tantrāloka* as a single, extra-comprehensive and authoritative source book appears to have been projected by Abhinavagupta himself. The central theme of the *Tantrāloka*, according to Abhinavagupta in his *Locana*[5], however revolves round

1. यदुक्तमस्मद्गुरुभिः अशेषागमोपनिषदालोके तन्त्रालोके ।
Ibid., III, p. 268

2. तस्मात् वैदिकात् प्रभृति पारमेश्वरसिद्धान्ततन्त्रकुलोच्छुष्मादिशास्त्रोक्तोऽपि यो नियमो विधिः वा निषेधो वा तथैव च उक्तं श्रीपूर्वादौ वितत्य तन्त्रालोकात् अन्वेष्यम् । T.S., p. 32

3. वितत्य चैतत् निर्णीतं तन्त्रालोके । Ibid., p. 97

* * *

एतच्च प्रपञ्चितं प्रथमत एव, तथा नवधा मुख्यतयैश्वरः शक्तिपातः इति सुविवेचितं श्रीतन्त्रालोकादौ । I.P.V.V., III, p. 279

* * *

एतच्च विस्तरतस्तत्प्रधानेषु तन्त्रालोकसारादिषु मया निर्णीतम् ।
I.P.V(Bh.), II, p. 242

* * *

एतदेव च वितत्य श्रीतंत्रालोके प्रतिपादितम् ।
Janma-maraṇa-vicāra, Bhaṭṭavāmadeva, KSS, 1918, p. 19

4. अत्र च परस्परं भेदकलनया अवान्तरभेदज्ञानकुतूहली तन्त्रालोकमेव अवधारयेत् । J.M.V., p. 99

5. ये अप्यविभक्तं स्फोटं वाक्यं तदर्थरूपमाहुस्तैरप्यविद्यापदपतितैः सर्वैयमनुसरणीया प्रक्रिया । तदुत्तीर्णत्वे तु सर्वं परमेश्वराद्वयं ब्रह्मेत्यस्मच्छास्त्रानुसारेण विदितं तन्त्रालोकग्रन्थं विचारयतेत्यास्ताम् ।
Dhvanyāloka-locana, K.M., IV, N.S., 1928, p. 19

the transcendental Absolutic reality called Brahman (i.e. Anuttara). The prime concern of the *Tantrāloka* was to explain, to unfold and to explore. It therefore assumed the form of a gloss, or a commentary and was therefore termed as the *Vārtika*[1] (gloss), *Śloka-vārtika*[2] (versified gloss) and *Ṣaḍardhaślokavārtika* (versified gloss on Trika system).[3] Possibly in designating the *Tantrāloka* as *Vārtika* Abhinavagupta was inspired by Kātyāyana's example in whose case Vārtika is defined as "an explanatory or supplementary rule which explains the meaning of that which is said, of that which is left unsaid, and of that which is imperfectly said."[4] This amply applies to the *Tantrāloka* as we shall have occasion to see later. Elsewhere in a very significant remark Abhinavagupta describes the *Tantrāloka* as a mix of all the varieties (e.g. brief, regular and large) of glossarial work based on Āgamas. Thus it is a Vārtika, a Bhāṣya and a Vṛtti all at

1. मया च वार्तिके एतत् व्याख्यातम् । I.P.V.V., III, p. 259
The verses purportedly quoted from the Vārtika here are the same as the T.A. 1.152-155.

2. अन्वर्थं चात्र दर्शितं तन्त्रालोके श्लोकवार्तिके च । Ibid., pp. 106-7
The use of 'ca' is very ambiguous and may lead one to conclude that the *Tantrāloka* and *Ślokavārtika* were two independent texts (vide K.T., p. 159). But in view of the overwhelming collateral textual evidence as produced above and non-discovery of any text by the name of the *Ślokavārtika* (pertaining to K.S.) so far it seems appropriate to identify the two. My earlier view on this stands modified (vide K.T., p. 159). In such a situation the text is to be construed as under—

अन्वर्थं चात्र दर्शितं श्लोकवार्तिके तन्त्रालोके च ।

3. यथोक्तं मयैव श्रीषडर्धश्लोकवार्तिके तन्त्रालोके । I.P.V.V., I, p. 33

4. उक्तानुक्तदुरुक्तार्थव्यक्ति (चिंता) कारि तु वार्तिकम् ।
The Student's Sanskrit-English Dictionary, V.S. Apte, Delhi, 1959, p. 503

a time.[1] It is perhaps the reason why Abhinava's interpretations-cum-explanations on specific issues in the *Tantrāloka* are recalled as testimony.[2] The *Tantrāloka* was also known as *Tantrāvaloka*.[3]

(ii) *Four motives behind the composition*

(a) Saṁgraha-Grantha

Abhinavagupta composed the *Tantrāloka* from several angles. Obviously the first and the most striking intention of his is to present a digest of the available tantric literature and lore.[4] Technically, therefore, the *Tantrāloka* is a compendium (Saṁgraha-grantha)[5]. In creating a compendium Abhinavagupta's primary objective seems to handle not only the Trika material alone in its tantric sources, but the non-Trika material in its agamic sources as well.[6] Abhinavagupta himself sets at rest all conjectures in this regard. His avowed intention is to introduce all the agamic material in its varied sources[7]. Abhinavagupta has been, therefore, quite appropriately hailed

1. अस्गाभिस्तु आगमग्रन्थनिष्ठे वार्तिकभाष्यवृत्तिग्रन्थे श्रीतंत्रालोकादौ प्रपञ्चो न्यक्षेण दर्शितः । I.P.V.V., III, p. 304

2. तदुक्तं निशाटनाख्यागमव्याख्याने तंत्रालोके । Paraśurāmakalpasūtra, Baroda, 1950, p. 44

3. तदुक्तं तन्त्रावलोके । Śrīnivāsabudha in his Dīpikā on the Tripurā-rahasya, Jñānakhaṇḍa, Varanasi, p. 193

4. इदमभिनवगुप्तप्रोम्भितं शास्त्रसारं
शिव निशमय तावत् सर्वतः श्रोत्रतन्त्रः । T.A. 37.85

5. ग्रन्थकृता निखिलषडर्धशास्त्रसारसंग्रहभूतग्रन्थकरणेऽप्यधिकारः कटाक्षीकृतः । T.A.V., I, pp. 14-15

6. अस्य ग्रन्थस्यापि निखिलशास्त्रान्तरसारसंग्रहाभिप्रायत्वं प्रकाशितम् । Ibid., I, pp. 29-30

7. अध्युष्टसंततिस्रोतः सारभूतरसाहृतिम् ।
विधाय तन्त्रालोकोऽयं स्यन्दते सकलान् रसान् ॥ T.A. 36.15

as Saṁgrahakāra[1] and the *Tantrāloka* as the *Saṁgraha*[2] by Jayaratha.

(b) Prakriyā or Paddhati Grantha

Abhinavagupta's second, but rather more significant, intention is to produce a Prakriyā or Paddhati, perhaps employed as interchangeable terms in the context. Abhinavagupta was perturbed over the fact that there was no Paddhati text in his source-system, i.e. the system of transcendental triad (Anuttara-ṣaḍardhārthakrama), although there were plenty of them in other source systems.[3] In order to overcome this drawback he decided to write the present *Prakriyā* i.e., *Tantrāloka*, complete in all respects.[4] Abhinavagupta and Jayaratha both do not give any clue to Abhinavagupta's concept of a Prakriyā-grantha, although Jayaratha is full of references to Abhinavagupta's professed aim to undertake a Prakriyāgrantha.[5] In this context one comes across four observations:

(i) The Prakriyā under reference namely, the *Tantrāloka*, is totally based on the *M.V.T*;[6]

Jayaratha's introductory observation preceding the above verse is very suggestive—

ननु इह त्रैयम्बिकैव मठिका वक्तुं न्याय्या यद्द्वारा अस्य शास्त्रस्य आयातिः किं मठिकान्तरव्यावर्णनेनेत्याशंक्याह T.A.V., XII, p. 389

1. एतच्चोत्तानतयैव गृहीत्वा संग्रहकाराः प्रवृत्ताः. . . . . . . । T.A.V., V, p. 19 (8th Āh.)
2. इह. . . . . . . .प्रक्रान्तेऽपि संग्रहे स्वकण्ठेनैव पाठेऽयमाशयो. . . . . । Ibid., p. 186
3. सन्ति पद्धतयश्चित्राः स्रोतोभेदेषु भूयसा ।
अनुत्तरषडर्धार्थक्रमे त्वेकापि नेक्ष्यते ॥ T.A. 1.14
4. अर्थितो रचये स्पष्टां पूर्णार्थां प्रक्रियामिमाम् ॥ Ibid. 1.15
5. ननु सामान्येन त्रिकदर्शनप्रक्रियाकरणं प्रतिज्ञाय. . . . . । T.A.V., I, p. 35
6. न तदस्तीह यन्न श्रीमालिनीविजयोत्तरे । T.A. 1.17

(ii) There were two Prakriyās within the monistic fold namely, Kula-prakriyā and Tantra-prakriyā;

(iii) Kula Prakriyā is superior of the two;[1] and both together represent Trikaprakriyā;

(iv) A sizable section of the learned scholars subscribing to the system but not possessing uninterrupted tradition required a guide in respect of the matters they did not know. The *Tantrāloka's* composition as *Prakriyā* was a significant step towards fulfilling this desideratum.[2]

Now let us see what the *Tantrāloka* as a Prakriyā text means. If we compare the *T.A.* 1.14 and 1.15, we find that Prakriyā and Paddhati denote the same thing. Another thing to be noted is that both terms stand for a particular class of books. Naturally the grammarian's usage of Prakriyā in the sense of an etymological work does not fit in here. The *Vācaspatyam* includes among its meanings a chapter or a section (Prakaraṇa) which lays down an order[3] and the *Śabdakalpadruma* interprets it as a "definite procedure"[4] (Niyatavidhi). Similarly, Paddhati is taken to stand for a treatise that brings out the gist or the

1. एवं च तन्त्रप्रक्रियोपासन्नगुर्वभिमुखीकरणानन्तरं विश्रान्तिस्थानतया कुलप्रक्रियागुरुमपि उत्कर्षयति । T.A.V., I, p. 31

2. अतोऽत्रान्तर्गतं सर्वं संप्रदायोज्झितैर्बुधैः ।
अदृष्टं प्रकटीकुर्मो गुरुनाथाज्ञया वयम् ॥ T.A. 1.19
अत इति उक्तयुक्त्यास्यैव शास्त्रस्य प्राधान्यात्। "प्रकटीकुर्म" इति प्रक्रियाकरणेन । T.A.V., I, p. 50

3. प्रकरणे "सा प्रक्रिया या क्रममित्यपेक्ष्य" पार्थसारथिमिश्रः ।
Vācaspatyam, VI Part, Varanasi, 1962, p. 4438

4. नियतविधिः इति शब्दरत्नावली ।
Śabdakalpadruma, Part III, Varanasi, 1967, p. 245

essential meaning. The *Vācaspatyam*[1] and *Śabdakalpadruma*[2], both lexicons agree and both cite Hemacandra[3] in support. Thus we see that according to these lexicographers a Prakriyā text constitutes a work or a section thereof composed to convey the essential purport of the subject and to lay bare the procedure, if any, involved in realizing the primary purpose. A close examination of Abhinava will reveal that his concept of the Prakriyā or Paddhati was closer to the above definition.

Abhinava refers to the *P.T.V.* as *Anuttaraprakriyā*.[4] It will simply amount to saying that the *P.T.V.* was also a Prakriyā-grantha.[5] Abhinava's use of the word Prakriyā elsewhere reminds[6] one of something relat-

1. पन्थस्य निष्कृष्टार्थबोधके ग्रन्थभेदे (हेमचन्द्रः) ।
Vācaspatyam, Vol. V, p. 4225

2. "ग्रन्थार्थबोधकग्रन्थः" इति हेमचंद्रः ।
Śabdakalpadruma, Part III, p. 40

3. Hemacandra's observations as per footnotes above assume significance because Hemacandra was quite close to Abhinava chronologically—a gap of a century obtained between the two—and was in know of Abhinava's works as his treatment of Rasa in the *Kāvyānuśāsana* betrays unmistakeable impact of Abhinava's *Abhinavabhāratī*.

4. अनुत्तरप्रक्रियायां वैतत्येन प्रदर्शितम् । T.A. 9.313

5. A question may naturally arise as to whether there were two Prakriyās on Anuttaratrika System, because as Abhinava has already said, that (vide Fn. 3, p.5 supra) there were no Prakriyā texts or Paddhatis on his system. The answer perhaps lies in the fact that, as we shall see later, the *P.T.V.*, *M.V.V.* and *T.A.* constitute one whole and as such may be part of a larger textual framework.

6. तत्राध्वैवं निरूप्योऽयं यतस्तत्प्रक्रियाक्रमम् ।
अनुसंदधेव द्राग् योगी भैरवतां व्रजेत् ॥
T.A., 8.5; Jayaratha explains
प्रक्रियाक्रमम् as कालाग्न्यादेरनाश्रितपर्यन्तं तथातथानुपूर्व्येण अवस्थानम् ।
T.A.V., V, p. 4

ing to practice or Sādhanā. The idea becomes clearer when Abhinava concludes that in the *SV.T.* knowledge does not involve action or practice.[1] Jayaratha leaves no doubt that the mutual difference between the several Tantras, even though sometimes belonging to the same sect, stems from the practices enjoined.[2] This leaves us in no doubt that Prakriyā must have meant a special practice—intra- and trans-ritualistic both—and the text that lays down the relative code is a Prakriyā-grantha. The other term used in this context by Abhinava is Paddhati, as we all know. What was his model we do not know. However he refers to one *Paddhati* by Īśānaśiva[3] which clearly brought out the essential procedure as laid down in the famous Krama Āgama *Devyāyāmala.* This Īśānaśiva is, no doubt, different from his namesake author of the *Gurudevapaddhati* or *Tantrapaddhati* and who definitely flourished after 1073 A.D. and was, according to Dwivedi, identical with the great-grand tea-

1. न प्रक्रियापरं ज्ञानमिति स्वच्छन्दशासने ।

TA., 8.11; Jayaratha adds

यदुक्तं तत्र "नास्ति दीक्षासमो मोक्षो न विद्या मातृका परा ।
न प्रक्रियापरं ज्ञानं नास्ति योगस्त्वलक्षकः ॥" (SV. T. 11.198)

2. इह (त्रिशिरोभैरवे) च अनन्तस्य श्रीसिद्धातन्त्रोक्तं भुवनमानं न ग्राह्यमेव "क्रियादिभेदभेदेन तन्त्रभेदो यतः स्मृतः ।
तस्माद् यत्र यदेवोक्तं तत्कार्यं नान्यतन्त्रतः ॥" इत्याद्युक्त्या तत्प्रक्रियाया भिन्नत्वात् ।
T.A.V., V, p. 16

3. मोक्षायैव न भोगाय भोगायाप्यभ्युपायतः ।
इत्युक्तवान् स्वपद्धत्यामीशानशिवदेशिकः ॥
श्रीदेव्यायामलीयोक्तितत्त्वसम्यक्प्रवेदकः । T.A. 22.30-31

Jayaratha's interpretation of the term Abhyupāya removes the last tinge of difference between Paddhati and Prakriyā—

अभ्युपायत इति भोगोपायभूतशास्त्रप्रक्रियाद्यनुसारेणेत्यर्थः ।

Ibid., X, p. 254

cher of Somaśambhu, the author of the *Karmakāṇḍa-kramāvalī.*[1] Dharmaśiva, a teacher of Abhinava—if we go by the authority of Kṣemarāja[2]—also wrote one *Paddhati* which had the 'indirect initiation' as its central theme and it is which has been referred to by Abhinava[3], though not by name. These are possibly the Paddhatis whose presence led Abhinava to lament the absence of one in his own system. The *Siddha-siddhānta-paddhati*, the famous text of Nātha cult, which is much later, a text full of references to Pratyabhijñā system, similarly seems to be a work in Paddhati tradition. Dwivedi refers to several Paddhatis such as the *Udayākarapaddhati*[4] and *Varuṇa Paddhati*[5] and Maheśvarānanda in his *M.M.P.* refers to one *Mahānayapaddhati.*[6] It may be, therefore, quite logical to conclude that the *Tantrāloka* was a text in Paddhati or Prakriyā tradition and was composed as a complete manual for the adherents of the Trika way of life.

(c) Śāstra Grantha

The third intention of Abhinava was to project the *Tantrāloka* as a full-fledged Śāstra (scripture) or Śāsana.[7] As such it turned out to be a Prakriyā Śāstra

1. For details see Upodghāta, p. 21. Also see 'History of Śaiva Cult in Northern India', B.S. Pathak, Delhi, 1980, pp. 46-50.
2. एते च धर्मशिवाचार्येण स्वपद्धतौ "एतेषां लक्षणं वच्मो गुरुपरम्परागतम्" इत्युपक्रम्य इत्थं व्याख्याताः । SV. T.U., VI, pp. 8-9
3. T.A. 21.50-55.
4. Upodghāta, p. 36
5. Ibid., p. 65
6. M.M.P., pp. 11-12; also see K.T., p. 244
7. इति ज्ञानचतुष्कं यत्सिद्धिमुक्तिमहोदयम् ।
तन्मया तन्त्र्यते तन्त्रालोकनाम्न्यत्र शासने ॥ T.A. 1.245

(manualistic scripture), to be precise.[1] It is why Jayaratha frequently remembers Abhinava as Śāstrakāra.[2] Jayaratha, while summing up the initial sentence (Ādivākya i.e., T.A. 1.1 to 1.21) tries to highlight the formal Śāstric character of the *Tantrāloka* as under—

(i) T.A. 1.1 to 1.5— अभिधेयम्=त्रिकार्थः (it is manifold).

(ii) T.A. 1.16 to 1.20—(a) प्रयोजनम्=त्रिकार्थस्य सातिशयत्वम्
(b) मुख्य-प्रयोजनम्=प्रत्यभिज्ञानाद् जीवन्मुक्तिप्रदत्वम्

(iii) T.A. 1.7 to 1.13—अधिकारः=गुरूपरम्परोपात्ततत्वम् परमेश्वरशक्तिपातपवित्रितत्वं च[3]

(iv) T.A. 1.14 to 1.15 & 1.245[4]—संबंधः=(a) वाच्य-वाचकभावः (वाच्य is प्रक्रिया and वाचक is तंत्रालोक).

1. "अर्थितो रचये" (१.१५) इति प्रतिज्ञायाः प्रक्रियायाश्च "तन्मया तन्त्र्यते तन्त्रालोकनाम्न्यत्र शासने (१.२४५) इत्यादिवक्ष्यमाणोपजीवनेन तन्त्रालोक इत्यभिधानम्। T.A.V., I, p. 53

2. वक्ष्यमाणषडर्धशास्त्रार्थगर्भीकारेण शास्त्रकारः परामृशति। T.A.V., I, p. 3; तथापि शास्त्रकाराणामियं शैली। Ibid., I, p. 52 etc.

3. Abhinava defines Adhikārin in T.A. 1.337 eloquently—

इह गलितमलाः परावरज्ञाः शिवसद्भावमया अधिक्रियन्ते।
गुरवः प्रविचारणे यतस्तद् विफला द्वेषकलंकहानियाञ्चा॥

The same may well be compared with the second concluding verse of the *Viveka*—

योऽधीती निखिलागमेषु पदविद् यो योगशास्त्रश्रमी
यो वाक्यार्थसमन्वये कृतरतिः श्रीप्रत्यभिज्ञामृते।
यस्तर्कान्तरविश्रुतश्रुततया द्वैताद्वयाज्ञानवित्
सोऽस्मिन्स्यादधिकारवान् कलकलप्रायं परेषां वचः॥

(T.A.V., XII, p. 428)

Abhinava makes it abundantly clear that such a 'competent' person is difficult to locate—

तत्र तत्र च शास्त्रेषु न्यरूप्यत महेशिना।
एतावत्यधिकारी यः स दुर्लभ इति स्फुटम्॥ T.A. 35.43

4. Jayaratha does not suggest the specific portions and their explications from the T.A. on this issue, but they are too patent to require an authoritative citation.

(b) अभिधेयप्रयोजनयोः साध्यसाधनभावः (साध्य is अनुत्तरत्रिकज्ञप्ति and साधन is तंत्रालोकोक्त उपायचतुष्टय or प्रक्रिया).

(v) T.A. 1.6—उपलब्धौ संभवद्विघ्ननिरासाय गणेशवटुकयोः स्तुतिः[1]

(d) Stuti Grantha

The fourth and the final approach consists in Abhinava's contemplation of the *Tanrāloka* as a full scale Stuti (prayer hymn). In the concluding part of the initial sentence[2] as well as in the ultimate verse[3] Abhinava leaves no ambiguity about his intention. Whenever he gets an opportunity he grabs the occassion to project the devotional theme of the *Tantrāloka*. In his eyes the entire subject matter of the *Tantrāloka* acquires meaning when it leads one to attain Śivahood owing to His grace alone. The *Tantrāloka* outlines the path and procedure to invoke such divine grace and once it is attained the clouds of nescient doubts disappear and one shines in one's pristine splendour.[4] Such an approach lends credence to the views of many a modern scholar who takes Kashmir Śaivism as theology or transcendental theology hoping to reach and realize the personalistic Godhead and not as a pure metaphysics concentrating on an

1. According to Jayaratha Abhinava wants to make it sure that the *Tantrāloka* is a Tantric Scripture and as such must contain veneration to Gaṇeśa and Vaṭuka.

2. अभिनवगुप्तहृदम्बुजमेतद्विचिनुत महेशपूजनहेतोः। T.A. 1.21

3. तव किल नुतिरेषा सा हि त्वद्रूपचर्चेत्यभिनवपरितुष्टो लोकमात्मीकुरुष्व ॥ Ibid. 37.85

4. गुरोर्वाक्याद्युक्तिप्रचयरचनोन्मार्जनवशात्
समाश्वासाच्छास्त्रं प्रति समुदिताद्वापि कथितात्।
विलीने शंकाभ्रे हृदयगगनोद्भासिमहसः
प्रभोः सूर्यस्येव स्पृशत चरणान्ध्वान्तजयिनः ॥ T.A.2.49

abstract Absolute. It is only from this deep religious point of view that the Prakriyā character of the *Tantrāloka* can be more meaningfully explained. Possibly this is the significance of this view being vouched in the beginning and in the end (Uparkrama and Upasaṁhāra, to put it traditionally) of the *Tantrāloka*.

(iii) *Five objectives behind the composition of the Tantrāloka*

(a-i) ATTAINMENT OF BHAIRAVAHOOD

After examination of the underlying motives of Abhinava a study of Abhinava's objectives behind his composition of the *Tantrāloka* will be immensely helpful. The fundamental aim is the same as that of his philosophical discipline in general. It is the achievement of Bhairavahood i.e., the divination of the mundane. Abhinava proudly declares that one who constantly practises all the tenets of thirtyseven Āhnikas is oneself transformed into Bhairava, the Absolute.[1] If a consistent perusal of 37 chapters leads to one's attainment of essential divinity, it is all the more reason to conclude that the microscopically finite being is capable of attaining cosmic personality.

(a-ii) PROPOUNDING FOURFOLD REDEMTIVE KNOWLEDGE

Abhinava is never tired of reiterating his preferences. He says that the original commitment of the *Tantrāloka* is to understand the nature of Absolute Awareness[2].

1. इति सप्ताधिकामेनां त्रिशतं यः सदा बुधः ।
आह्निकानां समभ्यस्येत्स साक्षाद् भैरवो भवेत् ॥
सप्तत्रिंशत्सु संपूर्णबोधो यद्भैरवो भवेत् ।
किं चित्रमणवोऽप्यस्य दृशा भैरवतामियुः ॥ T.A. 1. 284-86

2. तंत्रालोकेऽभिनवविरचितेऽमुत्र . . . . . .
यत्तत्राद्यं पदमविरतानुत्तरज्ञप्तिरूपं तन्निर्णेतुम् . . . . ॥ Ibid. 2.1

The four varieties of redemptive knowledge, as discussed in the *Tantrāloka*, are primarily designed to master both the worldly accomplishment and the spiritual transcendence.[1] While making a passing reference in his *Locana*,[2] as we had occasion to note earlier, Abhinava finds the transcendental Godhead as occupying the central focus of the *Tantrāloka*. It is descent of His grace (Śaktipāta) that alone constitutes the driving force for the aspirant's movements and it is why the problems of bondage and emancipation assume a kind of primacy over other issues.[3] Abhinava goes on positing that the basic purpose of the *Tantrāloka* is inculcation of the 'intuitive awareness'[4] (Prātibha-saṁvitti) which once thoroughly inculcated transforms the discursive perspective of mankind into the unitive one.[5] Abhinava (and his commentator Jayaratha also) refutes the charge of being arrogant in self-eulogy, as to him it is just a statement of facts.[6]

1. इति ज्ञानचतुष्कं यत्सिद्धिमुक्तिमहोदयम् ।
तन्मया तन्त्र्यते तन्त्रालोकनाम्न्यत्र शासने ॥ Ibid. 1.245

2. तदुत्तीर्णत्वे तु सर्वं परमेश्वराद्वयं ब्रह्म इत्यस्मच्छास्त्रानुसारेण विदितं तन्त्रालोकग्रन्थं विचारयतेत्यास्ताम् । Dh.L., K.M., IV, p. 19

3. इह यद्यपि परमेश्वरशक्तिपातमंतरेण तच्छास्त्रश्रवणादावन्यत् प्रवृत्ति-निमित्तं नाभ्युपेयते . . . . . इति तत्साक्षात्कारेणैव अज्ञानापगमान्मोक्षावाप्तिः . . . . तथापि . . . . . तदेकनियतं ज्ञानाज्ञानयोः स्वरूपं न ज्ञानम् इति . . . . तत्परीक्षणस्य . . . . . प्राधान्यमपि कटाक्षयितुमुपक्रम एव बंधमोक्षपरीक्षामुट्टङ्कयति ग्रन्थ-कारः । T.A.V., I, pp. 52-54.

4. ततः प्रातिभसंवित्त्यै शास्त्रमस्मत्कृतं त्विदम् ।
योऽभ्यसेत्स गुरुर्नैव वस्त्वर्था हि विडम्बकाः ॥ T.A. 13.160

5. ततस्तरतमभावेन प्रातिभोदयाद्हेतोर्यः पुनरिदं श्रीतन्त्रालोकसंज्ञम् अस्मत्कृतं शास्त्रं प्रातिभत्वं संवेदयितुम् अभ्यसेत् स समनन्तरमेव संपूर्णबोधत्वात् प्रातिभो गुरुर्भवेत् यद्दृक्पातमात्रात्सर्वोऽप्ययं लोकस्ताद्रूप्यमियात् ।
T.A.V., VIII, p. 102

6. ननु महतीयं विडम्बना यत्स्वयमेव स्वकृतिं प्रत्येवं प्रशंसा नाम,
इत्याशंक्योक्तं नैव वस्त्वर्था हि विडम्बका इति । T.A.V., VIII, p.102

(b) Presenting the ultimate textual authority

This brings us to another objective of Abhinava in presenting the *Tantrāloka* as the ultimate textual authority. Self-realization is the goal of all spiritual disciplines and the standard effective tool conceived by them is the power of the Godhead. No other text has been able to drive this truth home more than the *Tantrāloka* and the reason for it lay in Abhinava's taking recourse to his own discerning judgement, unfailing sense of right logic, vast command over Śaivistic scriptures and above all his deep insight into Trika ideology, in that order.[1] All these combined together lent enormous width and intense depth to Abhinava's treatment. Knowledge in order to earn transcendence has to pass through three successive stages:

(i) it must emanate from a scripture;
(ii) it must be thoroughly investigated under a knowledgeable guide; and
(iii) it must ultimately form basic core of one's experience.[2]

Jayaratha throws a veiled hint that Abhinava's intellectual/spiritual equipment very much betrayed such a wholistic framework of mind.[3] Under such circumstances the *Tantrāloka* could not but become the most ideal, complete and reliable textual autho-

1. इति यज्ज्ञेयसतत्त्वं दर्श्यते तच्छिवाज्ञया ।
मया स्वसंवित्सत्तर्कपतिशास्त्रत्रिकक्रमात् ॥ T.A. 1.106

2. यतः शास्त्रक्रमात्तज्ज्ञगुरुप्रज्ञानुशीलनात् ।
आत्मप्रत्ययितं ज्ञानं पूर्णत्वाद् भैरवायते ॥ T.A. 4.77

3. While commenting on T.A. 7.1 (इति कालतत्त्वमुदितं शास्त्रमुखागमनिजानुभवसिद्धम्) Jayaratha explains सिद्धम् as "यतः शास्त्रक्रमात् भैरवायते ॥" इत्याद्युक्त्या पारिपूर्ण्येन लब्धसिद्धिरिति (सिद्धीति ?) शिवम् । T.A.V., IV, p. 203

rity. We are, therefore, tempted to suggest that three-fold epistemic methodology consisting of verbal testimony, reasoning and perception (Āgama, Yukti and Pratyakṣa) emerged from the triple sources of agamic understanding—scripture, guide and self.

(c) Easy comprehension of the tantric wisdom

Easy comprehension of the tantric wisdom was the third objective of Abhinava.[1] It was from this point of view that he concentrated mainly on those issues or opinions which would be useful for all. Not that he shunned controversial issues rather, on the contrary, he took them up in his other works for a specialist's treatment.[2]

(d) Restoration and preservation of the tradition

A careful look into the *Tantrāloka* brings out one more objective which is however treated by Abhinava in a low key. His three references, one (Sampradāyojjhitaiḥ)[3] in the beginning and two others (Viḍaṁbitāḥ[4] and Bhraṣṭe Viddhau[5]) in the middle of the *Tantrāloka* are quite conspicuous by their mention.

1. संकलय्योच्यते सर्वमधुना सुखसंविदे । T.A. 11.51
2. नहि सर्वंसर्विकया एतदापादयितुं पार्यते इति किमशक्यार्थाभिनिवेशेन । T.A.V., X, p. 57
3. अतोऽत्रान्तर्गतं सर्वं सम्प्रदायोज्झितैः बुधैः ।
   अदृष्टं प्रकटीकुर्मो गुरुनाथाज्ञया वयम् ॥ T.A. 1.19
4. येन यत्प्राहुराख्यानसादृश्येन विडम्बिताः ।
   गुरूपासां विनैवात्तपुस्तकाभीष्टदृष्टयः ॥ Ibid. 9.55
5. तेन भ्रष्टे विधौ वीर्ये स्वरूपे वानया परम् ॥
   मन्त्रा न्यस्ताः पुनर्न्यासात्पूर्यन्ते तत्फलप्रदाः । Ibid. 15.134-35

Jayaratha adds तेन शक्त्यात्मत्वेन हेतुना निजनिजतन्त्रप्रसिद्धविद्याभ्रंशेऽपि तन्त्रान्तरीया मन्त्रा न्यस्ताः. . . .मालिन्या . . . . .पुनर्न्यासात् . . . . .स्वाम्नायाम्नातफलदानोन्मुखाः संपाद्यन्ते इत्यर्थः । T.A.V., IX, p. 71

In the first, Abhinava seems to suggest that there were people who, though learned, were deprived of the uninterrupted tradition and hence did not have access to the doctrinal secrets. In the second, he hints at the existence of the people who were neither conversant with the text nor had waited upon the teacher for guidance. As such, being easily misled by the similarity of expression, they showed considerable gap in their knowledge. In the third, he implies that in certain sections the traditional secrets or specific procedures were lost or corrupted beyond recognition. In the first and second case, he undertook to propound the traditional wisdom inherited by him and in the third, he enjoins alternative course to be followed by taking recourse to the assignment (Nyāsa) called Mālinī. Jayaratha's observation, that whenever Abhinava quotes an agamic authority and recites a particular reading he does so to remove any misgivings about that source,[1] further strengthens the above premises. The foregoing discussion leads us to conclude that one of the undeclared objectives of Abhinava is to restore and preserve the existing and traditionally acquired tantric literature and practices. We will have to say something on this aspect again while examining his style and method.

From the above noted account we note that Abhinava's motives and objectives could be classified into two groups i.e., the one declared and the other undeclared, and may be briefed as under:

1. इह....स्वकण्ठेनैव पाठेऽयमाशयो–यदत्र बहूनि शास्त्रान्तरेष्वसमंजसानि पाठान्तराणि संभवन्ति–इति श्रोतॄणां मा भूत्संमोहः ।

T.A.V., V, p. 186

Motives

(a) DECLARED

To compose the *Tantrāloka*

(i) as a compendium,
(ii) as a manual,
(iii) as a prayer.

(b) UNDECLARED

(i) To produce a scripturistic treatise (Śāstra).

Objectives

(a) DECLARED

(i) (a) To realise self and make others realise the same,
(b) To propound fourfold redemptive knowledge,
(ii) To afford easy comprehension of the abstruse traditional secrets.

(b) UNDECLARED

(i) To devise an-overriding textual authority,
(ii) To restore the tantric learning and practices.

CHAPTER TWO

ABOUT THE AUTHOR

(ABHINAVAGUPTA)

(i) *Biographical data*

It will be appropriate if we begin with the biographical data as made available by Abhinavagupta in the *Tantrāloka*. Abhinavagupta gives graphic details of his ancestry, parentage, teachers, pupils and circumstances under which the *Tantrāloka* was written.[1]

(a) NAME

According to the *Tantrāloka* Abhinavagupta was not his actual name. It was a title which he earned from his teachers in recognition of his devotion to and reflection upon Śiva.[2] This fact has already been emphasized earlier[3] where, according to Jayaratha, his name implied authoritativeness.[4] Abhinavagupta is never tired of repeating this fact. He calls himself competent.[5] This leads to the natural conclusion that

1. The reader is advised, for further details, to see Abhi. (pp. 1-77), K.T. (pp. 157-165), Kane's The History of Sanskrit Poetics, Bombay, 1951 (pp. 226-233) and Raghavan's posthumous work, Abhinavagupta and His Works (pp. 17-30), which is the reprint from JORI, Vol. XIV, IV, 1933.

2. अभिनवगुप्तस्य कृतिः सेयं यस्योदिता गुरुभिराख्या ।
त्रिनयनचरणसरोरुहचिन्तनलब्धप्रसिद्धिरिति ॥ T.A. 1.20

3. बोधान्यपाशविषनुत्तदुपासनोत्थ-
बोधोज्ज्वलोऽभिनवगुप्त इदं करोति ॥ Ibid. 1.16

4. अभिनवगुप्त इति सकललोकप्रसिद्धनामोदीरणेनापि आप्तत्वमेव उपोद्वलितम् । T.A.V., I, p. 34

5. योग्योऽभिनवगुप्तोऽस्मिन् कोऽपि यागविधौ बुधः ॥ T.A. 4.278

he alone was competent to undertake a work like *Tantrāloka* which was professedly a digest of the entire Ṣaḍardha (lit. half of six i.e., Trika) scriptural literature.[1] Abhinava's academic, intellectual, spiritual and yogic attainments were of very high order. The very nature of his physical birth, in the tantric parlance, underlies this. In the first verse itself which refers to his parents he suggests his Yoginībhūtva[2] (i.e., arising from Yoginīs.). Such a suggestion assumes added significance in the context of the *Tantrāloka* whose committed goal, as we have seen, is to enable the listener-aspirant achieve Bhairavahood (Absolutic being). Here the parents achieve Bhairavahood which is transmitted to progeny.[3] Thus there is very suggestive relationship between his birth and composition of the *Tantrāloka*. This view gets strengthened by another remark of Jayaratha. In the thirteenth Āhnika while discussing the various kinds of fall of

1. तदेवम् एवंविधसिद्धयोगिनीप्रायपितृमेलकसमुत्थतया...स्वात्मनि निरुत्तरपदाद्वयज्ञानपात्रतामभिदधता ग्रन्थकृता निखिलषडर्धशास्त्रसारसंग्रहभूतग्रन्थकरणेऽप्यधिकारः कटाक्षीकृतः । T.A.V., I, pp. 14-15

2. Yoginībhū is a typical Kula concept. In the 29th Āhnika called 'Rahasyavidhiprakāśana', this concept has been discussed under Dautavidhi (i.e., practice relating to the female messenger). When parents unite identifying themselves with Śiva and Śakti giving birth to progeny, the latter who is the Śiva-incarnate and instant repository of knowledge is designated as Yoginībhū—

तादृङ्मेलककलिकाकलिततनुः कोऽपि यो भवेद्गर्भे ॥
उक्तः स योगिनीभूः स्वयमेव ज्ञानभाजनं रुद्रः ।
श्रीश्रीवीरावलिशास्त्रे बालोऽपि च गर्भगो हि शिवरूपः ॥
T.A. 29.162-63

Also see fn. 1 above.

3. कुण्डं शक्तिः शिवो लिङ्गं मेलकं परमं पदम् ॥ . . . .
एवं कर्मणि कर्मणि यत्र क्वापि स्मरन् व्याप्तिम् ॥
सततमलेपो जीवन्मुक्तः परभैरवीभवति । Ibid. 29.141, 161-62

grace (Śaktipāta), Abhinava points out to the characteristics,[1] laid down in the *Śrīpūrvaśāstra*, of an aspirant who is endowed with Madhyatīvraśaktipāta:

1. Unflinching faith in God;
2. Realization of Mantras;
3. Control over all the objective principles;
4. Successful conclusion of the activities undertaken;
5. Poetic creativity; and
6. Sudden or spontaneous knowledge of all the disciplines.

All these signs or a few of them show themselves in varying degrees according to the quantum of grace bestowed. But, Jayaratha, on the authority of his teachers, says all these signs were patently visible in the author of the *Tantrāloka*.[2] This is why such a man whose wisdom (Sattarka—right logic) dawns on its own is said to be initiated by one's own deified awareness and exercises universal jurisdiction.[3] It is, therefore, not difficult to understand as to why Abhinava assumes the role of an Ācārya (teacher) throughout his work.[4]

1. रुद्रशक्तिसमाविष्ट इत्यनेनास्य वर्ण्यते ।
चिह्नवर्गो य उक्तोऽत्र रुद्रे भक्तिः सुनिश्चला ॥
मन्त्रसिद्धिः सर्वतत्त्ववशित्वं कृत्यसंपदः ।
कवित्वं सर्वशास्त्रार्थबोद्धृत्वमिति क्रमात् ॥ Ibid. 13.214-215

Pandey refers to five characteristics leaving 'Kavitva' (Abhi., p. 17) which needs review.

2 समस्तं चेदं चिह्नजातं अस्मिन्नेव ग्रन्थकारे प्रादुरभूद् इति प्रसिद्धिः । यद्गुरवः—
अकस्मात्सर्वशास्त्रार्थज्ञत्वाद्यं लक्ष्मपञ्चकम् ।
यस्मिञ्श्रीपूर्वशास्त्रोक्तमदृश्यत जनैः स्फुटम् ॥
T.A.V., VIII, p. 137

3. यस्य स्वतोऽयं सत्तर्कः सर्वत्रैवाधिकारवान् ॥
अभिषिक्तः स्वसंवित्तिदेवीभिर्दीक्षितश्च सः ॥ T.A. 4.42-43

4. अभिनवगुप्तेनार्यात्रयमुक्तं संग्रहाय शिष्येभ्यः । Ibid., 11.53

(b) PUPILS, COLLEAGUES AND FAMILY CIRCLE

Two factors prompted Abhinavagupta to undertake the writing of the *Tantrāloka*. He was implored by his students and colleagues[1] and was ordained by his teacher Śambhunātha[2] to write a complete manual and bring out the aspects that the heretics were not able to see. Abhinavagupta in his concluding remarks even names his important pupils who were instrumental to his writing the *Tantrāloka*. Manoratha, who happened to be his brother[3], was foremost among them. However, before he could go ahead to favour Manoratha, other disciples including his cousins also approached him with a similar request.[4] Of

---

जय० remarks—स्वनामोदीरणस्यायमाशयो यदेतावत्प्रमेयजातं विस्तरीतुमिव संग्रहीतुमप्यनन्यसाधारणं ममैव परं प्रावीण्यम् इति ।
T.A.V., VII, p. 44 (11th Āh)

Also see आचार्यमभ्यर्थयते स्म गाढं— T.A. 37.70

1. इत्यहं बहुशः सद्भिः शिष्यसब्रह्मचारिभिः ।
अर्थितो रचये स्पष्टां पूर्णार्थां प्रक्रियामिमाम् ॥ Ibid. 1.15

2. अतोऽत्रान्तर्गतं सर्वं संप्रदायोज्झितैर्बुधैः ।
अदृष्टं प्रकटीकुर्मो गुरुनाथाज्ञया वयम् ॥ Ibid. 1.19

3. सोऽनुग्रहीतुमथ शांभवभक्तिभाजं
स्वं भ्रातरमखिलशास्त्रविमर्शपूर्णम् ।
यावन्मनः प्रणिदधाति मनोरथाख्यं
तावज्जनः कतिपयस्तमुपाससाद ॥ T.A. 17.64

Pandey (Abhi., p. 13) takes Manoratha as Abhinava's younger brother. It is, however, difficult to maintain for the reasons coming later.

4. श्रीशौरिसंज्ञतनयः किल कर्णनामा यो यौवने विदितशांभवतत्त्वसारः ।
देहं त्यजन्प्रथयति स्म जनस्य सत्यं योगच्युतं प्रति महामुनिकृष्णवाक्यम् ॥
तद्बालमित्रमथ मन्त्रिसुतः प्रसिद्धः श्रीमन्द्र इत्यखिलसारगुणाभिरामः ।
लक्ष्मीसरस्वति समं यमलंचकार सापत्नकं तिरयते सुभगप्रभावः ॥
अन्ये पितृव्यतनयाः शिवशक्तिशुभ्राः क्षेमोत्पलाभिनवचक्रकपद्मगुप्ताः ।
ये संपदं तृणममंसत शंभुसेवासंपूरितं स्वहृदयं हृदि भावयन्तः ॥
षडर्धशास्त्रेषु समस्तमेव येनाधिजग्मे विधिमण्डलादि ।

these Karṇa—the son of Śauri, Mandra—Karṇa's boyhood friend and son of a minister, Kṣema, Utpala, Abhinava, Cakraka, Padmagupta—all cousins, and Rāmagupta are remembered by name. A few others also beseached Abhinava who accommodated all of them as it was against his training to turn down a request. We have already come across his brother Manoratha, Karṇa and Rāmadeva in the concluding verses of the *Parātriṁśikāvivaraṇa*[1] being described in extremely eloquent terms. His brother was a great devotee of Śiva and displayed command over all the disciplines. Karṇa, though quite young, had grasped the essence of Śaiva principles and was totally averse to mundane attractions. He is the same Karṇa who, together with Mandra, requested Abhinava time and again to write a commentary on the *Mālinī-vijayottaratantra*.[2] Karṇa had one son, Yogeśvaridatta by name, who displayed personal qualities justifying his name.[3] Karṇa's young wife Ambā[4] also grew detached from the worldly affairs and devoted herself exclusively to the worship of Śiva when her husband died later at an advanced age.[5] It is clear from Abhi-

---

स रामगुप्तो गुरुशंभुशास्त्रसेवाविधिव्यग्रसमग्रमार्गः ॥
अन्योऽपि कश्चन जनः शिवशक्तिपातसंप्रेरणापरवशस्वकशक्तिसार्थः ।
अभ्यर्थनाविमुखभावमशिक्षितेन तेनाऽप्यनुग्रहपदं कृत एष वर्गः ॥
T.A. 37.65-69

1. P.T.V. 7-9 (Concluding verses, pp. 279-80)
2. सच्छिष्यकर्णमन्द्राभ्यामर्थितोऽहं पुनः पुनः ।
वाक्यार्थं कथये श्रीमन्मालिन्यां यत्क्वचित् क्वचित् ॥ M.V.V. 1.11
3. तस्य स्नुषा कर्णवधूर्विधूतसंसारवृत्तिः सुतमेकमेव ।
यासूत योगेश्वरिदत्तसंज्ञं नामानुरूपस्फुरदर्थतत्त्वम् ॥ T.A. 37.76
4. अम्बाभिधाना Ibid. 37.79
5. यामग्रे वयसि भर्तृवियोगदीनामन्वग्रहीत् त्रिनयनः स्वयमेव भक्त्या ।
भाविप्रभावरभसेषु जनेष्वनर्थः सत्यं समाकृषति सोऽर्थपरम्पराणाम् ॥
Ibid. 37.77

nava's remarks that although Karṇa's entreaty was a forceful factor behind Abhinava's undertaking, the former did not live long to see the work complete. Ambā, Karṇa's wife, was perhaps Abhinava's sister, elder or younger it is difficult to say. Because, on the strength of Abhinava's own statement, she looked upon Abhinava as her teacher and Śiva personified although he happened to be her real brother and as such she was successful in keeping the filial emotions at bay.[1] And when it came to Abhinava, though a brother, he justified her trust, respect and faith in him as a teacher by his virtuous conduct where the joy of knowledge aggravated his lust for further knowledge,[2] but who also actively nurtured all the efforts annulling the sense of delimited existence from heart. This perhaps explains why Abhinava devotes so much space to the description of Karṇa and his family.

Next comes Rāmagupta who is referred to as Rāmadeva in the *P.T.V.* He was exclusively given to the study of Śaiva scriptures and having fully comprehended the nuances of Vidhi and Maṇḍala in Trika scriptures was rather impatient to serve his teacher, Śiva as well as scriptures. From the *P.T.V.*

भक्त्युल्लसत्पुलकतां स्फुटमङ्गभूषां श्रीशंभुनाथनतिमेव ललाटिकां च ।
शैवश्रुतिं श्रवणभूषणमप्यवाप्य सौभाग्यमप्यधिकमुद्वहति स्म यान्तः ॥
T.A. 57.58

1. अम्बाभिधाना किल सा गुरुं तं स्वं भ्रातरं शम्भुदृशाभ्यपश्यत् ।
भाविप्रभावोज्ज्वलभव्यबुद्धिः सतोऽवजानाति न बन्धुबुद्ध्या ॥
Ibid. 37.79

2. भ्राता तदीयोऽभिनवश्च नाम्ना न केवलं सच्चरितैरपि स्वैः ।
पीतेन विज्ञानरसेन यस्य तत्रैव तृष्णा ववृधे निकामम् ॥
सोऽन्यश्च शांभवमरीचिचयप्रणश्यत्संकोचहार्दनलिनीघटितोज्ज्वलश्रीः ।
तं लुम्पकः परिचचार समुद्यमेषु साधुः समावहति हन्त करावलम्बम् ॥
Ibid. 37.80-81

we learn that he had thoroughly mastered grammar, Mīmāṁsā and logic also.[1]

The list includes his five cousins including Kṣema and one his namesake. All these cousins showed in common their absolute devotion to Śiva and rejection of worldly possessions. We do not know if Kṣema amongst them was identical with Abhinava's illustrious disciple Kṣemarāja, the author of several erudite works. But all the circumstantial evidence tends to favour this identification. Although all these are mentioned as 'Pitṛvyatanayāḥ', Abhinava in his *Tantrāloka* does not indicate who his uncle (Pitṛvya) was. According to Pandey he mentions his uncle as Vāmanagupta in the *Abhinavabhāratī*.[2] From this quotation he appears to be a man of literature. While discussing Abhinava's teachers we shall revert to him. Since he is the only person alluded to as his uncle, it may not be illogical if Kṣema's father and Vāmanadatta are identified.

The only pupil we have yet to talk about is Mandra. He happens to be a boyhood friend of Karṇa and his cousin also, as is gathered from the fact that Vatsalikā, Śauri's wife, has been called his aunt (Pitṛvyavadhū).[3] The possession of all the necessary basic qualities makes his personality very pleasing and he was gifted with enormous riches and learning in equal measure. It was he who made Abhinava's stay at his suburban residence where all the members of house-

1. पदवाक्यप्रमाणवित् । P.T.V. 9 (concluding verses, p. 280)
2. तत्र हास्याभासो यथास्मत्पितृव्यस्य वामनगुप्तस्य A. Bh., Vol. I, p. 297, quoted, Abhi., p. 735
3. तस्याभवत् किल पितृव्यवधूर्विधात्रा । T.A. 37.73

hold including children were dedicated to the divine worship.[1]

It was the combined request of all these pupils and his fellow-students[2] who were longing to learn the entire tantric literature that he could not desist from writing the *Tantrāloka*.[3] In fact it was his own deep rooted desire that was awaiting an excuse for an outlet just as a dancer, desiring to dance, cannot resist stepping when he gets an instrument for accompaniment. Not only the request from students, but also the advice of his teachers to this effect was found by him full of great benign possibilities.[4]

(c) Place of composition

The *Tantrāloka* was, thus, written in the suburban residence of Mandra, where his aunt Vatsalikā[5] looked after Abhinava with so much care and concern that Abhinava found her name equal to her merits and felt constrained to attribute the success of his work to the all-caring presence of Vatsalikā.[6] His

1. विक्षिप्तभावपरिहारमथो चिकीर्षन् मन्द्रः स्वके पुरवरे स्थितिमस्य वव्रे ।
आबालगोपमपि अत्र महेश्वरस्य दास्यं जनश्चरति पीठनिवासकल्पे ॥
T.A. 37.72

2. T.A. 1.15 (fn. 1 on p. 22 supra). Abhinava is silent about his fellow-students. Could the phrase, therefore, be explained as not 'his' fellow-students but as 'their' (pupils') classmates?

3. आचार्यमभ्यर्थये स्म गाढं संपूर्णतन्त्राधिगमाय सम्यक् ।
जायेत दैवानुगृहीतबुद्धेः संपत्प्रबन्धैकरसैव संपत् ॥ T.A. 37.70

4. सोऽप्यभ्युपागमदभीप्सितमस्य यद्वा स्वातोद्यमेव हि निनर्तिषतोऽवतीर्णम्
सोऽनुग्रहप्रवण एव हि सद्गुरूणामाज्ञावशेन शुभसूतिमहाङ्कुरेण ॥
Ibid. 37.71

5. तस्याभवत् किल पितृव्यवधूर्विधात्रा वा निर्ममे गलितसंसृतिचित्रचिन्ता ।
शीतांशुमौलिचरणाब्जपरागमात्रभूषाविधिर्विहितवत्सलिकोचिताख्या ॥
Ibid. 37.73

6. इत्थं गृहे वत्सलिकावितीर्णे स्थितः समाधाय मतिं बहूनि ।
. . . . स तन्निबन्धं विदधे महार्थम् . . . . . . Ibid. 37.82-83

gratitude is reflected in every word of the poetic appreciation he has showered on her.[1] Vatsalikā was the wife of Śauri who was king's minister and had later resigned the job when his mind became pure owing to devotion to Śiva.[2]

(d) TIME

Out of the material covered so far, the portion relating to Karṇa and Śauri etc. is relevant from yet another point of view. Abhinava, though ever ready to provide sufficient biographical data about himself and his environ, does not throw any direct hint on his time in the *Tantrāloka* itself. Abhinava's time is no doubt fairly certain (he is placed around 950-1020 A.D.).[3] It is here that we get some clues on the matter. Śauri appears to be a senior contemporary of Abhinava because the latter has seen all the three generations of Śauri e.g.,—Śauri, Karṇa and Yogeśvaridatta. Abhinava in fact was the contemporary of Karṇa, his brother-in-law, husband of his sister Ambā. Abhinava also witnessed the death of Karṇa, his close relative and an ardent disciple. Karṇa died at fairly advanced age (*Agrage Vayasi* T.A. 37.77) when his son, Yogeśvaridatta, was already grown up. Cons-

1. मूर्ता क्षमेव करुणेव गृहीतदेहा धारेव विग्रहवती शुभशीलतायाः ।
वैराग्यसारपरिपाकदशेव पूर्णा तत्त्वार्थरत्नरुचिरस्थितरोहणोर्वी ॥
T.A. 37.74

2. भ्रातापि (? भर्तापि) तस्याः शशिशुभ्रमौलैर्भक्त्या परं पावितचित्तवृत्तिः ।
स शौरिरात्तैश्वरमन्त्रिभावस्तत्याज यो भूपतिमन्त्रिभावम् ॥ Ibid. 37.75

Here the word 'bhrātā' does not stand logical scrutiny. We have therefore suggested the correction within brackets. Śauri was Vatsalikā's husband and not brother—is proved by collateral evidence.

3. Abhi., pp. 8-10; K.T., pp. 157-159.

truing the present data with those in the *P.T.V.*[1] we come to learn that Śauri was son of Vallabha who was a Brahmin and a senior minister or the prime minister of king Yaśaskara who definitely ruled in the year 939 A.D. Thus, Abhinava who belonged to the third[2] generation from king Yaśaskara should have undertaken the writing of the *Tantrāloka* at quite mature age; his accepted date (circa 950-1025 A.D.) continues to remain the same which may be shown in the following tabular form:

King Yaśaskara (939 A.D.)	=Vallabha	
	↓	
	Śauri=Vatsalikā	
	V	
	Karṇa=Ambā	=Abhinavagupta (950-1025 A.D.)
	V	
	Yogeśvaridatta	

(e) Ancestors & parents

Abhinava has provided sufficient insight into his place of origin, ancestors and teachers. Apart from scattered references throughout the text of the *Tantrāloka* he has devoted sizable space in the first and the thirtyseventh Āhnikas. His earliest known ancestor Atrigupta was born in Madhyadeśa which falls

1. कश्मीरेषु यशस्करस्य नृपतेरासीदमात्याग्रणीः
श्रीमान्वल्लभ इत्युदाहृततनुर्यः प्राग्र्यजन्मा द्विजः ।
तस्य स्वाङ्गभवः प्रसिद्धिपदवीपात्रं समग्रैर्गुणैः
श्रीशौरिः शिशुचन्द्रचूडचरणध्यानैकरत्नाकरः ॥....
श्रीमद्वत्सलिकाभिधा सहचरी तस्यैव भक्त्युल्लसत्-
प्रोद्रिक्तान्तरवृत्ति शंकरनुतौ यस्या मनो जृम्भते ॥
तस्यैवात्मभवो......कर्णाभिधानो द्विजः ।
P.T.V. 5-7 (concluding verses, p. 279)

2. To this extent we revise our opinion in the K.T., p. 159.

in Kumārikā region (earth).[1] Construed with the material from the *P.T.V.* Madhyadeśa is found to be synonymous with Antarvedi[2] (i.e., land between Gaṅgā and Yamunā) which might be identified with modern Kannauj and was the centre of all learning. His surname was Gupta and his proper as well as Gotra names were Atri,[3] if we go by the explanation of Jayaratha. He was brought to Kashmir by king Lalitāditya-Muktāpīḍa of Karkoṭaka dynasty (725-761 A.D.) out of great love and respect possibly[4] when the latter conquered the king Yaśovarman of Kannauja (730-740 A.D.). Abhinava has paid glowing tributes to Kashmir, the land of learning, beauty and eternal bliss. Atrigupta was settled in Pravarapura, a decent beautiful town founded by an earlier king Pravarasena[5] (c. 5th-6th century) on the banks of

1. कन्याह्वयेऽपि भुवनेऽत्र परं महीयान् ।
निःशेषशास्त्रसदनं किल मध्यदेशस्तस्मिन्नजायत गुणाभ्यधिको द्विजन्मा ।
कोऽप्यत्रिगुप्त इति नामनिरुक्तगोत्रः शास्त्राब्धिचर्वणकलोद्यगस्त्यगोत्रः ॥
T.A. 37.37-38
The meaning of the last Pāda of T.A. 37.38 is not clear. Does it mean that because of his swallowing the scriptural water he was named Agastya also?
2. अन्तर्वेद्यामत्रिगुप्ताभिधानः प्राप्योत्पत्तिं प्राविशत्प्राग्र्यजन्मा ।
P.T.V. 11 (concluding verses, p. 280)
3. नामनिरुक्तगोत्र इति अत्रिगोत्र इत्यर्थः । गोत्रनामश्लिष्टतया निर्दिष्टम् ।
T.A.V., XII, p. 412
4. तमथ ललितादित्यो राजा निजं पुरमानयत्
प्रणयरभसात् कश्मीराख्यं हिमालयमूर्धगम् । T.A. 37.39
5. श्रीमत्परं प्रवरनाम पुरं च तत्र यन्निर्ममे प्रवरसेन इति क्षितीशः ।
यः स्वप्रतिष्ठितमहेश्वरपूजनान्ते व्योमोत्पतन्नुदसृजत्किल धूपघण्टाम् ॥
Ibid. 37.47
तस्मिन्कुबेरपुरचारिसितांशुमौलिसांमुख्यदर्शनविरूढपवित्रभावे ।
वैतस्तरोधसि निवासममुष्य चक्रे राजा द्विजस्वपरिकल्पितभूरिसंपत् ॥
Ibid. 37.52
यत् प्रवरसेन इति क्षितीशः पुरं निर्ममे तस्मिन्नमुष्य द्विजस्य ललितादित्यो राजा निवासं चक्रे इति दूरेण संबंध : । T.A.V., XII, p. 413

Vitastā, modern Jhelum. We do not know if he is the same as the illustrious composer of the *Setubandha*, because Abhinava is silent on this aspect. A house was built on the bank of Jhelum by king Lalitāditya for his residence facing the temple of Śiva creating an environ of sanctity around the whole place. The temple, too, was located on the river bank and had a Siddhaliṅga enshrined in it.[1] The king also granted enough property and wealth for Atrigupta's maintenance.[2] After a sufficient gap of about 150 years in the lineage of the immigrant family of Atrigupta, Abhinava's grandfather Varāhagupta was born. He was an eminent scholar.[3] It appears all through the intervening generations, about which nothing is known, traditions of learning and devotion to Śiva continued unabated. Varāhagupta's son Narasiṁhagupta, also popularly known as Cukhalaka, was Abhinava's father. His intellect was sharp, mind pure as a result of his deep access into all the branches of learning and heart full of devout devotion to Śiva.[4]

On the authority of Jayaratha we know that the name of Abhinava's mother was Vimalā.[5] In fact

1. रोधः प्रतिष्ठितमहेश्वरसिद्धलिङ्गस्वायम्भुवार्चनविलेपनगन्धपुष्पैः ।
T.A. 37.50

2. Pandey (Abhi., p. 19) reads 'bhūmisaṁpat' for 'bhūrisaṁpat' in the printed text which is equally a good reading. We have, however, interpreted it as 'property and wealth' instead of 'jagir' following the printed text.

3. तस्यान्वये महति कोऽपि वराहगुप्तनामा बभूव भगवान्स्वयमन्तकाले ।
गीर्वाणसिन्धुलहरीकलिताग्रमूर्धा यस्याकरोत् परमनुग्रहमाग्रहेण ॥
T.A. 37.53

4. तस्यात्मजश्चुखलकेति जने प्रसिद्धश्चन्द्रावदातधिषणो नरसिंहगुप्तः ।
यं सर्वशास्त्ररसमज्जनशुभ्रचित्तं माहेश्वरी परमलंकुरुते स्म भक्तिः ॥
T.A. 37.54

5. अस्य हि ग्रन्थकृतः श्रीनरसिंहगुप्तविमलाख्यौ पितरौ इति गुरवः ।
T.A.V., I, p. 14

Abhinava himself suggests it in the very first word (Vimalakalā) of the *Tantrāloka*[1]. His mother died when Abhinava was a child[2] and was brought up by his father. His father though young was in the least distracted by deviations natural to the young age and had developed acute devotion to Śiva as a result of complete aversion to the worldly attractions[3]. Mother's premature death brought a sea change in Abhinava's spiritual life and with the removal of the staunchest cause of attachment, he instantly attained salvation in his lifetime itself.[4] His father reared Abhinava not only physically, but intellectually also. We shall have occasion to dilate upon it later.

Now a brief pause. In this context Abhinava makes no mention of his brother and sister though we have already noted that Manoratha and Ambā were his brother and sister respectively. It is difficult to say among the three who was younger and who was elder. From Abhinava's account we know that his mother died in his childhood and he was tended by his young father; it is quite possible that Abhinava might be the youngest. The reason for our holding so lies in the fact that he was a Yoginībhū in whose birth

1. विमलकलाश्रयाभिनवसृष्टिमहा जननी T.A. 1.1

By a strange coincidence, this verse forms the first introductory verse of the P.T.V. and M.V.V. also.

2. माता व्ययूयुजदमुं किल बाल्य एव ।
दैवं हि भाविपरिकर्मणि संस्करोति ॥ Ibid. 37.56

3. तारुण्यसागरभरानपोह्य वैराग्यपोतमधिरुह्य दृढं हठेन ।
यो भक्तिरोहणमवाप्य महेशचिन्तारत्नैरलं दलयति स्म भवापदस्ताः ॥
तस्यात्मजोऽभिनवगुप्त इति प्रसिद्धः श्रीचन्द्रचूडचरणाब्जपरागपूतः ।
Ibid. 37.55-56

4. माता परं बंधुरिति प्रवादः स्नेहोऽतिगाढीकुरुते हि पाशान् ।
तन्मूलबन्धे गलिते किलास्य मन्ये स्थिता जीवत एव मुक्तिः ॥ Ibid.37.57

parental union did not take place for the satisfaction of carnal instinct but as a matter of spiritual necessity. Abhinava's parents must have taken some time before they were able to develop such a frame of mind. Thus his brother and sister should have been born in the evolutionary phase. In any case the mutual gap between their birth must be small as the father was quite young when he turned away from worldly allurements and mother passed away quite early. Regarding Abhinava's own family, the *Tantrāloka* is not of much help. It is from the I.P.V.V. we learn that he was a celibate throughout his life and as such the question of having wife or son etc. did never arise.[1]

From the foregoing account the following picture of Abhinava and his family emerges :

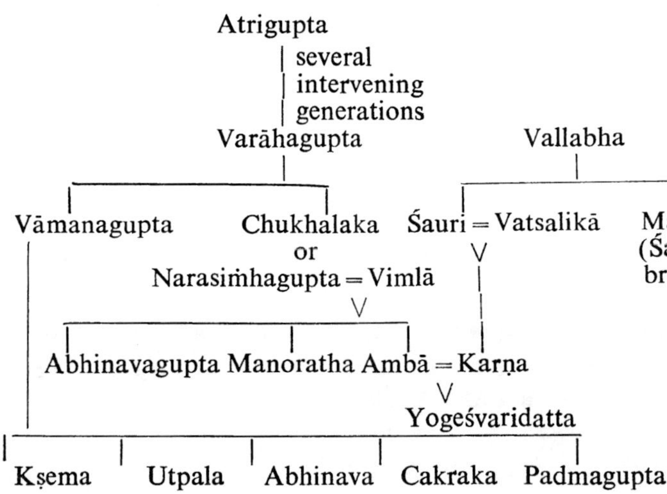

(f) TEACHERS

Coming to his teachers we find Abhinava very in-

1. दारात्मजप्रभृतिबन्धुकथामनाप्तः ।

I.P.V.V., III, concluding verse 2.

formative. He received his first lessons from his father, Narasiṁhagupta alias Cukhalaka. Grammar, logic and literature were the three fields which he mastered under the guidance of his father,[1] but the lessons with his father were just the beginning of his extraordinary intellectual pursuit. It appears while he was enjoying his lessons in literature, he was overtaken by irresistible devotion to Śiva which made him serve numerous teachers at their own seats.[2] In pursuing his ever-increasing lust he did not even bother for the normal decorum and accepted serfdom of his teachers to acquire knowledge.

It appears Abhinava had to face tremendous criticism for going from one teacher to the other.[3] Although he is an ardent follower of the *Śrīpūrvaśāstra*, he quotes from the *Mataśāstra* twice[4] in the *Tantrāloka* to emphasize that as a black bee (Bhṛṅga) moves from flower to flower to collect scent, in the same way a student, desirous of knowledge, should visit from teacher to teacher. It is why he flocked at the gates of logicians, Mīmāṁsists, Buddhists, Ārhats and Vaiṣṇavas.[5] He also suggests the order in which he

1. पित्रा स शब्दगहने कृतसंप्रवेशस्तर्कार्णवोर्मिपृषतामलपूतचित्तः ।
साहित्यसान्द्ररसभोगपरो महेशभक्त्या स्वयंग्रहणदुर्मदया गृहीतः ॥
T.A. 37.58

2. स तन्मयीभूय न लोकवर्तनीमजीगणत् कामपि केवलं पुनः ।
तदीयसंभोगविवृद्धये पुरा करोति दास्यं गुरुवेश्मसु स्वयम् ॥ Ibid. 37.59

3. तस्मान्न गुरुभूयस्त्वे विशङ्केत कदाचन ।
गुर्वन्तररते मूढे आगमान्तरसेवके ॥
प्रत्यवायो य आम्नातः स इत्थमिति गृह्यताम् । Ibid. 13.349-50

4. आमोदार्थी यथा भृङ्गः पुष्पात्पुष्पान्तरं व्रजेत् ।
विज्ञानार्थी तथा शिष्यो गुरोर्गुर्वन्तरं व्रजेत् ॥
Ibid. 13.335; also cf. T.A. 22.45-6

5. अहमप्यत एवाधःशास्त्रदृष्टिकुतूहलात् ॥
तार्किकश्रौतबौद्धार्हद्वैष्णवादीन्नसेविषि । Ibid. 13.345-46

approached the teachers of respective disciplines. He first approached Vaiṣṇavas, then Buddhists, then Śiddhānta Śaivists, and finally Trika scholars.[1] It is a very terse proposition to identify all his teachers by name in different disciplines, yet we get a reasonably adequate account in this respect.

(i) MAṬHIKĀGURUS & (ii) JÑĀNAGURUS

Abhinava's teachers may be divided in two broad groups—(1) Maṭhikāgurus (teachers representing a preceptorial school and thereby a definite spiritual approach) and (2) Jñānagurus (teachers imparting knowledge in general in some specific area). In the opening verses of the first Āhnika he deals with the Maṭhikāgurus[2] (except Amardaka Maṭhikā) and towards close of the *Tantrāloka* (37th Āh.) he first discusses Maṭhikāgurus and then other teachers. Under Maṭhikāgurus he first refers to Bhūtirāja.[3] Bhūtirāja and his son, whose name Abhinava does not disclose, represent the Nātha Maṭhikā, representing dualist-cum-monist school.[4] Traiyamba Maṭhikā, which is related to Tantra-prakriyā, is represented by Lakṣmaṇagupta who steps into the shoes of Utpala and Somānanda, Abhinava's grand and great-grand teachers respectively.[5] Lakṣmaṇagupta is followed by

1. प्राग्वैष्णवाः सौगताश्च सिद्धान्तादिविदस्ततः ।
क्रमात्त्रिकार्थविज्ञानचन्द्रोत्सुकितदृष्टयः ॥ T.A. 13.348
2. For Maṭhikās see K.T. pp. 32-34.
3. तदपरमूर्तिर्भगवान् महेश्वरो भूतिराजश्च । T.A. 1.9
4. श्रीनाथसंततिमहाम्बरघर्मकान्तिः श्रीभूतिराजतनयः स्वपितृप्रसादः । Ibid. 37.60
5. श्रीसोमानन्दबोधश्रीमदुत्पलविनिःसृताः ।
जयन्ति संविदामोदसंदर्भा दिक्प्रसर्पिणः ॥
तदास्वादभरावेशबृंहितां मतिषट्पदीम् ।
गुरोर्लक्ष्मणगुप्तस्य नादसंमोहिनीं नुमः ॥ Ibid. 1.10.11

Śambhunātha, who represents the Fourth School[1], which also goes by the name of Ardha-traiyambaka and is supposed to be identical with Kula Prakriyā.[2] Śambhunātha appears to be the main inspiration behind the *Tantrāloka*. Although Abhinava has left out teachers of the Āmardaka school in the beginning, possibly because they fell outside the purview of Tantraprakriyā, he utilizes the first apportunity in the concluding verses to refer to Vāmanātha who was the son or pupil of Eraka and represented the dualist school founded by Amardaka or Ānanda.[3]

After discussing Maṭhikāgurus, he switches over to give out a long list of his main teachers[4] who perhaps taught him secular subjects. The list reads as under: (i) Śrīcandra Śarmā, (ii) Bhava,[5] (iii) Bhaktivilāsa, (iv) Yogānanda, (v) Abhinanda, (vi) Śivaśakti,[6]

---

also see त्रैयम्बकप्रसरसागरशायिसोमा—
नन्दात्मजोत्पलजलक्ष्मणगुप्तनाथः । T.A. 37.61

1. तुर्याख्यसंततिमहोदधिपूर्णचन्द्रः श्रीसोमतः सकलवित्किल शंभुनाथः । Ibid. 37.61

2. विश्रान्तिस्थानतया कुलप्रक्रियागुरुमपि उत्कर्षयति—
जयताज्जगदुद्धृतिक्षमौऽसौ भगवत्या सह शंभुनाथ एकः ।
यदुदीरितशासनांशुभिर्मे प्रकटोऽयं गहनोऽपि शास्त्रमार्गः ॥
(T.A. 1.13) T.A.V., I, p. 31

3. आनन्दसंततिमहार्णवकर्णधारः सद्दैशिकवरात्मजवामनाथः । T.A. 37.6

4. श्रीचन्द्रशर्मभवभक्तिविलासयोगानन्दाभिनन्दशिवशक्तिविचित्रनाथाः ।
अन्येऽपि धर्मशिववामनकोद्भटश्रीभूतेशभास्करप्रमुखप्रमुखा महान्तः ॥
Ibid. 37.62

5. The name of Candravara, mentioned at No. 11 by Pandey (Abhi., p. 12) is not found in the text cited above. Instead, we have some Bhava in his place. The text as it is may also mean "Bhaktivilāsa, the son of Candra Śarmā". Pandey adopts a different text, possibly from the MS in his possession—

श्रीचन्द्रचन्द्रवरभक्तिविलासयोगानन्दाभिनन्दशिवभक्तिविचित्रनाथाः ।
अन्येऽपि धर्मशिववामनकोद्भटश्रीभूतीशभास्करमुखप्रमुखा महान्त : ॥

6. Pandey reads Śivabhakti. Ibid.

(vii) Vicitranātha, (viii) Dharmaśiva,[1] (ix) Vāmanaka, (x) Udbhaṭa, (xi) Śrībhūteśa[2] and (xii) Bhāskara.

All these teachers, whose favour was earned by Abhinava due to their service and attendance, conveyed whatever they knew in their branches to Abhinava helping him become self-contented and truly dedicated to exploring reality.[3] Since these are his principal teachers, there might have been some not-so-important teachers, about whom we hardly know anything. Abhinava, however, refers to his several teachers in the body of the text quite often, but use of the term 'Guru' or 'Guravaḥ' is so loose that it is difficult to take a definite stand. Sometimes it refers to a mythical figure,[4] sometimes to a preceptorial ancestor much anterior to him,[5] sometimes to the legendary Kṛṣṇa[6] and sometimes to the earlier commentators including even his opponents[7]. Moreover, it does not have an exact chronological connotation. However, on the basis of available evidence, a conjecture can be made. Abhinava studied the *Mātaṅga Āgama* with some Aniruddha[8] who also commented

1. Pandey takes Dharma and Śiva separately (Abhi., p. 12), but they are one as subsequent discussion will bring out.
2. Pandey reads Bhūtīśa. Ibid.
3. एते सेवारसरचितानुग्रहाः शास्त्रसारप्रौढादेशप्रकटसुभगं स्वाधिकारं किलास्मै ।
   यत्संप्रादुर्यदपि च जनान्नैक्षताक्षेत्रभूतान् स्वात्मारामस्तदयमनिशं तत्त्वसेवारसोऽभूत् ॥ T.A. 37.63
4. Vide ibid. 8.9
5. Ibid. 1.100; 9. 278
6. Ibid. 1.124
7. Ibid. 8.101; 9.173
8. श्रीमताप्यनिरुद्धेन शक्तिमुन्मालिनीं विभोः ॥
   व्याचक्षाणेन मातङ्गे वर्णिता निरपेक्षता । Ibid. 13.293-94

× × ×

upon the *Mataṅga Śāstra*. an Āgama of Siddhānta Śaivism. Jayaratha seems to have quoted a long extract from this commentary in his *Viveka* on the *Tantrāloka* 8.433-34.[1] In addition, Abhinava also furnishes some useful information about some of his teachers. Dharmaśiva, mentioned at serial No. (viii) above, seems to have imparted lessons on some of the matters connected with Parokṣa Dīkṣā (indirect initiation). His views are quoted in the context of judging the comparative strength of the rites (Saṁskāras)[2] which were slightly different from those enunciated by Śambhunātha. His method is then discussed from the T.A. 21.50 to 21.55. Abhinava has referred to two Vāmanas above with slight variation in name—one is Vāmanātha, his teacher in Śaiva dualism and other Vāmanaka about whom we perhaps know nothing. According to Pandey one of the Vāmanas (which one?) is identical with Abhinava's uncle Vāmanagupta[3] and has been mentioned in the list of his teachers. Possibly it is Vāmanaka which goes more in

---

तत्स्थाने वृत्तिमन्तीति मतङ्गे गुरवो मम । T.A. 9.261

Jayaratha remarks—न चैतदस्माभिः स्वोपज्ञमित्युक्तम् 'मतङ्गे गुरवो मम' इति । मतङ्गशास्त्रव्याख्यातारः श्रीमदनिरुद्धप्रभृतय इत्यर्थः ।
T.A.V., VI, p. 211

For other details see Dwivedi's Upodghāta, pp. 16-17.

1. यदाहुः "कालाग्निर्नरकाणां. . . . . .केचिदेव तु" इति । अत्र च साक्षादागमे (मतङ्गागमे) संवादिते ग्रन्थविस्तरः स्यात् इति तद्वृत्तिकृदुक्तं संवादितम् ।
T.A.V., V, p. 275

2. श्रीमान् धर्मशिवोप्याह पारोक्ष्यां कर्मपद्धतौ । T.A. 21.50

Dwivedi takes him as a scholar of Siddhānta Śaivism or dualistic Śaivism so to say, who wrote a Paddhati text and quotes Kṣemarāja's statement in support "धर्मशिवाचार्येण स्वपद्धतौ"
(Uddyota on SV.T. 11.6-7).

Vide Upodghāta, p. 42; also see p. 20 thereof.

3. Abhi, pp. 13, 735

line with Vāmanagupta. But Abhinava nowhere refers to Vāmanaka as his uncle in the *Tantrāloka* nor does he give the slightest idea about the discipline taught. He, however, refers to one Vāmanadatta, who on the testimony of Jayaratha, was the author of one *Saṁvitprakāśa*.[1] This Vāmanadatta has definitely been referred to as 'Gurubhiḥ' and not by name. From the content and context it appears that this Vāmanadatta talked of variety in the instrumental knowledge without affecting the overall unity of divine consciousness. In all probability Vāmanaka is Vāmanadatta who was a teacher of Abhinava, but not his uncle.[2] Amongst the remaining Jñānagurus our informations about Bhāskara are in much better shape, though his name does not figure in the *Tan-*

1. नीले पीते सुखे दुःखे संविद्रूपमखण्डितम् ॥
गुरुभिर्भाषितं तस्मादुपायेषु विचित्रता । T.A. 5.154-55
Jayaratha adds गुरुभिः वामनदत्ताचार्येण भाषितमिति संवित्प्रकाशे ।
T.A.V., III, p. 467

2. Dwivedi in his Upodghāta (pp. 15-16, 65-66, 72-73, 78, 83) has dwelt in detail on the issue except student-teacher relationship between Abhinava and Vāmana. He has identified Hrasvanātha, the author of the Advaya-saṁpattivārtika with Vāmanadatta, the author of the Saṁvitprakāśa. The view needs further examination. His other informations are important. According to him the Saṁvitprakāśa was a text with Vaiṣṇava leanings. Its MS is available in B.H.U. Library (Nos. C4003 and C5186). Vāmanadatta seems to have written two more books Subodhamañjarī (C4235 at B.H.U.) and Svabodhamañjarīmātṛkā (C100 at B.H.U.). If Hrasvanātha, the son of Harṣadatta, is none other than the author of the Saṁvitprakāśa—if Dwivedi's hypothesis prevails—he should be credited with the authorship of the Bodhavilāsa also (K.T., pp. 182-83, fn. 3). Dwivedi has disputed duality of Hrasvanāthas (Upodghāta, p. 66) suggested by us (K.T., pp. 176-183), but without assigning any reason whatsoever for disagreement.

trāloka elsewhere.[1] From other sources we know that he was the renowned author of the *Vārtika* on the *Śivasūtras*, in addition to the *Vivekāñjana* and *Kakṣyāstotra*. His father was one Divākara and he was a disciple of Śrīkaṇṭha in Spanda branch and of the Stotrakāra Siddhinātha in Krama.[2] Some liberty may be taken for certain conjectures with regard to Bhava mentioned at Serial No. (ii) above. Abhinava has referred to a series of teachers coming in preceptorial succession who commented on the *Parātrīśikā Śāstra* running as under—Somānanda, Kalyāṇa and Bhavabhūti.[3] If Abhinava's description depicts the chronological succession of teacher-commentators Bhavabhūti occupies exactly the same point of time (calculating from Somānanda) which is occupied by Bhava as teacher of Abhinavagupta. In that case 'Bhava' would be an abbreviated form of Bhavabhūti or should we be justified in reading in the text "Bhavabhūtivilāsayogānanda" in place of "Bhavabhaktivilāsayogānanda"? We leave it for future investigation.

In this group figures Udbhaṭa also, about whom Abhinava's commentator Jayaratha gives us some information. This Udbhaṭa is different from his earlier namesake, who was a poetician and a prominent figure in king Jayāpīḍa's court (779-813 A.D.). The latter Udbhaṭa followed Ujjaṭa in succession and happened to be the grand disciple of Bhānuka (850-

1. Bhāskara is included in the list in T.A. 37.62. The reference to Bhāskara in T.A. 1.21 is of dubious value (Abhi, p. 917) and is more figurative than informative.

2. See K.T., pp. 144-146.

3. असदेतदिति प्राहुर्गुरवस्तत्त्वदर्शिनः ।
श्रीसोमानंदकल्याणभवभूतिपुरोगमाः ॥ T.A. 13.149

900 A.D.), an early Krama teacher.[1] This tradition descended down to Jayaratha intact through intervening generations of teachers. However if both the accounts—Abhinava's as well as Jayaratha's—are construed together, it would appear that Abhinava was in possession of both the Krama traditions—one descending through Govindarāja→Somānanda→Lakṣmaṇagupta and the other through Bhānuka→Ujjaṭa→Udbhaṭa. Since Abhinava subscribed to the tradition headed by Somānanda, he is avowedly indebted to Lakṣmaṇagupta for his lessons in the whole of Tantra-prakriyā comprising Krama, Trika and Pratyabhijñā systems. Udbhaṭa comes in for a lone reference, because Abhinava, though, learnt Krama dicta from Udbhaṭa, his lessons were limited to the sphere of Udbhaṭa's branch of Krama alone and his heart did not lie there.

Coming to the Maṭhikāgurus our first encounter takes place with one Vāmanātha who taught tantras of the dualistic schools to Abhinava.[2] He has nowhere been remembered except once. From Abhinava's statement[3] we simply know that he was either son or pupil of Eraka,[4] who happened to be an excellent teacher. This Eraka, the teacher in dualism, is not to be confused with his earlier namesake who

1. तत्राद्यः (गोविन्दराजः) . . . . चेदं रहस्यं श्रीसोमानन्दाभिधानाय गुरवे संचारयाम्बभूव। द्वितीयोऽपि एवमास्त, तस्यैव चैषा श्रीमदुज्जटोद्भट्टादिनानागुरु-परिपाटीसंततिः यत्प्रसादासादितमहिमभिरस्माभिरेतत् प्रदर्शितम् ।

T.A.V., III, p. 192-3; cf. K.T., pp. 137-138

2. See fn. 3 on page 35 supra.

3. T.A. 37.60

4. 'Ātmaja' in T.A. 37.60 may not necessarily mean son, it may mean disciple also. See K.T., pp. 135-137. To this extent the views regarding Eraka in K.T., p. 122 stand modified.

was a Stotrakāra and a Krama propagator (850-900 A.D.).[1] We are in dark about any further details.

Next come Bhūtirāja (900-950 A.D.) and his son as representative teachers of dualism-cum-nondualism[2] initiated by Śrīnātha. It appears that Abhinava took his lessons from father and son both. As we have seen, Bhūtirāja is remembered in the beginning and his son towards the end of the *Tantrāloka*. The *Tantrāloka* is silent about his son. From other sources he may be identified with Helārāja, the illustrious commentator of the *Vākyapadīya* and brother of Indurāja, the latter being Abhinava's teacher in literary criticism.[3] Bhūtirāja has claimed highest veneration from Abhinava who views him as another form of the Godhead.[4] Bhūtirāja seems to have excelled in many branches of learning in addition to the dualistic-monistic discipline. Perhaps his full name was Bhūtirājamiśra. He seems to have initiated Abhinava in the science of the 'size of all the regions' (Bhuvanas)[5] and 'purifiability of all of them' and propounded the theory of hundred Rudras (Śatarudras)[6] in the context of the treatment of Bhuvanādhvan and Pratiṣṭhā Kalā. Another major item which Abhinava learnt

1. See K.T., p. 122
2. The view that the system taught was dualism in the K.T., p. 155 needs be rectified.
3. K.T., pp. 154-155; Abhi., p. 214
4. तदपरमूर्तिर्भगवान् महेश्वरो भूतिराजश्च । T.A.19.
Cp. गुरुभ्योऽपि गरीयांसं युक्तं श्रीचुखलाभिधम् ।
ततो गुरुतरः श्रीमान्भूतिराजो महामतिः । M.V.V. 1.5-6
5. अथ सकलभुवनमानं यन्मह्यं निगदितं निजैर्गुरुभिः ॥
तद्वक्ष्यते समासात् बुद्धौ येनाशु संक्रमेत् । T.A. 8.406-7
6. अन्ये तु समस्तानां शोध्यत्वं वर्णयन्ति भुवनानाम् ।
श्रीभूतिराजमिश्रा गुरवः प्राहुः पुनर्वहीरुद्रशतम् ॥ Ibid. 8.410

from Bhūtirāja was Brahmavidyā which consisted of such Mantras which if read at the time of death would lead to instant self-realization.[1] He also imparted three esoteric disciplines pertaining to Praṇava, Māyā and Bindu to Abhinava[2] in the course of discussion on Mantravīrya. Several references in the *Tantrāsāra* to Bhūtirāja in the context of Krama system gave rise to a suspicion among later scholars that Krama was also one of the domains in which Abhinava was introduced by Bhūtirāja. According to Jayaratha there was no substance in such statements.[3] Jayaratha has also taken exception to his being a pupil of Cakrabhānu (1050-1100 A.D.), an important[4] Krama teacher. Bhūtirāja is one person about whom we have some more informations, most of them provided by Abhinava himself. But we refrain from them at the moment as we are concentrating on the material in

1. अथोच्यते ब्रह्मविद्या सद्यःप्रत्ययदायिनी ॥
शिवः श्रीभूतिराजो यामस्मभ्यम् प्रत्यपादयत् ।
सर्वेषामेव भूतानां मरणे समुपस्थिते ॥
यया पठितयोत्क्रम्य जीवो याति निरञ्जनम् । T.A. 30.62-64
2. एतद्विद्यात्रयम् श्रीमान् भूतिराजो न्यरूपयत् ॥
यः साक्षादभजच्छ्रीमाञ्श्रीकण्ठो मानुषीं तनुम् । Ibid. 30. 120-121
3. श्रीदेवीपंचशतिकेऽपि अस्य श्रीसोमानन्दभट्टपादेभ्यः प्रभृति त्रिकदर्शनवदेव गुरवः इति न तत्राप्यस्य श्रीभूतिराजो गुरुत्वेन स्थितः, न च असावप्यस्य न गुरुः यद्वक्ष्यति ।
T.A.V., III, p. 194
4. अतश्चास्य गुरुक्रममजानानैरद्यतनैः
"श्रीभूतिराजनामाप्याचार्यश्चक्रभानुशिष्योऽन्यः ।
अभिनवगुप्तस्य गुरोर्यस्य हि कालीनये गुरुता ॥
इत्यादि यदुक्तं तत्स्वोत्प्रेक्षितमेव इत्युपेक्ष्यम् । Ibid., III, p. 193
Dwivedi accepts Bhūtirāja as the son of Cakrabhānu, which is not borne out by facts, vide Upodghāta, p. 52 and K.T., p. 156.

the *Tantrāloka*[1] alone. Thus Bhūtirāja emerges as an extremely celebrated scholar who was father of two eminent scholars e.g., Indurāja and Helārāja and teacher of Abhinavagupta and Helārāja.

Next comes Lakṣmaṇagupta who commands very high veneration from Abhinava. He comes in the preceptorial lineage of Traiyambaka and is responsible for Abhinava's training in the entire monistic thought of Kashmir including Krama, Trika and Pratyabhijñā branches, excepting Kula. He directly inherited the traditional secrets from Traiyambaka through Somānanda and Utpala. Thus he was direct disciple of the last.[2] We have already marked Abhinava referring in very eloquent words to him.[3]

In addition to Trika, Krama and Pratyabhijñā which constitute Tantra-prakriyā, Abhinava refers to his other views also. From the T.A. 15.247 to 254 Abhinava discusses a special type of Nyāsa, which according to Jayaratha was advocated by Lakṣmaṇagupta[4] in the overall context of Samayidīkṣā. This was one of the six original Nyāsas employed to invoke and realize Kālasaṁkarṣiṇī. Lakṣmaṇagupta differed from Śambhunātha in respect of Śāktanyāsa.[5]

1. See T.S., p. 30; M.M.P, p. 127; Bh. G.S., p. 186; M.P.(S), p. 115; I.P.V.V., III, p. 405; Abhi., pp. 165-66; and K.T., pp. 152-156.

2. त्रैयम्बकप्रसरसागरशायिसोमानन्दात्मजोत्पलजलक्ष्मणगुप्तनाथः ।

T.A. 37.61

The word Ātmaja is to be understood in the sense of pupil and not son. Pandey's views (Abhi., pp. 7, 164) need revision. See K.T., p. 135.

3. Vide fn. 5, p. 34 supra.

4. श्रीलक्ष्मणगुप्तः पुनरेतदन्यथा व्याचख्याविति याह T.A.V., IX, p. 122

5. While commenting on शंभुनाथो न्यासविधौ देवो हि कथमन्यथा T.A. 15.246 Jayaratha observes शंभुनाथ इति श्रीलक्ष्मणगुप्तमते हि अन्यथा न्यासविधिरित्याह । Ibid., IX, p. 122

Similarly Jayaratha points out that Lakṣmaṇagupta held a different construction of the Mantras[1] as opposed to the 'ancients'. The *Tantrāloka* and *Viveka* both do not go beyond this point. From it it appears that Lakṣmaṇagupta must have certain work or works to his credit of which we know very little. It is only from another source, the *I.P.V.V.*, that we know that he was the author of one *Śrīśāstra*[2] which, subject to further investigations, may be identified with *Śāradātilakatantra*.[3] It appears strange at the first sight that Abhinava neither refers nor quotes from the *S.T.* anywhere, perhaps due to the fact that the *S.T.* does not purport to be a work relating to the disciplines in which Abhinava was specifically groomed by Lakṣmaṇagupta. Future studies may investigate if the views appearing in the *Tantrāloka* or Jayaratha are traceable or not to the *S.T.*

We have now arrived at the ultimate phase of our enquiry regarding his teachers. Śambhunātha, the prime force and motivation behind the *Tantrāloka*, was Abhinava's guide in Kula system or Ardha-Traiyambaka school, a school emanating from Traiyambaka through his daughter. Kula system was also

1. Commenting on 'दीप्तैः' in T.A. 30.15 Jayaratha remarks—दीप्तैरिति

   श्रोकारादीनामकारादीनां ह्रस्वानामाग्नेयस्वभावत्वात्
   तेजोमयैरिति प्राच्याः, सरेफैरिति श्रीमल्लक्ष्मणगुप्तपादाः ।

   T.A.V., XII, p. 184

2. श्रीशास्त्रकृद्घटितलक्ष्मणगुप्तपादसत्योपदर्शितशिवाद्वयवाददृप्तः ।

   I.P.V.V., III, p. 406

3. The author of the *Śāradātilaka* has styled himself as Lakṣmaṇadeśika. Dwivedi takes them as two different persons, vide Upodghāta, p. 56. However he does not state reasons nor does he examine the reasons put forward so far. See K.T., pp. 146-150.

known as Kula-prakriyā.[1] Among all his teachers Śambhunātha is held in highest regard. He is compared to the sun whose rays removed the darkness caused by ignorance from the heart of Abhinava.[2] He is again described as the sun in the vast firmament of the lineage of Traiyambaka.[3] He is further described as the moon for the ocean of the Trika systems.[4] Bhaṭṭanātha was his other title or name.[5] It was because of him and his consort that Abhinava shone with spiritual splendour consequent upon the total removal of his sense of duality. It was due to this special calibre, Abhinava could embark upon writing the *Tantrāloka*. The consort here is some Bhagavatī, as we know it from another verse.[6] In fact she was the spiritual messenger (Dūtī) and has been specially mentioned because under Kula Prakriyā knowledge is transmitted through her alone. In other words Abhinava was favoured by Śambhunātha through his Dūtī Bhagavatī.[7]

Śambhunātha's preceptorial lineage may be presented like this—Sumatinātha→Somadeva→Śam-

1. See fn. 2 on p. 35 supra.
2. श्रीशंभुनाथभास्करचरणनिपातप्रभापगतसंकोचम् ।
अभिनवगुप्तहृदम्बुजमेतद्विचिनुत महेशपूजनहेतोः ॥ T.A. 1.21
3. श्री त्रैयम्बकसन्तानविततताम्बरभास्करः । Ibid. 6.88
4. श्री शंभुनाथ आदिक्षत् त्रिकार्थाम्बोधिचन्द्रमाः । Ibid. 29.95
5. श्रीभट्टनाथचरणाब्जयुगात्तथा श्रीभट्टारिकांघ्रियुगलाद्गुरुसंततिर्या ।
बोधान्यपाशविषनुत्तदुपासनोत्थबोधोज्ज्वलोऽभिनवगुप्त इदं करोति ॥ Ibid. 1.16
श्रीभट्टनाथ इति श्रीशम्भुनाथः । श्री भट्टारिका इति
भगवत्याख्या अस्य दूती । T.A.V., I, p. 34
6. जयताज्जगदुद्धृतिक्षमोऽसौ भगवत्या सह शंभुनाथ एकः । T.A. 1.13
7. कुलप्रक्रियां दूतीमुखेनैव शिष्यस्य ज्ञानप्रतिपादनाम्नायात् इह गुरुतद्दूत्योः समस्कन्धतया उपादानम् । T.A.V., I, p. 35

bhunātha→Abhinava.[1] Sometimes Abhinava speaks of Śambhunātha as the direct recipient of grace and knowledge from Sumati,[2] ignoring Somadeva. According to Jayaratha one should not get confused on such statements, because the 'teacher' here means the lineage teacher[3] or the word 'teacher' has to be understood to stand for teacher or grand-teacher, as the case may be. Jayaratha adds to our information by quoting from certain other source.[4] From it, it is clear that Śambhunātha hailed from some seat situated in south known as Jālandhara and was a competent authority in the system of five sources thriving on Atimārga. This is an important statement from the historical angle. As we know Krama has been called to have emanated from Northern seat.[5] As against this Jālandhara is described not as Southern Pīṭha but as being situated somewhere in south.

1. शाम्भवाख्यं समावेशं सुमत्यन्तेनिवासिनः । T.A. 1.213

Jayaratha remarks "सुमत्यन्तेनिवासिनः इति श्रीसोमदेवादयः । श्रीसुमतिनाथस्य श्रीसोमदेवः शिष्यः, तस्य श्रीशम्भुनाथः इति हि आयातिक्रमविदः ।
T.A.V., I, p. 236

cp. श्रीसोमतः सकलवित् किल शम्भुनाथः । T.A. 37.61

2. इति श्रीसुमतिप्रज्ञाचन्द्रिकाशान्ततामसः । श्रीशंभुनाथ . . . . . ॥
T.A. 10.287

Also see "श्रीशंभुनाथो मे तुष्टस्तस्मै श्रीसुमतिप्रभुः । T.A. 5.41

3. यत्तु "लोकेऽभूत्सुमतिः ततः समुदभूत् तस्यैव शिष्याग्रणीः । श्रीमान्शंभुरिति . . . . . ." इत्यन्यत्रोक्तं तत्परमगुर्वभिप्रायेण योज्यम् । यद्वा "यावानस्य संतानस्तावानेको गुरुर्मतः" इत्यादिवक्ष्यमाणनीत्या अवलम्बनेन व्याख्येयम् ।
T.A.V., I, p. 236

4. कश्चिद्दक्षिणभूमिपीठवसतिः श्रीमान्विभुर्भैरवः
पञ्चस्रोतसि सातिमार्गविभवे शास्त्रे विधाता च यः ।
लोकेऽभूत्सुमतिस्ततः समुदभूत्तस्यैव शिष्याग्रणीः
श्रीमाञ्छम्भुरिति प्रसिद्धिमगमज्जालन्धरात्पीठतः ॥ Ibid., I, p. 236

5. उत्तरपीठलब्धोपदेशात् Ibid., III, p. 192

Geographically, present Jālandhara falls towards south of Kashmir. Could we therefore surmise that Śambhunātha belonged to modern Jālandhara and Abhinava walked down to him in pursuit of his studies, since former's fame had already spread far and wide from his spiritual seat itself. The other significant point that merits consideration is that he excelled in Atimārga, which was perhaps more akin to Tripurā system. This problem has occupied our attention elsewhere[1] and our information has remained static so far.

Śambhunātha's learning was not confined to Kula system alone. Jayaratha while explaining the *T.A.* 1.13[2] says that the choice of diction implies his having contributed to the disciplines like Trika etc.[3] In order to endorse his statement he quotes a verse from Abhinava suggesting that Abhinava's commentary on one of the Trika Śāstras, incorporated his learning from Śambhunātha who had mastered all the scriptures. However, as the verse could not be traced to any of Abhinava's published works, it is difficult to precisely pinpoint the system. It may, however, be observed in passing that Śambhunātha exercised considerable impact on Abhinava in respect of his

1. Vide K.T., pp. 27-29. If Atimārga is synonymous with Tripurā, it is curious that Jayaratha nowhere refers to Śambhunātha in his V.M.V, a text devoted to Tripurā school. It is now for the future studies to decide on it.

2. यदुदीरितशासनांशुभिर्मे प्रकटोऽयं गहनोऽपि शास्त्रमार्गः ॥ T.A. 1.13

3. शास्त्रमार्गो विमलो जातः इत्यनेनास्य त्रिकाद्यागमव्याख्यातृत्वमपि प्रकाशितम् । यदुक्तमनेनैव—

"इत्यागमं सकलशास्त्रमहानिधानाच्छ्रीशंभुनाथवदनादधिगम्य सम्यक् ।
शास्त्रे रहस्यरससंततिसुन्दरेऽस्मिन् गंभीरवाचि रचिता विवृतिर्मयेयम् ॥

T.A.V., I, p. 32

two other texts e.g., *P.T.V.*[1] and *M.V.V.*[2]. Since other sources are not our immediate concern we have to refrain from alluding to them unless it is absolutely necessary.

Abhinava has cited Śambhunātha as an authority on several occasions and on different issues.[3] Abhinava learnt Dhyāna (meditation), as the first among Āṇava Upāyas, from him.[4] The second Upāya, consisting of articulation of the state of vital airs (Prāṇavṛttisamuccāra) is also credited to the teachings of Śambhunātha.[5] This included variety of blisses from Nirānanda, to Jagadānanda. Under the same Āṇavopāya presentation[6] of the 'day-night division'(Ahorātravibhāga—the second ancillary topic under the Kālādhvan, i.e. passage of time) and his criticism of other inferior views[7] carries the imprints of Śambhu-

1. P.T.V., Verse 18, pp. 281-82.
2. M.V.V. 1.4.
3. But for Jayaratha our task in this connection would have been impossible because of the indiscriminate use of the word Śambhu or Śambhunātha, sometimes meaning a deity and sometimes his teacher. Construing Abhinavagupta, Jayaratha and contextual circumstances we have tried to gather threads.

4. इत्येतत् प्रथमोपायरूपं ध्यानं न्यरूपयत् ।
श्रीशंभुनाथो मे तुष्टस्तस्मै श्रीसुमतिप्रभुः ॥ T.A. 5.43

5. अथ प्राणस्य या वृत्तिः प्राणनाद्या निरूपिता । . . . .
तदेव जगदानंदमस्मभ्यं शंभुरूचिवान् । Ibid. 5.43-52

Jayaratha remarks "तदेतत् प्रमात्रात्म चिदेकरूपं परं तत्त्वं जगता निजानंदाद्यात्मना विश्वेन रूपेण आनन्दो यत्र यतश्चेति जगदानन्दशब्दवाच्यम् अस्मभ्यं श्रीशंभुनाथ आदिशत्, न पुनरेतदस्माभिः स्वोपज्ञमेवोक्तमित्यर्थः ।
T.A.V., III, p. 356

6. दिनरात्रिक्रमं मे श्रीशम्भुरित्थमपप्रथत् ।
श्रीसन्तानगुरुस्त्वाह ध्यानं बुद्धाप्रबुद्धयोः ॥ T.A. 6.89

7. अलं वानेन नेदं वा मम प्राङमतमत्सरः ॥
हेये तु दर्शिते शिष्या सत्पथैकान्तदर्शिनः । Ibid. 6.91-92

nātha's teachings. In the overall context of passage of space (Deśādhvan)[1] Abhinava has openly acknowledged the debt of Śambhunātha in his treatment of the five stages of human experience such as wakefulness etc.,[2] being the third ancillary topic under the elaboration of the sub-categories (Tattvabheda). Similarly in the course of enunciating the second anciallary topic, i.e. the procedure of categories (Tattvavidhi), fifteen internal varieties of every category and the like have been discussed by Abhinavagupta only in the light of what Śambhunātha preached him by transmitting the entire tradition which the former secured from his teachers.[3] In the same context Abhinavagupta discusses the categories as symbolized by Prāṇic variety latent in the Khecarīcakra keeping within the instructions of Śambhunātha.[4] In the thirteenth Āhnika while dwelling upon the fifth ancillary topic i.e., variety of disappearance (Tirobhāvavaicitrya), Abhinavagupta invokes the criteria as laid down by Śambhunātha as to who ought to be preferred as a teacher between a Yogin and a Jñānin.[5] It is in this Āhnika

1. इति देशाध्वविभागः कथितः श्रीशंभुना समादिष्टः । T.A. 8.452
Jayaratha explains श्री शंभुना as परमेश्वरेण गुरुणा च ।
T.A.V., V, p. 283
2. तस्यामेकः प्रमाता चेदवस्थं जाग्रदादिकम् ।
तद्दर्श्यते शंभुनाथप्रसादाद्विदितं मया ॥ T.A. 10.230
× × ×
श्री शंभुनाथः सद्भावं जाग्रदादौ न्यरूपयत् । Ibid. 10.287
3. अधुना प्राणशक्तिस्थे तत्त्वजाले विविच्यते ॥
भेदोऽयं पाञ्चदश्यादिर्यथा श्रीशंभुरादिशत् । T.A. 10. 186-87
Jayaratha adds—श्रीशंभुरादिशदित्यनेन गुरुपरम्परागतत्वादविगीतप्रसिद्धिनिबन्धत्वमस्य ध्वनितम् । T.A.V., VII, p. 129
4. स इत्थं प्राणगो भेदः खेचरीचक्रगोपितः ॥
मया प्रकटितः श्रीमच्छाम्भवाज्ञानुवर्तिना । T.A. 10.226-27
5. विभागस्त्वेष मे प्रोक्तः श्रीशंभुनाथेन दर्श्यते । Ibid. 13.333

that Abhinavagupta does not accept Bhedavādin's view regarding existence of gradation in the descent of grace on the strength of Śambhunātha's teachings.[1] Moving further we notice Abhinava discussing the varieties of 'general assignment' (Sāmānyanyāsa) as a third ancillary topic under Samayidīkṣā and ascribing it to his teacher.[2] In the same Āhnika Abhinavagupta expresses his indebtedness to him in the presentation of various types of 'special assignment' (Viśeṣanyāsa) and underscores the difference between the two lines adopted by Śambhunātha and Lakṣmaṇagupta, his two teachers, in respect of the *Śripūrvaśāstra.* Abhinavagupta reconciles the two positions saying that one should first practice sixfold Śāktā Nyāsas as advocated by Lakṣmaṇagupta and then switchover to sixfold Śaiva Nyāsas enjoined by Śambhunātha.[3] Samayīdīkṣā pertains to the daily functions (Nityakarma) of the aspirants. All round worship of the cycle aiming at adoring the ultimate principle of effulgence is the sixteenth ancillary topic[4] while the fire-

1. तस्मान्न मन्महे कोऽयं शक्तिपातविधेः क्रमः ॥
इत्थं भ्रान्तिविषावेशमूर्च्छानिर्मोकदायिनीम् ।
श्रीशंभुवदनोद्गीर्णां वच्म्यागममहोषधिम् ॥ T.A. 13.102
2. संहारदानादानादिशक्तियुक्ता यतो रलौ ॥
एकत्वेन स्मरन्तीति शंभुनाथो निरूचिवान् । Ibid. 15.132-33
3. इत्थं श्रीपूर्वशास्त्रे मे संप्रदायं न्यरूपयत् ॥
शंभुनाथो न्यासविधौ देवो हि कथमन्यथा ।
न्यासे विवर्ज्यतेऽमुष्मिन्नङ्गान्यप्यस्य सन्ति हि ॥ T.A. 15.245-246
Jayaratha makes a significant remark—शंभुनाथ इति श्रीलक्ष्मणगुप्तमते हि अन्यथा न्यासविधिरित्याशयः। T.A.V., IX, p.122
4. एतच्च गुरुशास्त्रसंप्रदायेन अस्माभिरुक्तमित्याह—
इति भैरवपरपूजा तत्त्वं श्रीडामरे महायागे ।
स्वयमेव सुप्रसन्नः श्रीमान्शंभुर्ममादिक्षत् ।
(T.A. 15-352)—Ibid., IX, p. 177

rites (Vahnikarma) constituted by Saṁskāras (Saṁskriyātattva) is the twentyfirst ancillary topic[1]—both these items have been reproduced by Abhinavagupta as he imbibed them from Śambhunātha. Another item of esoteric value was Jālayoga which was a major constituent of the indirect initiation (Parokṣa Dīkṣā).[2] In the context of the eighth ancillary topic under the occasional functions (Naimittika Vidhi) Abhinavagupta examines the phenomenon of death eliminating the fear thereof and while rejecting other views he swears by one propagated by Śaṁbhunātha. The whole of the twentyninth Āhnika is devoted to Kulayāga or the esoteric practices according to Kula-prakriyā, the specific area where Śambhunātha excelled. But even here certain items were propounded with greater emphasis on the authority of Śambhunātha[3]. For instance, the method of worship (Arcāvidhi, the third ancillary topic in the Āhnika) included the doctrine of ten aspects of Homa (offering oblation to fire) which emanated from Śambhunātha.[4] In the thirtyfifth Āhnika Abhinavagupta's attempt to strike a synthesis and project a harmonious construction of the different scriptures is again inspired by the teachings of Śambhunātha.[5]

From the foregoing account it is obvious that

1. इत्येतत्संस्क्रियातत्त्वं श्रीशंभुर्मे न्यरूपयत् । T.A. 15.408
2. योगः श्रीशंभुनाथागमपरिगमितो जालनामा मयोक्तः । Ibid. 21.26
3. न च तद्दर्शितं मिथ्या स्वान्तसम्मोहदायकम् ।
   तदित्थं प्रयाणस्यैतत्तत्त्वं श्रीशंभुनाथतः ॥
   अधिगम्योदितं तेन मृत्योर्भीतिर्विनश्यति । Ibid. 28.366-67
4. दशान्यास्तदुपायायेत्येवं होमे दशांशताम् ।
   श्रीशंभुनाथ आदिक्षत्त्रिकार्थाम्बोधिचन्द्रमाः ॥ T.A. 29.95
5. इत्थं श्रीशंभुनाथेन ममोक्तं शास्त्रमेलनम् । Ibid. 35.44

Śambhunātha exercised tremendous influence not over Abhinavagupta's knowledge alone but also over his basic approach towards tantric wisdom and life. It is a matter of great misfortune that none of his works is extant today.[1] In certain circles he has also been equated with Siddhinātha, the author of the

1. However, Pandey assigns one *Tantrasadbhāva* to Śambhunātha on the basis of the T.A. 30.99[a]—

तुलामेलकयोगः श्रीतन्त्रसद्भावशासने ।

य उक्तः शम्भुनाथेन स मया दर्शितक्रमात् ॥ (Abhi., p. 583)

Dwivedi agrees with Pandey's views [NST (Upodghāta) p. 37 and also Upodghāta, p. 38]. This view is further strengthened when we find the same idea echoed in the *T.A.* 29.212—

शंभुनाथेनोपदिष्टां दृष्टां सद्भावशासने ।

According to Jayaratha this *Sadbhāvaśāsana* is none other than the *Tantrasadbhāva* [सद्भावशासने इति श्रीतन्त्रसद्भावे T.A.V. (29th Āh.), XI, p. 136]. However the equation does not hold further. As we have already pointed out earlier, the use of 'Śambhunātha' is not definitive—sometimes it stands for the divine and sometimes for the teacher. Here and in most contexts it denotes the divine source. In the *T.A.* 20.12 Abhinavagupta ascribes the authorship of the *Tantrasadbhāva* to the Godhead—

यथा श्रीतन्त्रसद्भावे कथिता परमेशिना ।

श्रीपूर्वशास्त्रेऽप्येषा च सूचिता परमेशिना ॥

a. Abhinavagupta reiterates his views regarding the revelatory character of the text in the T.A. 30.59—

व्योमस्विति शिवेनोक्तं तन्त्रसद्भावशासने ।

Even in continuation with the T.A. 30.99, cited above, Abhinavagupta explicates his stand in the T.A. 30.101—

प्रकर्तव्या यथा दीक्षा श्रीसन्तत्यागमोदिता ।

कथ्यते ह्राटकेशानपातालाधिपचोदिता ॥

Then on the strength of Abhinavagupta's own statements the *Tantrasadbhāva* is a work of divine origin and Śambhunātha, his teacher, could not be its author. According to Dwivedi (Upodghāta, p. 38) the work is available in M.S. and the quotes from it in the *T.A.V.* are traceable to it.

Krama Stotra, but on a close scrutiny the view is difficult to maintain.[1]

Thus, the known part of the glittering galaxy of Abhinavagupta's teachers comes to a close. However, it does not wind up the list altogether, because several references[2] in the *Tantrāloka* to his teachers are either obscure or doubtful and thereby they strengthen the possibility of there being several other teachers. From the quotations it appears that Abhinavagupta, in addition to different disciplines, learnt different texts in the same discipline from different teachers, but at the present juncture our informations are severely handicapped. Moreover, his teachers in Buddhism, Vaiṣṇavism and Jainism etc. are not known to us. A few of them may be from the list furnished by Abhinavagupta and a few not-so-important might have escaped any mention at all. To recapitulate, the following chart may give a brief idea of his teachers and the subjects they taught on the basis of the material in the *Tantrāloka*:

1. K.T., pp. 140-143; for other details see Abhi., pp. 489, 577 and Upodghāta, pp. 76, 79.

2. अथ स्थूलोदयोऽर्णानां भण्यते गुरुणोदितः । T.A. 6.240

× × ×

इति सप्तकमाख्यातं गुरुपंक्तिविधौ प्रपूज्यमस्मद्परमगुरुभिः ।

Ibid. 16.10

× × ×

अभिनवगुप्तगुरुः पुनराह हि सति वित्तदेशकालादौ ॥

अपवर्गे हि विस्तीर्णकर्मविज्ञानसंग्रहः कार्यः । Ibid. 16.195-96

× × ×

आवाहने मातृकार्णं मालिन्यर्णं च पूजने ॥

कुर्यादिति गुरुः प्राह स्वरूपाप्यायनद्वयात् । Ibid. 17.10-11

× × ×

आवाह्येष्ट्वा प्रतर्प्येति श्रीस्वच्छन्दे निरूपितम् ॥

अनेनैव पथा नेयमित्यस्मद्गुरवो जगुः । Ibid. 17.18-19

	Name	*Subject*
	MAṬHIKĀGURUS	
1.	Narasiṁhagupta (father) alias Cukhalaka	Grammar, literature and logic
2.	Vāmanātha	Dualistic Śaivism
3.	Bhūtirāja	Dualistic-cum-monistic Śaivism, Brahmavidyā, Vidyātraya and Śatarudrīya
4.	Bhūtirājatanaya (Helārāja)	Dualistic-cum-monistic Śaivism (and perhaps philosophy of grammar ?)
5.	Lakṣmaṇagupta	Tantra-prakriyā (Krama, Trika and Pratyabhijñā or Traiyambaka school of monism) and the *Devīpañcaśatika* plus Śāktanyāsa
6.	Śambhunātha	Kulaprakriyā (Ardhatraiyambaka school of monism) and the *Śrīpūrvaśāstra* plus several other matters.
	JÑĀNAGURUS	
7.	Śrīcandra Śarmā	?
8.	Bhava (? Bhavabhūti)	*Trīśikāśāstra* (?)
9.	Bhaktivilāsa	?
10.	Yogānanda	?
11.	Abhinanda	?
12.	Śivaśakti	?
13.	Vicitranātha	?
14.	Dharmaśiva	Parokṣa-dīkṣā (partly)
15.	Vāmanaka (? Vāmanadatta)	Upāya-bheda

16. Udbhaṭa	Sister tradition of Krama system
17. Śrībhūtīśa	?
18. Bhāskara	*Śivasūtras* and Spanda school (?)
19. Aniruddha	*Mataṅga Āgama.*

(II) *Works*

From Abhinava's teachers we now turn to his works[1] confining our enquiry to the titles cited in the *Tantrāloka* alone. Interestingly the number of own works mentioned is not large. His first ever reference has been made to one *Anuttaraprakriyā*[2] which has been found identical with the *Parātriṁśikāvivaraṇa* by Jayaratha. It is to be noted that Abhinavagupta makes no mention of its authorship. He has referred to other *Vivṛtis* on the *P.T.* but they are all by his predecessors[3] and goes on citing views from one such *Vivṛti* in the *T.A.* 13.150-154. In view of Abhinavagupta's silence on the authorship are we justified in branding the *Anuttaraprakriyā* as his work? Perhaps yes, for (i) Jayaratha interprets *Anuttaraprakriyā* as *Parātriśikāvivaraṇa*, which is exactly the title of Abhinavagupta's published work, (ii) Abhinavagupta has

1. For material from additional sources see Abhi. pp. 27-131; Abhinavagupta and His works, Raghavan, Varanasi, pp. 17-32 and also pp. 33-77; K.T., pp. 159-165.

2. अनुत्तरप्रक्रियायां वैतत्येन प्रदर्शितम् ।
एतत् तस्माततः पश्येद्विस्तरार्थी विवेचकः ॥ T.A. 9.313

Jayaratha explains—

अनुत्तरप्रक्रियायामिति श्रीपरात्रिंशिकाविवरणादौ इत्यर्थः ।
T.A.V., VI, p. 249

3. श्रीसोमानन्दकल्याणभवभूतिपुरोगमाः ॥
तथाहि श्रीत्रीशिकाशास्त्रविवृतौ तेऽभ्यधुर्बुधाः । T.A. 13.149-50

shunned detailed discussion on the *inter se* relationship amongst categories where each succeeding category represents the power and each preceding the powerful and commends his another work for a detailed understanding. The problem, *inter alia*, has been treated in detail in the *P.T.V.* by Abhinavagupta (pp. 99-218). Abhinavagupta's commendation, coming as it does in the *Tantrāloka*, assumes special significance because the *Parātriṁśikā* has been called the *Trikasūtra* elsewhere and has been shown to serve as an index to the entire subject matter of Trika System,[1] (iii) The word "Purogamāḥ" (i.e. pilots or precursors) clearly implies that he authored a commentary on the *P.T.* which was preceded by his teachers namely Somānanda, Kalyāṇa and Bhavabhūti. Profuse references to Somānanda and his univocal acknowledgement of debt to the former towards the end of his *P.T.V.*[2] leave no doubt about the fact that the reference to the *Anuttaraprakriyā* is to his own work.

The other work which has found mention is the *Mālinīślokavārtika* where the nature of five sources starting with their origin from the transcendental base has been taken up for elaborate treatment. One, eager to learn, may refer to it because Abhinavagupta is not in the habit of unnecessary repetition.[3] This text

1. उक्तं श्रीत्रिकसूत्रे च जायते यजनं प्रति । T.A. 12.15
Jayaratha adds श्रीत्रिकसूत्र इति त्रिकप्रमेयसूचिकायां श्रीपरात्रीशिकायाम् इत्यर्थः । T.A.V., VII, p. 101 (12th Āhnika)

2. तत्तत्त्वनिर्मलस्थितिविभागिहृदये स्वयं प्रविष्टमिव ।
श्रीसोमानन्दमतं विमृश्य मया निबद्धमिदम् ॥
P.T.V., concluding verse 19, p. 282

3. मयैतत्स्रोतसां रूपमनुत्तरपदाद्ध्रुवात् ।
आरभ्य विस्तरेणोक्तं मालिनीश्लोकवार्तिके ॥
जिज्ञासुस्तत एवेदमवधारयितुं क्षमः ।
वयं तूक्तानुवचनमफलं नाद्रियामहे ॥ T.A. 37.30-31

is identical with the *Mālinīvijayavārtika* and is a versicular running commentary on the *Mālinīvijayottara Tantra*. This is none other than the famous *Śrīpūrvaśāstra*, the scriptural backbone of the *Tantrāloka*. Pandey has successfully visualized a chronological order[1] among all the three works under reference which is as follows—*M.V.V.*, *P.T.V.* and *T.A.*—each coming in succession.

In this very context it is significant to note that Abhinavagupta makes an indirect reference to one of his works called *Pañcikā*. While commenting on the *T.A.* 23.75[2] Jayaratha yields sufficient information.[3] It was a commentary which bore the title *Pañcikā* and was composed in versicular form as a quotation from it suggests. One thing is absolutely sure that the treatise was available to Jayaratha. Here again Abhinavagupta's reticence on its authorship is intriguing. It is Jayaratha who in another context refers to the *Pañcikā* as Abhinavagupta's composition.[4] The relevant reference does not give an idea of the original text as to whose commentary it was. Banking on the contextual evidence (Abhinavagupta is discussing removal of inferior knowledge from an aspirant belonging to the lesser disciplines as pro-

1. Abhi., pp. 30-33
2. अतएवाम्बुजन्मार्कदृष्टान्तोऽत्र निरूपितः ॥
3. निरूपित इत्येतद्विवरण एव पंचिकायाम् । यदुक्तं तत्र–
   दिवाकरकरासारविरहात्संकुचत्कजम् ।
   सत्स्वप्यन्यग्रहमहः स्वेति नैव विकासिताम् ॥
   एवं शिष्यहृदम्भोजं गुरुपादविवर्जितम् ।
   निमीलद्विकसत्येव पुनस्तत्पादपाततः ॥ T.A.V., X, p. 292
4. यत्पुनरनेन पंचिकायां व्याख्यातं . . . . . . तत्
   तत्त्वक्रमसाम्यापादनहेवाकिनां केषांचन मतमिति ।
   Ibid., X, pp 56-57.

pounded in the *Śrīpūrvaśāstra*)[1] it, in all probability, should have been an exposition of the *Śrīpūrvaśāstra*. If it be so, the work would be identical with one *Pūrvapañcikā* included by Pandey among the works of Abhinavagupta.[2] The contention gets support if we coordinate the statement of Jayaratha on the *T.A.* 16.135-36 where Abhinavagupta dwells on the 'assignment of the passage of a syllable' (Padādhvanyāsa) in the context of 'variety of the purifiables' (Śodhyavaicitrya) under Putrakadīkṣā (initiation concerning aspirant of Putraka class) with the one in the *P.T.V.*[3] The work, as held by Pandey, might be an extremely large work if one remembers that the *M.V.V.* was a running commentary on the first verse of the *M.V.T.*[4], of course briefly incorporating the total subject matter of all the 18 chapters. Since the *P.T.V.* alludes to this text, the chronological sequence of the four works would emerge somewhat like this—*Mālinīvijayavārtika*, *Pūrvapañcikā*, *Pratyabhijñā Vimarśinī* and *Tantrāloka*. It will be proper to conclude that all these works constituted a complete whole on the Tāntrika material in a cognate field. It is significant to note that the *Mālinīvijayavārtika* was written in the same house[5] in which the *Tantrāloka* was under-

1. श्रीपूर्वशास्त्रे तेनोक्तं यावत्तेनैव नोद्धृतः
अत्र ह्यर्थोऽयमेतावत्पूर्वोक्तज्ञानवृंहितः ।
. . . . .दृष्टान्तोऽत्रनिरूपितः ॥ T.A. 23.73-75
2. Abhi., p. 37. Śrīpūrvapañcikā would be the better title.
3. वर्णमन्त्रपदरूपता शोध्यांशवृत्तिः—इत्यास्ताम्, अप्रकृतमेतत्, निर्णीतं च
मयैव श्रीपूर्वप्रभृतिपञ्चिकासु । P.T.V., p. 147
4. प्रवरपुरनामधेये पुरे पूर्वे काश्मीरिकोऽभिनवगुप्तः ।
मालिन्यादिवाक्ये वार्तिकमेतद् रचयति स्म ॥ M.V.V. 2.335
5. Ibid.

taken.[1] It aimed at pleasing Śambhunātha[2] and was undertaken at the instance of Karṇa and Mandra.[3] Similar was the case with the *P.T.V.* at the time of whose writing, like the *Tantrāloka*, Abhinavagupta was under the care of Vatsalikā[4] and which was written at the request of Karṇa among others.[5] The benedictory verse is common to all the three works. The ideas that have been dealt with in one text are skipped over or just referred to in other works. It is an irony of fate that the *Pūrvapañcikā* or *Pañcikā* is perhaps lost to us.

Only one more work that is available from references is the *Prakīrṇakavivaraṇa*. Although the work is not cited by name in the *Tantrāloka*—it is alluded to as 'elsewhere' (Anyatra),[6] Jayaratha interprets the word 'Anyatra' as *Prakīrṇakavivaraṇa*. According to Abhinavagupta the causative operation (Prayojaka-vyāpāra) indicated in Sanskrit by the suffix Ṇic loses its primary meaning if it is related to the insentient prompter. The problem is: what is that constitutes the proper object of causative operation—one about which the relative action has already commenced or is yet to commence? Abhinavagupta says he has dealt with the issue in detail elsewhere, hence the reader should better not concentrate on this point here. In the *Tantrāloka* and for that matter in whole of the Abhi-

1. T.A. 37.72
2. M.V.V. 1.4
3. Ibid. 1.11
4. Ibid., concluding verse 6, p. 279.
5. P.T.V., concluding verse 7, pp. 279-80.
6. इत्थं जडेन संबंधे न मुख्या ण्यर्थसंगतिः ।
   आस्तामन्यत्र विततमेतद्विस्तरतो मया ॥ T.A. 10.44
   अन्यत्रेति प्रकीर्णकविवरणादौ । T.A.V., VII, p. 33

navan writings there is absolute lack of any other reference to this work. Whether the work is identical with or different from his own *Prakaraṇavivaraṇa* has been discussed elsewhere.[1] It is, however, difficult to surmise about the precise nature of its contents. However, the word 'Prakīrṇaka' stands for 'miscellaneous'. Hence Abhinavagupta appears to have focussed on several relevant miscellaneous issues which were not primarily philosophical but, all the same, carried philosophical 'implications'. Such a hypothesis appears harmonious with the admission of Abhinavagupta that philosophical implications of grammatical issues (e.g., whether an inanimate entity can be endowed with causative action) received detailed consideration in this work.

Abhinava's most works are interspersed with the sprinklings of Stotras. In the *Tantrāloka*, too, we find Abhinavagupta referring to his *Stotras* at least twice.[2] In the 26th Āhnika Abhinavagupta quotes one Āryā and two Śārdūlavikrīḍitas as the *T.A.* 26.63-65.[3] One verse is quoted again as the T.A. 29.76. But the striking point about this *Stotra* is that it has not been quoted or cited, it has rather been assimilated into the text and made part of it. Since Abhinavagupta employs the word Stotra in plural

1. Contribution of Kashmir to Sanskrit Literature (unpublished), K.S. Nagarajan, thesis submitted to the University of Poona for the degree of Ph.D., 1961, p. 356; K.T., pp. 163-64. Also See Abhi, pp. 28,38.

2. स्तोत्रेषु बहुधा चैतन्मया प्रोक्तं निजाह्निके ॥ T.A. 26.62

3. The verses have been translated by me in my unpublished postgraduate dissertation "Abhinavagupta Ke Stotra; Eka Adhyayana" (Hindi) pp. 275-76. These verses form part of Naimittika Vidhi in the *T.S.*, pp. 180-81 and one verse i.e., कृत्वाधारधरां etc. has been incorporated as *M.V.V.* 2.126.

(i.e., Stotreṣu) he seems to imply that he has been giving vent to his ideas through Stotras as and when occasion warrants so. In the *Tantrāloka* we quite often come across with such verses which are replete with intense devotion.[1] But in the absence of any definite statement to this effect we assign the sorting out of such portions to the future ventures.

Before closing the discussion on Abhinavagupta's writings let us examine an intriguing statement from him. He says that one of the secondary items namely Naimittika (occasional functions) with its varieties has been dealt with in the *Tantrasāra*.[2] The *Tantrasarā* which is another work by the same pen, resounds the statement.[3] Now the problem is that the *Tantrasāra*, as we know, is a shorter version of the *Tantrāloka* on the admission of Abhinavagupta himself.[4] In all probability the *Tantrāloka* must precede the *Tantrasāra*; how could the *Tantrāloka*, therefore, contain a reference to the *Tantrasāra*? One thing is certain that the *Tantrasāra* is posterior in chronological order—it was a summary in simple words intended to enlighten all and sundry.

1. Cp. विदितमृतिसतत्त्वाः संविदम्भोनिधाना-
दचलहृदयवीर्याकर्षनिष्पीठनोत्थम् ।
अमृतमिति निगीर्णे कालकूटेऽत्र देवा
यदि पिबथ तदानीं निश्चितं वः शिवत्वम् ।। T.A. 28.367

2. इति नैमित्तिकं श्रीमत्तन्त्रसारे निरूपितम् ।
त्रयोविंशतिभेदेन विशेषार्चानिबन्धनम् ।। Ibid. 28.9

3. नैमित्तिकं ज्ञानलाभः. . . . . .समयनिष्कृतिलाभः इत्येतत् नैमित्तिकं विशेषार्चाकारणम् । T.S., KSS XVII, p. 179

4. विततस्तन्त्रालोको विगाहितुं नैव शक्यते सर्वैः ।
ऋजुवचनविरचितमिदं तु तन्त्रसारं ततः शृणुत ।। Ibid., p. 2
(Opening verse 2). Also see pp. 96-97, 98, 99, 130, 170, 186-87, 194-95.

In all likelihood it seems to be a reference to some other work of the same name. Luckily Abhinavagupta in his *P.T.V.* refers twice to this work and quotes therefrom.[1] In the same work he further quotes twice from some *Trikatantrasāra*[2]. It appears that both of these texts were identical and were, perhaps, a scriptural work, on the Trīśikā offshoot of Kaulika discipline. According to Dwivedi[3] this work is also known variously as the *Saḍardhaśāstra*, *Saḍardhasāra*,[4] *Saḍardhahṛdaya*, *Sāraśāsana* and *Sāraśāstra* etc. However, the evidence is too sketchy to hazard a definite opinion. We are, however, inclined to think that while the *Tantrasāra* and the *Trikatantrasāra* formed one unit, Ṣaḍardhaśāstra etc. represented a separate unit standing perhaps for the *P.T.* which is reckoned as the *Trikasūtra* and *Saḍardhahṛdaya*[5] by the *Tantrāloka* itself. Sometimes these very names have

1. तथाहि श्रीतन्त्रसारे—
   त्रिशकार्थस्त्वया प्रोक्तः सार्धकोटिविस्तरः । इति । P.T.V., p. 17
   × × ×
   यदुक्तं श्रीतन्त्रसारे
   "धारयन्ति पशोः पाशान्भावान्स्वात्ममयांस्तथा ।
   विद्यामायानियत्याद्याः शोध्यास्तेन प्रयत्नतः ॥" इति । P.T.V., p. 117
2. अतएव तथाविधबीजकुसुमैकघनभावशिवशक्तिसंघट्टः स्वयं स्वात्मनैव पूज्य इति इत्युपदिष्टम् श्रीत्रिकतन्त्रसारे—
   "शिवशक्तिसमापत्त्या शिवशक्तिघनात्मकः ।
   शिवशक्तिसमापत्तित्रिकं संपूजयेत्परम् ॥" इति । Ibid, p. 184
   × × ×
   एवमानन्दयोग एव हृदयपूजा, यथोक्तं त्रिकतन्त्रसारे
   "आनन्दप्रसरः पूजा तां त्रिकोणे प्रकल्पयेत् ।
   पुष्पधूपादिगन्धैस्तु स्वहृत्संतोषकारिणीम् ॥ इति । Ibid, p. 223
3. Vide Upodghāta, pp. 39-40
4. T.A. 12.15
5. Ibid. 31.54

been used to refer to the *Tantrāloka* also.[1] In the absence of conclusive denotation, it will be better to leave the things as they are at the moment.

If we shift from the *Tantrāloka* to the material in Jayaratha we are likely to conclude that Abhinavagupta undertook one more book called the *Anupratyabhijñā*.[2] On a closer scrutiny the view cannot be conclusively maintained, because much will depend on how we construe the phrase "Anenaiva"[3] i.e., as qualifying 'Anupratyabhijñākṛtā or 'Abhiprāyeṇa'. In view of the obvious contextual emphasis sought to be laid down by Jayaratha, construing Anenaiva with Abhiprāyeṇa seems more logical. On such a view Anupratyabhijñā will not tend to be Abhinavagupta's but rather someone else's work. Our other informations about this work and its author are practically nil.

(III) *Methodology*

The undertaking of the *Tantrāloka* was a very ambitious, massive and intricate project for Abhinava. Covering the vast panorama of the anarchous tantric literature of varying hues was no mean task. It appears that Abhinava evolved certain guiding principles, criteria and methods to handle the mate-

1. See Upodghāta to N.S.T., Dwivedi, p. 37.
2. Vide K.T., p. 160. We revise our opinion as expressed there as per ensuing discussion. Also see Upodghāta, p. 17
3. यदुक्तं श्रीप्रत्यभिज्ञाकृता—"तत्र त्वर्पकादुपाधेस्तदाकारत्वं, चित्तत्त्वस्य तु निजैश्वर्यात् ।" इति । अनुप्रत्यभिज्ञाकृताऽप्यनेनैव अभिप्रायेण,
नाथ त्वया विना बिम्बं स्वच्छे स्वात्मनि दर्शितम् ।
प्रसेना दर्पणेनैव प्रभावाद्भावमण्डलम् ॥" इत्याद्युक्तम् ॥
T.A.V., II, pp. 72-73

rial in hand in such a manner as to weave a well-knit and coherent pattern. It is really amazing to see a subtle unity of purpose and presentation permeating the whole of the *Tantrāloka* without affecting the diversity of content and treatment.

(a) Guiding principles of explanation

Of all the characteristics of the *Tantrāloka*, the two are the most prominent—it is a comprehensive compendium and a glossorial treatise. Fused together they put the *Tantrāloka* in proper focus—it is a masterly compendium written in a glossorial style. As is quite usual with Abhinava, he does not keep us in suspense about his guiding principles. He devotes 10th and 11th ancillary topics—methods of explanation and listening respectively—under Naimittika Vidhi (28th Āhnika) and spells out the following imperatives of explanation relying upon the authority of the *Devyāyāmala Tantra*[1]—

1. सूत्रपदवाक्यपटलग्रन्थक्रमयोजनेन सम्बन्धात् ।
अव्याहतपूर्वापरमुपवृह्य नयेत वाक्यानि ।।
मण्डूकप्लवसिंहावलोकनाद्यैर्यथायथं न्यायैः ।
अविहतपूर्वापरकं शास्त्रार्थं योजयेदसङ्कीर्णम् ।।
तन्त्रावर्तनबाधप्रसङ्गतर्कादिभिश्च सन्न्यायैः ।
वस्तु वदेद् वाक्यज्ञो वस्त्वन्तरतो विविक्ततां विदधत् ।
यद्यत्व्याहृतिपदवीमायाति तदेव दृढतरैर्न्यायैः ।
बलवत्कुर्याद्दूष्यं यद्यप्यग्रे भविष्यत्स्यात् ।।
दृढरचितपूर्वपक्षप्रोद्धरणपथेन वस्तु यद्वाच्यम् ।।
शिष्यमतावारोहति तदाशु संशयविपर्ययैर्विकलम् ।।
भाषा न्यायो वादो लयः क्रमो यद्यदेति शिष्यस्य ।
सम्बोधोपायत्वं तथैव गुरुराश्रयेद्व्याख्याम् ।। T.A. 28.400-405

Jayaratha adds— "यागत्रयात्मकपौर्णमासाङ्गप्रयाजानुयाजवदेकमनेकसाधारणं तन्त्रम् । अवघातादेरिव यावद्द्रव्यमसकृत्प्रयुक्तिरावर्तनम् । चमसगोदोहनादिवदसक्तप्रतिषेधो बाधः । पशुपुरोडाशवत् परमध्यपातिनो निजतन्त्रनैरपेक्ष्येण

(i) Sentences must be interpreted keeping in view the total textual perspective and their consistent construction must take into account the aphorism, phrase, sentence, chapter and section of the text, etc.

(ii) For lucid perspectival interpretation selective handling of the material or its over-all viewing may be resorted to as demanded by the occasion.

(iii) The item under reference is to be distinguished from other objects by resorting to various methods defined by common application (Tantra), exclusive application (Āvartana), negation (Bādha), contextual or incidental discussion (Prasaṅga) and exploration of the potential options (Tarka) as well as transference of one attribute to another (Atideśa).

(iv) Each utterance must be vigorously subjected to scrutiny and the opposite view, though to be denounced later, ought to be fortified with stronger arguments.

(v) The substantiation of the relative issue by demolishing the strongly conceived prima facie defence leads to quicker grasp free from suspicions and contrary ideas.

परकीयेनैव तन्त्रेण सम्पादनं प्रसङ्गः। संशयनिर्णयान्तरालवर्ती भवितव्यतात्मकः प्रत्ययस्तर्कः । आदिशब्दादतिदेशादयः . . . . . . भाषा संस्कृतादिरूपा षोढा भिन्ना । न्यायः प्रागुक्तो लौकिकः शास्त्रीयो वा । वादस्तत्त्वनिश्चयफलरूपः पक्ष-प्रतिपक्षपरिग्रहः । लयो व्याख्येयवस्तुनिष्ठतल्लीनतात्मा व्याख्यानाभ्यासः । क्रमः पाठार्थपरिपाटीविशेषः । T.A.V., XI, pp. 172-174

It may, however, be noted in passing that the *T.S.* substitutes Prasaṅga and Tarka with Samuccaya (conjunction or aggregation) and Vikalpa (option). Abhinava does not explain these words. M.R. Shastri in his editorial footnote (p. 189) adds—अनेकक्रिया-कारकसंबंधः समुच्चयः, शब्दज्ञानानुपाती वस्तुशून्यो विकल्पः ।" Collective presentation of similar instances and statement of an optional instance, however, seem to be better explanations.

(vi) Linguistic variants (Bhāṣā), classical and conventional rules (Nyāya), close grasp of the pros and cons leading to conclusive appreciation of a theme (Vāda), regular homework at the theme (Laya), particular manner of textual interpretation (Krama)—these are the several alternatives out of which a teacher is supposed to employ one he finds most conducive and convenient for enlightening his student.

As an addendum another remark from Abhinava in some other text[1]—we are committed to confine ourselves to the pages of the *Tantrāloka* alone—may appear beneficial to refer to. The author of a scholastic treatise, according to him, has a multi-directional going—something he has to condense, something to enlarge, something he has to insert and something to skip. It is only then that he becomes a Śāstrakāra and is able to communicate adequately.

(b) Multi-tier handling of the source material

It is interesting to see how Abhinava employs all these—and many more norms—in his *Tantrāloka*. Quite in line with his extensive treatment his method has several tiers and we now propose to take an account of them. One, however, must be cautious that Abhinava has an extremely complex style serving various ends at a time, hence certain amount of overlapping will be unavoidable. The *Tantrāloka* being a digest of the Tantras the first thing that arrests our attention is his mathodical handling of the source

1. संकोच्य किंचिदिह किंचिदथ प्रसार्यं
प्रक्षिप्य किंचिदिव किंचिदथाप्यपास्य ।
विद्वांज्जनो भवतु संप्रति शास्त्रकृच्च
सम्यकप्रचारणविधिः स हि जन्म तस्य ।।
I.P.V.V., III, p. 404 (concluding verse 7)

material. In this area again his role is manifold. He has to identify the sources, make his pick, scrutinize it and then edit the same before it is reduced to writing. As we shall see later in detail he first sorts out the source material under three heads—(1) basic, (2) general and (3) specific. For instance, the *M.V.T.* is the basic source, the *SV.T.* and *Sp.K.* are the general sources and the remaining are the specific sources pertaining to the specific items. In culling material from them his first criterion is utility (upayoga)[1]. Even if a thing has been discussed at length in the original sources, Abhinava would avoid touching upon it if it does not serve the purpose in hand. The notion of utility includes that of relevance as well. Abhinava, though, categorically dispels doubts regarding his capacity for an elaborate treatment, he would scrupulously restrict himself to the relevant material[2] and move ahead. Abhinava's third criterion is to conform to the factual position. Even though a specific treatment may sometimes look at variance with his known stand, he would not feel shy of recording the same.[3] His fourth guiding principle behind a specific selection is its consistency with the general theme. Sometimes a text (the *M.V.T.* in this case) that may be wholly relevant as being advocate of a

1. श्रीमत्त्रैशिरसे तच्च कथिते विस्तराद्बहु ।
इह नो लिखितं व्यासभयाच्चानुपयोगतः ॥ T.A. 3.256-57
2. स च नो विस्तरः साक्षाच्छक्यो यद्यपि भाषितुम् ।
तथापि मार्गमात्रेण कथ्यमानो विविच्यताम् ॥ Ibid. 10.153

Jayaratha explains मार्गमात्रेण as दिङ्मात्रेण । T.A.V., VII, p. 107

3. तथापि वस्तुसत्तेयमिहास्माभिर्निरूपिता T.A. 19.219
Mark the words इह अस्माभिः and also the prefatory remark of Jayaratha—ननु यद्येवं तत् कथं भोक्तृभोग्ययोर्युगपदुत्पादो भवतैव उक्तः, इत्याशङ्क्याह । T.A.V., VI, p. 175

consistent theory is quoted at random only to highlight its uniform approach.[1] His choice is quite deliberate being invariably guided by the twin canons of consistency and relevance and in so doing he would not desist from rearranging the whole thing.[2] This will perhaps explain the two conflicting approaches in the 16th and 19th Āhnikas. It is the demand of relevance that they, though opposed to one another, fit in the two different chapters dealing with the 'assignment of purifying Mantras' in respect of the 'purifiable categories' and the 'assignment of words' in respect of the 'instant passing away' respectively.[3] His unflinching faith in relevance and utility is further exemplified by his handling of Dhyāna (meditation) —a sub-upāya under Āṇava. Āṇava-upāya in a sense is a series of sub-upāyas where, as per agamic order, Uccāra comes first followed by Karaṇa, Dhyāna and Varṇa respectively. Abhinava here interferes with the agamic sequence and places Dhyāna in the beginning to be followed by Uccāra, Karaṇa and Varṇa in that succession owing to their respective superior efficacy.[4]

1. अष्टादशपटलस्य एकवाक्यतां दर्शयितुमालूनविशीर्णतया अयं ग्रन्थः संवादितः । T.A.V., III, p. 114
2. एतच्च यद्यपि श्रीस्वच्छन्दे त्रिविधादहंकारादनन्तरमुक्तं तथापि इह विकारषोडशकसाजात्येनैव व्याख्यातम् । Ibid. V, p. 199
3. केवलशोधकमन्त्रन्यासाभिप्रायतो महादेवः ।
   तत्त्वक्रमोदितमपि न्यासं पुनराह तद्विरुद्धमपि ॥ T.A. 16.231
   Jayaratha adds महादेवो हि शोध्यानां षट्त्रिंशत्तत्त्वानां क्रमेण तन्न्यासपुरःसरीकारेण उदितमपि शोधकमन्त्रन्यासाभिप्रायेण पुनस्तद्विरुद्धमपि एकान्नविंशतेः (19th Āhnika devoted to सद्य उत्क्रान्तिनिरूपण) पदानां न्यासमाह तदन्यथात्वेनापि अकथयदित्यर्थः । T.A.V., X, p. 89
4. उच्चारकरणध्यानवर्णैरेभिः प्रदर्शितः ॥
   अनुत्तरपदप्राप्तावभ्युपायविधिक्रमः ।

One of the reasons for selective treatment lies in the difficulty in understanding the original source. He prefers dealing with the incomprehensible material omitting the easier one.[1] But that does not mean he would compromise authenticity for convenience. He would not commit an agamic source even when he is sure of its stand, to a particular thesis, if the same has not been unequivocally propounded.[2] Thus while authenticity guides enumeration, easy comprehension guides omission. According to Jayaratha one of the criteria that guided the selective treatment was practicability and general applicability. It is possible he might have propounded different views of different people in some other writings, but it is impossible and impractical to take cognizance of all the views at one place.[3] Notwithstanding adherence to these

---

अकिंचिच्चिन्तनं वीर्यं भावनायां च सा पुनः ॥
ध्याने तदपि चोच्चारे करणे सोऽपि तद्ध्वनौ ।
स स्थानकल्पने बाह्यमिति क्रममुपाश्रयेत् ॥ T.A. 5.155-57

Jayaratha supplies the proper context—

ननु उच्चारादीनाम् आगमेऽप्यनेनैव क्रमेण पाठः इति कथमिह तदुल्लङ्घनेन ध्यानोपक्रममेषां निर्देशः कृतः इत्याशंक्याह...... एवं पूर्वं पूर्वमुत्तरत्र वीर्यमिति पाठक्रममपहाय...... अर्थक्रमावलम्बनेन अन्यथैवं निर्देशः कृतः ।
T.A.V., III, pp. 468-469

1. शेषास्तु सुगमरूपाः शब्दास्तत्रार्थमूहयेदुचितम् ॥ T.A. 9.88

2. अनया तु दिशा प्रायः सर्वभेदेषु विद्यते ॥
भेदो मन्त्रमहेशान्तेष्वेष पञ्चदशात्मकः ।
तथापि स्फुटताभावात्सन्नप्येष न चर्चितः ॥ Ibid. 10.183-84

Abhinava says, although the thirteenfold character is also possible in water, like earth, the same has not been propounded as it has not been clearly, unambiguously, discussed in the *Śrīpūrvaśāstra*.

3. अत्र च चतुर्भिरङ्गुलैः...... इति । यत्पुनरनेन पञ्चिकायां व्याख्यातं ...... तत् तत्त्वक्रमसाम्यापादनहेवाकिनां केषांचन मतमिति । नहि सर्वसर्विकया एतदापादयितुं पार्यते इति किमशक्यार्थाभिनिवेशेन ।
(Comm. on T.A. 16.135-138). T.A.V., X, 11.56-57

norms occasionally, though sparsely, there appears to be an element of casualness in Abhinava's treatment. At such places Abhinava does not go deep, but restricts himself to the surface material. For example, Ananta, the presiding deity of the earthy regions (regions finding berth in the category called earth), is depicted as seated on a boat 'within' waters.[1] Now the word 'within' (Antāḥ) is either interpreted as 'residing above' (i.e., outside) or as 'gradual presence' (of 100 Rudras beginning with Ananta) but in no case as 'inside'. Why did Abhinava, instead, not choose a clearer expression to avoid likely confusion? Jayaratha suggests that as Abhinava's main preoccupation was to produce a compendium he made a cursory choice of the material as it appeared on the face of it, if it did not affect his logical position. This type of choice has been designated as 'expanded' or 'shallow'[2] (Uttāna) and Abhinava takes recourse to it several times. Reasons of space and fear of unwieldy size of the text also placed certain constraints on Abhinava in the final selection of his material.[3] But such a situation is consequent upon one of the three courses adopted by Abhinava—(1) He has already dealt with the similar material from other sour-

1. नेता कटाहरुद्राणामनन्तः कामसेविनाम् ।
पोतारुढो जलस्यान्तर्मद्यपानविर्घूणितः ॥ T.A. 8.21

2. जलस्यान्तरित्यर्थात् तदुपरि संस्थितः । .... क्रममात्रमेवाभिधित्सितं न त्वन्तर्बहीरूपत्वमपि .... । ...... एवं .... इत्यादावपि व्याख्येयम् । एतच्च उत्तानतयैव गृहीत्वा संग्रहकाराः प्रवृत्ताः, इति तत्र तथाभ्यधुः, येनास्य अन्तरवस्थाने भ्रान्तिबीजत्वं प्ररूढम् । T.A.V., V, pp. 14-19

3. Cp. अनयैव दिशा नेयं मतङ्गकिरणादिकम् ।
ग्रन्थगौरवभीत्या तु तल्लिखित्वा न योजितम् ॥
T.A. 13.284; also see the fn. 2 on p. 67 supra.

ces and candidly admits existence of the additional connected material which he has not deliberately used. In this context he occasionally advises the reader to refer to the original text itself;[1] (2) Sometimes he implies that his treatment is strictly confined to the basic sources and further reference to other sources will add only unnecessary bulk to the work;[2] (3) A thing may be relevant and contextually justifiable to refer to, but it leads to innumerable varieties depending upon the individual preferences. For example, in the *M.V.T.* (Śrīpūrvaśāstra) elemental submergence (Bhautāveśa) finds place after fifty varieties of Rudraśakti-samāveśa, but Abhinava though admitting its relevance and utility chooses to skip it.[3] But he continues to have an open mind. As and when he finds his 'basic' sources less vocal, he does not shirk laying his hands on other cognate sources.[4]

1. Cp. इत्यादिगह्वरोक्तं तत एव पठेद्बहु । T.A. 28.226
Jayaratha remarks—तत एव बहु पठेदिति अस्माभिस्तु ग्रन्थविस्तरभयान्न पठितमित्यभिप्रायः । T.A.V., XI, p. 89

2. Cp. प्रत्येकवर्णगोऽप्युक्तः सिद्धयोगीश्वरे मते ॥
देवताचक्रविन्यासः स बहुत्वान्न लिप्यते । T.A. 30.25-26
Jayaratha's observation is important—
बहुत्वादिति ग्रन्थविस्तरभयादिति प्रक्रान्ते श्रीपूर्वशास्त्रे हि एतत्पूजनं न आम्नातम् इत्याशयः । T.A.V., XII, pp. 187-88

3. रुद्रशक्तिसमावेशः पञ्चधा ननु चर्च्यते ।
कोऽवकाशो भवेत्तत्र भौतावेशादिवर्णने ॥
प्रसंगादिति चेत्समाधिः संभवन्नयम् ।
नास्माकं मानसावर्जी लोको भिन्नरुचिर्यतः ॥ T.A. 1. 192-93

4. Vide इह (अप्तत्त्वे भुवनेशाष्टकताप्रसंगे) श्रीस्वच्छन्दशास्त्रानुसारं प्रक्रमेऽपि (श्री) पूर्वशास्त्रप्रक्रियया एषां पाठे, अयमाशयो—यदेतदेव भुवनेशाष्टकमप्तत्त्वे सर्वागमेषु प्रधानतया उक्तम् इत्यत एव प्रतिष्ठायाम् एतदाद्यष्टकसप्तकस्वीकारेणैव सर्वत्र भुवनानां संकलनम् । T.A.V., V, p. 145

(c) Interpretation and its norms

Likewise Abhinava has tried to fashion a model for interpreting the source material. In all his writing Abhinava's obsession with three aims is obvious. They are (1) authenticity (2) unambiguity and (3) communicability. First of all, therefore, he tries to find out the meaning of the word employed, then grapples with the sentence[1] and then discovers its implication[2] and if the same still lacks in clarity, he picks up a suitable illustration.[3] While looking for denotation of a word he tries to fix up a modality for interpretation—whether it is to be explained literally,[4] etymologically or by implication. Sometimes even if some scriptural authority on an etymology or linguistic construction is not readily available, Abhinava would like one to exercise one's common sense, as it is not always possible to lay down everything in a book.[5] He always calls upon the intelligent reader to make his own guesses and draw inferences from a logical construction of the source texts, even if there is no explicit averment.[6] Abhinava is very methodical and meticulous. In interpreting a text he first decides upon the reading and critically edits it, if there are more readings than one or if there is confusion or

1. पदार्थयोजनानन्तरं वाक्यार्थमपि योजयितुमाह । T.A.V. I, p. 206
2. एवमेतत्पदार्थद्वारेण व्याख्याय तात्पर्यमुखेनाप्यभिधत्ते । ननु विसर्गशब्दो शक्तौ केन निमित्तेन प्रवृत्तः. . . . . Ibid. II, p. 99
3. इत्याशंकां दृष्टान्तोपदर्शनद्वारेण उपशमयति Ibid., II, p. 146
4. इह सर्वत्र शब्दानामन्वर्थं चर्चयेद्यतः । T.A. 6.30
5. cp. अतोऽध्वशब्दस्योक्तेयं निरुक्तिर्नोदिताऽपि चेत् ।
क्वचित्स्वबुद्धया साप्यूह्या कियल्लेख्यं हि पुस्तके ॥ T.A. 6.33
6. cp. इत्येवं शुद्धतत्त्वानां सृष्ट्या शिष्योऽपि तन्मयः ।
भवेद्ध्येतत्सूचितं श्रीमालिनीविजयोत्तरे ॥ Ibid.17.111

difference of opinion.[1] He further examines the various interpretations already offered and finally puts his stamp on one. In agamic circles there was a dispute as to whether Avyakta springs from Māyā or Kalā. While the *Rauravasaṁgraha* of Bṛhaspati subscribed to the former premise, the *Śrīpūrvaśāstra* swore by the latter. Abhinava sides with the *Rauravasaṁgraha* and declares all other alternative views as inconsistent and misleading.[2] In fact he seems to have an air of finality about his interpretation. In the process of interpretation he sometimes replaces the original agamic phrase thereby eliminating confusion and according proper meaning to both at the same time.[3] He then identifies the difficult portions. Sometimes it is a word[4] and sometimes it is a sizable part of the text. In the latter case he will leave out the easy portion and take up the difficult one. This offers one of the reasons why Abhinava calls his *Tantrāloka* as the *Vārtika*. In this connection a reference may be made to the *Tantrāloka* 8.171-178

1. इह सर्वत्र भुवनेश्वराणाम् आदिग्रहणेनैव प्रक्रान्तेऽपि संग्रहे स्वकण्ठेनैव पाठेऽयमाशयो—यदत्र बहूनि शास्त्रान्तरेषु असमञ्जसानि पाठान्तराणि संभवन्ति—इति श्रोतॄणां भाभूत्संमोहः। T.A.V., V, p. 186
2. तत एव निशाख्यानात्कलीभूतादलिङ्गकम् ॥
इति व्याख्यास्मदुक्तेऽस्मिन् सति न्यायेऽतिनिष्फला। T.A. 9.41-42
Jayaratha explains निशाख्यानात् as मायाख्यात् तत्वात् and अलिङ्गकम् as अव्यक्तम्. His prefatory remark is important—अतएव च एवं विसंवादाशङ्कया अत्र यदन्यैरन्यथा व्याख्यातं तदप्रयोजकमेव, इत्याह
T.A.V., VI, p. 41
3. Vide धारिकाप्यायिनी बोद्ध्री पवित्री चावकाशदा ॥
T.A. 11.33
Jayaratha comments on the word—
पवित्री—"पूञ् पवने" इत्यस्य ह्ययं प्रयोगः। उत्पूयिनी तु ऐशः पाठः।
T.A.V., VII, p. 30 (11th Āh)
4. Vide शेषास्तु सुगमरूपाः शब्दास्तत्रार्थमूहयेदुन्नितम् T.A.9.88

where Abhinava devotes full eight verses to the explanation of the 1st of the two verses quoted by him earlier (*T.A.* 8.169-170) from the *Raurava Vṛtti* varbatim, as he felt it might be difficult to comprehend[1] otherwise. Since he does not want to leave anything at the mercy of an unintelligent reader, he once even cites a long portion (*T.A.* 13.164-195) from the *Nandīśikhātantra* word by word so that even an ordinary reader may be able to grasp the proper import.[2] He then, for a proper interpretation, sets upon both the stages of textual investigation—internal as well as external. In the first instance he analyses the whole text and arranges the entire subject-matter in a logical order and in the second he contrasts and compares the basic sources with the cognate sources and also the cognate sources with the basic ones so as to get a clearer and more detailed picture of the issues at hand. For example, in the 13th[3] and 15th[4] Āhnikas

1. इत्याशङ्क्याह्. . .तद्ग्रन्थमेव पठति. . .तत्राद्यं श्लोकं विषमत्वात् स्वयमेव व्याचष्टे, द्वितीयस्तु सुगमत्वात् स्वयं न व्याकृतः ।
T.A.V., V, pp. 122-128

2. श्रीमन्नन्दिशिखातन्त्रे वितत्यैतन्निरूपितम् ॥
प्रश्नोत्तरमुखेनेति तदभग्नं निरूप्यते । T.A. 13.163-64
... ...
इत्येष पठितो ग्रन्थः स्वयं ये बोद्धुमक्षमाः ।
तेषां शिवोक्तिसंवादाद् बोधो दाढ्र्यं व्रजेदिति ॥ Ibid. 13.196

3. एवं प्राग्विषयो ग्रन्थ इयानन्यत्त्र तु स्फुटम् ।
ग्रन्थान्तरं मध्यतीव्रशक्तिपातांशसूचकम् ॥ T.A. 13. 212
... ...
स इत्यन्तो ग्रन्थ एष द्वितीयविषयः स्फुटः ॥
अन्यस्तु मन्दतीव्राख्यशक्तिपातविधिं प्रति । Ibid. 13.216-17
... ...
अन्ये यियासुरित्यादि ग्रन्थं प्राग्ग्रन्थसंगतम् ॥
कुर्वन्ति मध्यतीव्राख्यशक्तिसंपातगोचरम् । Ibid. 13.246-47
तमाराध्येति तु ग्रन्थो मन्दतीव्रैकगोचरः ॥ Ibid. 13.253

4. न चाधिकारिता दीक्षां विना योगेऽस्ति शांकरे ।
न च योगाधिकारित्वमेकमेवानया भवेत् ॥

Abhinava makes a first hand, direct analysis of the contents of the *Śrīpūrvaśāstra* and while reconciling the whole text, he even pin-points the textual portions that supposedly have bearing on the relevant theses (here 'descent of grace' and 'initiation' respectively) being propounded. The second phase (i.e., external) of his enquiry is seen where he abides by the authority of the *Nandīśikhātantra*[1] or *Svacchandatantra* when he finds it more comprehensive but quite in tune with his basic scripture the *M.V.T.*[2] The moment he notices variation, he strikes a note of caution and amends his treatment accordingly. In pursuance to this he discusses five gross elements (constituting physiological fetters) not after threefold egoity, as is done in the *Svacchandatantra*, but as constituting sixteen modifications of Prakṛti.[3]

(d) PRESENTATION : MULTI-ENDED STYLE

There is a system about his presentation also. The

अपि मन्त्राधिकारित्वं मुक्तिश्च शिवदीक्षया ।
इत्यस्मिन्मालिनीवाक्ये साक्षान्मोक्षाभ्युपायता ॥
दीक्षायाः कथिता प्राच्यग्रन्थेन पुनरुच्यते ।
पारम्पर्येण संस्कृत्या मोक्षभोगाभ्युपायता ॥ T.A. 15.4-7

The same thing he does in connection with the *Mataṅga śāstra*. See सम्यग्ज्ञानस्वभावा हि विद्या साक्षाद्विमोचिका ॥
उक्तं तत्रैव तत्त्वानां कार्यकारणभावतः ।
हेयादेयत्वकथने विद्यापाद इति स्फुटम् ॥ Ibid. 15.9-10

1. ननु श्रीपूर्वशास्त्रमधिकृत्य इदम् (i.e. प्रातिभेन शंका शाम्यते) उच्यते इत्युपक्रान्तं, तत्किमिह श्रीमन्नन्दिशिखाद्यवान्तरग्रन्थार्थकथनेन इत्याशङ्क्याह—
एनमेवार्थमन्तःस्थं गृहीत्वा मालिनीमते ॥ Ibid. 13.199
मालिनीमते निरूपितम् इति प्राच्येन संबंधः । T.A.V., VIII, p. 127

2. Vide ibid, V, p. 145.

3. एतच्च यद्यपि श्रीस्वच्छन्दे त्रिविधादहंकारादनन्तरमुक्तं तथापि इह विकार-षोडशकसाजात्येनैवं व्याख्यातम्। T.A.V., V, p. 199

first thing that appeals even to a casual reader is awareness of this mission that is reflected in his style. He conceives the *Tantrāloka* as an organic whole and every section is so interwoven in order to serve a continuing integrated purpose that it is difficult to view one section in complete isolation from the other. He adopts twofold strategy to achieve this objective—one, notwithstanding his commitment to contextual relevance Abhinava does not consolidate his treatment of a particular issue at one place, instead he spreads it over several places catering for the demand of related issues;[1] two, he lets one chapter slide into the next and thereby maintains the structural unity. The second strategy is called Sañcaya Nyāya (i.e., analogy of an aggregate or accumulation) by Jayaratha,[2] where the first half of the concluding verse in every chapter marks the end of the current chapter

1. For example, Karaṇas (Karaṇa means 'intelligent practice' —करणं सप्तधा प्राहुरभ्यासं बोधपूर्वकम्— T.A. 5.129) which ought to have been exhausted under Āṇava-upāya (5th Āhnika) are discussed in at least five different chapters namely 11th, 15th, 16th, 29th and 32nd. Similarly, one of the ancillary issues called Paratattvāṇtaḥpraveśalakṣaṇāni was a proper topic under Kulopāya (3rd and 29th Āhnikas) but which has been considered under Āṇava-upāya. Abhinava and Jayaratha, who closely follows him, no doubt have their justifications but they only strengthen our contention that the *Tantrāloka* has to be looked into as a 'whole'. See Jayaratha—

ननु भेदप्राणविकल्पसंस्काराधायित्वत्वाद् बुद्धिध्यानादीनां स्पष्टमेवाणवोपायत्वम् इति युक्तमत्र तदभिधानम्, परतत्त्वान्तःप्रवेशलक्षणः पुनरयमुपायो निर्विकल्पस्वरूपत्वान्न तथा, इति कथमस्यात्राभिधानम् ? इत्याशंक्याह—

T.A.V. III, p. 433

2. इह आह्निकादाह्निकान्तरस्य संचयन्यायेन परस्परमनुस्यूततां दर्शयितुम् एकेनैव श्लोकेन तत्पर्यन्तप्रारम्भयोरुपसंहारक्रमौ करोति इति अस्य ग्रन्थकारस्य शैली इति।

T.A.V., I, p. 309

while the second half the beginning of the next chapter. He breaks this rule only once at the end of the 36th chapter where he uses one single half to denote conclusion and commencement both.[1] The third connected strategy aims at complete fusion of the quoted agamic text in the body of the *Tantrāloka*. But for Jayaratha we would never know what is the precise source material and what is Abhinava's treatment of it. Quite often we know it from Jayaratha's obvious comments and sometimes by contrasting it against the excerpts cited from the original by Jayaratha. For the sake of clarity we cite just one example in the footnote below.[2]

This fusion of original, however, with his own treatment is Abhinava's peculiar tool which he has used with master precision and canny skill to serve diverse ends and is not so simple a mechanism as it sounds at the first instance. As we have already seen, Abhinava (i) sometimes simply refers to the text[3], (ii) sometimes reproduces agamic authority[4]

1. इह आह्निकादाह्निकान्तरस्य परस्परमनुस्यूततां दर्शयितुम् आद्यन्तयोरेकेन श्लोकेन पृथगुपसंहारोपक्रमयोरुपनिबन्धेऽपि सांप्रतं ग्रन्थान्ते तदाश्लेषमत्यन्तमवद्योतयितुमेकेनैव अर्धेन युगपत्तदुपनिबन्ध इति । T.A.V., XII, p. 390

2. The text of the *Tantrāloka* runs as—

तदैव मोक्ष इत्युक्तं धात्रा श्रीमन्निशाटने ॥
विकल्पयुक्तचित्तस्तु पिण्डपाताच्छिवं व्रजेत् ।
इतरस्तु तदैवेति शास्त्रस्यास्य प्रधानतः ॥ T.A. 1.50-51

Compare with the corresponding extract from the *Niśāṭana* as quoted by Jayaratha—

"विकल्पयुक्तचित्तस्तु पिण्डपाताच्छिवं ब्रजेत् ।
विकल्पहीनचित्तस्तु ह्यात्मानं शिवमव्ययम् ॥
पश्यते भावशुद्ध्या यो जीवन्मुक्तो न संशयः ।" T.A.V., I, p. 84

3. उपायभेदान्मोक्षेऽपि भेदः स्यादिति सूरयः । T.A. 1.165

4. तत्रत्यमेव ग्रन्थं पठति T.A.V., I, p. 202 (T.A. 1.168-170 is a reproduction from the M.V.T.)

verbatim, (iii) sometimes elects to present a gist in his words[1] and (iv) sometimes partly quotes and partly summarizes.[2] Each one of these alternatives is purpose-oriented. In quoting directly he is guided by his desire to remove confusion.[3] When he employs his own language, it is either in order to summarize[4] or to introduce next topic[5]/matter/text after incorporating relevant material from the authority concerned. Sometimes, while retaining the original Āgama intact, Abhinava reverses the order of subject and predicate and thereby tries by implication to uphold his stand as he has done in the case of the *Mataṅga Āgama*.[6] In modifying the quoted authority sometimes certain altogether different considerations have weighed. For instance, he alters the text of the *Śrīpūrvaśāstra* from 'Na dvaitam nāpi cādvaitam' to 'Na dvaitaṁ nāpi cādvyayam' (*T.A.* 4.106) just for metri-

1. एतदेवार्थद्वारेण दर्शयति Ibid., II, p. 121 (introducing T.A. 3.115 which refers to the *Bhagvadgītā*)

2. तत्रत्यमेव ग्रन्थमर्थतः शब्दतश्च पठति T.A.V. XIII, p. 150 (Reference is to the *Śrīgahvara Tantra* in T.A. 29. 240-41)

3. स्वकण्ठेनैव पाठेऽयमाशयो . . . . . इति श्रोतॄणां मा भूत्संमोहः इति । Ibid., V, p. 186

4. Cf. Jayaratha on T.A. 1.75-76—एतत्प्रश्नार्थ एव ग्रन्थकृता संक्षेपचिकीर्षया स्ववचसोपनिबद्धः Ibid., I, p. 117

5. Cf. Jayaratha on T.A. 1.84-86—एतदेव च "अथवा . . . ." इत्यादि "स्थिति . . ." इत्यन्ततत्रत्यग्रन्थार्थगर्भीकारेण ग्रन्थान्तरमुपक्षेप्तुकामो ग्रन्थकारः स्वोक्त्या योजयति "तस्य सर्वं प्रसिध्यति" इति Ibid., I, p. 130

6. तदुक्तं श्रीमतङ्गादौ स्वशक्तिकिरणात्मकम् ।
अथ पत्युरधिष्ठानमित्याद्युक्तं विशेषणैः ॥ T.A. 1.202

Jayaratha's remark is significant अथ पत्युरधिष्ठानं स्वशक्तिकिरणात्मकम् इत्येवंपाठः ऐशः, ग्रन्थकृता पुनरेवं विध्यनुवादभावदर्शनार्थम् अन्यथा पाठः कृतः T.A.V., I, p. 228; also see व्यत्यासपाठे च अयमाशयः—यत् उपायोपेयादिना द्वारद्वारिभावेन शाम्भवोपाये एव प्राधान्येन विश्रान्तिः । Ibid., I, p. 203

cal propriety.[1] Likewise, Abhinava's omissions or extremely brief treatments are equally pregnant with suggestion. He omits an item or deals in brief with it if he finds its meaning obvious.[2] Specific items are omitted to enlarge the scope or application of the relative subject matter. Abhinava, for example, presents the *Śivatanuśāstra* as propounding the contents of the *Śrīpūrvaśāstra* itself though with a difference in style. In this treatment among the five sheaths (Kañcukas—revealing agents of limited individuality), 'time' and 'determination' (Kāla and Niyati) have been purposely dropped so as to clear the path for purification of categories, through three sheaths[3] Kalā etc. Omission is also resorted to avoid unnecessary repetition or analytical arrangement. Abhinava defines Pūjā (worship) and though he thinks that Homa (rite of oblation to fire) is duly covered by his definition of worship, he does not say so because Homa, as an ingredient of worship, has already been discussed and is likely to be discussed in future.[4] Abhinava is wary of discussing Mala (i.e., dirt = ignorance) in the 13th chapter again, because he has al-

1. न द्वैतं नापि चाद्वैतम् इत्येवं वृत्तानुरोधान्न पठितम् ।
T.A.V, III, p. 112.

2. तदुक्तं मालिनीतंत्रे सिद्धं समयमण्डलम् ॥
येन दृष्टमात्रेति सिद्धमात्रपदद्वयात् ।
आकृतिर्दीप्तरूपा या मन्त्रस्तद्वत्सुदीप्तिकः ॥
शिष्टं स्पष्टमतो नेह कथितं विस्तरात्पुनः । T.A. 21.20-22

3. एवमाणवादिकञ्चुकत्रयेण सह षट् कञ्चुकानि इत्यत्र भङ्ग्यन्तरत्वम् । कालनियत्योस्तु अनभिधाने अयमाशयो यत् कलादिशुद्ध्या सत्तत्त्वशुद्धिरिति । T.A.V., VI, 169

4. एवं होमादीनामपि पूजोपकरणत्वादेव ईदृक्रूपमर्थं सिद्धम्, इति न साक्षादुक्तम्, तच्च प्राक् बहूक्तं वक्ष्यते च इति तत एवावधार्यम् ।
Ibid., III, p. 124

ready done so in the 9th chapter.[1] Abhinava, does not mind repeating if it really advances the argument, but he would just keep away from a superfluous repetition. This is the reason why he does not take up virility of Mantra (Mantravīrya) in the 30th Chapter which is the appropriate topic after Mantra and Vidyā.[2] Apart from repetition, the fear of unnecessary analytical arrangement or elaboration (Vyāsa) is also an inhibiting factor. Since in the *Traiśiras Āgama* cycles of power consisting of varying number of spokes (powers)—from one to thousand—have already been elaborated Abhinava prefers not to make a reference to them for fear of fruitless compilation and irrelevance.[3]

In fact, Abhinava equips us fully to have insight into his unique style. He has three regular practices (i) brief (ii) detailed and (iii) mixed and calls the first two as Saṁkṣepa or Samāsa, Vistāra or Vyāsa or Vikāsa respectively. Abhinava has been very informative about the style he adopts in a particular setting. He discusses the concept of Ṣaḍadhva (six ways) as part of Sthānaprakalpa under Āṇava Upāya in great detail and affirms this fact.[4] Yet at an other

1. अत्रोच्यते मलस्तावदित्थमेष न युज्यते ।
इति पूर्वाह्निके प्रोक्तं पुनरुक्तौ तु किं फलम् ॥ T.A. 13.53
2. अत्र वीर्यं पुरैवोक्तं सर्वत्रानुसरेद्गुरुः ॥
अर्थवीजप्रवेशान्तरुच्चाराद्यनुसारतः ।
नहि तत्किंचनाप्यस्ति यत्पुरा न निरूपितम् ॥
निष्फला पुनरुक्तिस्तु नास्मभ्यं जातु रोचते । Ibid. 30. 121-123
3. श्रीमत्त्रैशिरसे तच्च कथितं विस्तराद्बहु ॥
इह नो लिखितं व्यासभयाच्चानुपयोगतः । Ibid. 3.256-57
4. अनुत्तरपदाप्तये तदिदमाणवं दर्शिता—
भ्युपायमतिविस्तरान्ननु विदां कुरुध्वं बुधाः । Ibid. 12.26

place he tells us that he is going to follow the brief method in dealing with the problem of 'regional enumeration' (Purasaṁgraha) after treating the regional measurement (Bhuvanamāna) and scheme of categories (Tattva Yojana) at length.[1] In fact he forewarns us in the very beginning of the eighth Āhnika that he proposes to make use of brief and detailed styles[2] both intending thereby to use combined or mixed style in describing Deśādhva. While employing brief style Abhinava may go even extremely brief and present the abbreviated subject matter in a couple of Kārikās after handling it at length. He does so in respect of his treatment of three sub-passages—i.e., Pada, Mantra and Varṇa—of the principal cosmic way called Śabda (word).[3] Towards elaborate delineations, on the other hand, he normally adopts a three-tier strategy. He first puts forward the other available views, examines them and then enunciates his own stand. While embarking upon a comprehensive treatment of descent of grace in[4] the thirteenth Āhnika he initially introduces opposite views, Sāṁkhya being the main among them, from Kārikās 3 to 36, subjects them to critical scrutiny from Kārikās

1. अथ सकलभुवनमानं यन्मह्यं निगदितं निजैर्गुरुभिः ॥
तद्वक्ष्यते समासात् बुद्धौ येनाशु संक्रमेत । T.A. 8.406-407

For correct meaning we have to construe this verse in the light of the *Viveka*.

2. देशाध्वनोऽप्यथ समासविकासयोगात्संगीयते विधिरयं शिवशास्त्रदृष्टः ॥
Ibid. 8.1

3. अभिनवगुप्तेनार्यात्रयमुक्तं संग्रहाय शिष्येभ्यः ॥
Ibid. 11.531; also cf.
"शैवाः केचिदिहानन्ता श्रैकण्ठा इति संग्रह : । Ibid. 8.434

4. तत्र केचिदिति प्राहुः शक्तिपातइममू (? शक्तिपातमिमम्) विधिम् ।
तं प्रदर्श्य निराकृत्य स्वमतं दर्शयिष्यते ॥ Ibid. 13.2

37 to 101 and then dwells on his own thesis from Kārikā 102 onwards. In so doing, Abhinava is always seized of the related auxiliary matters as well. His frequent reversal to the 'original' or the 'subject in hand' may be understood only in this light.[1] In the context of Śivahastavidhi, a part of Samayidīkṣā, he starts discussing about various types of initiates such as Putraka, Ācārya and Daiśika finding them contextually relevant and reverts to Śivahastavidhi, the original item. Similarly as a part of his over-all organisational scheme the discussion on subordinate or particular issues (Anujoddeśa) follows that on principal or general issue (Pūrvaja Uddeśa). As we shall be seeing in detail subsequently he misses no opportunity to furnish proper background of the proposed subordinate topic. For instance, in the 15th Āhnika, assigned to Samayī initiation, Abhinava before discussing the first ancillary issue i.e., types of consecration or bath (Snānabheda), dwells on the necessary background.[2] The third phase of his style, which we have called as mixed, sometimes has a strange feature about it, that is, the detail refers to content while the condensation to body of the text, as for instance in Samayidīkṣā.[3] It means that Vistara and Saṅkṣepa have varied applications sometimes to the physical body of the text and sometimes to its contents.

1. एवं प्रसङ्गान्निर्णीतं प्रकृतं तु निरूप्यते । T.A. 15.472
2. एवमादौ शिष्याणां तत्तद्भेदभिन्नतया योग्यतालक्षणम् औचित्यं परीक्ष्य स्थानभेदादि प्रतिपादयितुं पीठिकाबन्धम् आरचयति ।
T.A.V., IX, p. 25
3. इति समयदीक्षणमिदं प्रकाशितं विस्तराच्च संक्षेपात् । T.A. 16.1
Jayaratha explains विस्तरादिति अर्थात् । संक्षेपादिति ग्रन्थतः ।
T.A.V., IX, p. 285

(e) PURPOSE-ORIENTED DICTION

Abhinava's multi-ended style is ably supported by the choice of diction. Since Abhinava is creating a Śāstra his vocabulary and its use has to be very precise and meaningful. His usage of the word 'Atha'[1] according to Jayaratha suggests his intention to treat the following treatment as an explanation of his own statement.[2] In this sense the *Tantrāloka* sometimes emerges as an auto-commentary. Sometimes 'Atha' indicates a fresh start.[3] Similarly the use of 'Samyak'[4] (adequately) implies a clearcut difference from the basic dualist texts like *Bhogakārikā* and *Mokṣakārikā* of Sadyojyoti.[5] In a continuing discussion specific repetition is aimed at clarifying the issues. For instance, the lunar eclipse takes place in a conjunction of Full Moon and New Moon and not in a pure New Moon[6]—the re-use of the word 'Pūrva' is just meant for this.

(f) PRESENTING THE ESOTERIC MATTER

The language and style both undergo a change when it comes to deal with the exclusively esoteric matter. As we have seen earlier, the first characte-

1. अथ समुचिताधिकारिण उद्दिश्य रहस्य उच्यतेऽत्र विधिः । T.A. 29.1

2. अत्र च स्वकृतप्रतिज्ञासूत्रवार्तिकप्रायतामभिद्योतयितुम् अथशब्दस्य उपादानम् । T.A.V., XI, p. 2 (29 th Āh.)

3. अथशब्द आनन्तर्ये, उद्देशानन्तरं हि लक्षणपरीक्षयोरवसरः इत्याशयः । Ibid., I, p. 74

4. इति तत्त्वस्वरूपस्य कृतं सम्यक्प्रकाशनम् । T.A. 9.314

5. सम्यक् इति अनेनात्र भोगकारिकादिभ्यो वैलक्षण्यम् कटाक्षितम् । T.A.V., VI, p. 250

6. एतच्च यद्यपि पूर्ववदित्यतिदेशाद्गतार्थमेव तथापि पूर्णिमाप्रतिपत्संभेदेनैवेन्दुग्रहो भवेत् न तु शुद्धायामेव प्रतिपद्यपि इति दर्शयितुम् न साक्षादुक्तम् । Ibid. IV, p. 97

ristic of his style of not divulging entire subject matter at one place at a time is found to be more pronounced in such matters—he reveals partly, he conceals partly. This is exactly what he has echoed in the *Tantrasāra*.[1] The esoteric matters, which are totally related to one's personal experience, must be transmitted orally by the teacher alone—it is the exclusive domain of the teacher and the taught—, yet he delves into it only to preserve the agamic secrets for posterity and in so doing he disperses its discussion over several chapters[2] as has been done in the case of Karaṇas.

In addition to the dispersal of subject matter Abhinava abjures the use of direct language. It has to be subtle.[3] There are four pedestals of a system or scripture specially in the Ādi Yāga—Vidyā, Mantra, Mudrā and Maṇḍala. After covering Mantra and Mudrā he initiates discussion on Vidyā and implies that the topic of Maṇḍala is included in that of Vidyā and needs no open description.[4] As an outcome of the same attitude Abhinava has a guarded style to suggest the precise Mantras etc. to be used in esoteric performances. This aspect is adequately illustrated in prescription of the Mantra 'Naiṛti bhoḥ'.[5] Al-

1. न अतिरहस्यम् एकत्र ख्याप्यं न च सर्वथा गोप्यम् इति हि अस्मद्गुरवः । T.S., p. 31. Cp. एवं च व्यावर्णने यदेकप्रघट्टकेनैव रहस्यार्थोपदेशो न न्याय इति । T.A.V., III, p. 443
2. गुरुवक्त्राच्च बोद्धव्यं करणं यद्यपि स्फुटम् ।
तथाप्यागमरक्षार्थं तदग्रे वर्णयिष्यते ॥ T.A. 5.130
3. तेषामतिसूक्ष्माणामेतावत्त्वं न वर्ण्यते विधिषु ॥ Ibid. 8.310
4. न पठ्यते रहस्यत्वात्स्पष्टैः शब्दैर्मया पुनः ।
कुतूहली तूक्तशास्त्रसंपाठादेव लक्षयेत् ॥ Ibid. 29.169
5. न्यक्षरे निर्ऋतिप्राये नाम्नि भोः शब्दमेककम् ॥
अपासयेप्यतो मन्त्रश्छन्दोबद्धोऽयमीरितः । Ibid. 15.383-4

though there is no set rule, the quantum of disclosure depends upon the previously discussed norm of utility.[1]

So far we concentrated on Abhinavagupta and tried to analyse the material offered by the *Tantrāloka* covering his biodata, his objectives and circumstances behind writing the *Tantrāloka*, the methodology adopted by him and the principles governing his approach and his basic aim. This part of the Introduction therefore should serve as a backdrop setting. From here we propose to study his illustrious commentator Jayaratha on more or less similar lines before reverting to our observations on the text.

Only Jayaratha knows how to unravel the mystery—

निर्ऋतिप्राये इति तेन "नैऋति भोः" इत्यादि पठनीयम् । छन्दोबद्ध इति छंदोभंगे हि मन्त्र एवं अयं न भवेदिति भावः । T.A.V., IX, p. 194

1. इह चैतदतिरहस्यादप्रस्तुतत्वाच्च न प्रपञ्चितं यथोपयोगमूह्यते एव केवलम् । Ibid., II, pp. 94-95

CHAPTER THREE

ABOUT THE COMMENTATOR

JAYARATHA

The illustrious author of the *Viveka* commentary, Jayaratha, is next to Abhinavagupta alone in importance. He is no ordinary commentator. He religiously follows the methodology adopted by his master and creates a sort of complete independent text which not only expatiates upon the *Tantrāloka* but also supplements, complements and defends as it were. But for the *Viveka* we would never understand the *Tantrāloka*. An attempt will be made to evaluate and appreciate Jayaratha's contribution in the pages that follow.

Following our usual practice that we adopted in the case of Abhinavagupta, we are supposed to begin with the biodata of Jayaratha on the basis of the material available in the pages of the *Viveka*. But since in our *Krama Tantricism, Vol. I* (pp. 209-215) most of these data have already been used it will be better for the reader to refer to those pages. Here we will recapitulate only certain salient features to give a bird's eye view incorporating additional information, if any.

(I) *Biographical Data*

(a) Ancestral and preceptorial lineage and rich parental heritage

Jayaratha provides graphic details about his parental and preceptorial geneologies, emanating from the vicinity of Abhinava's period itself. He represented the tenth generation from his earliest mentioned ancestor Pūrṇamanoratha who was a court minister of King Yaśaskara (939 AD).[1] He was the grandson of one Śṛṅgāraratha who was also a minister of king Rājarāja[2] whose identity is not yet finally established but who is generally identified with King Jayasiṁha (1127-1155 A.D.). This Śṛṅgāraratha, whose father Guṅgaratha died prematurely at young age,[3] was different from one Śṛṅgāra who was the son of Dāśī Rājānaka and was the grand teacher of Jayaratha in statecraft.[4] Jayaratha throws some subtle hints about his ancestry and his age-long connection with Abhinava. 'Ratha' was perhaps the family title or surname as all the members of his ancestral lineage carried this appendage with them and so was the subtitle 'Datta' which embellished all the members of his preceptorial clan. Pūrṇamanoratha, the first known ancestor of Jayaratha, was a colleague of Vallabha in king Yaśaskara's court, whose son Śauri was Abhinava's senior contemporary and whose grandson Karṇa was married to Abhinava's sister. Thus, there was a close nexus between Abhinava and the earlier ancestors of Jayaratha in addition to the academic and spiritual ties that knitted them together. Another thing that Jayaratha wants to drive home is

1. श्रीमान् यशस्करनृपः सचिवं समस्तधर्म्यस्थितिष्वकृत पूर्णमनोरथाख्यम् ।
T.A.V., XII, p. 430, (verse 8)

2. तया स श्रृंगाररथाभिधानो बालो विवृद्धिं गमितो जनन्या ।
सत्त्वाख्यया ख्यातगुणः क्रमेण श्रीराजराजः सचिवं व्यधाद्यम् ॥
Ibid., p. 432, verse 28

3. सूत्वा सुतं गुङ्गरथो युवैव प्रमयं ययौ । Ibid., p. 431, verse 26

4. अप्यस्य राजतन्त्रे चिन्तयतो राजतन्त्रमास्त गुरुः ।
दाशीराजानकजन्मा श्रीश्रृंगारो ममापि गुरुः ॥
Ibid., XII, p. 433, Verse 36

that all the generations preceding him enjoyed virtuous conduct,[1] power,[2] plenty of worldly riches,[3] fame,[4] learning[5] and devotion to Śiva[6] and thus created the proper psychological environment that Jayaratha inherited from his forefathers. Similarly the entire series of his preceptorial lineage was characterised by spiritual prowess,[7] Sādhanā,[8] systematic scholarship[9] and virtuousness[10] and thereby offered rich intellectual heritage.

Jayaratha provides an insight into some of the important episodes connected with his family. Amṛtaratha and Utpalaratha II, the two ancestors sixth from Jayaratha, established two seminaries as a means of support to virtuous Brahmins in a place

1. धर्म्यस्थितिषु T.A.V., XII, p. 430, verse 8;
   कृत्वा धर्म्यां स्थितिं Ibid., p. 431, verse 22;
   चारित्रसंचितमहासुकृतप्रपञ्चाम् Ibid., p. 432, verse 27
2. सचिवम्......अकृत Ibid., p. 430, verse 8;
   साचिव्यमाप्य, ibid, verse 14; सचिवं व्यधाद्यम् Ibid., p. 432, verse 28
3. सकलजनहृदयदयितान् अर्थान् Ibid., p. 430, verse 10;
   लक्ष्म्यालिङ्गननिपुणैः Ibid, verse 11
4. यद्यशः कौमुदी विश्वम् Ibid., p. 430, verse 90;
   यशोविवेकौ ibid., p. 431, verse 25; ख्यातगुणः, Ibid., p. 432, verse 28
5. पाण्डित्यमेवासूत Ibid., p. 431, verse 25.
6. व्यवहारे शर्वभक्तौ चैषां प्रागल्भ्यमीयुषाम्। Ibid., p. 431, verse 20; शिवानुगगात् ibid., verse 23
7. उचितां पद्धतिं मुक्तिमार्गे Ibid., XII, p. 430, verse 14
8. यन्मेलापमवाप्य कौलिकमहाज्ञानानुविद्धं महः Ibid., p. 430, verse 16
9. अध्याप्याखिलसंहिता Ibid, verse 15; संहितापारगं ibid., p. 431, verse 17
10. सुकृतिमुख्यम् Ibid., p. 431, verse 17

where a school or a metal workshop existed.[1] Utpalaratha II was appointed as a minister by king Ananta (1028-1063 A.D.) whose writ ran upto Trigarta (modern Jalandhar in the north-west) and who brutally crushed the forces of the King of Darads.[2] It was he (Utpalaratha II) who received lessons from his maternal uncle Vibhūtidatta when the elder son of the latter died within seven days of his initiation and out of indifference and aversion arising from this tragic death Vibhūtidatta did not consecrate his younger son[3] and chose, at the divine instance, to transmit knowledge to his younger son through him, i.e. Utpalaratha II. Utpalaratha learnt the entire concept of spiritual union (Melāpa) characterised by Kaulika knowledge which he conveyed to Śrīcakra, an ardent pupil of Vibhūtidatta. From Śrīcakra, the parental spiritual heritage was handed down to Viśvadatta,[4] whom

1. शालास्थाने वर्तकारे मठौ सुकृतकर्मठौ ।
तेषूत्पलामृतरथौ चक्राते द्विजसंश्रयौ ॥
T.A.V., XII, p. 430, verse 12

2. त्रैगतोर्वीनिवेशा गजमदसलिलैर्लम्बिता म्लानिमानं
तत्रत्यक्ष्मापकीर्तिप्रसरमलिनतां यस्य संसूचयन्ति ।
तस्यानन्तक्षितीन्दोर्बलबहलदरद्राजविद्रावणस्य
प्रापत्साचिव्यमाप्योत्पलरथ उचितां पद्धतिं मुक्तिमार्गे ॥
Ibid., verse 14

3. अध्याप्याखिलसंहिता अपि सुतस्नेहान्निषिक्ते मृते
पुत्रे ज्यायसि देवतापरिहृतासेके दिनैः सप्तभिः ।
वैरस्यान्न कनीयसे स यददाद्बालाय सेकं ततो
देव्या स्वप्नविबोधितोऽस्य तनयस्यैतन्मुखेनास्त्विति ॥
Ibid., verse 15

4. यन्मेलापमवाप्य कौलिकमहाज्ञानानुविद्धं महः
शिष्यायैकतमाय देयमपुनर्भावार्थमासादितम् ।
श्रीचक्राय ददौ द्विजः स भगवानुर्वीधरोऽस्मिन्नसौ
श्रीचक्रात् स्वपितृक्रमाप्तमखिलं तत्साधिकारं व्यधात् ॥
Ibid., pp. 430-31, verse 16

Utpalaratha brought to his own residence after his teacher and maternal uncle passed away.[1] Viśvadatta soon acquired knowledge of scriptures and mastered his ancestral legacy. He was then shifted to a convent in the front yard of the temple constructed by some Kanakadatta, whose identity we have not been able to establish so far (but who may be a kith of Vibhūtidatta's clan, as the title 'datta' indicates), for permanent residence and was provided with a lot of movable and immovable assets for future maintenance.[2] Utpalaratha II, though a minister, gave himself up for the pursuance of spiritual emancipation[3] and the same thing was true of his eldest son Śivaratha who, though a minister of king Ucchala, dedicated all that he inherited from his father for human salvation and later resigned his exalted job.[4] Similarly Guṇaratha, Jayaratha's great grandfather, erected a new convent called 'Acalaśrīmaṭha' which survived, even when the whole city (i.e., Pravapura—modern Srinagar) was

1. अथ स परमधामैकात्म्यमाप्ते गुरौ स्वे निजगृहमुपनिन्ये तत्सुतं विश्वदत्तम् ।
अकृत सुकृतिमुख्यं संहितापारगं च प्रथितगुणममुं चाजिग्रहत्स्वाधिकारम् ।।
T.A.V., XII, p. 431, verse 17

2. श्रीकनकदत्तविरचितदेवगृहाग्रे मठं निवासाय ।
कृत्वा ददौ स तस्मै स्थावरधनकनकसंपूर्णम् ।। Ibid., verse 18

3. प्रापत्साचिव्यमाप्योत्पलरथ उचितां पद्धतिं मुक्तिमार्गे ।।
Ibid., p. 430, verse 14

4. सर्वार्थसेविनां मोक्षसेवां शिवरथोऽग्रहीत् ।।
पित्राहृत्य नृपद्मेन पारिपाल्यं हि सोऽर्पितम् ।
त्यक्त्वार्थदोषविदभूदरागो निष्परिग्रहः ।।
अधिकारं ग्राहितः स विद्वानुच्चलभूभुजा ।
कृत्वा धर्म्यां स्थितिं कंचित्कालं तत्याज निःस्पृहः ।।
Ibid., p. 431, verses 20-22

engulfed by fire, perhaps due to his right conduct.[1] His grandfather Guṅgaratha died prematurely[2] when his father Śṛṅgāraratha was still a child and it was his grandmother Sattvā who reared and brought him up to become a minister of king Rājarāja.[3] Thus a combined tabular chart of Jayaratha's both lineages—parental and preceptorial—emerges as on the facing page.[4]

Jayaratha's time does not present much problem. He has furnished enough evidence to conclude—it is unnecessary to go into details right now—[5] that he flourished somewhere during second half of the twelfth century (1150-1200 A.D.).

Jayaratha speaks very eloquently of his father Śṛṅgāraratha.[6] He was very close to king Rājarāja or Jayasiṁha, like mind to soul. The king fully depended on him whether the matter related to collection of money involving intermediaries or to rivers like Ledari which did not involve others.[7] He was given unrestricted authority over all the infantries and armies falling under the tributary princes and

1. निर्दग्धमनलदग्धे नगरेऽपि सत्पथप्रथितः ।
अचलश्रीमठमकरोदभिनवमनयोर्गुणरथाख्यः ॥
T.A.V., XII, p. 431, verse 24

2. सूत्वा सुतं गुङ्गरथो युवैव प्रमयं ययौ । Ibid., verse 26

3. Ibid., p. 432, verse 28.

4. Also see K.T. Appendix 'A'. Here the tables have been combined and modified specially in respect of Viśvadatta and his progeny plus disciples.

5. Vide K.T., pp. 210-12 for details.

6. श्रीशृंगाररथादवाप्य कृतिनो जन्मानवद्यक्रमम् ।
T.A.V., I, p. 310

7. तस्यात्मनो मन इवान्यमुखार्थलब्धिष्वासाद्य साधकतमत्वमरोधचारम् ।
साक्षाद्बभार विषयेषु स किंच लेदर्यादिष्वनन्यविषयेष्वपि भूमिभर्तुः ॥
Ibid., XII, p. 430, verse 32

ANCESTRAL GENEALOGY

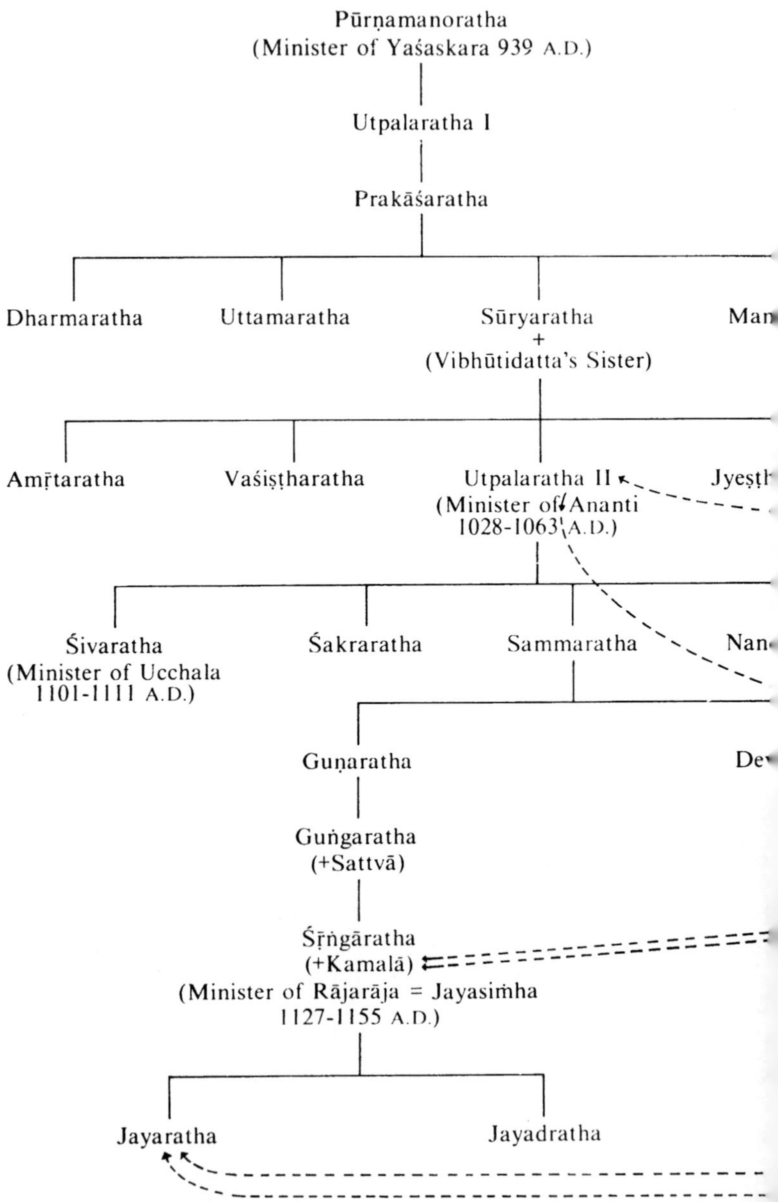

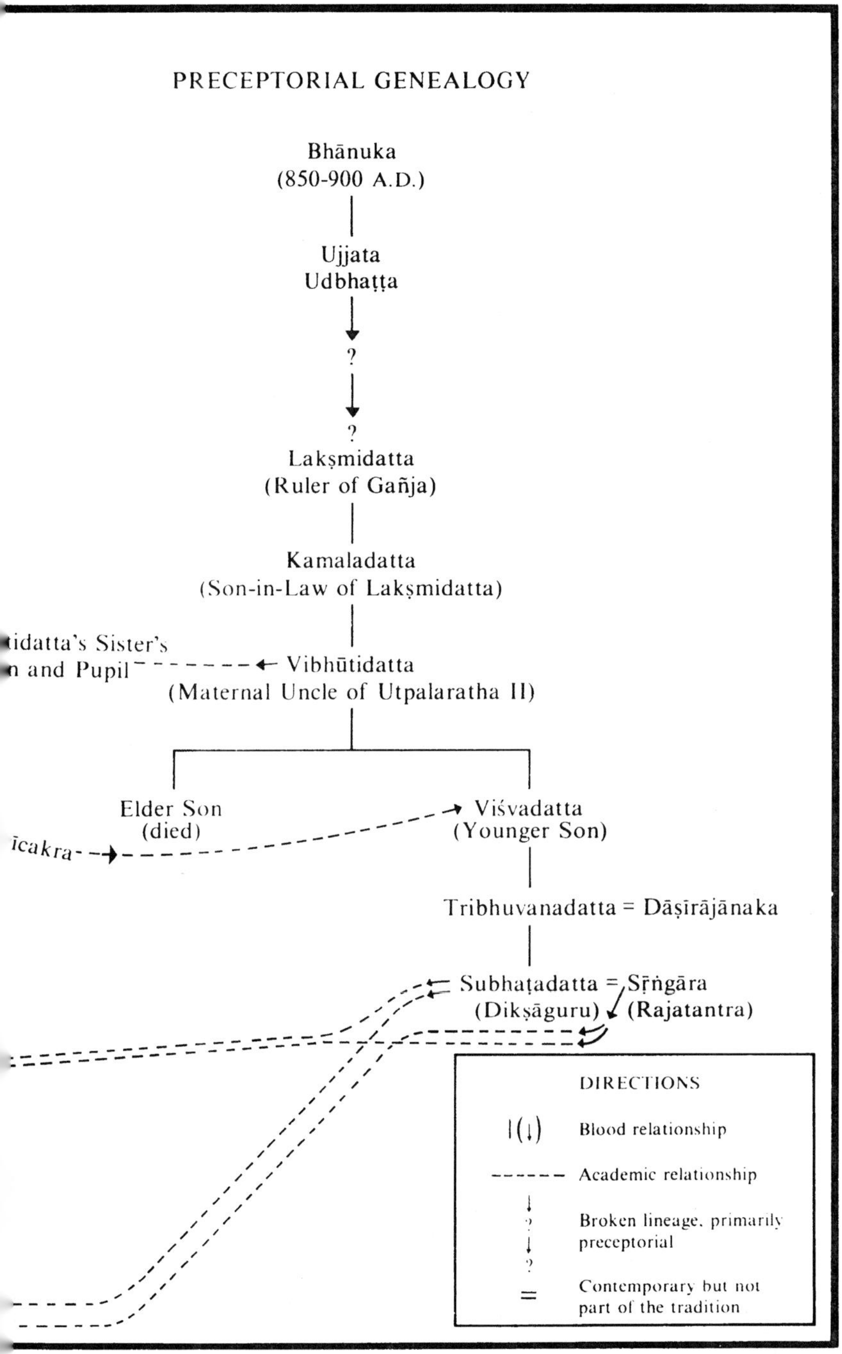
PRECEPTORIAL GENEALOGY
Bhānuka
(850-900 A.D.)
Ujjata
Udbhaṭṭa
?
?
Lakṣmidatta
(Ruler of Gañja)
Kamaladatta
(Son-in-Law of Lakṣmidatta)
idatta's Sister's
n and Pupil
Vibhūtidatta
(Maternal Uncle of Utpalaratha II)
Elder Son
(died)
Viśvadatta
(Younger Son)
īcakra
Tribhuvanadatta = Dāṣīrājānaka
Subhaṭadatta = Sṛṅgāra
(Dikṣāguru)
(Rajatantra)
DIRECTIONS
Blood relationship
Academic relationship
Broken lineage, primarily preceptorial
Contemporary but not part of the tradition

while exercising his powers as the top brass (Sarvādhikārin) he introduced a major innovation by keeping the regular forces and mercenaries separately.[1] He devoted his energies for welfare of the common man and encouraged pursuit of excellence by suitable financial gifts and grants. He created an atmosphere free from terror and subsequently developed acute devotion for Śiva, something behoving his noble heritage.[2] He was initiated into Śaivite practices by Subhaṭa Datta who later performed initiation ceremony of Jayaratha also.[3] He owed his extensive training in statecraft to Śṛngāra, son of Dāśī Rājānaka, who again seems to have imparted lessons to Jayaratha also.[4] Disgusted to see the ruinous state of some new constructions due to vagaries of nature, he carried out five renovations on the Mahādeva mountain.[5] To him and his wife Kamalā, Jayaratha and his brother Jayadratha were born exactly as nectre and moon came out from the ocean, the abode of Kamalā (Viṣṇu's spouse, goddess of riches in Hindu pantheon). These two brothers were delight to every-

1. सामन्तसन्ततिसमाश्रितसर्वमौलपादातशस्त्रिनिचयेऽप्यधिकारमाप्य ।
सर्वाधिकारिणि पदे स विभोः सहायः सेनाभटान् पृथगपि प्रथयाञ्चकार ।
T.Ā.V., p. 431, verse 33

2. तस्य सर्वजनतोपकारिणः पुष्णतो गुणिगणान् धनर्द्धिभिः ।
साधुसाध्वसमुषः कुलोचिता शर्वभक्तिरतिवल्लभाभवत् ।।
Ibid., verse 34

3. श्रीविश्वदत्तपौत्रत्रिभुवनदत्तात्मजः कुलक्रमतः ।
श्रीसुभटदत्त आसीदस्य गुरुर्यो ममाप्यकृत दीक्षाम् ।।
Ibid., p. 433, verse 35

4. अप्यस्य राजतंत्रे चिन्तयतो राजतंत्रमास्त गुरुः ।
दाशीराजानकजन्मा श्रीशृङ्गारो ममापि परमगुरुः ।।
Ibid., verse 36

5. सावद्यां नवनिर्मितिमालोच्य देशकालदौरात्म्यात् ।
पञ्च महादेवाद्रौ जीर्णोद्धारान् व्यधतत सुधीः ।। Ibid., verse 37

body and were equal in merit.[1] Jayaratha was elder of the two.[2] Jayaratha, however, does not remember his mother Kamalā so much as his grandmother Sattvā who, though a young widow, displayed tremendous forbearance and sacrifice into moulding his father what he was—a profound and versatile man. She in her own right won the unsolicited respect from the people for her virtuous conduct and total exemplary dedication to the ways of the gods and ancestors.[3]

Jayaratha speaks highly of his brother Jayadratha who though younger was his junior by a very nominal age gap and was intellectually and academically at par with his elder brother Jayaratha. Jayaratha does not throw any further light on his brother in the *Tantrāloka*.[4] Similarly Jayaratha, who has several works to his credit, does not refer to them in his *Viveka*. Per-

1. जयरथजयद्रथाख्यौ सकलजनानन्दकौ समगुणद्र्धी ।
अमृतशशिनाविवाब्धेरस्मात्कमलाश्रयादुदितौ ॥
T.A.V., XII, p. 433, verse 38

2. ....कृती जयरथाख्यः ।
ज्येष्ठोरनयोरकार्षीत्........ ॥
Ibid., p. 434, verse 41

3. यां हव्यकव्यविधिबन्धधियं सिताच्छ–
निर्यन्नखच्छविमिषात्पदधूलिलुब्धा ।
संसेवते स्म सुरसिन्धुरिवावदात–
चारित्रसंचितमहासुकृतप्रपंचाम् ॥
तया स शृंगाररथाभिधानो बालो विवृद्धिं गमितो जनन्या ।
सत्त्वाख्यया........ ॥ Ibid., p. 432, verse 27-28

4. The title of *Haracaritacintāmaṇi* (K.M., reprinted from the same by Bhāratīya Vidyā Prakashan, Delhi-Varanasi) mentions Jayaratha as the author while all the colophons except that of the Ist Prakāśa (where there are two readings) record Jayadratha as the author. See K.T., p. 212-13.

haps he wanted to compose his *Viveka* as a touchstone for evaluation of his scholarship by posterity.[1]

(b) Two groups of teachers: second group casting stronger formative influence

Coming to his teachers he mentions four by name who fall into two groups of two each. The first group consisted of Subhaṭa Datta and Śṛṅgāra and the other of Kalyāṇa and Śaṅkhadhara. Jayaratha gratefully acknowledges the deeprooted contribution of the second group in sharpening his academic and spiritual calibre. Subhaṭa Datta, being the linear descendent in the official tradition, was the natural choice to perform his initiation.[2] He seems to be an older contemporary of Jayaratha because he initiated Jayaratha's father also as we have already seen. Subhaṭa Datta wrote a commentary[3] on the *Tantrāloka* for the sake of Śṛṅgāraratha[4] who acquired substantial command over the Śaiva scriptures from him. Jayaratha makes it absolutely clear that while Subhaṭa Datta was his father's teacher, he was responsible for Jayaratha's initiation only. Subhaṭa Datta was the son of Tribhuvana Datta and grandson of Viśvadatta. It is this Viśvadatta who is perhaps remembered as

1. K.T., pp. 213-215.
2. श्रीविश्वदत्तपौत्रस्त्रिभुवनदत्तात्मजकुलक्रमतः ।
श्रीसुभटदत्त आसीद् अस्य गुरुर् यो ममाप्यकृत दीक्षाम् ॥
T.A.V., XII, p. 433, verse 35
3. व्यधुस्तन्त्रालोके किल सुभटपादा विवरणं
यदर्थं यश्चैभ्यो निखिलशिवशास्त्रार्थविदभूत् ।
Ibid., p. 433, verse 39
4. The context may very well apply to Jayaratha in place of Śṛṅgāraratha. But we prefer to take it as referring to Śṛṅgāraratha because of the use of pronoun Yaḥ in singular number, whereas

'Parameṣṭhīguru' (great grandteacher) by Jayaratha who ascribes a verse to him and presumably presents him as a Krama author.[1]

There is one more reference to Jayaratha's grand teacher (Paramaguru) whose authority has been once invoked by Jayaratha in quelling doubts about one's preference for a particular tradition (out of several options prevailing) as authentic and final. He is credited with the view that one's preference will ultimately depend upon one's preceptorial stand.[2] This view is cited to support Jayaratha's contention that his treatment of Krama tradition bears the stamp of his teacher's authority. It is difficult to say if this Paramaguru was Tribhuvanadatta or Subhaṭadatta. Chances are that Jayaratha's reference tends towards Tribhuvana datta because Subhaṭadatta, circumstantially though Paramaguru, was technically Guru as it was he who initiated Jayaratha into Śaiva spiritualism. It is, however, very interesting to note that Jayaratha claims direct access to Krama tradition emanating from Bhānuka (850-900 A.D.). While Govindarāja, Bhānuka's classmate, handed down the

---

the immediate referant in the preceding verse is in dual number covering Jayaratha and his brother Jayadratha.

1. यदुक्तमस्मत्परमगुरुभिः—

क्रमत्रयसमाश्रयव्यतिकरेण या संततं
क्रमत्रितयलंघनं विदधती विभात्युच्चकैः ।
क्रमैकवपुरक्रमप्रकृतिरेव या द्योतते
करोमि हृदि तामहं भगवतीं परां संविदम् ॥ T.A.V., I, p. 11

See for detailed discussion K.T., pp. 189-91 and also Upodghāta, p. 34.

2. इत्येकतरपरिग्रहे यथास्वं गुरूपदेश एव निबन्धनम्, यथोक्तमस्मत्परमगुरुभिः "यो यस्य गुर्वादेशः तस्य मोचक इति" ।

T.A.V., III, p. 203

tradition through Somānanda,[1] the parallel tradition was lineally transmitted to Jayaratha through Ujjaṭa and Udbhaṭa etc.[2] Although Jayaratha claims to be in possession of both the traditions as also the others, he is direct lineal repository of the tradition from Bhānuka. Since we have no trace of any other person having mastered Krama secrets in the whole preceptorial genealogy other than Viśvadatta, Jayaratha's great grandteacher, it may not be absolutely off the mark to surmise that Jayaratha's regular linear preceptorial ancestors emanating from Lakṣmī Datta, who also happend to be the ruler of a place called Gañja and perhaps flourished around last quarter of the tenth century (975-1023) and was chronologically quite close to Udbhaṭa (900-950 A.D.) and Ujjaṭa (875-925 A.D.) with a few missing links in between, constituted the regular vehicle for the transmission of that tradition.[3] Our knowledge about Subhaṭadatta does not go beyond this point. The other teacher in this group is Śṛṅgāra, teacher of Śṛṅgāraratha —Jayaratha's father—in political science. However, by the use of 'also' (Api in Mamāpi) Jayaratha seems to imply that he also learnt something of political affairs from Śṛṅgāra.[4]

It is the second group of teachers that wielded con-

1. तत्राद्यः (गोविन्दराजः) . . . . . स चेदं रहस्यं श्रीसोमानन्दाभिधानाय गुरवे संचारयाम्बभूव । T.A.V., III, p. 192
Also see "यदधिकारेण श्रीगोविन्दराजादीनामुपदेशः प्रवृत्तो योऽस्मत्पर्यन्तमपि प्राप्तः । Ibid., p. 198

2. द्वितीयोऽपि (भानुकोऽपि) एवमेवास्त तस्यैव चैषा श्रीमदुज्जटोद्भट्टादिनानागुरुपरिपाटीसंततिः यत्प्रासादासादितमहिमभिरस्माभिरेतत्प्रदर्शितम् । Ibid, p. 192-93

3. Also see K.T., pp. 110-111, 120-22.

4. श्रीश्रृङ्गारो ममापि गुरुः । T.A.V., XII, p. 433, verse 36

siderable influence on the making of Jayaratha—as an academician and as a top grade spiritualist both. He is avowedly indebted to Śaṅkhadhara for his proficiency in all the secular sciences[1] including the science of grammar, the science of linguistic interpretation propounded by Jaimini and all other empirical disciplines.[2] Śaṅkhadhara was perhaps known as Saṅgadhara[3] (if it is not a scribal aberration) also. He owed his acquisition of all the Śaivite learning and insight into Śaiva scriptures to Kalyāṇa, who was an embodiment of the divine.[4] In fact Jayaratha's blissful experience flowing from the realization of oneness of Śiva is exclusively due to him, who was instrumental in removing all the dirt and mental fickleness.[5] No other teacher except Kalyāṇa has claimed reverence from Jayaratha in glowing terms in the opening verses of the *Tantrālokaviveka* where he is likened to an ocean whose drops of compassion made Jayaratha self-realized without the fall of mortal frame[6] and whose sermons were carried out with the

1. श्रीमच्छंखधरात्परं परिचयं विद्यासु सर्वास्वपि । T.A.V., I, p. 310
2. अधिगतपदविद्यस्त्रीन्मुनीन्योऽधिशेते
   प्रथयति च लघुत्वं जैमिनेर्वाक्यबोधे ।
   निखिलनयपथेषु प्राप यश्चाधिराज्यं
   त्रितयमपि कथानां यत्र पर्याप्तिमेति ॥
   Ibid., XII, p. 433, verse 40
3. तस्माच्छ्रीसङ्गधरादवाप्तविद्यः कृती जयरथाख्यः ।
   Ibid., p. 434, verse 41
4. श्रीकल्याणतनोः शिवादधिगमं सर्वागमानामपि । Ibid., I, p. 310
5. शिवाद्वैतज्ञप्तिप्रकटितमहानन्दविदितं
   गुरुं श्रीकल्याणाभिधममुमवाप्यास्तरजसम् ॥
   Ibid., XII, p. 433, verse 39
6. देहे विमुक्त एवास्मि श्रीमत्कल्याणवारिधेः ।
   यस्य कारुण्यविप्रुड्भिः सद्गुरुं तं हृदि श्रये ॥
   T.A.V., I, p. 2, verse 2

same zeal by the kings, as crowns over their heads.[1]

Jayaratha offers a very intimate insight into the matters of his personal teachers. While commenting upon the *T.A.* 13.342[2]—blessed is the disciple who gets a teacher perfect in wisdom—Jayaratha cites his own example.[3] Jayaratha considers himself extremely fortunate in having attended on Kalyāṇa and Śaṅkhadhara who were teachers of perfect knowledge—Kalyāṇa in Śaiva spiritualism of monistic-dualistic character and Śaṅkhadhara in the secular disciplines of grammar, linguistics and logic. Incidentally our knowledge is highly deficient in regard to the written contribution, if at all, made by his teachers. Jayaratha cites the views of his teacher only thrice in the whole of *Viveka*—once in connection with the interpretation of the term Mūla in the *Tantrāloka*[4], the second time while stating the reasons behind his opting for the *Devyāyāmala's* standpoint on Śikhābīja in preference to the *Triśirobhairava's*[5] and the third time while sub-

1. मूर्ध्न्युत्तंस इव क्ष्मापैः सर्वैर्यस्यानुशासनम् ।
हृदये भवसंभारकर्कशेऽप्याशु शिश्रिये ॥ T.A.V., I, p. 2, verse 3
2. धन्यस्तु पूर्णविज्ञानं ज्ञानार्थी लभते गुरुम् ॥
3. अत्र च अहमेव उदाहरणं यद्विज्ञानार्थिना मया लोकोत्तरे द्वयाद्वयात्मनि शैवशास्त्रादौ अभिख्यामात्रप्रख्यापितपरश्रेयःसंश्रयः श्रीमान्कल्याणः पूर्णविज्ञानवानेक एव गुरुर्लब्धः पदवाक्यप्रमाणादौ लौकिके श्रीमान् सुगृहीतनामधेयः शङ्खधरश्चेति ।
T.A.V., VIII, p. 205
4. निमज्जेत्साङ्गमूलाख्यं जपन्ना तन्मयत्वतः । T.A. 15.50
मूलं च अत्र परेति गुरवः । T.A.V., IX, p. 30
5. अत्र च शिखायां कवचबीजमिति श्रीत्रिशिरोभैरवानुयायिनः चतुष्कलमिति श्रीदेव्यायामलोपजीविनः अस्मदगुरवस्तु द्वितीयमेव पक्षमामनन्ति यदिह श्रीपूर्वशास्त्रानुदितस्यापि नेत्रमन्त्रस्य श्रीत्रिशिरोभैरवीयं मतमपहाय श्रीदेव्यायामलप्रक्रमेणाभिधानात् तदर्थ एव विवक्षितः । Ibid., XII, p. 198

stantiating Abhinava's description of real Homa[1] (In fact the third one is the only direct statement from his teacher). Presumably these views belong to Kalyāṇa as the context is patently Śaivite one. Jayaratha owes three things to his teacher—one, he was able to annihilate all the distracting determinate ideas;[2] two, he was not easily vulnerable;[3] and three, he had imbibed the Kaulika experience personally.[4] In fact Jayaratha was a self-realized person during his lifetime.[5] By any standard these are not mean achievements and speak highly of the calibre of his teacher.

(c) Personal achievements

Going by the gleanings from his statements Jayaratha, to top everything, was a Jīvanmukta[6]—the summum bonum of all spiritual seekers. He was constantly in the state of mental harmony marked by divine ecstacy.[7] He also suggests that he was the

1. यदभिप्रायेणैव अस्मदगुरुभिरपि—
   शश्वद्विश्वमनश्वरप्रकृतयो विश्वस्तचित्ता भृशं
   ये विज्ञानतनूनपाति विततोन्मेषा वषट्कुर्वते ।
   तेषां संततसर्वमेययजनक्रीडामहायज्वनां
   नो मन्येऽवभृथक्षणः क्षणमपि क्षीणस्थितिर्लक्ष्यते ॥
   इत्याद्युक्तम् । T.A.V., III, p. 233
2. गुरुचरणप्रसादप्रध्वस्तसमस्तदुर्विकल्पौघः । Ibid., III, p. 471
3. श्रीसद्गुरुसेवारससनातनाभ्यासदुर्ललितवृत्तः । Ibid., X, p. 305
4. श्रीमद्गुरूपदेशप्रक्रमसंक्रान्तकौलिकानुभवः ।
   Ibid., XI, p. 172 (29th Āh.)
5. देहे विमुक्त एवास्मि श्रीमत्कल्याणवारिधेः । Ibid., I, p. 2
6. Ibid.
7. शैवावेशवशोल्लसदसमरसास्वादसामरस्यमयः । Ibid., II, p. 264
   (Colophon, 3rd Āhnika)
   Also cp. "शाक्तसमावेशवशप्रोन्मीलितसद्विकल्पविभवेन
   Ibid., III, p. 307

"blessed" one having smelt the intense fall of divine grace,[1] which autómatically meant attainment of perfect knowledge. He was an accomplished Yogin who exercised excellent command over the contemplation of the movement of breath—respiratory and downward both.[2] Free from all doubts he was imbued with a sense of beatific serenity and his realization of Absolutic harmony induced a feeling of total resignation from mundane affairs.[3] Yet his synthetic personality remains transparent as ever. In the last concluding verse of his *Viveka* he proudly portrays himself as an encyclopaedic genius springing from a unique blend of empirical and metempirical disciplines.[4] Thus he appears to be well-versed in grammar, linguistics, logic, secrets of all Śaiva scriptures and none could excel his ingenuity whether it was Trika philosophy or Krama metaphysics. According to the colophon of the *Tantrāloka*, he earned the same title of being a super-teacher in

1. तीव्रशक्तिपाताघ्रातः पुनः पूर्णज्ञानमेव गुरुमासादयेत् यत्प्रसादादनायासमेवास्य स्वात्मनो विज्ञानपारिपूर्ण्यं समुदियादित्याह—अत्र चाहमेवोदाहरणम् । T.A.V., VIII, p. 205
2. प्राणापानसमाश्रयचारविचारचातुरीनिष्ठः Ibid., IV, p. 471
3. निरस्तः संदेहः शममुपगता संसृतिरुजा
विवेकः सोत्सेकः सपदि हृदि गाढं समुदितः ।
अतः संप्राप्तोऽहम् निरुपधिचिदद्वैतमयता–
मसामान्यामन्यैः किमिव तदिदानीं व्यवसितैः ।।
Ibid., XII, p. 434, verse 46
4. पदे वाक्ये माने निखिलशिवशास्त्रोपनिषदि
प्रतिष्ठां यातोऽहं यदपि निरवद्यं जयरथः ।
तथाप्यास्यामङ्ग क्वचन भुवि नास्ति त्रिकदृशि
क्रमार्थे वा मत्तः सपदि कुशलः कश्चिदपरः ।।
Ibid., pp. 434-35, verse 47

Maheśvara's cult[1] as did his master Abhinava. He seems to have enjoyed a fairly long life, as he talks of being quite ripe in age when he completed the remained *Tantrāloka Viveka*.[2] His mission might have abortive had it not received tremendous encouragement from his royal patron Rājarāja alias Jayasiṁha, whose inspiration proved to be the real instrument behind the writing of the *Viveka*.[3]

(II) *The Tantrālokaviveka*

(a) AN EXTENSION OF AND SUPPLEMENT TO THE TANTRĀLOKA

Composition of the *Tantrālokaviveka* was a lifetime mission for Jayaratha. He worked assiduously for a major part of his life and the day his mammoth undertaking reached fruition, a feeling of creative joy overtook him.[4] It was the result of a persistent, regular, long-drawn hard work in discovering the essential meaning of Abhinava's magnum opus. The successful completion seems to be the end result of his exploiting all the existing source material. In this sense the *Tantrālokaviveka* is not just a commentary, it is the continued extension of the *Tantrāloka*.

1. कृतिः श्रीराजानकमहामाहेश्वराचार्यजयरथस्य ॥
T.A.V., XII, p. 435

2. . . . .सम्यक्परिणतवयसा . . . . . . ।
Ibid., p. 434, verse 45

3. इह मम गतस्तन्त्रालोके विवेचयतो यतो
निरवधिमभिप्रेतोत्साहः स एव निमित्तताम् ।
Ibid., p. 432, verse 30

4. वाचस्तत्त्वार्थगर्भाः श्रवसि कृतवतो वल्लकी क्वाणहृदया
नित्याभ्यासेन सम्यक्परिणतवयसा चिन्तयासेव्यमानान् ।
आश्लिष्यन्ती नवोढा निविडतरमियं भावना लम्भयिष्य–
त्यानन्दास्रप्रवाहामलमुखकमलान् सांप्रतं निर्वृतिं नः ॥
Ibid., p. 434, verse 45

At every step he is aware of the complexity and massiveness of the project because it demanded close familiarity with practically all sources of knowledge and highlighted one's apparent difficulty in treading the impassable jungle of Śaivite discipline made all the more impervious by the perplexity in bringing out real intent of the scriptures belonging to the conflicting source-bases.[1] He, therefore, owns up full responsibility for all the failings that might have crept in and humbly craves for indulgence from the sympathetic readers. Among his immediate supporting sources, it appears, were certain commentaries. One such commentary was *Vivaraṇa*, authored by his family preceptor Subhaṭa Datta, which however seems to have cast little impact on him[2] despite the fact that it greatly enlightened Jayaratha's father. In the *Tantrāloka* he is invariably guided by his teacher Kalyāṇa, and not Subhaṭa Datta. Perhaps, another commentary was *Unmeṣa* by an unknown author[3] whose views were ignored by Jayaratha. In any case there were several, numerous one may add, interpreta-

1. विद्यास्थानैरशेषैरपि परिचयतो दुर्गमे शैवशास्त्रे
स्रोतोभिन्नागमार्थप्रकटनविकटे नैव कश्चित्प्रगल्भः ।
तन्त्रालोकेऽत्र यस्मात्स्खलितमपि महत्कुत्रकुत्रचिच्चेत्
स्यान्नूनं ते हि तस्मान्मम न विमुखतां हन्त सन्तः प्रयान्तु ॥
T.A.V., XII, p. 434, verse 43

2. The opinion in K.T., p. 213 that Subhaṭadatta served as a model stands modified.

3. अत्र चोन्मेषकृता क्लिष्टकल्पनया यत् व्याख्यातं, तदाग्रहमात्रपरतया तदुपेक्ष्यम् । T.A.V., X, p. 221
The above conclusion is a qualified one and will hold true if the *Unmeṣa* is not a commentary on the *Śrīmṛtuñjaya-siddhatantra* which is central subject in the context. However, we are inclined to construe it as above.

tions[1] of various portions and whether they crystallised into book form—today we are not in a position to say. We are, however, inclined to believe that there did exist commentaries which invited criticism from Jayaratha.[2] Indeed it is our misfortune that these are not extant today. It may, therefore, be propounded with certain amount of certainty that criticism of existing commentaries was one of the devices resorted to by Jayaratha to build up his work. From the very beginning of his *Viveka*, Jayaratha leaves us in little doubt about his motives. He took up the *Viveka* not because he wanted to establish himself as an author, nor was he keen to display his unique felicity in expression. It was his sole urge to let the determinate ideas culminate into perfect awareness[3] consequent upon careful consideration of its meaning. Jayaratha seems to have had three types of audience in mind—(1) the ignorant, (ii) the hostile or envious, and (iii) the doubtful. While he does not mount any attack on those who were yet to arrive on the scene he is determined to address his work to all the three classes of audience[4]—whether past or present—alike

1. केषांचिदपि व्याख्यान्तराणामासमञ्जस्यमतीव संभवदपि न प्रकाशितम्।
T.A.V., I, p. 15
Also cf. '''तस्मादस्मदुक्तमेव व्याख्यानं युक्तमित्यन्यदुपेक्ष्यम्।
Ibid., V, p. 260

2. अतश्च.....इति पठित्वा....चेत्याद्यभिधाय पूर्वापरानुसारितया उभयपक्षमीलनयाङ्गुलव्यत्यासेन व्याख्यायाम्....इति दोषाः।
Ibid., X, p. 91-92

3. न ग्रन्थकारपदमाप्तुमथास्म्यपूर्वं
वाक्कौशलं च न निदर्शयितुं प्रवृत्तः।
किं त्वेतदर्थपरिशीलनतो विकल्पः
संस्कारवांश्च समियादिति वाञ्छितं नः॥ Ibid., I, p. 2

4. यातायाताः स्थिताः केचिदज्ञा मत्सरिणः परे।
संदिग्धा केऽपि किं ब्रूयां श्रोतारो यदनागताः॥

who without grasping the inherent purport have indulged in deliberate show of their expressionist talent. Thus he primarily assumes the role of an educator, a critic and an umpire all blended into one. He indeed sets himself to a formidable task.

The sense of mission was so profound that it led him to procure each and every text, having slightest bearing on the subject. It was a sort of hunting spree and he was constantly on the search, on his own admission, to devise innumerable devices in order to get hold of such texts.[1] As is natural, his ceaseless effort made it possible for him to take the glossorial job in his stride and a moment came when he did not take time to explain[2], yet he was able to turn out the greatest or the most exalted commentary[3].

(b) TITLE

This superb commentary is now commonly known as the *Viveka* (i.e., discernment) and has been so designated in the introductory lines appearing in the beginning of the text.[4] But subsequently in most of

---

तदनाकर्ण्य गूढार्थं स्वादु स्वाशयकौशलम् ।
साकूतमुक्तमन्यैर्यत्तेन दोलायते मनः ॥ Ibid., p. 3

1. तत्तद्ग्रन्थाधिगमोपायशतान्वेषणप्रसक्तेन ।
T.A.V., I, p. 42 (2nd Āh.)

It is significant that Jayaratha in the Ist Āhnika lays down his purpose and in the very next Āhnika gives out his method.

2. ....एतद्व्याख्यातं जयरथेनाशु । Ibid.

3. ....वरिष्ठां विवृतिमिमां जयरथश्चक्रे ॥
Ibid., IV, p. 203

4. अथ श्री तन्त्रालोकः श्रीमन्माहेश्वराचार्यवर्यश्रीमदभिनगुप्तविरचितः ।
श्रीमदाचार्यवर्यजयरथविरचितविवेकाभिख्यव्याख्यानोपेतः ।
Ibid., I, p.1

the title lines[1] as well as the colophons[2] it is remembered as the *Prakāśa* (light). Sometimes name *Viveka* has been retained in chapter-colophons[3] also. Once Jayaratha describes it as the *Vivaraṇa* also.[4] It, therefore, transpires that Jayaratha was not very fastidious about the name and himself allowed both the nomenclatures to be used alternatively.

(c) Fundamental motives

(*i*) *Attainment of the Godhead*

The basic aim of Jayaratha in attempting a gloss on the *Tantraloka* is the same as Abhinava's—to inculcate intellectual framework necessary for attainment of the Godhead or Self-Absolute,[5] yet he does not unnecessarily drag on with this. Unlike Abhinava, who is out to secure divine grace for all creatures, Jayaratha would be content if his attempt succeeds in enlightening just one man. In fact, he prefers to remain self-confined and dedicates, like his glorious master, his work as an offering to the Godhead.[6]

1. अथ श्रीतन्त्रालोकस्य श्रीमन्महामाहेश्वराचार्याभिनवगुप्तपादविरचितस्य श्रीमदाचार्यजयरथकृतप्रकाशाख्यव्याख्योपेतस्य ।
T.AV., I, p. 1 (2nd Āh.)
2. ......श्रीजयरथाचार्यकृतप्रकाशाख्यव्याख्योपेते Ibid., p. 42
3. ......श्रीजयरथविरचितविवेकाभिख्यव्याख्योपेते.......
Ibid.., IV, p. 58 (7th Āh.)
4. विवरणमेतदरचयज्जयरथ इति पञ्चमाह्निके कश्चित् ॥
Ibid., III, p. 471
5. यस्मादेषणवित्क्रिया यदुदिता ह्यानन्दचिद्भूमयो
यस्यैवोद्धुरशक्तिवैभवमिदं सर्वं यदेवंविधम् ।
तद्धाम त्रिकतत्त्वमद्वयमयं स्वातन्त्र्यपूर्णप्रथं
चित्ते स्ताच्छिवशासनागमरहस्याच्छादनध्वंसि मे । Ibid., I, p. 1
6. सत्सु प्रार्थनयानया न किमिह तेषां प्रवृत्तिः स्वतो
दुर्जातिष्वपि चार्थिता अपि यतः कुर्युः प्रवृत्तिं न ते ।

(ii) Resurrection of tradition and
(iii) Restoration and preservation of the Tantrāloka

The undercurrent of his entire effort, nevertheless, remains to explore and project the *Tantrāloka* as he steers it clear through the mess that had pervaded all ranks of the scholarship by his time.

Jayaratha is replete with unmistakeable signs towards the existence of this anarchy. Often he becomes very harsh on these confusion-mongering elements. During his examination of the actual chronology of the propagators of Krama system and their traditional viewpoint, he asks the reader to ignore such people who lack scholastic tradition, have not applied their brain to the scripture as well as preceptorial school and are devoid of any commonsense of their own.[1] Sometimes he himself overlooks many apparent discrepancies.[2] We shall soon see several instances of such confusion where Jayaratha's reconciliatory instinct comes to the fore. By the time of Jayaratha, the *Tantrāloka's* text seems to have acquired several interpretations—sometimes equally weighty—all of which were admitted by him as possible

---

सर्वाकारमिति प्ररोहति मनो न प्रार्थनायां यदि
स्वात्मन्येव तदास्महे परमुखप्रेक्षित्वदैन्येन किम् ॥
हंहो दैव सदैव मां प्रति कथंकारं पराधीनता-
मायातोऽस्यधुना प्रसीद भगवन्नेकं वचः श्रूयताम् ।
सदयः कंचन तज्ज्ञमेकमपि तं कुर्याः कृतिं मामकी-
मेतां यः प्रमदोदितास्तु निभृतश्रोत्रं क्षणं श्रोष्यति ॥

Ibid, XII, p. 434, verses 43-44

1. तस्माददृष्टगुरुभिरपरिशीलितशास्त्रसंप्रदायैः
स्वविमर्शशून्यैर्देवानांप्रियैर्यत् किंचिदत्रोच्यते तदुपेक्ष्यमेव ।

T.A.V., III, p. 203

2. एवमनेकप्रकारमासमञ्जस्यं संभवदपि अनङ्गत्वान्न प्रदर्शितम् ।

Ibid., p. 179

alternatives. Take for instance the word 'Sadṛśa' (similar) in the *T.A.* 3.5,[1] or 'Kāṭhinyābhāvataḥ' (because of the lack of solidity[2]) in the *T.A.* 3.20 which attracted two alternative explanations. This could be equally probable that Jayaratha himself, for want of absolute certainty, offers alternative explanations. Opposition to Abhinava's views in the internal circle appears to have gained considerable ground and Jayaratha has to take upon himself to re-establish Abhinava. His frequent tips of endorsement[3] bring us to the same conclusion. Similarly Jayaratha suggests that there was great opposition from one section of scholars to the concept of Tattva-bheda (sub-division of categories), particularly the theory of fifteen subdivisions, since he asks his counterparts to shun antagonism and see reason.[4] Jayaratha himself draws our attention to the complete anarchy that prevailed with regard to the textual reading and order of certain particular portions among the various commenta-

1. सदृशमिति सजातीयम् । ......शरीरसंस्थानप्रतिबिंबं दृश्यते । यद्वा विषयान्तरोपलक्षणपरतया शब्दप्रतिबिम्बविषयत्वेन व्याख्येयम् ।
T.A.V., II, p. 5

2. इह तु सर्वतः स्वच्छत्वात् एकेन भागेन प्रतिसंक्रान्तमपि मुखादि न लक्ष्यते भागान्तरेण—अन्ततः आलोकादिना प्रतिसंक्रान्तेन तस्यावृतत्वात् । यद्वा यथा काचस्फटिकशकलादयः सर्वतः स्वच्छत्वात् तद्व्यवहितवस्तुदर्शनान्यथानुपपत्त्या नायनानां रश्मीनां न प्रतिघातकास्तथा दीपादयोऽपि, काठिन्याभावे सति सर्वतः स्वच्छत्वाद् भागान्तरेण निर्गच्छतः प्रतिबिम्बस्येति न तत्र तत्र प्ररोहमेति—मलिनस्य तत्प्रतीघातकस्य भागान्तरस्याभावात् । Ibid., p. 25

3. For instance in his commentary on just one verse(T.A. 3.31) Jayaratha uses phrases like—
युक्तमित्युक्तम्, इति वक्तुं युक्तम्, इति साधु दृष्टान्तितम्, युक्तयुक्तम्, at least four times.

4. इति भेदानुप्राणितः समग्र एवायं व्यवहारः सोढव्य इति किमनया पाञ्चदश्यादिक्रमकल्पनयापराद्धं यदेवमस्याः प्रद्वेषः ।
Ibid., VII, pp. 64-65

tors.[1] The illustrations may be multiplied to show that the atmosphere inherited by Jayaratha was surcharged with suspicion, confusion and ignorance and Jayaratha discharged a formidable task in restoring the correct order and resurrecting the genuine traditional position.

Jayaratha's obsession with restoring the correct traditional thesis is so ardent and deep-rooted, and in a sense essential, if we keep in view his professed mission, that he raises stormy controversies, investigates into them and then outlines the exact traditional stand.

One of several controversies hinted at by Abhinava relates to the exact number of Kālīs ordained by the *Kramastotra* (by Siddhanātha). Abhinava was a great champion of twelve-Kālīs theory in his *Tantrāloka*, but the confusion resulted from misapprehending the proper approach of Abhinava on the issue whose sole aim was to present Saṁvit-krama while others including the *Pañcaśatika* and a section of the *Kramastotra*'s commentators were guided by their eagerness to conceal Saṁvitkrama and present Pūjākrama.[2] This problem arose in the wake of Abhinava's bringing in Raktakālī, instead

1. सर्वेषामेव च विवरणकृतामत्रं प्रतिपदं पाठानां श्लोकानां व्यत्यासो दृश्यते, इत्यस्मद्दृष्ट एव पाठे क इवायं प्रद्वेषः । T.A.V., III, p. 202

We are, however, not quite sure if विवरणकृताम् here refers to the *Kramastotra* (K.T. p. 179) alone or the *Tantrāloka*.

2. इह तु पूजाक्रमगोपनाय स्वशय्ययैव स्थापनम्, यदधिकृत्य संवित्क्रमः परिनिष्ठितिमियात्, अतएवागमैकशरणतया प्रवृत्तेऽपि श्रीक्रमस्तोत्रे ग्रन्थकृतां अभिनवगुप्तानां संवित्क्रममेव प्रदर्शयितुं तद्विवृतौ . . . . इत्याद्युक्तम् ।

Ibid., p. 162

of Sthitīkālī, after Sṛṣṭikālī.[1] Similarly Abhinava's exclusion of Sukālī from the list of Kālīs evoked a furore among die-hards because it made Abhinava subscribe to the notion of twelve Kālīs admitted in Anākhyacakra according to the *Sārdhaśatika*. Jayaratha examines the objection from every possible angle—scriptural authority, textual testimony, doctrinal consistency, chronological continuity, contextual propriety, scribal authenticity and colateral evidence—and resolves that Abhinava's stand in entertaining only twelve Kālīs in Anākhyacakra is unimpeachable.[2] In the same vain Jayaratha goes on scrutinizing even the historical inaccuracies and sets the chronological record straight. He says with a pinch of salt that these contemporaries do not know anything[3] about Abhinava's preceptorial tradition and claims to be in direct receipt of the traditional secrets supplying several missing links on Cakrabhānu, Kakāradevī, Somarāja, Hrasvanātha, etc. and the real purport of the *Kramastotra*.[4] He then comes to the well-settled

1. ननु सर्वत्रैवान्यत्र श्रीसृष्टिकाल्यनन्तरं श्रीस्थितिकाल्या अभिधानम्, यदुक्तं श्रीसार्धशतिके. . . .इति तत्कथमिह तदनन्तरं श्रीरक्तकाल्यादिनिर्देशः कृतः, एवं हि आगमविरोधः स्यात् ? T.A.V., III, p. 161

2. ननु क्रमदर्शने सर्वत्रैव श्रीसृष्ट्यादिदेवीनां मध्ये श्री सुकाल्या भगवत्या अभिधानं येनानाख्यचक्रे त्रयोदश देव्यः. . . . .तदत्र क्रमनयसमानकक्ष्यत्वविवक्षायामपि कथमेतद्विरुद्धमभिहितं "द्वादशैव देव्यः" इति ? अत्रोच्यते इह क्रमदर्शने सर्वसर्विकया अनाख्यचक्रे त्रयोदशैव देव्यः पूज्यत्वेनाभिमताः इति तावन्नास्ति नियमः. . . . . .एवमिह सुकालीं विना द्वादशैव देव्यः पूज्यतया यद्युक्ताः, तत्को दोषः । Ibid., pp. 189-191

3. अतश्चास्य एवं गुरुक्रममजानानैरद्यतनैः . . . .इत्यादि यदुक्तं तत्स्वोत्प्रेक्षितमेव-इत्युपेक्ष्यम् । नहि चक्रभानुना प्रायः कस्यचिदपि एवमुपदिष्टम् तन्मूलतयैव इदानीमस्योपदेशस्य शतशो दर्शनात् । Ibid., p. 193

4. Ibid., pp. 193-202

principle that one cannot extract a piece in isolation —the text has to be accepted or rejected as a whole —and although in the case of alternative positions one's sheet anchor is bound to be one's preceptorial teaching, Jayaratha finds his conclusion unaffected on either version of the original text.[1] This controversy has been raised earlier also on more philosophical footing with the conclusion that there is no scope at all for the thirteenth form otherwise it will render the twelve forms as non-modes of consciousness.[2] Although the theory of thirteen forms may be justified with reference to the empirical subject, it has no ground metaphysically.[3] In fact such a sharp division of respective standpoints led to two different schools within Krama system and was responsible for historically different lines of growth.

Jayaratha refers to another controversy in the course of his treatment of the 'passage of space' (Deśādhva). The context relates to the regions as obtaining within the category of earth. There were

1. नन्वेवं तर्हि "अयं पाठः साधुरयमसाधुः" इति विचारः किं नाश्रीयते यद्य एव समूलः पाठः स एव साधुरितरस्तु इतरथेति मूलं चात्रोभयत्रापि प्रदर्शितेन क्रमेण समानमुत्पश्यामः—, इत्येकतरपरिग्रहे यथास्वं गुरूपदेश एव निबन्धनम् ।

T.A.V., III, p. 203

2. ननु अस्यास्त्रयोदशात्मकत्वमपि अन्यैरुक्तं तत्कथमिह द्वादशात्मकत्वमेवोच्यते ? . . . . संविदो हि अतिरेके द्वादशरूपाणि असंविद्रूपत्वात् न चकास्युरेव इति निराभासा संविदेकैव अवशिष्येत, इति को नाम त्रयोदशरूपत्वस्यावकाशः ।

Ibid., pp. 127-129

3. तत्कथमेतत् प्रतिसमाधीयते इत्युच्यताम् ? उच्यते—इह भेदाधिवासिता मायाप्रमातारस्तावदुपदेश्याः, इति समानार्थचर्यावत् तदानुगुण्येन अत्र प्रवृत्तः उपदेशः सुखेन प्ररोहमियात्, इति विकल्पबलोपनतं भेदमाश्रित्य संविदस्त्रयोदशरूपत्वमुक्तम्, इह पुनर्वास्तवमभेदमेवावलम्ब्य एवमुपदेशः इति सर्वमेव प्रतिसमाहितम् ।

Ibid., pp. 133-34

varying agamic positions. For example, the stands taken up by the *Nandiśikhātantra* and the *Triśirsobhairava* did not tally with that by the *Siddhātantra*. Similarly there was some difference of opinion if the region presided over by the god Ananta lay within waters or above it. Jayaratha examines all aspects in detail and concludes that internal existtence has to be construed as external existence and in fact internality or externality was not the point at issue, what was intended was the 'sequence' alone. Viewed in this light the alleged opposition between the *Siddhātantra* and others will evaporate. This does not even militate against the position accepted by the *Tantrarāja Bhaṭṭāraka*. Jayaratha does not deny the distinctive character of various positions; what he wants to bring home is their structural and scholastic compatibility.[1]

It is neither possible nor advisable to take stock of all such situations for reasons of space. We will, therefore, refer to one more instance and then proceed further. In the course of discussion on the cosmic passage called Kalā (crest) Abhinava does not stop at the ultimate reality, i.e. Śiva, being 36th category but talks of thirtyseventh and thirtyeighth category also ruling out any scope for the fallacy

1. The controversy consumes about 8 pages (T.A.V., V, pp. 15-22) but the following remark from the *Viveka* is significant—

यच्च श्रीसिद्धातन्त्रोक्तं भुवनमानमिह न ग्राह्यम्—इत्युक्तं तदप्ययुक्तम्, यतो यदि नाम नरकादिवदनन्तभुवनस्येह मानं किंचिदुच्येत तत्प्रकियाभेदादन्यतन्त्रोक्तमग्राह्यमेव इति स्यात्। भुवनस्य मानमवश्यंभावि तच्चेह नोक्तम्, इति तदाकांक्षायामेव अवश्यमेवान्यतः कुतश्चिदपेक्षणीयम् इति को नाम श्रीसिद्धातंत्रे प्रद्वेषः। यद्वा श्रीतन्त्रराजभट्टारकेऽपि अस्य लक्षोच्छ्रितत्वमुक्तम् इति तदपेक्ष्यतां, को नाम नो निर्बन्धः, यावता हि अस्माकमन्तर्भुवनमानसंख्याया आसमञ्जस्यमभिधानीयं तच्च उभयथापि सिद्ध्येत् इत्यलं बहुना। T.A.V., V, pp. 20-21

called infinite regress.[1] Abhinava's view, Jayaratha suggests, was first attacked on the counts of (i) lack of reason[2] and (ii) absence of scriptural evidence[3] and then on those of (iii) doubtful support[4] and (iv) deviation from the normally accepted position.[5] Jayaratha again gets quite harsh on the critics who having avoided pains of sitting at the feet of a teacher are utterly confused about real intent of Abhinava or the scriptural position.[6] Although the ultimate reality is correctly accepted as thirtysixth category yet the problem is how to account for immanence if it is considered transcendent and for objectivity or knowability if

1. न चानवस्था ह्येवं स्याद्दृश्यतां हि महात्मभिः ॥
यद्वेद्यं किंचिदाभाति तत्क्षये यत्प्रकाशते ।
तत्तत्त्वमिति निर्णीतं षट्त्रिंशं हृदि भासते ॥
तत्किं न किंचिद्वा किंचिदित्याकांक्षावशे वपुः ।
चिदानन्दस्वतन्त्रैकरूपं तदिति देशने ॥
सप्तत्रिंशं समाभाति तत्राकांक्षा च नापरा ।
तथापि क्लृप्तवेद्यत्वं यत्र भाति स चिन्मयः ॥
अष्टात्रिंशत्तमः सोऽपि भावनायोपदिश्यते ।
यदि नाम ततः सप्तत्रिंश एव पुनर्भवेत् ॥ T.A. 11.23-27

2. विरुद्धधर्माध्यासस्तावद्भेदहेतुरित्यविवादः । सर्वाविभागात्मत्वादेश्चाविशेषात् स एवात्र नास्ति इति कुतस्त्योऽयमनयोर्भेदः । T.A.V., VII, p. 18 (11th Āh.)

3. एवंविधश्च कश्चिदागमोऽपि न संवादितः । Ibid., p. 19

4. नन्वत्र (श्रीकुलरत्नमालायाम्). . . .का वार्ता तु सप्तत्रिंशाष्टात्रिंशयोः प्रत्युत म्लिष्टप्रायमालूनविशीर्णं किं तावदप्रातीतिकमुक्तम् । Ibid., p. 20

5. वस्तुतो हि सर्वशास्त्रेषु षट्त्रिंशत्त्वेन गीयमानमनवच्छिन्नं बोधमात्रमेव परतत्त्वमित्युक्तम् । Ibid., p. 19

6. सप्तत्रिंशाष्टात्रिंशयोरपूर्वतयाभिधानेन सुकुमारहृदयानामागमिकानां संमोहो मा भूदिति करुणापरस्य परमेश्वरस्य गूढार्थतया यथोक्तनीत्या मायाप्रमात्रपेक्षया कल्पनामात्रसारमेवमभिधानं तच्च गुरूपसेवनादावदृष्टकष्टैः स्वावमर्शशून्यैश्च कथमेवमेवावगम्यते । Ibid., VII, p. 21 (11th Āh.)

it is viewed as subject or knower. Jayaratha finds both of these anomalies resolved by the enunciation of the 37th and 38th stages.[1] He also says that Abhinava's basic approach is to expatiate upon the agamic viewpoint even in preference to the generally accepted thesis.[2]

(iv) *Furnishing chronological continuity*

As a part of his ardent responsibility Jayaratha, as we have pointed out earlier also, has worked hard on chronological accounts of the preceptorial lineages and has always abided by the preceptorial authority. Jayaratha himself recognizes this to be his prime contribution in the *Viveka*. In his *Vāmakeśvarīmatavivaraṇa* he emphatically avers that those who have interpreted or referred to the *Tantrāloka* without having access to the teacher and for that matter uninterrupted tradition have only lent themselves to great ridicule[3]. In fact his account of Krama and Kula histories and several other important authors on Kashmir Śaivism is invaluable. For instance Niṣkriyānandanātha, Vidyānanda, Śaktyānanda, Śivānanda and his three female disciples,

1. यावता हि एकस्यैव षट्त्रिंशस्य तत्त्वस्य मायाप्रमातृपेक्षया विश्वोत्तीर्णत्वेऽपि विश्वमयत्वं प्रमातृत्वेऽपि प्रमेयत्वं च कथं नाम संगच्छताम् . . . . तच्चोभयमपि सप्तत्रिंशाष्टात्रिंशयोरेवोपकल्पनेनोपशाम्यति, द्वयोरपि भिन्नविषयत्वेनैव कृतार्थत्वस्योक्तत्वात्। T.A.V., VII, p. 26 (11th Āh.)

2. वस्तुतस्तु षट्त्रिंशमेव सर्वंसहमित्युक्तप्रायम् । . . . . . .ग्रन्थकृता पुनस्तदेव भित्तितयावलम्ब्य तदागमार्थव्याचिकीर्षापरतयैवमभिहितम् । Ibid., p. 26

3. यत् पुनरत्र अन्यैरन्यत्र वा साक्षात् गुरुस्तदर्थंसतत्त्वमनवगम्य श्रीतंत्रालोकसंवादनं तदर्थप्रकाशनं वा कृतं तत् सर्वं पितृपितामहक्रमोपनतं प्रकृतं स्पष्टं मार्गमपि अजानतामश्रुतामपूर्वामदृष्टचरां च गहनगहनां तत्सरणिं तज्ज्ञानं प्रति प्रकाशयतां तेषामेव महतीमुपहास्यतामावहति । VMV, KSS 66, p. 76

Govindarāja, Bhānuka, Eraka, Ujjaṭa, Udbhaṭṭa, the Stotrakāra alias Siddhanātha, Bhāskara, Bhūtirāja I, Kuladhara, Bhojarāja, Somarāja, Śivānanda II, own ancestral and doctrinal lineages, linear expanse of Traiyambaka, Sumatinātha, Somadeva and Śambhunātha are some of those celebrated personages about whom our knowledge depends on Jayaratha sometimes exclusively and sometimes in a very large measure. For fear of detail and reasons of space and propriety we propose to abandon our enquiry here.[1] One thing, however, is absolutely certain that not only he has direct access to the tradition but also deep insight into it and leaves no stone unturned to make sure that the reader is convinced about the stamp of finality and authenticity that he puts on it.[2]

(d) HANDLING OF THE SOURCE MATERIAL

(i) *Four progressive phases and their several dimensions*

Jayaratha closely follows the footsteps of his master. His major contribution lies in opening floodgates of our information on the source-material. Thus like the *Tantrāloka*, the *Viveka*, too, emerges as a major reliable sourcebook on the basic sources with several dimensions to it. There is a discernible progression in Jayaratha's handling of the material and it passes through the following phases—

(I) *Material drawn upon by Abhinava*—Identi-

1. See for details K.T., Chapter Six, pp. 82-248; Abhi., Chap. 5, pp. 132-251, Chap. 7, pp. 545-549; Upodghāta, Pūrvārdha.

2. तस्मादस्मदुक्तमेव व्याख्यानं युक्तमित्यन्यदुपेक्ष्यम् ।
T.A.V., V, p. 260

fication, structural information, citation, possible and relevant restoration, critical determination and interpretation;

(II) *Material produced after Abhinavagupta*—allusion, scrutinization, possible restoration, textual settlement and discovery of *inter se* relationship;

(III) *Gaps creating deviations or controversies*—enumeration and reconciliation; and

(IV) *Additional information*—substantiation, textual determination, rationalization, underlining potentialities, textual restoration and the furnishing of cultural information.

(ii) Material drawn upon by Abhinava

We are afraid that in an attempt like the present 'Introduction' it is well nigh impossible to do away with overlapping altogether as emphases vary with angles, approaches and context. Towards supplying the source material Jayaratha's job is manifold. The first is identification of the text or source, if Abhinava makes an unassertive reference. The second in the same connection is to identify the exact portion of the source and to cite from it, if necessary, in case Abhinava names a source but withholds further information. For instance, the word Ādi in the *T.A.* 1.46,[1] according to Jayaratha, stands for an agamic text belonging to the dualistic branch of Śaivism called *Cillācakreśvarī-mata* followed by an extract.[2] Similarly the *Ratnamālā* in the *Tantrā-*

1. मतङ्गादौ कृतं श्रीमत्खेटपालादिदैशिकैः ।

2. आदिशब्देन चिल्लाचक्रेश्वरीमतादेर्ग्रहणम् । तदुक्तं तत्र–
"बौद्धं च पौरुषेयं च द्विविधं तन्मलं स्मृतम् ।
तत्र दीक्षादिना याति पौरुषेयं मलं क्षयम् ।।

loka[1] is identified as the *Kularatnamālā*[2] (we get the complete title). Jayaratha also enlightens us that this reference is to the content and purport of the *Ratnamālā* and not to its language. He then goes on giving several excerpts from it.[3] The verb 'Pracakṣate'[4] (i.e., say), though vague, stands for the *Parātriṁśikā* according to Jayaratha who mentions the exact relevant spot in the mentioned text.[5] Similarly 'Āgame'[6] in the *T.A.* 4.148 stands for the *Pañcaśatika*[7]—it is only on the authority of Jayaratha that we know it. Jayaratha cites the relevant portion as well. Jayaratha, it seems, abhors vagueness and scrupulously furnishes zero-error information. While discussing Abhinava's allusion to the *Mataṅgaśāstra*[8], Jayaratha specifically reminds the reader that the actual reference is to the *commentary* on the *Mataṅgaśāstra* and not to the Āgama proper[9] in order to avoid

---

बौद्धमक्षयमेवास्ते तावत्तावत्समुद्रितम् ।
यावन्न बौद्धमेवास्य सजातीयविलापकम् ।।
ज्ञानमभ्युदितं सम्यक्सारेतरविभागकृत् ।" इति ।
T.A.V., I, pp. 85-86

1. यथोक्तं रत्नमालायाम् । T.A. 1.274

2. रत्नमालायामिति श्रीकुलरत्नमालायामिति उक्तमिति अर्थतो, न तु शब्दतः । T.A.V., I, p. 281

3. Ibid., pp. 282-283

4. तदेव ब्रह्म परममविभक्तं प्रचक्षते ।। T.A. 3.167

5. प्रचक्षत इति श्रीपरात्रिंशकादौ तथाहि तत्र पराबीजोद्धारे "तृतीयं ब्रह्म सुश्रोणि" इत्युक्तम् । T.A.V., II, p. 166

6. सृष्टिं कलयते देवी तन्नाम्नागम उच्यते । T.A. 4.148

7. आगमे श्रीपञ्चशतिकादौ उच्यते अभिधीयते इत्यर्थः । तदुक्तं तत्र । T.A.V., III, p. 158

8. श्रीमन्मतङ्गशास्त्रे च क्रमोऽयं पुरपूगगः । T.A. 8.428

9. अत्र च साक्षादागमे संवादिते ग्रन्थविस्तरः स्यात् इति तद्वृत्तिकृदुक्तं संवादितम् । T.A.V., V, p. 275

unnecessary elaboration. He then offers us a glimpse of the versicular commentary under reference. In fact it is impossible to understand the *Tantrāloka* without the aid of the *Viveka*. In a single continued treatment Abhinava alludes to the respective orders of the five sheaths (Kañcukas) according to the *Sarvajñānottara*, *Svāyambhuva*, *Kiraṇa* and *Mātaṅga-pārameśvara*,[1] but in the *Tantrāloka's* text the *Svāyambhuva* is nowhere mentioned even obliquely. It is by the analysis of the contents that Jayaratha finds an unmistakeable appeal to the authority of the *Svāyambhuva*.[2] On the same pattern Jayaratha hints that Abhinavagupta is not simply referring to but also quoting and in such a case he completes[3] an incomplete quote.[4] Thus we see that Jayaratha does not restrict himself to the provision of name alone, he tries to discover the underlying source. This attitude is profusely reflected in places like the discussion of Mālinīnyāsa[5] (an assignment called Mālinī) where Abhinavagupta does not take us into confidence about his agamic base, but Jayaratha

1. पुंरागवित्कलाकालमाया ज्ञानोत्तरे क्रमात् ॥
नियतिर्नास्ति वैरिञ्चे कलोर्ध्वे नियतिः श्रता ।
पुंरागवित्त्रयादूर्ध्वं कलानियतिसंपुटम् ॥
कालो मायेति कथितः क्रमः किरणशास्त्रगः ।
पुमान्नियत्या कालश्च रागविद्याकलान्वितः ॥
इत्येष क्रम उद्दिष्टो मातङ्गे पारमेश्वरे । T.A. 9.45-48

2. नियतिर्नास्तीति सर्वज्ञानोत्तरे तस्या अनभिधानात्, वैरिञ्च इति—स्वायम्भुवे, यदुक्तं तत्र– T.A.V., VI, p. 46

3. इति देवो न्यरूपयद् इति प्राच्येन संबंधः । Ibid., IX, p. 28

4. श्रीमदानन्दशास्त्रे च नाशुद्धिः स्याद्विपश्चितः ।
किन्तु स्नानं सुवस्त्रत्वं तुष्टिसंजननं भवेत् ॥ T.A. 15.45

5. इत्येष मातृकान्यासो मालिन्यास्तु निरूप्यते । Ibid. 15.120

comes forward with references to and quotations from the *Siddhātantra as* well as the *Triśirobhairava* and underscores the similarity they have with other tantras like the *Matabhaṭṭāraka* on this issue.[1]

In addition to the above-noted information Jayaratha's job includes the furnishing of structural information in respect of the cited source material. It is rendered possible by affording an insight into the quoted extract. Abhinavagupta, for example, quotes the *Kiraṇāgama* to substantiate the relationship of path and destination (Upāya-upeya-bhāva) as subsisting between the power and the power-ful.[2] Here Jayaratha comes to our rescue saying that this *Āgama* had a question-answer format where Garuḍa is the inquirer while the Godhead assumes the role of the answerer. It is this long dialogue between the two (of which specific portions have been earmarked by Jayaratha) that has been drawn upon by Abhinavagupta and put in his own words for the sake of brevity.[3] Likewise the *Triśirobhairava* was also in the form of a dialogue between the Goddess and the God where Devī asks and Śiva answers. We owe this information to Jayaratha, who pinpoints the portion actually quoted by Abhinavagupta.[4]

1. T.A.V., IX, pp. 63-65
2. श्रीमत्किरणशास्त्रे च तत्प्रश्नोत्तरपूर्वकम् ।
   अनुभावो विकल्पोऽपि मानसो न मनः शिवे ॥
   अविज्ञाय शिवं दीक्षा कथमित्यत्र चोत्तरम् । T.A., 1.75-76
3. तत्र गरुडेन .... पृष्टे भगवता .... इत्यादिना .... इत्यन्तेन... प्रतिसमाहितम् । एतच्च पुनरप्यागूर्य गरुडेन .... इत्यादिना पृष्टम् । एतत्प्रश्नार्थ एव ग्रन्थकृता संक्षेपचिकीर्षया स्ववचसोपनिबद्धः । T.A.V., I, pp. 116-117
4. श्रीमत्त्रिशरसि प्रोक्तं परज्ञानस्वरूपकम् ।
   शक्त्या गर्भान्तर्वर्तिन्या शक्तिगर्भं परं पदम् ॥ T.A. 2.32

This Āgama was divided into several chapters called Paṭalas.[1] Similarly the *Ūrmimahāśāstrasiddha Santānarūpaka* as presented by Abhinavagupta[2] happened to be identical with Kula text *Ūrmikaulasiddhasantānarūpaka* and was in the form of a dialogue between Devī and Śiva and had one of the chapters called Pādovallī dealing with preceptorial genealogy.[3]

It is no use multiplying instances. Jayaratha's another major contribution lies in retaining certain important pre-Abhinavan sources in more or less complete form. The preservation of the *Kramastotra*, attributed by us to *Siddhanātha* elsewhere,[4] in somewhat intact shape[5] in the pages of fourth Āhnika[6] is a classic example of the same. Similar is the case with the *Pañcaśatika*, etc. In a sense Jayaratha's coverage is no less wider than that of his master.

The greatest task, however, consists in his editing the text critically and determining the precise reading. Jayaratha seems to have worked religiously on it. Here his job is twofold. On the one he handles the

---

Jayaratha adds—"परं ज्ञानं कथं देव" इति देवीप्रश्ननिर्णयार्थं ह्येतदत्र परज्ञानरूपं भगवतोक्तमित्याशयः, तदेव पठति "शक्त्या" इत्यादि ।
T.A.V., I, p. 26 (2nd Āh.)

1. श्रीत्रिशिरोभैरवप्रथमपटलाच्च अयमर्थः स्वयमेवाधिगन्तव्यः ।
Ibid., I, p. 150

2. श्रीमदूर्मिमहाशास्त्रे सिद्धसंतानरूपके ।
इदमुक्तम्. . . . . T.A. 2.48

3. ऊर्मिमहाशास्त्र इति श्रीमदूर्मिकौलसिद्धसंतानरूपके इत्यनेन पादोवल्ल्यां पारम्पर्येऽप्यम्लानत्वं दर्शितम् तत्र-हि . . . . इति भगवत्या पृष्टो भगवान् . . . . इत्याद्युपक्रम्य . . . . इत्यादिपर्यन्तं बहूक्तवान् । T.A.V., I, p. 40 (2nd Āh).

4. Vide K.T., pp. 142-43

5. Also see Upodghāta, p. 31

6. Vide T.A.V., III, pp. 150, 160, 165, 167, 169, 173, 178, 181, 183, 185, 187, 202

agamic texts alluded to and/or quoted by Abhinavagupta or by himself and on the other he handles the text of the *Tantrāloka*. For the timebeing we concentrate on the former alone. In critically handling the source texts he rectifies the incorrect reading—whether due to scribal mistake or due to misinformation—, indicates his preference out of the two or more seemingly equal readings, reconciles differing scriptural positions, criticizes his own schoolmen for their deviations and preferences for other readings, and finally arranges the texts in a natural and logical order. To appreciate better, let us look into some illustrative instances. At one place[1] Jayaratha discusses the original Āgama, i.e. *Svāyambhuva*, and holds that the reading Kalā, which he chanced to see in older manuscripts, has to be accepted in preference to the common reading Kāla without which the Abhinavan text would militate against the *Kiraṇa Āgama*.[2] At another, Jayaratha retains Dvitīyām in the quoted text in preference to Tṛtīyām Caturthīm,[3] as adopted by a section of misguided scholars while commenting upon Abhinavagupta

1. नियतिर्नास्ति वैरिञ्चे कलोर्ध्वे नियतिः श्रुता ।
   पुंरागवित्त्रयादूर्ध्वं कलयानितिसंपुटम् ॥ T.A. 9.46
2. वैरिञ्च इति स्वायम्भुवे यदुक्तं तत्र–
   मायातत्त्वात्कालतत्त्वं संस्थितं तत्पदद्वये ।
   संस्थान्यस्मिन्कला तद्वद्विद्याप्येवं ततः पुन ॥ इति, अत्र हि संस्थापयति नियच्छति भोगेषु, अणूनिति संस्था नियतिरिति व्याख्यातारः, अत्र च कालो नियतिसंपुटः, कलेत्येवमात्मैव जरत्पुस्तकदृष्टः पाठो ग्राह्यः अन्यथा हि कैरणोऽर्थो विसंवदेत् । T.A.V., VI, p. 46
3. "अथात्माख्यां द्वितीयां परिकल्पयेत्" इत्यत्र च तृतीयां चतुर्थीं वेति पाठो भवेत्, सिद्धातंत्रे च सैकार्णत्यादिना वक्ष्यमाणेन ग्रन्थेन पौनरुक्त्यं प्रसज्येदिति अलं गुर्वागमसंप्रदायशून्यैः सह संलापेन । Ibid., IX, pp. 162-63

who draws upon the *Siddhayogīśvaramata* in respect of the seat-worship (Āsanārcana) and invokes the contents thereof[1], because it will lead to unnecessary repetition when construed with the *Siddhātantra*. In the same context he resolves the textual order and implies that 'Sārdhākṣarāṃ' qualifies 'Dvayīṃ'—the two are not independent.[2] As seen earlier, Jayaratha not only identifies the quoted text but goes a step further. He pinpoints exact reading[3] in the original source in case Abhinavagupta does not strictly adhere to the 'original'.[4] Here Abhinavagupta reads Pūrṇāṁ and Kṛśāṁ while it is Pīnāṁ and Durbalāṁ in the original *Vijñānabhairava*. Jayaratha, at a different place, quotes from a tantra, probably the *Siddhātantra* if one goes by the contextual evidence, after correction of Ūnā into Ūnāṃ stating his reasons for doing so.[5] He meets the anticipated criticism by further reasoning.[6] At another place[7] Abhinava draws upon the *Mṛtyuñjaya-tantra*

1. तत्रासने पुरा मूर्तिभूतां सार्धाक्षरां द्वयीम्
न्यस्येद्व्याप्तृतयेत्युक्तं सिद्धयोगीश्वरीमते ॥
विद्यामूर्तिमथात्माख्यां द्वितीयां परिकल्पयेत् । T.A. 15.321, 323

2. अत्र च सार्धाक्षरामिति पठित्वा द्वयीं मातृकां मालिनीं च न्यस्येदिति न वाच्यम् । एवं हि अत्र श्रौन्मनसस्य पङ्कजत्रयस्य वाचकमभिहितं स्यात् ।
T.A.V., IX, p. 162

3. उक्तमिति श्रीविज्ञानभैरवे ।
तत्र च पीनां दुर्बलां चैवेति पाठः । Ibid., p. 243

4. उक्तं च पूर्णां च कृशां ध्यात्वा द्वादशगोचरे ॥ T.A. 15.480

5. "शूलानि स्युः षट्सहस्राण्यूनं सार्धशतद्वयात् ।" इति ऊनमिति ऊना इति वा अपपाठ एव अनन्वितत्वात् तृतीया स्थाने पञ्चम्यनुपपत्तेः ।
T.A.V., XII, p. 246

6. Ibid, pp. 246-7

7. एकैकं द्वयङ्गुलं ज्ञेयं तत्र पूर्वं पदत्रयम् ।
अष्टाङ्गुलानि चत्वारि दशाङ्गुलमतः परम् ॥ etc. T.A. 16.234-36

for his notion of independent assignment (Svatantra Nyāsa) pertaining to the ultimate-cum-nonultimate deity. Jayaratha has adopted the reading 'Ekaikam dvayaṅgulam' in preference to 'Ekaikadyaṅgulam' and vehemently ridicules those who opt for such a reading by a curious mixture of the preceding and the following confusing both because such a reading clearly nullifies the original agamic reading, brings in the element of farfetched imagination, lacks the use of the word 'again' and also violates the explanations offered by the teachers.[1] These examples, though handful, will indeed help us gather an idea about Jayaratha's careful diligence.

The next step Jayaratha takes is to accord a proper interpretation. He addresses himself to the task of giving the most appropriate and relevant interpretation. As a rule he feels shy of bringing in other interpretations in spite of their probability. Nor does he harp on their patent mutual inconsistency, if the same is irrelevant. It is of course very natural for Jayaratha to hunt out the exact basic source behind Abhinava's specific thesis or pronouncement. For example, while initiating discussion on the 'division of day and night' as a sequel to the 'movement of breath' (Prāṇacāramāna) he underscores Abhinava's heavy dependence upon the *Svacchanda Tantra.* But it is also his bounden duty to point out the lines on which the source authority is to be understood with a warning of the impending negative results. Abhinava invokes the authority of the *Parā-*

1. अस्य न्यासस्य एकैकद्वयङ्गुलमिति पठित्वा. . .चेत्यभिधाय पूर्वापरानुसारितया उभयपक्षमीलनया अङ्गुलव्यत्यासेन व्याख्यायामार्षपाठपरित्यागः कष्टकल्पना पुनर्वचनानुपयोगः श्रीमद्गुरुव्याख्यातिक्रमाश्चेति दोषाः ।
T.A.V., X, pp.91-92

triśikā[1], also known as the *Trikaśāsana*, for his treatment of the principle of right teacher and his initiation and quotes two verses from it[2] leaving out intervening verses.[3] Jayaratha immediately steps in to say that the omission is purposive and the first line of the quoted text is quite capable of covering even the unquoted portion of the quoted last verse.[4] Sometimes Jayaratha accords an apparently incon-

1. यत्तु (S.T. 7.36 and 7.39)........ इत्याद्युक्तं तत्केवलमेव प्राणावाहमधिकृत्यापानवाहं चेत्यधिगन्तव्यम् । एवं (S.T. 7.68).... इत्यादौ पक्षसन्धिग्रन्थेऽपि अयमेवाशयो योज्यः । अन्यथा ह्येका त्रुटिरकृतविनियोगा स्यात् ।
T.A.V., IV, p. 57

2. अदृष्टमण्डलोऽप्येवं यः कश्चिद्वेत्ति तत्त्वतः ।
स सिद्धिभाग्भवेन्नित्यं स योगी स च दीक्षितः ॥
एवं यो वेत्ति तत्त्वेन तस्य निर्वाणगामिनी ।
दीक्षा भवेदिति प्रोक्तं तच्छ्रीत्रिंशकशासने ॥ T.A. 4.50

3. Luckily the text of the P.T.V. is printed with the commentary of Abhinava in KSS as Volume No. 18 (1918). The verses under reference, traceable at Nos. 18 to 25, are as under—

अदृष्टमण्डलोऽप्येवं यः कश्चिद्वेत्ति तत्त्वतः ।
स सिद्धिभाग्भवेन्नित्यं स योगी स च दीक्षितः ॥
अनेन ज्ञातमात्रेण ज्ञायते सर्वशक्तिभिः ।
शाकिनीकुलसामान्यो भवेद्योगं विनापि हि ॥
अविधिज्ञो विधानज्ञो जायते यजनं प्रति ॥
कालाग्निमादितः कृत्वा मायान्तं ब्रह्मदेहगम् ।
शिवो विश्वाद्यनन्तान्तः परे शक्तित्रयं मतम् ॥
तदन्तर्वर्ति यत्किंचित् शुद्धमार्गे व्यवस्थितम् ।
अणुर्विशुद्धमचिरादैश्वरं ज्ञानमश्नुते ॥
तच्चोदकः शिवो ज्ञेयः सर्वज्ञः परमेश्वरः ।
सर्वगो निर्मलः स्वच्छस्तृप्तः स्वायतनः शुचिः ॥

4. तत्र च "अदृष्टमण्डलोप्येवम्..." इत्यादि श्लोकानन्तरम् "अनेन ज्ञातमात्रेण..." इत्यादिग्रन्थान्तरं संभवदपि प्रकृतानुपयोगात् न पठितम्, अदृष्टमण्डलत्वादेव च "तिलाज्याहुतिवर्जितत्वादि" अवसीयते, तदपि न पठितम् ।
T.A.V., III, p. 58

gruous interpretation. For instance, he explains the word Antaḥ in Abhinava's text, which is based on the *Devyāyāmala Tantra* in the context, not as 'within' but as 'just above it'.[1] But in arriving at this interpretation he has to compare and contrast a host of Āgamas and synthesize their anomalous stands and then to conclude that Abhinavagupta's leaning towards a general, and hence casual, survey is sometimes responsible for such expressions. Jayaratha intends his method to be a trend setter for interpretation of the cognate tantric material.[2]

(iii) *Pre-Abhinavan tantric material*

The same approach permeates his handling of the tantric material, whether of Abhinavan, pre-, or post-Abhinavan era. In the absence of a clearly worked-out chronological analysis of this material our remarks have to be limited to the works quoted by Jayaratha on his own. Very often he draws upon those sections of pre-Abhinavan material which have remained untouched by Abhinavagupta. Despite Abhinavagupta's extensive coverage, a lot of material from hitherto unknown sources has found its way into Jayaratha which is of immense value

1. जलस्यान्तरित्यर्थात् तदुपरि संस्थितः । T.A.V., V, p. 14

2. यदुक्तं श्रीनन्दिशिखायाम्. . . । श्रीत्रिशिरोभैरवेऽपि. . .इत्यादीनाम् अन्तःस्थितिविधायकानां वाक्यानां कोऽर्थः स्यात् । किंच. . .इदमत्र प्रतिपत्तव्यं— यदनन्तस्य बहिरवस्थानमिति। तथाहि श्रीतन्त्रराजभट्टारके. . .इत्यादिकमनन्तस्य नान्तःस्थितेर्विधायकं किंतु एवं शुद्धिक्रमस्य तदवस्थितेः पूर्वमुक्तत्वात् एतावन्मात्रस्यैवात्र विवक्षितत्वात्। यदुक्तं तत्र . . . . एवं . . . इत्यादावपि व्याख्येयम् । एतच्चोत्तानतयैव गृहीत्वा. . .तत्र तत्र तथाभ्यधुः येनास्य अन्तरवस्थाने भ्रान्तिबीजत्वं प्ररूढम् । तथा च सोमशंभुः. . . .इति न पूर्वापरव्याहतत्वम् । यद्वक्ष्यति. . . .
Ibid., pp. 14-19

for any future chronicle of tantric history. Of all the works referred to by Jayaratha, his allusions to the *Śrīkaṇṭhī* are highly significant[1] for the study of the ten Śiva tantras, eighteen Rudra tantras and sixtyfour Bhairava tantras (divided into eight groups) belonging to the dualistic, dualistic-cum-monistic and monistic schools. Jayaratha gives a few lengthy quotations incorporating the names of all the tantras.[2] Though it is difficult to ascertain its period, the first ever reference to it is found in the *Uddyota* of Kṣemarāja on the *Svacchanda Tantra*[3] which also testifies to Jayaratha's description about the subject-matter. Among other agamic texts he refers to the *Kramasadbhāva*, *Sārdhaśatika*, *Ānandeśvaratantra*, *Pañcāmṛta Bhūtakṣobha*, *Anantavijaya*, *Kulakramodaya* and *Kula-krīḍāvatāra* for the first time. As is usual he not only quotes but also informs about their formal structure, subject matter and crucial points which evoked special interest. For instance, the *Krama sadbhāva* was an Āgama of Nigama class and there was a sharp difference of opinion whether it advocated worship of sixteen or seventeen deities.[4]

1. एतच्च श्रीश्रीकण्ठ्यामभिधानपूर्वं विस्तरत उक्तं तद्यथा...एतच्च श्रीश्रीकण्ठ्यामभिधानपूर्वं विस्तरत उक्तम्। तद्यथा....यत्तु श्रीश्रीकण्ठ्यां तत्पुरुषवक्त्रमुद्दिश्य...इति। अतश्च भेदभेदाभेदाभेदप्रतिपादकं शिवरुद्रभैरवाख्यं त्रिधैवेदं शास्त्रमुद्भूतम् इति सिद्धान्तः। T.A.V., I, pp. 39-45

2. Dwivedi has given a very useful comparative chart of sixty-four tantras from several sources including the *Śrīkaṇṭhī* in his Upodghāta, pp. 94-111. See page 71 also. Further see his Upodghāta to N.S.T., p. 46.

3. पञ्चमन्त्रमहात्मनेत्यनेन श्रीकण्ठीयसंहिताद्युक्तनानास्रोतोभेदः सूचितः। तत्र.....स्रोतोभेदेन नानाशास्त्रप्रपञ्चोदयः प्रदर्शितः।
S.T.U., IV, p. 19

4. यदभिप्रायेणैव श्रीक्रमसद्भावभट्टारके अनाख्यचक्रे षोडशैव देव्यः पूज्य-

The *Sārdhaśatika*, which Jayaratha quotes four times[1], closely follows on the heels of the *Pañcaśatika* and explicitly differs from the *Kramasadbhāva* regarding the order. Similarly it is to his credit that we know that the *Ānandeśvara-tantra* comprised twelve thousand verses.[2] According to Dwivedi it was possibly a tantra belonging to the Left Path.[3] It advocated Tarpaṇa (offering libations of water) with the aid of the thumb and the middle finger. The *Bhūtakṣobha*[4] and *Pañcāmṛta*[5] were other two Āgamas that followed the trail. The *Anantavijaya* was a tantra belonging to Siddhānta Śaivism which Jayaratha considers extremely dissimilar.[6] He falls back upon it because the matter under reference has not been treated in sister tantras. The *Kulakramodaya*, perhaps a Kula tantra, was devoted to the discussion of the method of assignment in the body conceived as a spiritual seat. As one of the topics Jayaratha specifically mentions the part of the text that focussed on the issue.[7] Jayaratha's references to

---

त्वेन उक्ताः । T.A.V., III, p. 136; यतः श्रीक्रमसद्भावभट्टारके अनाख्यचक्रे सप्तदश पूज्यत्वेनोक्ताः ibid., III, p. 190; Also see ibid., III, pp. 166-7, 163, 173, 223. See K.T., pp. 233-235, for details.

1. T.A.V., III, pp. 161, 189; See Upodghāta, p. 76 and K.T., pp. 143, 232 for details.

2. अन्यत्र पुनर्मध्यमाङ्गुष्ठयोगेनापि तर्पणमुक्तम् । तथा च द्वादशसाहस्रे श्रीमदानन्देश्वरे — T.A.V., IX, p. 139

3. Upodghāta, p. 20

4-5. भूतक्षोभेऽपि....इति । श्रीपञ्चामृतेऽपि...इति तथा...इति। — T.A.V., IX, p. 140

6. इत्यपेक्षायां समानकल्पेऽपि शास्त्रे तदनुपलम्भात् अत्यन्तमसमानात् अनन्तविजयाख्यात् सिद्धान्तशास्त्रात् "उत्तानं...ह्येवम्" इत्याद्यपेक्षणीयम् । — Ibid., III, p. 280

7. श्रीशैलाख्यं तु तत्पीठमित्यर्थः । तदुक्तं श्रीकुलक्रमोदये—

श्रीशैले संस्थिता ब्राह्मी"...इत्यादि उपक्रम्य "पादाधारस्थिता ब्राह्मी" इति । — Ibid., XI, p. 44

the *Kulakrīḍāvatāra* are at par with those to the *Śrīkaṇṭhī* for a proper grasp of esoteric items like Ovallī, Mudrā, Chummā, Pallī, Pīṭha and Ghara of the six competent teacher-princes etc. There are also necessary to understand the precise internal character of a preceptorial tradition, because these vary from preceptor to preceptor.[1] Jayaratha quotes this Āgama on each of these topics. In addition, a substantial number of innumerable references to the unidentified Āgamas, which until independently distinguished, must belong to Āgamas of this period.

(*iv*) *Source material provided by the known authors*

The other segment of the source-material is provided by the works of known authors. Among these Abhinavagupta occupies the place of glory. Besides references to his famous treatises like *Īśvarpratyabhijñā-vimarśinī*, *Tantrasāra*, *Tantrāloka*, *Annuttrāṣṭikā* and *Paramārthasāra*, Jayaratha earns our gratitude for his reference to the *Kramakeli*, Abhinavagupta's celebrated commentary on the *Kramastotra* by Siddhanātha. The early history of Krama system would not be possible without the rich material provided by Jayaratha from this text.[2] Jayaratha, apparently cites a long quote throwing enormous

1. तदुक्तं श्रीकुलक्रीडावतारे—
तेषां मुद्राश्च छुम्माश्च पल्ली ओवल्लयस्तथा ।
पीठक्रमो घराश्चैव पित्रा विभजता तथा ।
इत्युपक्रम्य "बोधिश्चामरपादानां. . .कौलगिर्यंता" इति ।
T.A.V., XI (29th Āh.), pp. 28-29

A long citation of 24 sentences follows.

2. एवं क्रमकेलावपि एतद्गर्भीकारेण यदनेन ग्रन्थकृता व्याख्यातं तत्रापि अन्यथा न किंचित्संभाव्यम् । Ibid., III, p. 191

light on Krama system as it stood before Abhinavagupta.[1] Jayaratha also refers to other little known texts such as the *Anupratyābhijñā*.[2]

(v) Post-Abhinavagupta tantric material: general

Towards the post-Abhinavagupta period Jayaratha's references to Somarāja,[3] Bhojarāja and his suspected work *Kramakamala*[4] are very important towards reconstruction of the history of Krama system. It is for the first time again that we hear of some Praśastibhūtipāda[5] and Tapasvirāja[6] in the pages of the *Viveka*. Similarly his mention of his great grandteacher Viśvadatta, his grandteacher[7] Tribhuvanadatta and teacher Kalyāṇa,[8] as we have already noted in a different context, lend tremendous help towards capturing the evolution of monistic thought in Kashmir. His unnamed citations[9] which are traceable to the *Mahānayaprakāśa*,[10] published

1. T.A.V., III, p. 192. See K.T., pp. 83, 85, 90, 110, 128, 139, 144, 161, 163-64 and Upodghāta, p. 30 for details.
2. अनुप्रत्यभिज्ञाकृताप्यनेनैवाभिप्रायेण . . . इत्याद्युक्तम् ।
T.A.V., II, p. 73.
See K.T., p. 160 and Upodghāta, p. 17.
3. T.A.V., III, p. 196
4. Ibid.
5. अनेनैवाभिप्रायेण श्रीप्रशस्तिभूतिपादैरपि—
ये ये भावा ह्लादिन इह दृश्याः सुभगसुन्दराकृतयः ।
तेषामनुभवकाले स्वस्थितिपरिपोषणं सतामर्चा ॥ इत्याद्युक्तम् ॥
Ibid., II, p. 219
6. Ibid., I, p. 11
7. Ibid., III, p. 203
8. Ibid., p. 233
9. ननु अस्याः परस्याः संविदोऽन्यैरनयैव भङ्ग्या त्रयोदशात्मकत्वमुक्तम्, यदुक्तम्—"एकं स्वरूपरूपं हि. . . . .पूजनीयतया स्थिताः ।" इति
10. M.P. (T). 9.15-18

in Trivendrum Sanskrit Series and assigned to Śivānanda II by us,[1] offer unimpeachable evidence of direct North-South dialogue after Madhurāja Yogin, Abhinava's junior contemporary and author of the *Gurunāthaparāmarśa*.

(*a*) Jayaratha vs. Kṣemarāja

His treatment of Kṣemarāja, however, is by far the most remarkable event of this phase, which reflects his uncompromising fervour for a thoroughly scientific study of the tantric material. Notwithstanding his innocuous references to the *Pratyabhijñāhṛdaya*[2], he has virtually mounted an attack on Kṣemarāja when it comes to the precise handling of the agamic sources. It is here we find Jayaratha sincerely translating his abiding commitment of keeping the misguided and the confused at bay from the sacrosanct domain of the tantric studies.

The *Svacchanda Tantra* is one of the premier sources of authority for the *Tantrāloka* next in importance to the *Mālinīvijayottara Tantra*. Jayaratha, in his unswerving desire to supply the root material for correct understanding of the *Tantrāloka*, profusely quotes (more than 300 times) the relevant portions from the *SV.T.* and in this process he frequently finds Kṣemarāja's readings and organisation of the text as adopted in the latter's commentary "*Uddyota*" quite misleading. Luckily the text of the Kṣemarāja's commentary and the text as available to or adopted by him is available in print in KSTS (Vols. 31, 38, 44, 48, 51, 53, 56; pub. 1921-1935) and the same may be referred to for a handy appraisal. It also shows

1. K.T., pp. 202-203
2. T.A.V., II, p. 202

that the agamic text was in a fluid state and a critical edition of the same was attempted by Jayaratha and Kṣemarāja both. The size and number of regions (Purāṇāṁ Parimāṇam) in the eighth Āhnika, for example, is obviously based on the *SV.T.* According to Jayaratha the *T.A.* 8. 132-138 specifically covers *SV.T.* 10. 431-464. Here Jayaratha reproduces exact verses[1-2] from the *SV.T.* which correspond to the *SV.T.* 10.453-54[3] and 10.432[4] in the printed edition and warns the student not to be duped by Kṣemarāja's readings[5]. He accordingly settles down for Viṣāvarte and Pañcāśat for Saṁvarta and Śatād. In the same context Jayaratha upholds Abhinavagupta's mention of Rūpavratā[6] which is not found in Kṣema's text at all. He digs at Kṣemarāja that the latter possibly has missed the relevant second half of the

1. विषावर्ते महावायौ विद्याधरगणाः स्मृताः ।
   दश त्रिंशच्च कोट्यस्ते दिव्याभरणभूषिताः ॥ T.A.V., V., p. 102
2. योजनानां शतादूर्ध्वं वायुरोधः प्रकीर्तितः । Ibid., p. 103
3. संवर्तेऽपि महावायौ. . . . .भूषिताः । SV.T,.V., p. 192
4. योजनानां. . . . . .प्रकीर्तितः । Ibid., p. 184

Here the readings adopted by Jayaratha and Kṣemarāja both are same. The editors give a variant in the fn. I (SV.T., V., p. 184) as पंचाशयोजनादूर्ध्वं which seems to have been the reading, as available to Jayaratha, in Kṣema's text. This gains strength in view of Kṣema's commentary on the subsequent verse (SV.T. 10.433) and seems to have come in for criticism.

5. अत्र च संवर्तेऽपि महावायाविति उद्योतकारव्याख्यापाठान्न भ्रमणीयं-यत्संवर्ते कथं विद्याधरा नोक्ता विषावर्ते तु उक्ता इति, अस्मत्तर्कित एव हि पाठः साधुर्महाजनपरिगृहीतत्वात् । एवं "योजनानां शतादूर्ध्वं वायुरोधः प्रकीर्तितः" इत्यादावपि अस्मत्तर्कित एव पाठो ग्राह्यः अन्यथा हि "तस्मादूर्ध्वं तु तावद्भ्यः" (SV.T. 10.433) इत्यादौ तावदर्थस्तन्मतेऽपि न सङ्गतः स्यात् । T.A.V., V, pp. 102-103

6. ये च रूपव्रता लोका आवहे ते प्रतिष्ठिताः । T.A. 10.137

verse as quoted by Jayaratha and therefore we need not be confused by Kṣema's omission.[1] Jayaratha clearly implies that the correct text must have the additional half verse. Just on the contrary, Jayaratha does not have certain verses in the original text, though Kṣema has them. While commenting upon the *Tantrāloka* 8.73,[2] Jayaratha quotes two verses in succession[3] which correspond to the *SV.T.* 10.227 and 10.229 apparently omitting the *SV.T.* 10.228[4]. In the aquatic category (Jala-tattva) Abhinavagupta posits thirteen regions.[5] Kṣemarāja's relative reading seems to have different implication unacceptable to Jayaratha.[6] One may go deeper and

1. रूपव्रता इति रूपविडम्बकवद् रूपविधानं न तु वस्तुनिष्ठं वस्तु येषां तेन व्रत(ता)जीविन इत्यर्थः । तदुक्तं श्री स्वच्छन्दे—
"ये च रूपव्रता लोकास्तेषां तत्र समाश्रयः ।" इति । एतदर्धं च उद्योतकृता न दृष्टम् इति न भ्रमणीयम् । T.A.V., V, p. 104

2. कुरुवर्षस्योत्तरेऽथ वायव्येऽब्धौ क्रमाच्छराः ॥
दश चेति सहस्राणि दीपौ चन्द्रोऽथ भद्रकः ॥

3. अब्धौ इति अब्धिमध्ये । तदुक्तम्—
तस्य चोत्तरदिग्विभागे प्रविश्य लवणोदधिम् ।
योजनानां सहस्राणि चत्वार्येव वरानने ॥
एकाधिकानि विस्तीर्णं चन्द्रद्वीपं प्रकीर्तितम् ।
दशयोजनसाहस्रं द्वीपं भद्रं प्रकीर्तितम् ॥ Ibid., V, p. 57

4. पञ्चयोजनसाहस्रं चन्द्रद्वीपं प्रकीर्तितम् ।
तथा वायव्यदिग्विभागे प्रविश्य लवणोदधिम् ।
Editorial footnote (ibid, V. p. 57) takes note of it.

5. आवीरभद्रभुवनाद्रुद्रकाल्यालयात्तथा ॥
त्रयोदशभिरन्यैश्च भुवनैरुपशोभितम् । T.A. 8.199-200

6. उपशोभितमिति अर्थादप्तत्त्वम् एवंपाठ एव च आगम इति उद्योतकार-व्याख्यया न भ्रमितव्यम् । T.A.V., V, p. 142
We have not made any effort to trace out the specific portion in the printed edition that being beyond our scope presently.

deeper. In Abhinavagupta's scheme of categories (Tattvayojana) everything other than Śiva is to be deemed as bondage in nature and so all the nine powers from Vāmā to Manonmanī in the region of impure knowledge (Aśuddha-vidyā) turn out to be binding in character.[1] Jayaratha, as usual, traces the precise textual authority to back Abhinavagupta's statement and also exploits the occasion to castigate Kṣemarāja. He not only has a different reading but finds Kṣema's preference for male deities to female ones as absurd,[2] because those people are clumsy who talk of nine female powers instead of nine male deities simply because of textual reading.[3] In the continuing context of categories Abhinavagupta describes Śakti-category to be obscured by knowledge (Māna or Pramāṇa) and inhabited by the two Rudras namely Tejasvin and Dhruveśa.[4] According to Jayaratha, Abhinava has the sanction from the *SV.T.* and the *Nandiśikhātantra* but dis-

1. पुरं चाशुद्धविद्यायां स्याच्छक्तिनवकोज्ज्वलम् ।
मनोन्मन्यन्तगास्ताश्च वामाद्याः परिकीर्तिताः ॥ T.A. 8.297

2. ता इति शक्तयः । तदुक्तम्—
वामा ज्येष्ठा च रौद्री च काली विकरणी तथा ।
बलविकरणी चैव बलप्रमथनी तथा ॥
सर्वभूतदमनी च तथा चैव मनोन्मनी ।
(This corresponds to SV.T. 10.1145-46 where the last line reads differently—दमनी सर्वभूतानां तथा चैव मनोन्मनी। Vol. VB, p. 484) इति च । अत्र च स्त्रीपाठ एव साधुर्महाजनै : परिगृहीतत्वात् ।
T.A.V., V, p. 204

3. ये तु पूर्वमशुद्धविद्याया वामादयो नव देवाः स्त्रीलिङ्गपाठाद्वामाद्या वा नव शक्तय उक्ताः । ते एतदंशावताररूपाः स्थूला बोद्धव्याः ।
SV.T.U., Vol. VB, p. 485

4. शक्त्यावृतिः प्रमाणाख्या ततः शास्त्रे निरूपिता ।
शक्त्यावृतेस्तु तेजस्विध्रुवेशाभ्यामलङ्कृतम् ॥ T.A. 8.359

agrees with Kṣemarāja's reading which places Pramāṇa's obscurity just above Śakti and not at par.[1] According to Abhinavagupta the region called Sādākhya is the proper abode of Sadāśiva[2] and is covered or obscured by Śiva alone, while Kṣemarāja assigns Sadāśiva-region just above Īśvara and just below Sadāśiva. Jayaratha charges Kṣemarāja with tampering with the original *SV.T.* by imaginary interpolation of an half-verse which has been disregarded by the learned. Even if this addition be deemed to be genuine, argues Jayaratha, it does not vindicate Kṣema's contention. It supports Abhinavagupta's stand instead, because the abode and the resident have the same level of subsistence. It is only on such a construction that the *Nandiśikhātantra*, too, may yield a consistent meaning. One, therefore, must guard himself against the misguiding interpretation offered by Kṣemarāja[3]. It is indeed premature to

1. तत्र शक्त्यावृतौ रुद्रद्वयम् । तदुक्तम्—
'तेजस्वीशो ध्रुवेशश्च प्रमाणानां परं पदम् ।'
(Corresponding to the SV.T. 10.1174) इति । शक्त्यावरणमूर्ध्वं चेति प्रमाणावरणं चोर्ध्वमित्युद्योतकारदृष्टः पाठः पुनरसाधुर्महाजनैरपरिगृहीतत्वात् । श्रीनन्दिशिखायामपि—
'तेजेश्वरो ध्रुवेशश्च शक्त्यावरणसंस्थितौ ।' इत्यादिरास्माक एव पाठः ।
T.A.V., V, pp. 240-41

2. भुवनैः पञ्चभिर्गर्भीकृतानन्तसमावृति ।
सामयात्सौशिवं तत्र सादाख्यं भुवनं महत् ॥ T.A. 8.365

3. "सादाख्यं भुवनम्" इति सदाशिवभट्टारकस्य साक्षादधिष्ठानस्थानमित्यर्थः अतएव महदित्युक्तम् । उद्योतकृता पुनः "ईश्वरस्य तथोर्ध्वे तु अधश्चैव दाशिवात्" (SV.T. 10.1190) इत्यर्धं परिकल्प्य इतः प्रभृति सादाशिवं तत्त्वमिति यदुक्तं तदयुक्तम्, अस्य अर्धस्य महाजनैरगृहीतत्वात्। अतएव च एवमपि "ऊर्ध्वं" इति पुनरुक्तम्, "अधश्चैव सदाशिवात्" इत्यप्यसंगतं तत्रैव तस्योक्तत्वात्; अपरिकल्पितत्वेऽपि एतदित्थं यथाकथञ्चिदव्याख्येयं यदीश्वरस्येति रुद्रोङ्कारस्य, सदाशिवादिति अधिष्ठातुः, अधिष्ठेयं हि अधिष्ठातुरध एव भवेदिति। यत्तु श्रीनन्दि-

suspect whether Kṣemarāja and Jayaratha belonged to different preceptorial traditions or Jayaratha nursed some grouse against his senior Kṣemarāja in order to wrest the place of honour from him among the post-Abhinavan scholarship, yet what surprises the modern reader most is Jayaratha's going to the extreme of charging Kṣema with deliberate distortions. As another instance of such aberrations Jayaratha, while explaining Abhinavagupta's views on the purification of deed (Karmaśodhana) in respect of the spiritual apprentice called Śivadharmī[1], invokes the authority of the *SV.T.* and propounds that once the process of fruition has commenced in respect of one particular deed it cannot be reversed so far as that deed is concerned. On the contrary, Kṣemarāja who talks of purifying even that deed which has commenced fruition[2] is taken to task for tampering with the text, for going against the previous pronouncements and also for transgressing the scriptural injunctions.[3] Jayaratha finds no end to it on

---

शिखायाम् "कथितं त्वैश्वरं तत्त्वमत ऊर्ध्वं सदाशिवः" इतितत्र साक्षात्स्थित इति। अन्यथा हि उभयत्रापि ईश्वरतत्त्वोपसंहारग्रन्थस्य व्याघातः स्यात, तन्महाजनक्षुण्ण एव मार्गोऽनुगन्तव्यः इति उद्योतकारव्याख्यया न भ्रमितव्यमित्यलं बहुना।

T.A.V., V, pp. 243-44

1. साधकस्य तु भूत्यर्थमित्थमेव विशोधयेत्।
   शिवधर्मिण्यसौ दीक्षा लोकधर्मापहारिणी। T.A. 15.28

2. भूत्यर्थाद्यत्प्राग्देहारम्भि शुभाशुभं तत एकमशुभमेवास्य शोधयेत्, एवं हि निर्विघ्नं भोगसिद्धिर्भवति। SV.T.U., Vol. II, p. 88

3. यदुक्तम्——
   साधकस्य तु भूत्यर्थं प्राक्कर्मेत्थं तु शोधयेत्।
   प्राक्कर्मगामि चैकस्थं भावयित्वा तु दीक्षयेत्॥ (Corresponding to the SV.T. 4.142 which reads the first line as साधकस्य तु भूत्यर्थं प्राक्कर्मैकं तु शोधयेत्) इति। अत्र च उद्योतकृता यत् इत्थमिति अपास्य एकमिति

Kṣemarāja's part. In the course of Abhinava's discussion on Śivahastavidhi[1] a spiritual apprentice is said to be transformed into a Samayin by his teacher's recourse to this method leading to a kind of intimate union (Sāyujya) in Īśvara category. Jayaratha finds fault with Kṣema's interpretation of the word Īśvare as Kālāgnirudra existing below the category of earth and dubs it as lacking in scriptural testimony.[2]

(vi) Restoring tradition: fathoming inter se relationship among Āgamas

Jayaratha's critical zeal does not pause here. His abiding concern is to restore the real tradition. For this he checks up, over and above the already discussed functions, inter se relationship between the Āgamas, substantiates arguments, peeps into the background to rationalize the item under consideration, underlines latent possibilities and may even advance suggestion for a proper appraisal. While discussing the variety of dissolution (Saṁhāravaicitrya) in the sixth Āhnika he endorses Abhinava's view that Samanā represents Pralaya stage and is identical with Sadāśiva stage where the universe continues to exist in residual form. In this context

---

पठित्वा देहारम्भिशुभाशुभकर्ममध्यादेकमशुभमपि अस्य शोधयेदिति व्याख्यातं तदुपेक्ष्यम्, आरब्धकार्यदेहारम्भिकर्मोच्छेदाशक्यत्वस्य प्रागुपपादितत्वात् क्वचिदप्येवमनाम्नातत्वाच्च । T.A.V., IX, p. 19

1. उक्तं दीक्षोत्तरे चैतज्ज्वालासंपातशोभिना ॥
   दत्तेन शिवहस्तेन समयी स विधीयते ।
   सायुज्यमीश्वरे तत्त्वे जीवतोऽधीतियोग्यता ॥ T.A. 15.458-59

2. ईश्वरे इति श्रीविद्यातत्त्वोर्ध्ववर्तिनि न तु पृथिवीतत्त्वाधः स्थिते कालाग्निरुद्रे तथाश्रुतेरदर्शनात् । अत्र च उद्योगकृदेव कृतश्रम इति किमिह तेन उक्तेन तत एव अवधार्यम् । T.A.V., IX, p. 231

he quotes the views of a sub-group who thought Pralaya stage as being one with Śiva stage.[1] He criticises the view, reasons out his position and concludes that even when Samanā is taken to be eternal, it does not dilute monism.[2] Similarly he provides relevant contextual framework. While commenting upon the *Tantrāloka* 8.290 he notes that though the five gross elements succeed triple egoity in the *SV.T.*, Abhinavagupta is discussing them as part of the sixteen modifications which lead to bondage.[3] Any tantric system worth the name must discard the caste system. Hence the references to caste, according to Jayaratha's rationalization, must be construed as referring to the non-initiates or to the faithful of the lower grades.[4] Moreover, Jayaratha provides a rich source of cultural information. It appears Dinars had come in vogue as a legal tender of currency in his time.[5] It is from him that we learn that several varieties of wine were prevalent in his time and why they were distinguished. For instance Madya was produced

1. अतएव चान्यैरस्मच्छास्त्रप्रक्रियामजानानैः 'शक्त्यन्तं महाप्रलये वृत्ते सकलोऽयमणुवर्गः प्रलयान्त ऊर्ध्वोर्ध्वमवस्थितेरभिधानात् परिशिष्टं शिवतत्त्वमेवासादयेत्। तदासादनमेव च मुक्तिः, तदक्रमेण सर्वेषामनायासमेव सा सिध्येदिति किं शास्त्रानुष्ठानादिना' इत्यादि यच्चोदितं तदुत्थानोपहतमेव।

T.A.V., IV, p. 142

2. न चैवमपि शंभुवत्समनाया अपि नित्यत्वादभेदवादक्षतिर्भेदमेवाधिकृत्य सृष्टिप्रलयादिव्यवहारस्योत्थानात्। Ibid., p. 143

3. एतच्च यद्यपि श्रीस्वच्छन्दे त्रिविधादहंकारादनन्तरमुक्तं तथापि इह विकारषोडशकसाजात्येनैव व्याख्यातम्। Ibid., V, p. 199

4. इत्याद्युक्तं तददीक्षितविषयम्, किन्तु पूर्वत्र अस्मदुक्तार्चातर्पणश्रद्धालुविषयत्वमधिकमन्यथा जातिभेदो दुर्वचः स्यात्। Ibid., IX, p. 12 (29th Āh)

5. हन्यते टंक्यते दीनार इव राजाभिधानं शास्त्रार्थो यस्मिन्स तथा।

Ibid., I, p. 150

from grapes, Śīdhu from sugarcane and Surā from Vibhītaka (Latin, Terminalia Belerica) and then he goes on talking about such varieties of wine as Vāruṇī, Madirā, kādambarī, Ghanasurā and jagala etc.[1]

(e) AN EXCLUSIVE GUIDE TO THE TANTRĀLOKA

(*i*) *Sevenfold assistance*

Jayaratha's contribution to the understanding of the *Tantrāloka* is invaluable and indispensable. To begin with, Jayaratha provides connotative titles to all the Āhnikas. Though in most cases they reflect the clue provided by Abhinavagupta during the body of the text, it is he who offers captions. We shall discuss this aspect at the appropriate occasion. In the second place he clearly demarcates the precise textual portions dealing with general and ancillary topics, designated as Pūrvaja-and Anuja-uddeśas by Abhinavagupta.[2] We shall look into it in the course of our discussion on the arrangement and organisation of the *Tantrāloka*. In the third place, he acquaints us with the background view. For example he points out, notwithstanding Abhinava's silence, that in the ninth Āhnika his master wanted to criticise Tattva (category)-doctrine of the *Bhogakārikā* etc. (dualistic Śaivism)[3]. He not only leaves us at that but follows it up with the intermittent criti-

1. मद्यशीधुसुरादिनेति मद्यं मृद्वीकादिप्रभवमनेकप्रकारं मद्यादिशब्दव्यपदेश्यं, शीधुरैक्षवः, सुरा विभीतकादिकृता, आदिशब्दात् तत्प्रकाराणां वारुण्यादीनां परिग्रहः। T.A.V., IX, p. 39

2. तत्रोच्यते पुरोद्देशः पूर्वानुजभेदवान्। T.A. 1.278

3. सम्यगिति अनेनात्र भोगकारिकादिभ्यो वैलक्षण्यं कटाक्षितमिति। T.A.V., VI, p. 250

cism of Śaṅkaranandana, Sadyojyoti, Devabala and Vaiśeṣikas[1]. Similarly he suggests that main target in the tenth Āhnika was to point out discrepancies in Nyāya and Bhāṭṭa Mīmāṁsā schools[2], though Abhinavagupta himself is once again silent on this point.[3] In the fourth place, he fills in the omissions of Abhinavagupta. In the twentyeighth Āhnika, Abhinavagupta talks of 23 types of occasional functions (Naimittikavidhi)[4]. Jayaratha feels that a particular 'occasional' (Naimittika) called Śivarātri is also included in the quartet beginning with Vipatpratīkāra (*T.A.* 28.7), the reason behind omission being the universal treatment of this item in practically all the scriptures.[5] Similarly in Dūtīyāga Abhinavagupta talks of six varieties of Dūtīs e.g. consisting of Janyā, Janikā and Sahajā in twofold relationships—physical and cognitive, and invokes the authority of the *Sarvācāratantra.*[6] In a significant remark Jayaratha adds that there are several sub-varieties such as Vegavatī, Saṁhārī, Trailokyakṣobhiṇī etc.,

1. शंकरनन्दनसद्योज्योतिर्देववलकणभुगादिमतम् ।
   प्रत्याख्यास्यन्नवमं व्याचख्यावाह्निकं जयरथाख्यः ॥ T.A.V., VI, p. 250
2. कौमारिलनैयायिकमतविमतिसतत्त्वविज्जयरथाख्यः ।
   अख्यापयदतिविशदां दशमाह्निके विवृतिरीतिमिमाम् ॥
   Ibid., VII, p. 208
3. इत्येष दर्शितोऽस्माभिस्तत्त्वाध्वा विस्तरादथ ।
   T.A. 10th Āh., concluding verse
4. T.A. 28.6-9
5. अनेन च विपत्प्रतीकारादिना चतुष्टयेन शिवरात्रिसंज्ञकमपि नैमित्तिकं संगृहीतम् । तत्र हि एतदेव भगवतोऽभवदित्याम्नायः । तच्च साधारण्येनैव सर्वशास्त्रेषु आम्नातमिति नेह स्वकण्ठेनोक्तम् । T.A.V., XI, p. 6
6. श्रीसर्वाचारहृदये तदेतदुपसंहृतम् ।
   षडेता शक्तयः प्रोक्ता भुक्तिमुक्तिफलप्रदाः ॥ T.A. 29.103

but a reference to the same has been avoided[1] for fear of endless recounting. In the fifth place, he allows us a peep into Abhinavagupta's own preferences and presuppositions. The case of Rudrakālī offers a good example. Rudrakālī, which marks the seventh stage in cyclic progression of consciousness in Anākhyācakra, has been equally named as Bhadrakālī by the texts like *Pañcaśatika* etc., without any semantic distinction. Abhinavagupta, however, prefers the title Rudrakālī—this piece of intimation we gather from Jayaratha[2]. In the sixth place, one has to depend upon Jayaratha for a clear understanding of the esoteric implications of Abhinavagupta's treatment. For example, the textual portion dealing with the notion of virility of Mantra (Mantravīrya)[3] apparently has no esoteric semblances, yet Jayaratha finds that the first three verses deal with Parābīja (the ultimate seed) and the subsequent three with five Piṇḍanāthas.[4] Similarly Abhinavagupta's description of the six-fold movement of breath from the point of view of pervasion (Vyāpti)[5] is necessarily

1. "वेगवत्यथ संहारी त्रैलोक्यक्षोभणी तथा ।
अर्धवीरासना चैव वक्त्रकौला तु पञ्चमी ॥"
इत्यादि तु अवान्तरभेदप्रायं प्रत्येकं सम्भवदपि आनन्त्यादिह न परिगणितम् । T.A.V., XI, p. 74 (29th Āh.)

2. इति पञ्चशतिकादौ पुनरियं भद्रकाली इत्युक्ता,
इति नाम्नि भेदेऽपि वस्तुनि न कश्चिद्भेदो । . . . .एवं चात्र प्रमाणरूपत्वेऽपि तत्तदर्थसंहारकारिणः प्रमातुरेव प्राधान्यं येन ग्रन्थकृतो रुद्रशब्दे भरः ।
Ibid., III, pp. 173-74

3. T.A. 4.186-191

4. एवं संवित्क्रमेण श्रीपराबीजस्योदयमभिधाय एतत्समानस्कन्धताभिधित्सया श्रीपिण्डनाथस्यापि उदयमभिधत्ते । T.A.V., IV, p. 220

5. षट्प्राणोच्चारजं रूपमथ व्याप्त्या तदुच्यते । T.A. 5.54

from that of Mantravyāpti.[1] As we have discussed in a different context earlier, Abhinavagupta's esotericism and symbolism is not at all understandable without Jayaratha's wholistic approach. The nature of Karaṇas which is spread over from 11th to 32nd Āhnikas as per declaration of Abhinavagupta himself[2] is made known by Jayaratha alone by locating exact references. Thus the Karaṇa of intelligence is dealt with in the eleventh (*T.A.* 11.21), of Vyāpti in the fifteenth (*T.A.* 15.339), of knower-known combine in the sixteenth (*T.A.* 16.253), of imposition as well as that of rejection in the twenty-ninth (*T.A.* 29.147/182) and of absorption in the thirtysecond Āhnika (T.A. 32.10 onwards)[3] by way of discussion on postures.[4] No doubt Jayaratha is aware of the limit to which he may go. With regard to the filling of Arghapātra he advises one to learn it from the mouth of a teacher, he has not touched it lest it might violate his school's code.[5] But all the same he does not withhold any information he has. The word Dīptaiḥ in depicting the nature of Mantra[6] was open to two types of meaning and he

1. इदानीमेतदेव मन्त्रव्याप्तिमुखेनाप्यभिधीयते, इत्याह अथ इत्यादि ।
T.A.V., III, pp. 357-58

2. गुरुवक्त्राच्च बोद्धव्यं करणं यद्यपि स्फुटम् ॥
तथाप्यागमरक्षार्थं तदग्रे वर्णयिष्यते । T.A. 5.130-31

3. Jayaratha here indicates the Āhnika and not the exact verses. The insertion within bracket is ours.

4. तथाहि. . . .इत्यादिना षोडशाह्निके. . . .इत्यादिना. . . .तत्तन्मुद्रा-स्वरूपनिरूपण द्वारेण द्वाद्वत्रिंशाह्निके संनिवेशस्य स्वरूपं वक्ष्यति इति तत एवैतत्सतत्त्वं स्वयमेव अवधारणीयम् । T.A.V., III, pp. 442-43

5. यश्च अत्र एतत्पूरणे सम्प्रदायः स रहस्यत्वात् समयभङ्गभयाच्च न इह अस्माभिः प्रदर्शित इति । एतद्गुरुमुखादेव बोद्धव्यम् । T.A.V., XI, p. 19

6. यरवलबीजैस्तु दीप्तैर्बिन्दुविभूषितैः । T.A. 30.16

gives both.[1] And in the case of divergent opinions about a thing, particularly if the authority of the *Srīpūrvaśāstra* was not readily handy on such esoteric issues as Ekavīravidhāna,[2] he finally airs the view acceptable to him.[3] In the seventh place, Jayaratha brings out the inherent argument of Abhinavagupta—not only the substance but the form as well.[4] Sometimes he builds up on the syllogistic form latent in Abhinavagupta's discussion and presents the whole of it.[5]

(ii) Discharge of twin editrial obligations

The greatest contribution of Jayaratha, however, lies in his role as the editor of the text of the *Tantrāloka*. His handling of the *Tantrāloka's* text is the logical extension of his approach to the handling of the tantric source material. It has two phases. One, when he subjects the text of the *Tantrāloka* to rigorous criticism and undertakes to produce the standard version and two, when he critically looks into the arrangement and order of the verses in order to put a well organised text. Since we have already seen something of this in a different context, our job has become easier requiring a few samples. Jaya-

1. दीप्तैरिति ओकारादीनामकारादीनां ह्रस्वानामाग्नेयस्वभावत्वात् तेजोमयैरिति प्राच्याः, सरेफैरिति श्रीमल्लक्ष्मणगुप्तपादाः। T.A.V., XII, p. 184
2. अन्येप्येकाक्षरा ये तु एकवीरविधानतः ।
   गुप्ता गुप्तरास्ते ग्रंगाभिजनवर्जिताः ।। T.A. 30.24
3. अत्र च शिखायां कवचबीजमिति श्रीत्रिशिरोभैरवानुयायिनः, चतुष्कलमिति श्रीदेव्यायामलोपजीविनः, अस्मद्गुरवस्तु द्वितीयमेव पक्षमामनन्ति ।
   T.A.V., XII, p. 198
4. अत्र पञ्चावयवं परार्थमनुमानं निर्दिष्टं तद्यथा. . . .
   Ibid., VI, p. 119
5. नास्तीति काकाक्षिवद्योज्यम्-तेनायमत्र प्रयोगः . . . .। Ibid, p. 125

ratha prefers the reading Vyomādiśabda[1] in place of an equally good reading[2], i.e. Vyomādiṣaṭka. Even when he retains a particular reading[3], as all the MSS available support it, he suggests a better reading.[4] In Jayaratha's original copy of the *Tantrāloka* the verse 3.220[5] possibly reads Mātra-(kuṇḍalinībījam) which has been rectified as Śātra (-kuṇḍalinī-bījam) because such type of reading is not only non-agamic but even otherwise conveys incoherent meaning and involves improper diction.[6] One may hold with reasonable confidence that there were certain uncertainties about the text of the *Tantrāloka* during the time of Jayaratha. It is why he sometimes suggests equally good alternative readings. Thus the printed text e.g.,

शिवदहनकिरणजालैदाह्यत्वात् सा यतोऽन्यरूपैव (T.A. 9.207)

may also be read as—

विज्ञानामृतसरिता प्लाव्यत्वात् सा यतोऽन्यरूपैव

To lend authenticity to his suggestions he cites the authority of the relative scripture (here *Śivatanu-śāstra*).[7] The *Tantrāloka*'s actual text was often a

1. व्योमादिशब्दविज्ञानात् परो मोक्षो न संशयः । T.A. 1.64
2. व्योमादिषट्क इति पाठे तु . . . इति व्याख्येयम् ।
T.A.V., I, p. 103
3. In भैरव इति गुरुभिरिमैः । T.A. 1.100
4. इमैः इति चिन्त्यम् । गुरुगदितैरिति तु श्रेष्ठः पाठः । T.A.V., I, p. 143
5. सात्र कुण्डलिनी बीजं जीवभूता चिदात्मिका । T.A. 3.220
6. मात्रेत्यपपाठः—न ह्यनेन कश्चिदप्यागमिकोऽर्थः संग्राह्यो वर्तते यदर्थोऽयमेतत्प्रयोगः, प्रत्युत असंगतार्थत्वमसाधुशब्दत्वं च प्रसज्यते ।
T.A.V., II, pp. 20-87
7. यद्वा विज्ञानामृतसरिता प्लाव्यत्वादिति पाठो ग्राह्यः । तदुक्तं तत्र (शिवतनुशास्त्रे)—

विज्ञानमृतसरिता शिवशशिनः स्यन्दमानयामलया ।
प्रप्लाव्य यतस्तेभ्यो निरस्यतेऽधस्ततः सान्या ।। इति ।

Ibid., VI, p. 167

matter of doubt. Jayaratha did finalise his own version wherein he piled up several corrected readings. Displaying a rare scientific attitude he furnishes evidence behind his choice even at the slightest doubt. Thus the reading adopted by him in the *T.A.* 13.355[1] was not due to his whim, he himself saw it in the old manuscripts not once or twice, but hundred times over.[2] Similarly the text of the *SV.T.* (4.142), corresponding to the *T.A.* 15.28, has slightly different reading in the version of Kṣemarāja, target of bitter attack from Jayaratha for deliberate distortions. Jayaratha prefers to ignore the text of Kṣemarāja and preserves the original reading for the sake of propriety having culled support from Abhinavagupta's statement in the *Mṛgendrā*.[3] Even when the available reading is not defective, he assiduously gropes for a better reading. In the *Tantrāloka* 15.80[4] he finds the word 'Yad' somewhat vague and proposes 'Iha' as a relatively lucid reading.[5] Jayaratha's critical editing of the *Tantrāloka* and his handling of the source texts has to be viewed together in a larger perspective so as to be able to evaluate his concerted effort towards keeping the text of the *Tantrāloka* free from imagination, interpolation and alien material and preserving its faithfulness to the original source literature.

1. जुगुप्सते तत्तस्मिंश्च विफलेऽन्यत्समाश्रयेत् ।
दिनाद्दिनं ह्रसंस्त्वेवं पच्यते रौरवादिषु ॥ T.A. 13.355
2. एवंपाठश्च जरत्पुस्तकेषु शतशो दृष्टः । T.A.V., VIII, p. 211
3. अतएव श्रीमृगेन्द्रायामपि . . . . . इत्यादि उक्तं ग्रन्थकृता । औचित्याच्च अत्र अस्माभिरयं पाठो रक्षितः । Ibid., IX, p. 19
4. पर्वताग्रनदीतीरैकलिङ्गादि यदुच्यते ।
5. यदीति (? यदिति) स्थाने इहेति स्पष्टः पाठः । T.A.V., IX, p. 44

His second editorial function relates to the organisation of the text. For example, the verse 'Jñānahīno' etc.,[1] (now numbered as *T.A.* 23.25 in the printed edition) was wrongly placed by certain scribes after the verse "Annādidāna" etc.[2] (Ist half of the verse numbered as *T.A.* 23.23 in the printed edition) which is restored to its regular place by Jayaratha.[3] It appears that Jayaratha is guided by the model handscript on the basis of which he prepared his version of the *Tantrāloka*. But even in his basic handscript there are certain places which have attracted editorial whetting. The verses as given in the footnote below[4] appear twice in the body of the text as *T.A.* 37.4-5 and *T.A.* 37.11-13 (2nd half to 1st half). Though Jayaratha retains the double mention, he clearly advises its precise placement and also reverses the order,[5] besides offering tips for better reading.[6] We come across a similar instance when he suggests that the first half[7] of the *T.A.* 31.42 in all

1. ज्ञानहीनो गुरुः कर्मी स्वाधिकारं समर्प्य नो ।
दीक्षाद्यधिकृतिं कुर्याद् विना तस्याज्ञया पुनः ॥
2. अन्नादिदानमित्येतत्पालयेत्सप्तसत्रकम् ।
3. That is, T.A. 23. 25. See अयं च श्लोकः क्वचित् "पालयेत्सप्तसत्रकम्" इत्यनन्तरं भ्रमात् लेखकैर्लिखित इति तदुपेक्ष्यम् । T.A.V., X, p. 272
4. यथा खगेश्वरीभावनिःशङ्कत्वाद्विषं व्रजेत् ।
क्षयं कर्मस्थितिस्तद्वदशङ्काद्भैरवत्वतः ॥
यदार्षे पातहेतूक्तं तदस्मिन्वामशासने ।
आशुसिध्यै यतः सर्वमार्षं मायोदरस्थितम् ॥
5. अत्र च अन्तरा श्लोकद्वयमन्यथा लिखितमधरे व्यत्ययेन न्याय्यमिति तत्रैव व्याख्यास्यामः । T.A.V., XII, p. 393
6. पातहेतूक्तमिति ..... पातकार्युक्तमिति तु स्पष्टः पाठः ।
Ibid., p. 395
7. शूलयागाः षट् सहस्त्राण्येवं सार्धशतद्वयम् ।

propriety be placed before the *T.A.* 31.39 for ensuring coherent construction.[1] Such instances bring his conscientious and ever vigilant self into bold relief. This, however, does not mean that he never succumbs to general weaknesses of the scholars. He does, but very rarely. We find a glimpse of such a lapse in his interpretation of the word 'Anta'[2] forming part of the compound in the *T.A.* 22.12.[3] Here the use of the words 'Ādi' and 'Anta' in the text obviously limits the options, but Jayaratha looks for an implied meaning convenient to him. But such far-fetched interpretations are very few and far between and in no way undermine his importance.

(III) *Methodology*

(a) Guiding principles

(*i*) *Conformity to Abhinava, teacher and scripture*

Coming to the methodology employed and norms of writing adhered to by Jayaratha we notice that his first guiding principle in taking up an item is its absolute conformity which means it must conform in the first place to the stand of Abhinava—the original author, in the second to the preceptorial stand and in the third to the scriptural view. All the three together, not severally, spell out his idea of adherence to the tradition. While discussing the notion of Karaṇa (*T.A.* 5.130) he abstains from giving out everything at one place and in so doing leans on

1. प्रायश्च अयं श्लोकः 'ततो रजांसि देयानि......(T.A. 31.39) इत्यतः पूर्वं न्याय्यो येन सर्वं सङ्गतं स्यात् । T.A.V., XII p. 247
2. अन्तः सिद्धान्तः । उक्तं हि प्राक् Ibid., X, p. 249
3. अथ वैष्णवबौद्धादितन्त्रान्ताधरवर्तिनाम् ।

Abhinavagupta's authority.[1] Similarly, in final selection out of several options it is the preceptorial injunction that must prevail.[2] Moreover, he never ventures to rely on his imagination and propound a thing unless it is expressly enjoined in the Āgamas.[3] One of the reasons for rejecting the Uddyotakāra's interpretation was his lack of scriptural endorsement.[4] Same is the case with those who propound a different reading from one picked up by him.[5] To him the teaming up of all the three authorities, specially teacher and scripture, is very sacred. Hence, he rejects the alternative readings and resulting explanations since they digress from the authority of the scriptural text and the teacher.[6]

(ii) Thoroughness and authenticity; and
(iii) Absence of fascination for word-by-word comentary: eight key factors

Thoroughness and authenticity, thus, are the twin criteria that he ardently pursues but they do not come in the way of his concise and systematic presentation. That is why he never revels in word-by-word explanation. His staying away, however, from the

1. तदस्माकमपि एवं व्याख्याने श्रीमदभिनवगुप्तपादा एव प्रमाणम्—इति नात्र विद्वद्भिरस्मभ्यमसूयितव्यम् । T.A.V., III, p. 443

2. इत्येकतरपरिग्रहे यथास्वं गुरूपदेश एव निबन्धनम् । Ibid., p. 203

3. न चैतदस्माभिः स्वोत्प्रेक्षितमुक्तमिति साक्षादागम एव पठितः । Ibid., IV, p. 10

4. अत्र च उद्योतकृता यत् .... व्याख्यातम् तदुपेक्ष्यम् .... क्वचिदपि एवम् अनाम्नातत्वाच्च । Ibid., IX, p. 19

5. इत्यत्र च तृतीयां चतुर्थीं वेति पाठो भवेत् .... इत्यलं गुर्वागमसंप्रदायशून्यैः सह संलापेन । Ibid., pp. 162-63

6. अतश्च .... इति पठित्वा .... चेत्याद्यभिधाय .... व्याख्यायाम् आर्षपाठपरित्यागः .... श्रीमदगुरुव्याख्यातिक्रमाश्चेति दोषाः । Ibid., X, pp. 91-92

verbatim commentary is not arbitrary. He is guided by certain norms which he has set for himself. (i) Obvious clarity, (ii) future treatment, (iii) overdetailed discussions are some of the considerations that prevent him from embarking upon word-by-word commentary.[1] (iv) Fear of unnecessary repetition is another factor which he is very much scared of.[2] If the item is of esoteric importance, frequent repetion might cause leakage, or if it is of general importance and has been occasionally discussed, too much repetion will amount to wastage of effort. To the list of his norms he adds two more—(v) relevance or utility and (vi) propriety, which constitute the hallmark of his style characterised by his disdain for (vii) far-fetched imagination and (viii) breach of tradition. Undue extension of the text and irrelevance, however, are the twin factors that frighten him most. He refrains from gathering all the possible interpretations because of these two factors.[3] The same consideration does not allow him to enumerate all the aspects associated with each movement of breath[4] (Cāra) or the total number of days associated

1. इत्येतदस्माभिः स्पष्टत्वात्, ग्रन्थविस्तरभयात्, अग्रे च निर्णेष्यमाणत्वात् न प्रातिपद्येन व्याख्यातम् । T.A.V., I, pp. 299-300

2. अत्रामृतबीजाद्युद्धारः प्राग्व्याख्ययैव गतार्थः इत्यतिरहस्यत्वात् नेह पुनरायस्तम् । Ibid., III, p. 371

× × ×

एतच्च पूर्वमेव बहूक्तम् इतीह न पुनरायस्तम् ॥ Ibid., II, p. 65

× × ×

एतच्च सर्वमसकृत्त्वेनैव व्याख्यातम् इति न पुनरायस्तम् । Ibid., I, p. 33

3. अत्र च संभवन्त्यपि व्याख्यान्तराणि न कृतानि, ग्रन्थगौरवभयाच्च प्रकृतानुपयोगाच्च । Ibid., p. 15

4. अस्माभिरप्यत्र गणना विभज्य न दर्शिता ग्रन्थविस्तरभयादनुपयोगाच्च । Ibid., IV, p. 10

with the residents of the five sheaths.[1] Even when he is dwelling upon certain source text, he only picks up the relevant material from here and there insted of reproducing the whole text.[2] The idea behind the whole exercise is that the quoted text must be relevant to the issue under discussion,[3] and at the same time should not make the work bulkier.

(*iv*) *Fear of undue extension and deviation from the original line*

The notion of relevance is intertwined with the notion of propriety. Relevance minus propriety does not sound convincing. He, therefore, derives strength from his concern for propriety while he sticks to relevance. At one place, he openly admits it.[4] He remains faithful to this principle throughout and does not counter all the anomalies even when he notices them in the available account of a tradition.[5] One should not, therefore, consider it a defect if Jayaratha does not explain or cite every word of the text.[6] In such an approach, as mentioned earlier,

1. तत्सर्वेषां कञ्चुकवासिनां .... गणना तु ग्रन्थविस्तरभयान्न लिखिता । T.A.V., III, p. 135
2. एतच्च ग्रंथविस्तरभयात् यथोपयोगम् उच्चित्य उच्चित्य लिखितमिति तत एव यथाशय्यमनुसर्तव्यम् । Ibid., XI, p. 168
3. इत्यादिश्लोकानन्तरम् .... इत्यादिग्रन्थान्तरं सम्भवदपि प्रकृतानुपयोगात् न पठितम् । Ibid., III, p. 58
4. औचित्याच्च अत्र अस्माभिरयं पाठो रक्षितः । Ibid., IX, p. 19
5. तदुक्तं स्वपारम्पर्यं व्याचक्षाणेन श्रीसोमराजेन .... एवमनेकप्रकारमासमञ्जस्यं संभवदपि अनङ्गत्वान्न प्रदर्शितम् । Ibid., p. 197
6. अस्माभिस्तु ग्रन्थविस्तरभयात् न प्रातिपद्येन संवादितम् । Ibid., I, p. 157

× × ×

तच्च अस्माभिर्ग्रन्थविस्तरभयात् प्रातिपद्येन न दर्शितम् । Ibid., p. 180

× × ×

he derives additional strength from his disdain for laboured use of imagination[1] and his almost religious concern for retention of the tradition intact.[2] Obviously it does not mean that he leaves the portions unexplained. Instead, he believes in explaining a thing thoroughly even by supplying/importing a missing word on his own in the interest of consistency. There are several instances that illustrate it.[3] Usually, he first attempts an explanation of words and then gives out essence or gist of Kārikā in his own words.[4] In the case of doubt or necessity to furnish additional explanation he offers alternative explanations[5] and tries to reconcile various ends if there is difference of opinion or confusion—whether deliberate or accidental. As we have already seen lot

---

इह तु ग्रन्थविस्तरभयान्न प्रातिपद्येन संवादितम् ।
Ibid., VII, p. 80

× × ×

एतच्च .... स्वयमवगन्तुं शक्यत्वात् ग्रन्थविस्तरभयाच्च न प्रातिपद्येन व्याख्यातमिति न विद्वद्भिरस्मभ्यम् असूयितव्यम् ॥ Ibid., XII, p. 212

1. चेत्याद्यभिधाय .... व्याख्यायाम् .... कष्टकल्पना .... चेतिदोषाः । T.A.V., X, p. 91-92

2. यश्च अत्र एतत्पूरणे सम्प्रदायः स रहस्यत्वात् समयभङ्गभयाच्च न इह अस्माभिः प्रदर्शित इति । Ibid., XI, p. 19

3. न शब्दोऽत्र काकाक्षिवद्योज्यः। Ibid., II, p. 28

× × ×

न शब्दोऽत्रापि संबंधनीयः । Ibid.

4. Cp. एवं परमेश्वर एव स्वस्वातन्त्र्यमाहात्म्यात् तत्तद्बिम्बप्रतिबिम्बाद्याभासवैचित्र्येण अवभासते इति तात्पर्यार्थः । Ibid., II, p. 12

× × ×

एवं पूर्णज्ञानावाप्तौ अनेके उपायाः संभवन्ति इति तात्पर्यार्थः ।
Ibid., III, p. 63

5. यद्वा .... शब्दप्रतिबिम्बविषयत्वेन व्याख्येयम् । Ibid., II, p. 5

× × ×

यद्वा यथा— Ibid., p. 25

of it earlier we leave the matters here. He, however, continues to remain unswerving in his commitment to bring out the essence of Abhinavagupta's work,[1] and wherever he leaves out something, the scholars are expected to treat it as unnecessary.

(b) Differences from Abhinava & deviation from the original line

We, thus, see that Jayaratha is extremely faithful to Abhinavagupta and tradition, but he is not a blind follower at all. A person of his calibre and competence can never be. There are occasions, notwithstanding their rarity, when he does not endorse Abhinavagupta's reading or finds the latter's version wanting in certain respects. For example, he raises his finger at the use of word 'Padmagaṁ' by Abhinavagupta.[2] He once again questions Abhinavagupta's reading and suggests a better one.[3] Similarly, when Abhinavagupta embarks upon consideration of various stations or seats (Pīṭhas) from the *T.A.* 15.83 to 15.97 on the authority of the *Niśisañcara Āgama*, Jayaratha invites attention of the reader to the portion from the *T.A.* 15.86 to 15.88[4] and finds the first half of the *T.A.* 15.86 not only contradictory to the conclusion

1. इह चास्माभिस्तद्व्याख्यासारोच्चयस्यैव प्रतिज्ञातत्वात् तदेव क्रियते, इति तदिरत् स्वयमेव सर्वत्रासारतया चिन्वन्तु सचेतसः । T.A.V., I, p. 16

2. एकैकामथवां देवीं मन्त्रं वा पद्मगं यजेत् । T.A. 15.365

Jayaratha comments—मन्त्रमिति नवात्माद्यन्यतमम् । तच्च अत्र पद्मं (? पद्मगं) दलव्याप्तपाश्वराद्वयमासनत्वेन चिन्त्यम् । T.A.V., IX, p. 184

3. भैरव इति गुरुभिरिमैः । T.A. 1.100

Jayaratha observes इमैः इति चिन्त्यम् । गुरुगदितैरिति तु श्रेष्ठः पाठः । T.A.V., I, p. 134

4. ज्ञेयं संकल्पनारूपमर्धपीठमतः परम् ।
शाक्तं कुण्डलिनी वेदकलं च त्र्युपपीठकम् ॥

contained in the second half of the *T.A.* 15.88 but also devoid of agamic support and therefore asks the reader to simply ignore it.[1] We have already seen in detail how much new material has been introduced by Jayaratha to make the *Tantrāloka* more understandable and uptodate but never has he deviated from the main stream. The matter thus introduced is invariably either colateral or complementary in nature. But Jayaratha, for once, has deviated from the original line and may not be called so faithful in spite of his resorting to the usual commentatorial gimmic. One of the nine main topics incorporated under Krama system is 'non-utility or irrelevance of the limbs of Yoga' (Yogāṅgānupayogitva).[2] The Yoga which Abhinavagupta seeks to refer to is the eight-limbed Yoga of Patañjali, nowhere alluding to the Ṣaḍaṅga (six-limbed) Yoga at all.[3] Jayaratha, however, takes Ṣaḍaṅga, and not Aṣṭāṅga, as actually belonging to Krama system (Svadarśanoktāni). Then why does Abhinavagupta refer to Patañjali's Yoga? The logic behind Abhinavagupta's enumeration, according to Jayaratha, is that though the

---

देवीकोट्टोज्जयिन्यौ द्वे तथा कुलगिरिः परः ।
लालनं बैन्दवं व्याप्तिरिति संदोहकत्रयम् ॥
पुण्ड्रवर्धनवारेन्द्रे तथैकाग्रमिदं बहिः ।
नवधा कथितं पीठमन्तर्बाह्यक्रमेण तत् ॥

1. "ज्ञेयसंकल्पनारूपमर्धपीठमतः परम्" इति अर्धं "नवधा कथितं पीठमन्तर्बाह्यक्रमेण तत्" इत्युपसंहारविरुद्धमनागमिकं चेत्यनार्षत्वादुपेक्ष्यम् ।
T.A.V., IX, p. 48

We, however, consider our interpretation tentative at the moment.

2. एवं योगाङ्गमियति तर्क एव च चापरम् ।
अन्तरन्तःपरामर्शपाटवातिशयाय सः ॥ T.A. 4.86

3. T.A. 14.87-94

former subscribes to Ṣaḍaṅga theory, he wants to convey the upper limit of the number of the yogic limbs.[1] However, Jayaratha's deviation is too transparent to fool anybody. Why does he do so? There may be two possible reasons. Either he is under the spell of Buddhist tantricists who propogated the six-limbed Yoga and is out to wean the people away from them to his path or he inherits a Krama tradition different from Abhinavagupta's which enjoined Ṣaḍaṅga Yoga. It is interesting to note that Jayaratha nowhere tries to define the six limbs and quotes an unidentified source only once to enumerate them.[2] Although it is an interesting episode of Krama history we do not intend to pursue it further because our interest is limited to exploring the *inter se* relationship between Jayaratha and his master.[3]

1. यन्नाम अत्र योगस्य स्वदर्शनोक्तानि षडङ्गान्यपहाय पातञ्जलीयं यमाद्यङ्गाष्टकमुक्तं, तत्रायमाशयो यत् क्वचिदपि एतदङ्गाष्टातिरिक्तम् अन्यदङ्गान्तरं नास्ति। T.A.V., III, pp. 102-103
2. Ibid., p. 15
3. See K.T., pp. 58-61 for the proper perspective.

CHAPTER IV

ABOUT THE TEXT

(I) *KSTS Edition: editorial and printing lapses*

The *Tantrāloka* is a very voluminous work of Abhinavagupta and togetherwith Jayaratha's commentary covers twelve volumes in bold print brought out in the Kashmir Series of Texts and Studies spread over 3718 pages.[1] The *Tantrāloka*, as printed, comprises roughly 6000 verses, 5844 1/2 to be exact. The fact that two verses, *T.A.* 37.4-5, have been repeated as *T.A.* 37.10 1/2-12 1/2 does not reduce the number because this anomaly is a legacy from the time of Jayaratha himself having been retained in his script itself. The sum total of the printed verse-numbers at 5842, therefore, does not give the correct picture because of several printing mistakes and editorial lapses resulting in occasional duplication and omission of numbers as well as treatment of half-verses as full ones. An effort has been made to assemble all such cases in the chart given below to offer a tabular view.

1. If we go by the printed numbering of the pages the total rises to 3721, but the page No. 308 in the 3rd volume, page No. 92 in the 7th volume (between 11th and 12th Āhnikas) and page No. 128 in the 10th volume are blank. The text of the new edition has 3725 pages spread over six volumes (vols 2-7) with seven intervening pages left blank (925, 1088, 1292, 2184, 2440, 2726, 2854). Thus the actual number of pages tallies at 3718.

Volumes.	*Āhnikas*	*Misprints*	*Verses mising*	*Half-verses* Numbered	*Half-verses* Numbering omitted	*Repetition of number*	*Repetition of verses*	*Printed number of verses*	*Actual number of verses*	*Āhnika-wise pages*	*Total of printed number of pages in the volume*	*Remark*
(1)	(2)	(3)	(4)	(5)	(6)	(7)	(8)	(9)	(10)	(11)	(12)	(13)
	I	207 for 107	58		Between 200-201	136 (half-verse)		333	334	1-310		
					Between 244-245							
		105 for 205			After 333							
	II			17				50	49	1-42	352	(310+42)
				50								
	III			30	Before 1							
II				37	Between 64-65							
				38	,, 85-86							
				40	,, 107-8							
					,, 260-61							
					After 293			293	294	1-264	264	
III	IV			1	After 278			278	278	1-307		
	V			1	Between 157-58			158	158½	309-471		
					After 158					(163 Pages)	471	P. 308 blank

(1)	(2)	(3)	(4)	(5)	(6)	(7)	(8)	(9)	(10)	(11)	(12)	(13)
IV	VI			1	After 251			250	250½	1-203		
				251								
	VII			1	Between							
					70-71			71	71	1-58	261	(203 + 58)
V	VIII	33 for 330										
		332for331		1				452	451½	1-284	284	
		352for351										
VI	IX			1								
				314				314	313	1-250	250	
VII	X			1	After 309			309	309	1-208		
	XI			1								
				60								
				118				118	116½	1-91		
	XII			1				26	25½	93-108	316	(208 + 108)
										(16 pages)		P. 92 blank between XI & XII Āhnikas.
VIII	XIII			129	Between							
					,, 127-28							
				208	,, 206-207							
					After 361			361	361½	1-214		
	ZIV				After 46			46	46½	215-239		
										(25 pages)	239	
IX	XV	389 for 379		378	After 612 (two half verses)			612	612⅓	1-285	285	

(1)	(2)	(3)	(4)	(5)	(6)	(7)	(8)	(9)	(10)	(11)	(12)	(13)
X	XVI			204	Before 1			311	311	1-127		P. 128 blank
	XVII							122	122	129-176 (48 pages)		
	XVIII				Before 1			11	11½	177-181 (5 pages)		
	XIX			56	Before 1			56	56	182-205 (24 pages)		
	XX			1	After 15			15	15	206-212 (7 pages)		
	XXI			1				61	60½	213-243 (31 pages)		
	XXII			1				48	47½	244-261 (18 pages)		
	XXIII			1				103	102½	262-305 (44 pages)		
	XXIV			1 24				24	23	306-314 (9 pages)		
	XXV			1				29	28½	315-327 (13 pages)		
	XXVI			1				76	75½	328-356 (29 pages)		
	XXVII			1				59	58½	357-380 (24 pages)	380	
XI	XXVIII			1	After 434			434	434	1-184		
	XXIX			1	Before 1 After 291			291	291½	1-172	356	(184+172)

(1)	(2)	(3)	(4)	(5)	(6)	(7)	(8)	(9)	(10)	(11)	(12)	(13)
XII	XXX			1	Before 1			123	123	173-222 (50 pages)		Pagination begins at 173
	XXXI				After 163			163	163½	223-302 (80 pages)		
	XXXII				Before 1 After 67			67	68	303-335 (33 pages)		
	XXXIII				Before 1			32	32½	336-351 (16 pages)		
	XXXIV				Before 1 After 2 (1 + ½ Verses)			2	4	352-354 (3 pages)		
	XXXV							44	44	355-380 (26 pages)		
	XXXVI				Before 1 After 15			15	16	381-390 (10 pages)		
	XXXVII				Between 32-33		37.4-5 as 37.10½ — 12½	85	85½	391-435 (45 pages)	263	

(a) Two types of textual anarchisms

Coming to the KSTS edition of which the MLBD[1] edition is a reprint, we find that it requires a through critical editing. It suffers from two types of textual anarchisms—(i) those which were confronted by Jayaratha and have been taken care of in the course of our treatment of his and which offer really serious problems of textual reconstruction and (ii) others which concern editing and printing errors which are not so serious but often create misleading situations. It is the latter we propose to look into briefly for the present.

(b) Basic MSS of the KSTS edition

In the absence of any editorial note or preface we have practically no idea about the MSS on which this edition is based. From the occasional footnotes, however, Mukund Ram Shastri, the editor, seems to have consulted four MSS which have been referred to by Nāgarī letters Ka, Kha and Ga plus one on which rests the text and which has not been indicated by any letter.[2] Out of the remaining MSS the Ga manuscript seems to be most complete as several missing portions have been filled only with the aid of this MS.[3] Notwithstanding our ignorance about

1. Motilal Banarsidass

2. It is equally probable to think that there were only three MSS from which the model MS was prepared by M.R. Shastri. Whatever the case it does not alter the position much.

3. "वेद्या हि" (T.A. 1.126) इति संपूर्णपद्यं ग० पुस्तकात् पूरितमस्ति ।
T.A.V., 1, p. 165, fn.

× × ×

प्रवृत्तोहम् इत्यारभ्य प्रत्ययवाच्य इत्यन्तः पाठो ग० पुस्तकात् पूरितोऽस्ति ।
Ibid., p. I66

वक्ष्याम इति आरभ्य बहुप्रकारम् इत्यन्तः पाठो ग० पुस्तकात् पूरितोऽस्ति ।
(Ibid., p. 179.) etc. etc.

the principles employed in finalization of the printed text the sustained and patient labour put in by the editor and his team of Panditas is easily visible with the result that a largely readable and complete text of an important treatise is in our hands.[1] Besides determining the acceptable readings and pointing out the respective variants, the editor has also corrected the patently corrupt readings.[2] Of course it is not a very frequent activity. It appears that the text of the Āhnikas from first to thirteen was more corrupt than the later ones as the profusion and frequency of footnotes suggest. Even among the initial Āhnikas the Ist was most defective and the incidence of mistakes has been gradually on the declining scale in the subsequent ones. From 14th onwards footnotes become conspicuous by their absence. At some places he offers interpretive comments,[3] but he does so very rarely. Wherever feasible, the editor has tried to trace the portions of the cited text to its published edition, if available. Although he is not absolutely regular on this score, his efforts have proved quite

1. Except the following portions which show some unfilled gaps—

(i) T.A. 15.378

(ii) T.A.V., I, p. 40 (on T.A. 1.18, quotation from the Śrī-kaṇṭhī)

(iii) Ibid., III, p. 107 (on T.A. 4. 100)

(iv) Ibid., VII, p.66 (on T.A. 10.83-84)

(v) Ibid., VII, p.67 (on T.A. 10.85)

(vi) Ibid., XI, p.38 (on T.A. 29.52-54, quotation)

2. पं० ५ ख०पु० श्रीमद्भट्टादिरिति शोधितः पाठः ।

Fn., ibid, I, p. 29

3. Vide, ibid, I, p. 4, fn. 1, which deals with the concept of Jagadānanda. Also see, ibid., I, p. 15 fn. 3, on

समयलोपावहं महात्मनाम् महागुरूणां निन्दाबीजम् ।

helpful. For example, he has tried to identify Jayaratha's citations from the *SV.T.* in the printed edition and at times has even pointed out to the variations, if any.[1] Out of the twelve volumes he has appended a verse-index to six from 3rd to 8th and has also purveyed citation-index in the 3rd and 6th volumes.

(c) PRINTING MISTAKES

It will not be out of place to refer the reader to the patently glaring printing mistakes in the printed edition. Some of which may be sampled as below—

(i) T.A. 19 reads अ्रदृष्टप्रकटीकुर्मो for अदृष्टं प्रकटीकुर्मो
(ii) T.A. 1.291 reads समुच्चारश्चिदात्मता for समुच्चारश्चिदात्मनो[2]
(iii) T.A. 1.298 reads संख्याधिक्यं for सांख्याधिक्यम्[3] (i.e., सांख्याद् आधिक्यम्)
(iv) T.A. 1.301 reads स्थानभित् for स्नानभित्[4]
(v) T.A. 1.302 reads द्रव्ययोग्यमर्चा for द्रव्ययोग्यत्वमर्चा[5]
(vi) T.A. 1.312 reads कलावेक्षा for कालापेक्षा[6]
(vii) T.A. 1.316 reads परीक्षाचार्यकरणं for परीक्ष्याचार्यकरणम्[7]
(viii) T.A. 1.324 reads बोधः for वेधः[8]
(ix) T.A. 37.75 reads भ्रातापि तस्याः for भर्तापि तस्याः[9]
(x) T.A.V., V, p. 145 reads सर्वत्र पूर्वशास्त्रप्रक्रियया for सर्वत्र श्रीपूर्वशास्त्रप्रक्रियया

1. श्रीस्वच्छन्दे तु लवणोदधिमित्यस्यानन्तरं .... इत्यधिकः पाठः । T.A.V., V, p. 57 Fn. 1

2. This reading becomes clear when construed with reference to its proper place of treatment in the 5th Àhnika, specially T.A. 5.62.

3. Cp. T.A. 13.3

4. Cp. ibid. 15.38

5. Cp. ibid. 15.160 and 15.180

6. Cp. ibid. 19.7

7. Cp. ibid. 23.2

8. Cp. ibid. 29.169

9. Retention of such readings creates historical anomalies.

These printing mistakes are such as to give wrong idea of the subject matter proposed to be discussed in the *Tantrāloka*. There are others which are quite obvious but do not injure the spirit of the text. Some instances may be sampled as under—

(i) T.A.V., III, p. 160 reads मोयोपरञ्जनं for मेयोपरंजनम्
(ii) T.A. 4.271 reads न तस्य च निषोधो for न तस्य च निषेधो
(iii) T.A.V., IV, p. 203 reads लब्धसिद्धीति for लब्धसिद्धिरिति
(iv) T.A. 7.63 reads स स्पदे खे for स स्पन्दे खे
(v) T.A.V., VIII, p. 1 reads अधिकारभेदम् उपदिष्टं for अधिकारभेद उपदिष्टः
(vi) T.A.V., VIII, p. 86 reads मतादीनां तत्त्वं for मलादीनां तत्त्वं
(vii) T.A.V., IX, p. 44 reads यदीति स्थाने for यदिति स्थाने
(viii) T.A.V., IX, p. 48 reads ज्ञेयसंकल्पनारूपम् for ज्ञेयं संकल्पनारूपम् (T.A. 15.86)
(ix) T.A. 29.255 reads वेदं गुरवो रहस्यविदः for वेधं गुरवो रहस्यविदः
(x) 37.72 reads परिहारमथो चिकीर्षन for परिहारमथ चिकीर्षन्

In the case of certain readings the problem is complicated when the MSS under reference do not have other variants than the printed one and the same text is retained in the *Tantrāloka* and the *Tantrāloka-viveka* both. For instance the *T.A.* 1.264 reads Lakṣyaṁ which is retained by Jayaratha in his *Viveka.* It, however, must be Lakṣaṇaṁ if a coherent meaning is to be derived. Sometimes one comes across a very interesting phenomenon. The editor retains चन्द्रिकाशांततापसः in the *T.A.* 10.287 whereas in the *Viveka*

(Vol. I, p. 236) he adopts चन्द्रिकापास्ततामसः while referring to the same verse. It is, therefore, apparent that the required editorial vigilance has been wanting and as a result the two portions were never coordinated, as it were.

(d) NUMBERING ERRORS

Besides printing, there is a variety of numbering errors. The simplest one is that of printing error. For instance, commentary on the *T.A.* 8.285 is printed as 8.281. Similarly, while the commentary is marked as relating to the *T.A.* 1.58 the verse bearing number 1.58 is not indicated. Another anomaly that is visible from the chart appearing on pp. 156-159 is that several verses have been left unnumbered. For example, the half-verse between *T.A.* 37.32 and *T.A.* 37.33 has been left unnumbered. Such instances are many and they have been duly shown in the table. This has made the problem of correct serialization more chaotic. While considering the style of Abhinavagupta we noted that he has adopted a style in which each preceding Āhnika ends with the first half of the concluding verse and the succeeding one begins with the latter half. This is what has been termed as Saṁcayanyāya by Jayaratha. In such an event there could have been one of the two editorial choices—to treat the verses as always marking either the chaptorial conclusions or the beginnings and number them accordingly. But the editorial practice has not been uniform in this regard. In some Āhnikas last verse has been treated as the concluding verse and has been numbered accordingly leaving the remaining half unnumbered as has been done in the 17th Āhnika. In some other Āhnikas this practice has been abandoned. The first concluding half has not been marked, instead the next commencing verse has been given a number, as has been the practice in the 16th Āhnika. Another anomaly that is very conspicuous is that quite often the concluding half and the introductory half both have been marked as two full independent verses. For example Āhnikas 7-8, 12-13, 19-20, 21-22, 25-26 and 30-31 may be taken up. Another prevailing anarchy consists in not providing any number to such verses. This is evident from a perusal of the Āhnikas 28-29, 29-30, 32-33 and 33-34. An interesting aspect of such anarchous behaviour has resulted in one half being treated as one verse while the other half being conjoined with another and made part of it. This is very well illustrated by Āhnikas 16-17, where the concluding verse is numbered as 16.311 while the introductory half is merged with the first half of the second verse (17.2) and numbered as 17.1. Similar thing seems to have happened in the 13-14th Āhnikas also. The same practice has been reversed elsewhere, i.e. the last half has been fused with the penultimate verse making it appear as one full verse. For example, the *T.A.* 8.452, being the concluding one, should have been half and numbered either as 8.453 or as 9.1, but it is not so as it has been assimilated with the preceding half, i.e. *T.A.* 8.452 and allotted its number. Sometimes the concluding as well as the introductory verses both have not been numbered at all, as has happened in the Āhnikas 34-35. From these illustrations one gets a fairly adequate idea of the discrepansies abounding in the whole of the KSTS edition and the scope of improvements to be effected.

Lack of a uniform editorial policy coupled with printing errors has spread to the other areas of the text. When it relates to internal references by the *Viveka*, the quoted numbers differ from the actual ones. For instance, the quoted verse shown as *T.A.* 9.244 is in fact *T.A.* 9.246. The same thing has been frequently repeated. Following are some such instances—

(i) T.A.V., VI, p. 180 quotes T.A. 8.260 but numbers it as 8.255.
(ii) T.A.V., VI, p. 179 quotes T.A. 8.253-260 but numbers it as 8.248-258.
(iii) T.A.V., VIII, p. 80 quotes T.A. 13.256 but numbers it as 13.252.

The problem is compounded when we notice that the reference appearing in the *T.A.V.*, III, p. 443 are not found in the *Tantrāloka* under the given numbers and one quotation which the editor shows as constituting the *Tantrāloka* 25.172 is found at variance with Jayaratha's statement who takes it as from the 29th Āhnika (i.e., *T.A.* 29.182).

Apart from these, there are some serious lacuna leading to interesting conclusions. For example, the colophon of the 17th Āhnika reading Vikṣipta Dīkṣā has led to the naming of the Āhnika as Vikṣiptadīkṣāprakāśana. It is only by examining the contents of the Āhnika we come to know that the reading in all probability should have been Vistṛtadīkṣā,[1] and discover how funny the reading is.

1. Jayaratha in his commentary on the last verse of the 17th Āhnika says that जननादिसमन्विता दीक्षा in the text means विस्तृता दीक्षा, while in the 2nd half of the same verse (T.A. 18.1) Abhinavagupta proposes to discuss संक्षिप्तदीक्षा.

Similarly a uniform practice in respect of pagination is also wanting. While there is continuous pagination in all the volumes irrespective of the number of Āhnikas contained therein, some of the volumes, notably Vth and XIth, have Āhnika-wise pagination. Likewise all the volumes have fresh pagination, but volume XII continues it from volume XI.[1]

On all counts, thus, the greatest single handicap seems to be the absence of critical textual editing and uniform editorial practice.

(II) *Metres employed*

The *Tantrāloka* is a versicular text like most Sanskrit works and though Abhinavagupta displays his poetic skill occasionally his main occupation is scholastic treatment. He seems to be quite at home in employment of a variety of metres and the following appear to be his favourite choice—Nardataka,[2] Anuṣṭup[3], Upendravajrā,[4] Vasantatilakā,[5] Āryā,[6] Rathoddhatā,[7] Sragdharā,[8] Mandākrāntā[9], Śārdūlavikrīḍita[10], Indravajrā[11], Śikhariṇī[12], Drutavilambita,[13]

1. This discrepancy does not exist in the new edition because of the running pagination in all the volumes.
2. T.A. 1.1
3. Ibid. 1.2, 3, 17, 32 etc.
4. Ibid. 1.5
5. Ibid. 1.8, 16; 37.48, 51, 60, 64, 67
6. Ibid. 1.20, 21; 26.63
7. Ibid. 1.201
8. Ibid. 1.330; 21.25
9. Ibid. 1.331; 2.39
10. Ibid. 1.332; 26.65
11. Ibid. 6.1
12. Ibid. 2.49; 3.23
13. Ibid. 2.50

Vaṁśastha[1], Pṛthvī[2] and Mālinī[3]. While he casts the *Tantrāloka* mostly in the traditional Anuṣṭup metre he seems to be quite fond of Āryā and Vasantatilakā also.

(III) *Topical organization and structural analysis*

(a) DIVISION INTO ĀHNIKAS

The whole *Tantrāloka* is divided into 37 Āhnikas (lit. daily lessons). Although at one place Abhinavagupta seems to use the word in its literal sense,[4] it usually stands for a chapter or section if the gross variation in the size of Āhnikas indicates anything. The fifteenth is the biggest Āhnika containing 612 verses and the thirtyfourth the smallest comprising just 4 verses. All other Āhnikas fall within these two extremes. The following exercise may be of some help in getting at the structural analysis of the *Tantrāloka*—

Number of verses	*Āhnikas*
(1) 451 and above	8, 9, 15
(2) 301 to 450	1, 10, 13, 16, 28
(3) 101 to 300	3, 4, 5, 6, 11, 17, 23, 29, 30, 31
(4) 51-100	7, 19, 21, 26, 27, 32, 37
(5) 1 to 50	2, 12, 14, 18, 20, 22, 24, 25, 33, 34, 35, 36

1. T.A. 3.39
2. Ibid. 12.26
3. Ibid. 28.367
4. इत्यनुत्तरपदप्रविकासे शाक्तमौपयिकमद्य विविक्तम् ।

Concluding verse after T.A. 4.278.

Jayaratha adds अद्य इत्यनेन आह्निकशब्दार्थस्तात्त्विकः इति प्रकाशितम ।

T.A.V., III, p. 307

The table pictures a very wide range. Although no clear cut guideline behind such a yawning gap is discernible, the nature of the subjectmatter to be treated seems to be the only answer. A feeble pattern, however, emerges in as much as the first half has claimed the larger slice of bigger chapters, whereas the second half abounds in the smaller ones. It is significant to note that while the earlier half is marked by preponderance of the theoritical discussion, the second by predominance of the procedural treatment.

(b) THREE DEVICES TO INDICATE SUBJECTMATTER

A welcome feature is that Abhinava has taken care to provide titles to all the Āhnikas focussing on their main subject matter. He utilizes three opportunities to ventilate his mind. He tries to entitle the chapters towards the end of the first Āhnika from verses 278 to 286 while discussing general topics and from verses 287 to 328 while discussing specific auxiliary topics. This is in the first place. He mentions theprecise prospective contents in the introductory as well as the concluding verse in such a way as to give a definite name to the Āhnika under reference.[1] This is in the second place. While cross-

1. This is the standard practice with Abhinavagupta and his prologue and epilogue usually correspond to one another. He, however, gives up this practice in the sixth Āhnika where he initially promises to discuss Sthānaprakalpa as part of the external means called Āṇava, but ends up with the discussion on Kālatattva. Such a phenomenon, however, does not constitute a serious lapse or deviation because Sthānaprakalpa is a broader theme which includes the notion of Kālatattva.[b]

a. स्थानप्रकल्पाख्यतया स्फुटस्तु बाह्योऽभ्युपायः प्रविविच्यतेऽथ ।

T.A. 6.1

referring to the contents of another Āhnika he occasionally, though not necessarily, alludes to the Āhnika in question by name. For instance, in the thirteenth Āhnika he refers to Liṅgoddhāradīkṣā which is the subject matter of the 22nd Āhnika[1] and to Dīkṣāprastāva[2] which occupies the 14th Āhnika or in the 9th Āhnika he refers to future Sadyonirvāṇadīkṣā[3] which is the main theme of the 19th Āhnika. Likewise, he refers to the 13th Āhnika by name in the 1st Āhnika.[4] Jayartha closely follows his master and provides captions to all the Āhnikas in the chapterwise colophons. The two colophons, however, relating to the 34th and 37th Āhnikas do not record any name. Jayaratha's titles are invariably followed by the word 'Prakāśana'. It lends credence to the view that Jayaratha perhaps preferred '*Prakāśa*' to '*Viveka*' as title for his commentary. Normally Jayaratha's nomenclatures echo those of Abhinavagupta but there have been some exceptions as well. This has happened in respect of the 16th and 17th Āhnikas. According to Abhinavagupta the 16th Āhinka dwells upon Putrakadīkṣā, but Jayaratha christens it as Prameyaprakāśana (revealing the subjectmatter)

---

b. इति कालतत्त्वमुदितं शास्त्रमुखागमनिजानुभवसिद्धम् ।
Concluding verse of the 6th Āhnika.

1. स्वातन्त्र्यात्तु महेशस्य तेऽपि चेच्छिवतोन्मुखाः ॥
द्विगुणा संस्क्रियास्त्येषां लिङ्गोद्धृत्याथ दीक्षया । T.A. 13.281-82

2. ज्ञानोपायस्तु दीक्षादिक्रिया ज्ञानवियोगिनाम् ।
इत्यधुनैवास्तां स्वप्रस्तावे भविष्यति ॥ Ibid. 13.155

3. सद्योनिर्वाणदीक्षोत्थपुंविश्लेषे हि सा सती ।
श्लिष्यन्त्यपि च नो सूते तथापि स्वफलं क्वचित् ॥ Ibid. 9.177

4. तद्विस्तरेण वक्ष्यामः शक्तिपातविनिर्णये ।
समाप्य परतां स्थौल्यप्रसंगे चर्चयिष्यते ॥ Ibid. 1.139

which, in a sense, is of no consequence. Similarly, the 17th, according to Abhinavagupta, focusses on Janānādisamanvitādīkṣā, but Jayaratha names it as Vistṛta-dīkṣā-prakāśana (Vikṣiptadīkṣā in the printed text which is wrong as already discussed elsewhere) in contrast to the 18th Āhnika which incorporates Saṁkṣiptadīkṣā. In some places, notwithstanding Jayaratha's total dependence on Abhinava, his nomenclatures are somewhat less communicative or slightly wanting, if one may say so. For example, Abhinava designs the 19th Āhnika as discussing Sadyaḥ-samutkrāntipradā Dīkṣā while Jayaratha names it as Sadya-utkrānti-prakāśana (lit., revealing sudden death). In fact, Jayaratha adopts such a practice from here right upto the 25th Āhnika. Perhaps for the sake of brevity, he prefers dropping 'Dīkṣā' or 'Vidhi' as the case may be.

(c) Division of Āhnikas into groups

Abhinavagupta broadly divides all the 37 Āhnikas into two groups. First thirtytwo Āhnikas except the first constitute one set and the remaining five, from 33rd to 37th, constitute the other. Their basic difference lies in the fact that while the first set dilates upon both—general as well as ancillary topics, the second set has no ancillary material to fall back upon. This also provides one of the reasons for the smaller size of the later Āhnikas. As we have already seen, Abhinavagupta directs all energies to nurture the *Tantrāloka* as a Śāstra. A scripture worth the name must have three essential parts—(i) topic or proposition to be enquired into, (ii) definition and (iii) examination (Uddeśa, Lakṣaṇa and Parīkṣā) respectively. Uddeśa is nothing but an averment of the topic by name which normally takes the form of question-answer between the teacher and the taught.[1] In fact this imparts tantric semblance to the tantric texts.[2] Lakṣaṇa consists in deciphering the distinctive character of the thing and Parīkṣā marks the total view which emerges after a thorough scrutiny of all the opposite positions.[3] From this angle he attempts a second classification of Āhnikas. As such, he devotes the first Āhnika to the positing of Uddeśas while other Āhnikas, from two to thirtyseven, focus on Lakṣaṇa and Parīkṣā both. Here again, as pointed out earlier, in his treatment of Uddeśas he underlines two categories of topics—general as well as ancillary—and discusses them from T.A. 1.278 to 1.284 and from T.A. 1.286 to 1.326 respectively. He has coined a special nomenclature as Pūrvaja (lit. anterior) and Anuja (posterior) standing for Sāmānya and Viśeṣa—in that order.[4] As we pointed out towards the beginning of this paragraph, thirtyone Āhnikas, from 2 to 32, define and examine general

1. तेनानुद्धाटितात्मत्वभावप्रथनमेव यत् ।
प्रथमं स इहोद्देशः प्रश्नः संशय एव च ॥
स्वयमेवं विबोधश्च तथा प्रश्नोत्तरात्मकः ।
गुरुशिष्यपदेऽप्येष देहभेदो ह्यतात्त्विकः ॥ T.A. 1.252/256

2. Cp. गुरुशिष्यपदे स्थित्वा स्वयं देवः सदाशिवः ।
पूर्वोत्तरपदैर्वाक्यैस्तन्त्रं समवतारयत् ॥ T.A.V., I, p. 268

quoted by Jayaratha from some unknown source, probably from the SV.T.

3. तस्याथ वस्तुनः स्वात्मवीर्याक्रमणपाटवात् ।
उन्मुद्रणं तयाकृत्या लक्षणोत्तरनिर्णयाः ॥
निर्णीततावद्धर्मांशपृष्ठपातितया पुनः ।
भूयो भूयः समुद्देशलक्षणात्मपरीक्षणम् ॥ T.A. 1.260-61

4. तत्रोच्यते पुरोद्देशः पूर्वजानुजभेदवान् । Ibid. 1.278

and ancillary topics both, while Āhnikas from 33 to 37 define and examine general topics alone.

(d) Demarcation of the primary and secondary topics

We are highly indebted to Abhinavagupta for enumeration of the primary and secondary topics he touches upon in course of his treatment. Jayaratha, his dedicated commentator, takes upon himself to demarcate as to where an ancillary topic begins and where another takes over. Yet there are places where Jayaratha does not give any direct indication. As a result precise positioning has been a difficult task in such cases. An effort, however, has been made to demarcate the precise places of all the ancillary topics dealt with in the *Tantrāloka* in the chart below indicating the items.

Number of Āhnika	Caption of Āhnika acc. to Jayaratha[1]	Caption of Āhnika acc. to Abhinava[2]	General topic[3] (Purvajoddeśa)	Ancillary topic (Anujoddeśa)[4]	Point of commencement of the ancillary topic
1	2	3	4	5	6
प्रथम	विज्ञानभेदप्रकाशन	विज्ञानसत्ताभेदोद्गार-प्रकटनपटु आह्निक or विज्ञानभित्प्रकरण[5]	विज्ञानभेद	सर्वोद्देशन[6]X	१.२२
द्वितीय	अनुपायप्रकाशन	अनुत्तरज्ञप्तिरूपनिर्णया-त्मक प्रकरण	गतोपाय or अनुपाय	—	—
तृतीय	शांभवोपाय-प्रकाशन	परौपयिक प्रणिगदन or शाम्भवात्मवेदनकथन	परोपाय or शांभवोपाय	१. विश्वचित्प्रतिबिम्बत्व[7]X २. परामर्शोदयक्रम ३. मन्त्राद्यभिन्नरूपत्व	३.४ ३.६६ ३.२००

X Jayaratha does not indicate commencement. In such a situation it has been suggested by us.
1. Available in respective chaptorial colophons, hence specific mention of the source not made.
2. Generally available in the introductory and concludding verses of the respective Āhnika, hence specific mention avoided.
3. Vide T.A. 1.278-286
4. Vide ibid., 1.287-328
5-6. T.A. 1.287
7. Ibid. 1.288

1	2	3	4	5	6
चतुर्थ	शाक्तोपाय-प्रकाशन or शाक्तसमावेश-प्रकाशन	शाक्तोपायपण्डलकथन or शाक्तोपायविवेचन	शाक्तोपाय	१. विकल्पसंस्कार[1]	४.२
				२. तर्कतत्त्व	४.१३
				३. गुरुसतत्त्व	४.३३
				४. योगाङ्गानुपयोगित्व	४.८६
				५. कल्पितार्चाद्यनादर	४.११५
				६. संविच्चक्रोदय	४.१२३
				७. मन्त्रवीर्य	४.१८१
				८. वास्तवजप्य	४.१९४
				९. निषेधविधितुल्यत्व	४.२१३
पंचम	आणवोपाय-प्रकाशन	आणवाऽनुत्तरताभ्यु-पायकथन	नरोपाय or आणवोपाय	१. बुद्धिध्यान[2]	५.१९
				२. प्राणसमुच्चार	५.४३
				३. चिदात्म-उच्चार	५.६२
				४. परतत्त्वान्तःप्रवेश	५.७४
				५. (अन्तःप्रवेश)पथलक्षण	५.१००
				६. करण	५.१२८
				७. वर्णतत्त्व	५.१३१

1. T.A. 1.288-289 2. Ibid. 1.291. चिदात्मता in the printed text is an obvious mistake for चिदात्मनः.

1	2	3	4	5	6
षष्ठ	कालतत्त्वप्रकाशन	कालतत्त्ववदन[1] (As part of स्थानप्रकल्प)	कालोपाय or कालाध्वन्	१. (प्राण) चारमान[2]X २. अहोरात्रसंक्रान्त्यादि[3] ३. संहारचित्रता[4] ४. वर्णोदय	६.२३ ६.६३ ६.१३९ ६.२१६
सप्तम	चक्रोदयप्रकाशन (कालतत्त्वानुषक्त)	चक्रोदय-रहस्यभणिति	चक्रोदय	१. चक्रभेद[5]X २. मन्त्रविद्याभेद	७.३ ७.४२
अष्टम	देशाध्वप्रकाशन	देशाध्वगान or देशाध्वविभागकथन	देशाध्वन्	१. पुरपरिमाण[6] २. पुरसंग्रह ३. तत्वयोजन[7]	८.२० ८.४०६ ८.२०४
नवम	तत्त्वप्रकाशन	तत्त्वप्रविभागकथन	तत्त्वाध्वन्	१. कार्यकारणभाव[8] २. तत्त्वक्रमनिरूपण	९.७ ९.४८-४९

1. Abhinavagupta professes to discuss स्थानप्रकल्प as part of आणवोपाय in the beginning, but ends with elucidation of कालतत्त्व.
2. T.A. 1.292-93. Here Ira Bajpai translates चारमान as सूर्यादिसंचार whereas it is प्राणचार. See Philosophy, p. 502.
3. It ought to be अहोरात्रसंक्रान्त्यादिकर्मविकल्पन if we go by Jayaratha.
4. In fact it ought to be सृष्टिसंहारचित्रता.
5. T.A. 1.293
6. Ibid. 1.294
7. In the body of the text the order enjoined in the Kārikā has been reversed.
8. T.A. 1.294-95

1	2	3	4	5	6
दशम	तत्वभेदप्रकाशन	तत्वभेदकथन	तत्वभेदन	१. वस्तुधर्म[1]	१०.१६
				२. तत्वविधि	१०.६७
				३. जाग्रदादिनिरूपण	१०.२२७
				४. प्रमातृभेद[2]	—
एकादश	कलादिप्रदर्शन[3]	कलाध्ववचन or कलाध्वविस्तरनिर्णय	कलाद्यध्वन्	१. कलास्वरूप[4]X	११.२
				२. एक-त्रि-पंचाद्यैस्ततत्वपरिकल्पन	११.३५
				३. वर्णभेदक्रम	११.४३
				४. सर्वाधारशक्तिनिरूपणX	११.१०६
द्वादश	अध्वोपयोगप्रकाशन	अध्वोपयोगप्रकाशन	अध्वोपयोग	१. अभेदभावना	१२.४
				२. कम्पह्रास	१२.१८
त्रयोदश	शक्तिपातप्रदर्शन[3]	शक्तिपातक्रमविवेचन	शक्तिपाततिरोहिति or शक्तिपातपरीक्षा	१. सांख्याधिक्य[5]X	१३.३
				२. मलादितत्वX	१३.४३
				३. शक्तिविचित्रता[6]X	१३.१२६
				४. अनपेक्षित्वसिद्धिX	१३.२८३
				५. तिरोभाववैचित्र्य	१३.३११

1. T.A. 1.295-96
2. Left undiscussed.
3. Jayaratha deviates from his usual nomenclature. Mark प्रदर्शन for प्रकाशन.
4. T.A. 1.296-97
5. Ibid. 1.298-99. Read सांख्याधिक्य for संख्याधिक्य in the Kārikā. It is not 'superiority of Sāṅkhya' as Ira Bajpai takes it (Philosophy, p. 504), but "superiority to Sāṅkhya".
6. Better read शक्तिपातविचित्रता.

1	2	3	4	5	6
चतुर्दश	दीक्षोपक्रमप्रकाशन	दीक्षोपक्रमप्रदर्शन	दीक्षोपक्रमण	१. तिरोभावव्यपगम[1]X	१४.२०
				२. ज्ञानपरिपूर्णता	१४.२७
				३. उत्क्रान्त्यनुपयोगित्व	१४.३२
पंचदश	समयदीक्षाप्रकाशन	समयदीक्षणप्रकाशन	समयित्वविधि	१. शिष्यौचित्यपरीक्षा[2]	१५.२०
		or	or	२. स्नानभेद[3]	१५.३०
		यागनिरूपण[4]	सामयी दीक्षा	३. स्थानकल्पन	१५.८०
				४. सामान्यन्यासभेद	१५.११५
				५. अर्घपात्र (विधि)	१५.१४६
				६. अर्घपात्रप्रयोजनX	१५.१५३
				७. द्रव्ययोग्यत्व	१५.१६०
				८. बहिरर्चा	१५.१८०
				९. द्वारार्चन or द्वारपूजाविधि	१५.१८३
				१०. प्रवेशX	१५.१९३
				११. दिक्स्वरूप	१५.१९४
				१२. देहप्राणादिशोधन	१५.२३२
				१३. विशेषन्यासवैचित्र्य	१५.२३९
				१४. सविशेषार्घभाजन or विशेषार्घपात्र	१५.२८८

1. T.A. 1.300
2. Ibid. 1.301-307
3. Read स्नानभित् for स्थानभित् in the Kārikā.
4. याग is नित्यकर्मात्मक. नित्यकर्म begins.

1	2	3	4	5	6
				१५. प्राणबुद्धिचित्स्वध्वन्यास-पूजने देहपूजाX	१५.२६५
				१६. अन्यशास्त्रगणोत्कर्ष	१५.३१०
				१७. सर्वतः चक्रपूजा[1]	१५.३२३
				१८. क्षेत्रग्रह	१५.३६६
				१९. पंचगव्यX	१५.३७१
				२०. भूगणेशपूजनX	१५.३७४
				२१. अस्त्रार्चाX	१५.३७६
				२२. वह्निकार्य	१५.३८८
				२३. अग्निग अधिवासन (चर्वादि-स्थापन)	१५.४११
				२४. तर्पण	१५.४१८
				२५. चरुसंसिद्धि	१५.४३६
				२६. दन्तकाष्ठान्तसंस्क्रिया[2]X	१५.४४७
				२७. शिवहस्तविधि	१५.४५६
				२८. शय्याक्लृप्ति	१५.४७४
				२९. स्वप्न-संबंधि सामयकर्म or सामयकर्म	१५.४९४
				३०. समय	१५.५२१

1. It is सर्वस्य मन्त्रचक्रस्य पूजा. 2. Jayaratha calls it दन्तसंस्कार.

1	2	3	4	5	6
षोडश	प्रमेयप्रकाशन	पुत्रकत्वसिद्धिनिरूपण[1] or पुत्रकदीक्षानिरूपण	प्रमेयप्रक्रिया (शक्तिपातावसरे गुरोर्दीक्षासंबंधिनी)	१. मण्डलात्मानुसंधान[2]X	१६.५
				२. निवेद्यपशुविस्तर	१६.२८
				३. अग्नितर्पणX	१६.४८
				४. स्वस्वभावदीपन	१६.८०
				५. शिष्यदेहग अध्वन्यासविधि	१६.८७
				६. शोध्यशोधकादिविचित्रता	१६.९७
				७. दीक्षाभेद	१६.१६३
				८. परन्यास	१६.२०७
				९. मन्त्रसत्ताप्रयोजनX	१६.२५२
				१०. योजनिकाभेद	१६.२९५
सप्तदश	विस्तृतदीक्षा-प्रकाशन[3]	भैरवतादात्म्यदायिनी-प्रक्रियानिरूपण or जननादिसमन्वितदीक्षा-कथन	पौत्रिकविधि	१. सूत्रक्लृप्ति[4]	१७.३
				२. तत्त्वशुद्धि[5]	१७.७
				३. पाशदाहX	१७.६७
				४. योजन[6]	१७.७८
				५. अध्वभेद	१७.११८

1. If we compare the T.A. 1.280-81 with the T.A. 1.310 and the contents of the 17th Āhnika it appears that there is some confusion in the order of the T.A. 1.280-81. पौत्रिकविधि should follow प्रमेयप्रक्रिया and not the other way round as is found in the text. 2. T.A. 1.307-309
3. As discussed elsewhere, Jayaratha's reading, i.e. विक्षिप्तदीक्षा-प्रकाशन is to be amended as above.
4. T.A. 1.310 5. This has earned the name of the Āhnika as तत्त्वदीक्षाप्रकरण, vide Jayaratha's remarks on T.A. 29.205 (T.A.V., XI, p. 133). 6. In fact it ought to be योजनिका.

1	2	3	4	5	6
अष्टादश	संक्षिप्तदीक्षा-प्रकाशन	(शिवतापत्तिदा)-संक्षिप्तदीक्षाकथन	संक्षिप्तदीक्षा	१. जननादिविहीनत्व[1]	१८.१
				२. मंत्रभेद	१८.३
एकोनत्रिंश[2]	सद्य उत्क्रान्ति-प्रकाशन	(सद्यःसमुत्क्रान्तिप्रदा-दीक्षानिरूपण) or सद्यः समुत्क्रम	सद्योनिर्वाणदीक्षा	१. कालापेक्षा[3]	१९.७
				२. क्षुपाण्यादिन्यास[4]	१९.१०
				३. शरीरग चार	१९.१५
				४. ब्रह्मविद्याविधि	१९.२४
विंशतितम	तुलादीक्षा-प्रकाशन	(जनाश्वासप्रदायिनीदीक्षा) or तुलाशुद्धिदीक्षाकथन	तुलादीक्षा	१. अधिकारिपरीक्षा[5]	२०.८
				२. अंतःसंस्कार	२०.१५
				३. तुलाविधि[6]	२०.११
एकविंश	परोक्षदीक्षा-प्रकाशन	परोक्षदीक्षानिगदन	पारोक्षी दीक्षा	१. मृतजीवद्विधि[7]	२१.६
				२. जालोपदेश[8]	२१.२४
				३. संस्क्रियागण	२१.३२
				४. (संस्क्रियागणगत) बलाबल-विचार	२१.४६

1. T.A. 1.311.
2. Not एकान्नत्रिंश as is usually printed.
3. T.A. 1.312. Read कालापेक्षा for कलावेक्षा in the Kārikā.
4. Jayaratha calls it क्षुरिकादिन्यास.
5. T.A. 1.313
6. In the body of the text the order between 2nd and 3rd अनुजोद्देशs has been reversed.
7. T.A. 1.314
8. Also known as महाजालप्रयोगविधि.

1	2	3	4	5	6
द्वाविंशतितम	लिङ्गोद्धार-प्रकाशन	लिङ्गोद्धारदीक्षाकथन	लिङ्गोद्धृतिक्रम or लिङ्गोद्धार	१. श्रवण[1]	२२.१४
				२. अभ्यनुज्ञान	२२.१७
				३. शोधन	२२.२२
				४. पातकच्युति	२२.२३
				५. शङ्काच्छेद	२२.४५
त्रयोविंशतितम	अभिषेकप्रकाशन	अभिषेकविधिनिरूपण	अभिषेकविधि	१. परीक्ष्याचार्यकरण[2]X	२३.२
				२. तद्व्रत (विद्याव्रत)X	२३.३१
				३. मतिहरण	२३.५१
				४. तद्विभागX (विषयविभाग)	२३.९९
				५. साधकत्व	२३.१०१
चतुर्विंश	अन्त्येष्टिप्रकाशन	अन्त्यसंस्क्रियाप्रतिपादन or अन्त्येष्टियागप्रतिपादन	अन्त्ययाग or अन्त्येष्टि or अन्त्येष्टिदीक्षा or सांन्यासिकी दीक्षा	१. अधिकारी[3]	२४.२
				२. संस्कारX	२४.१८
				३. संस्कारप्रयोजन	२४.२१
पंचविंशतितम	श्राद्धप्रकाशन	श्राद्धविधिनिगदन or श्राद्धप्रकाश	श्राद्धक्लृप्ति	१. प्रयोजन[4]	२५.८
				२. भोगमोक्षदानेन विधि (श्राद्धस्य भोगमोक्षदानहेतुता)	२५.२१

1. T.A. 1.315
2. T.A. 1.316. Read परीक्ष्याचार्यकरणम् for परीक्षाचार्यकरणम् in the Kārikā.
3. Ibid. 1.317
4. Ibid. 1.318

1	2	3	4	5	6
षड्विंश	स्थण्डिलपूजा-प्रकाशन	स्थण्डिलयागकथन or शेषवृत्तिनिरूपण	शेषवृत्ति[1]	१. शेषवृत्तिप्रयोजन[2]	२६.२
				२. स्थण्डिलगत परा नित्या अर्चा	२६.३६
सप्तविंश	लिङ्गार्चाप्रकाशन	लिङ्गार्चासंप्रकाशन or लिङ्गपूजाकथन	लिङ्गार्चा	१. लिङ्गभेद[3] (बहुधा लिङ्ग-स्वरूप)	२७.१२
			(नित्यावशेषरूपा पूजा)	२. अक्षसूत्रनिरूपण	२७.३०
				३. पूजाभेद	२७.५६
अष्टाविंश	पर्वपवित्रकादि-प्रकाशन	नैमित्तिकप्रकाश or नैमित्तिकविधिकथन or पर्वपवित्रप्रभृतिप्रभेदि-नैमित्तिककर्म[6]	निमित्तज बहुभित्पर्वपवि-त्रादि	१. नैमित्तिकविभाग[4]	२८.६
				२. नैमित्तिकप्रयोजनविधि	२८.९
				३. पर्वभेद	२८.१०
				४. पर्वभेदविशेषX	२८.३१
				५. चक्रचर्चा[5]	२८.६०
				६. चक्रार्चन	२८.७६

1. Also described as अनुयागविधि in later Āhnikas vide T.A. 28. 60; 29. 175 and 29.178.
2. Ibid. 1.319
3. Ibid. 1.319-20
4. Ibid. 1.320-323
5. Jayaratha inserts two more ancillary topics—one Pavitrakavidhi after the 6th and the other, i.e. तीर्थायतनचर्चा after the 8th topic. See discussion below.
6. नैमित्तिककर्म begins.

1	2	3	4	5	6
				७. गुर्वाद्यन्तदिनाद्यर्चाप्रयोजन-निरूपण[1]X	२८.१९२
				८. मृतिपरीक्षा	२८.२१६
				९. योगीशीमेलकादिविधि	२८.३७१
				१०. व्याख्याविधि	२८.३८५
				११. श्रुतविधि	२८.३९५
				१२. गुरुपूजाविधि	२८.४२३
एकोनत्रिंश	रहस्यविधि-प्रकाशन	रहस्यविध्यभिधान or रहस्यविधिपरिचर्चा	रहस्यचर्या	१. अधिकारिभेद[2]	२९.२
				२. सिद्धपत्नीकुलक्रम	२९.२९
				३. अर्चाविधि	२९.५६
				४. दौतविधि	२९.९६
				५. रहस्योपनिषत्क्रमX	२९.१६९
				६. दीक्षाविधि	२९.१८६
				७. अभिषेक	२९.२२५
				८. वेध (दीक्षा)[3]	२९.२३६

1. Jayaratha explains it as गुर्वादिजन्मदीक्षाप्रायणादिना अर्चाप्रयोजनादिनिरूपणम्. T.A.V., XI, p. 85

2. T.A. 1.323-24

3. Read वेध for बोध in the Kārikā.

1	2	3	4	5	6
त्रिंश	मन्त्रादिप्रकाशन	त्रिककुलक्रमयोगिमन्त्र-कदम्बकनिरूपण or मन्त्रविद्यादिस्वरूपोपवर्णन	मन्त्रौघ	१. मन्त्रस्वरूप[1]	३०.४
				२. मन्त्रवीर्य	३०.२१
एकत्रिंश	मण्डलप्रकाशन	मण्डलसद्भावसंक्षेपा-भिधान or मण्डलविधिकथन	मण्डल	१. शूलाब्जभेद[2]X	३१.७
				२. व्योमेशस्वस्तिकादिनिरूपण	३१.१३२
द्वात्रिंश	मुद्राप्रकाशन	मुद्रासंप्रकाशन or मुद्राविधिकथन	मुद्रिकादिविधि[3]	१. गुणप्रधानताभेद[4]	३२.४
				२. स्वरूप	३२.१०
				३. वीर्यचर्चन	३२.६३
				४. कालभेद[5]	३२.६६
त्रयस्त्रिंश	एकीकारप्रकाशन	चक्रभेदैकीकारनिरूपण or शास्त्रार्थैकीकारोदय	एकीकार[6]		
चतुस्त्रिंश	[7]	स्वस्वरूपप्रवेशकथन	स्वस्वरूपप्रवेश		

1. T.A. 1.325
2. Ibid. 1.325-26
3. मुद्रा is necessary for काम्य कर्म which, however, is not discussed by the *Tantrāloka*. Cf. T.A. 32.8
4. Ibid. 1.326-27
5. Read कालभेद for कलाभेद in T.A. 1.327
6. From here onwards the distinction between primary and secondary topics disappears. In a sense, only the general issues are now discussed. As such, the commencement of ancillary issues has not been indicated.
7. Jayaratha's colophon does not indicate any title for this Āhnika.

1	2	3	4	5	6
पंचत्रिंश	शास्त्रसंमेलन	समस्तशास्त्रमेलनकथा	शास्त्रमेलन		
षट्त्रिंश	आयातिक्रम-निरूपण	शास्त्रायातिकथन	आयाति		
सप्तत्रिंश	उपादेयभावादि-निरूपण	उपादेयभावनिर्णय	उपादेयभाव		

(e) TREATMENT OF ANCILLARY TOPICS

Even a cursory perusal of the above chart indicates that Abhinavagupta has been very thorough and exact in the handling of his treatise. Yet there seem to have happened certain modifications to his original scheme as we proceed with the actual treatment. As usual Jayaratha is a great help at such places. According to Abhinavagupta the ancillary topics under Āṇavopāya (Vth Āhnika) are seven in number. While subscribing to the scheme of Abhinavagupta, Jayaratha suggests that these seven items may be easily grouped under four Prameyas (topics) namely Uccāra, Dhyāna, Karaṇa and Varṇa. However, after the fourth Prameya or ancillary topic as discussed in the 5th Āhnika, Abhinavagupta undertakes to discuss the 5th Prameya called Sthānaprakalpa[1] in the sixth Āhnika which also focusses on other aspects of Āṇavopāya.

In the 7th Āhnika, the second ancillary topic i.e., Mantravidyābheda, is purportedly treated as one topic by Abhinavagupta while Mantra and Vidyā both have to be taken separately and understood, consequently, as Mantracakrabheda and Vidyācakrabheda. In the 8th Āhnika the original order of the 2nd and 3rd ancillary items as outlined in the prefatory remark[2] has been reversed in the course of treatment. Thus the 2nd topic, Purasaṁgraha, commences at *T.A.* 8.406 while the third, Tattvayojanā, at *T.A.* 8.204. Perhaps the reason was Abhinavagupta's

1. इदानीमाणवोपायस्यैवाङ्गभूतमुच्चारादिप्रमेयचतुष्टयानन्तरोद्दिष्टं स्थानकल्पनाख्यं परमं प्रमेयं द्वितीयेनार्धेन अवतारयितुमुपक्रमते ।
T.A.V., IV, p. 5

2. परिमाणं पुराणां च संग्रहस्तत्त्वयोजनम् । T.A. 1.294

desire to treat the 1st and 3rd topics in detail and the 2nd in brief.[1]

Coming to the 10th Āhnika one notices that the declared focus of the chapter is on the subdivisions of categories (Tattvabhedavidhi), but Abhinavagupta in the same sequence enters into an elaborate discussion on the subdivisions of regions (Bhuvanabhedavidhi, commencing at *T.A.* 10.151) without openly enlarging the scope of the chapter. Moreover, the fourth ancillary topic, variety of knowing subjects (Pramātṛabheda), finds a specific mention in the prefatory enumeration of ancillary items[2], yet it has not been taken up for a separate treatment by Abhinavagupta later. Jayaratha has tried to justify it as a deliberate omission since subjective variety is inherent in all the preceding sub-topics.[3] Next comes consideration of the twin cosmic passages called word-passage and meaning-passage (Śabdādhvan and Arthādhvan). The former consists of Bhuvana, Tattva and Kalā; and the latter of Varṇa, Pada and Mantra. Abhinavagupta devotes five full chapters and a part of the sixth chapter to the treatment of passage of meaning (Arthādhvan) whereas he spares only part of one chapter i.e., 11th (in addition to certain occasional references in the 6th and 7th Āhnikas), which is avowedly devoted to the treatment of the subpassage of Kalā (one of the three sub-passages constituting Arthā-

1. अथ सकलभुवनमानं यन्मह्यं निगदितं निजैर्गुरुभिः ॥
तद्वक्ष्यते समासाद् बुद्धौ येनाशु संक्रमेत् । T.A. 8.406-7

2. वस्तुधर्मस्तत्त्वविधिर्जाग्रदादिनिरूपणम् ॥
प्रमातृभेद इत्येतत्तत्त्वभेदे विचार्यते । Ibid. 1.295-96

3. प्रमातृभेदश्च वस्तुधर्मादिषु त्रिष्वपि प्रमेयेषु अन्तः प्रतिपदमुक्तः, इति तेन नेह पृथगुपात्तः । T.A.V., VII, p. 207

dhvan), for the treatment of Śabdādhvan. All the three sub-passages of word namely Varṇādhvan, Padādhvan and Mantrādhvan have been subsumed under the third ancillary item called Varṇabhedakrama commencing at the *T.A.* 11.43. The subsequent Āhnikas till 14th do not call for any comment. In the 15th Āhnika two things attract our attention. One, the 28th ancillary topic is introduced as Sāmaya Karma by Jayaratha,[1] while Abhinavagupta takes it as Sāmaya Karma relating to sleep[2]. Two, Āhnikas from 15th to 27th form a cluster dealing with daily rites (Nityakarma) whereas the 28th deals with occasional rites (Naimittikakarma). However, the colophon of the 15th Āhnika in Jayaratha's commentary also hints at inclusion of Naimittika in the 15th.[3] If our understanding of the text is adequate, it offers a fit case for future investigation as to how Naimittika could prematurely creep in at this point. Similarly the tenth ancillary issue in the 16th Āhnika i.e., Mantrasattāprayojanam is a bit confusing. From the prefatory remark[4] it looks like single item meaning 'purpose of the existence of Mantra' whereas in treatment it actually has twin elements, the phrase meaning "existence and purpose of Mantra".[5] In a sense, two simple ancillary issues instead of one complex item would have been far better. But Abhinavagupta prefers it that way.

1. इदानीं सामयं कर्म अभिधातुमाह — T.A.V., IX, p. 245
2. स्वप्नस्य सामयं कर्म समयाश्चेति संग्रहः ॥ — T.A. 1.306
3. नित्यनिमित्तादिबहुप्रकारकर्मप्रपञ्चपञ्चमुखः ।
   पञ्चदशकमाह्निकमिदं व्यपञ्चयज्जयरथाभिख्यः ॥
   T.A.V., IX, p. 285
4. दीक्षाभेदः परो न्यासो मन्त्रसत्ताप्रयोजनम् । — T.A. 1.309
5. एवं मन्त्राणां सत्तामभिधाय प्रयोजनमप्याह ॥ — T.A.V., X, p. 114

As we march ahead we are further confronted with deviations from the original scheme. The 20th Āhnika is titled as Tulādīkṣāprakāśana which actually constitutes the 3rd ancillary topic as envisaged in the prefatory verse.[1] In this verse Antaḥsaṁskāra figures as the 2nd ancillary theme. Abhinavagupta, however, reverses the order during treatment and discusses Tulāvidhi first and Antaḥsaṁskāra later. Jayaratha takes due congnizance of this drift.[2] We come across a slightly different phenomenon in the 21st Āhnika. Abhinavagupta talks of four ancillary topics under this Āhnika in his prefatory remarks[3], but Jayaratha seems to have dropped the 3rd item namely Saṁskriyāgaṇa. In his view the fourth item, Balābalavicāra, immediately follows the 2nd i.e., Jālopadeśa.[4] Perhaps this is the reason Jayaratha does not indicate the beginning of the 3rd ancillary theme. Sometimes Jayaratha adds certain ancillary item not provided for by Abhinavagupta originally. In the 28th Āhnika Jayaratha suggests inclusion of Pavitrakavidhi after Cakrārcana (the 6th Anujoddeśa)[5] and Tīrthāyatanacarcā after Mṛtiparīkṣā (the 8th Anuja). According to Jayaratha, Tīrthāyatanacarcā should have followed the discus-

1. अधिकारपरीक्षान्तःसंस्कारोऽथ तुलाविधिः ।
इत्येतद्वाच्यसर्वस्वं स्याद्विंशतितमाह्निके ॥ T.A. 1.313

2. अत्र च संस्कारस्य अधिकारिपरीक्षानन्तरं समुद्देशेऽपि उभयशेषत्ववचनाशयेन तुलाविध्यनन्तरमभिधानम् । T.A.V., X, p. 212

3. मृतजीवद्विधिर्जालोपदेशः संस्क्रियागणः ।
बलाबलविचारश्चेत्येकविंशाह्निके विधिः ॥ T.A. 1.314

4. एवं जालोपदेशमुपदिश्य संस्क्रियागणस्य बलाबलविचारमभिधातुमाह । T.A.V., X, p. 237

5. एवं चक्रार्चनमभिधाय पवित्रकविधिमभिधातुमाह । Ibid., XI, p. 47

sion on Pavitrakavidhi but since its usefulness is linked with death, its consideration after Mṛtiparīkṣā is only proper.[1] Now both of these suggested ancillary items do not figure in the opening list of Abhinavagupta.[2] In that case Pavitrakavidhi should have commenced at *T.A.* 28.112 and Tīrthāyatanacarcā at 28.247. Abhinavagupta's own style occasionally seems quite complicated. He proclaims to have dedicated the 30th Āhnika to the treatment of Mantras and accordingly he decides on two suitable ancillaries namely Mantrasvarūpa and Mantravīrya. Jayaratha dittoes it by naming the Āhnika as Mantrādiprakāśana. Abhinavagupta himself observes in his concluding remark that he has dealt not only with Mantra but also with Vidyā (i.e. Brahmavidyā) in the 30th Āhnika yet he does not devise any independent Anuja to earmark discussion on Vidyā. It is difficult to say at this stage if Vidyā constitutes another ancillary item, but if at all it does, it should commence with *T.A.* 30.62.

(f) THREE BROAD DIVISIONS OF THE TEXT AND OTHER SCHEMATISATION BY JAYARATHA

Jayaratha offers several insights into the scheme and contents of the *Tantrāloka* from various angles. From one such clue[3] we infer that he visualizes three

1. यद्यपि च अत्र पवित्रकविध्यनन्तरं तीर्थायतनचर्चनमुद्दिष्टं तथापि तत् मरणोपयोगित्वात् तत्परीक्षान्तरुपक्षिप्तमिति न कश्चित् पूर्वापरव्याघातः ।
T.A.V., XI., p. 97
2. T.A. 1.320-323
3. Commenting on the T.A. 6.1 he observes—
अथ शब्दोऽधिकारे। तेन इतः प्रभृति आद्वादशाह्निकं यत्किंचिदुच्यते तत्सर्वं स्थानकल्पनाधिकारेण, इति पञ्चदशाह्निकात् प्रभृति पुनरेतदेव बाह्यस्थण्डिल-

broad divisions of the text, one dealing with the general issues, the other with Upāyas and the remaining with the specific notion of Sthānaprakalpa (a sub-concept under Āṇava-upāya meaning devising or allotting places). The first group consists of the 1st, 13th and 14th Āhnikas dealing with the varieties of knowledge, descent of grace and process of initiation respectively. The second group includes Āhnikas from 2nd to 5th pertaining to specific Upāyas. The third group comprises Āhnikas from 6th to 12th and from 15th to 37th. By far this is the largest group. This does not amount to say that these Āhnikas have nothing else to discuss. It simply means that Sthānaprakalpa sets their predominant undertone. Even here it may, however, be remembered that Āhnikas from 6th to 12th are directly addressed to this item. It merely implies that the discussion on the doctrine of six passages (Ṣaḍadhva) is essentially an offshoot of the doctrine of Sthānaprakalpa which again is a corollary of Āṇavopāya. Although it is not feasible at the moment, for reasons of space, to dilate upon the concept of Sthāna, it may be stated that Sthāna has three varieties—Prāṇa (breath), Deha (body) and Bahiḥ (exterior). Prāṇa is fivefold—Prāṇa, Apāna, Samāna, Udāna and Vyāna. Deha is twofold—internal and external. And Bāhya has eleven varieties in the main—Maṇḍala, Sthaṇḍila, Pātra, Akṣasūtra, Pustaka, Liṅga, Tūra, Paṭa, Pusta, Pratimā and

---

मण्डलाद्यधिकृत्य अभिधीयते इत्याग्रन्थसमाप्तेः प्राधान्यात् स्थानकल्पनस्यैव सकलोऽयं प्रपञ्च इति । T.A.V., IV, p. 2

Though here Jayaratha is quite silent about the contents of the 1st five Āhnikas and also about those of intervening Āhnikas between 12th and 15th, the conclusions drawn above will not appear incoherent when viewed in totality of Jayaratha's treatment.

Mūrti to the exclusion of innumerable sub-varieties. Though Ṣaḍadhva is primarily related to Prāṇavidhi, it encompasses other varieties of Sthāna as well. Perusing through the pages of the *Tantrāloka* one will easily see the logic behind Jayaratha's statement that Sthānaprakalpa constitutes the main undercurrent of almost all the Āhnikas after the 6th excepting the 13th and 14th. This is borne out by two additional factors. One is Jayaratha's observation[1] on the *T.A.* 5.157[2] and other happens to be Abhinavagupta's devising of Sthānaprakalpa as the 2nd ancillary topic (commencing at *T.A.* 15.80) in the 15th Āhnika assigned to Samayadīkṣā where he covers the concepts of Pīṭha, Ardhapīṭha, Upapīṭha, Sandohaka, Kṣetrāṣṭaka, Upakṣetrāṣṭaka etc. These are the items that specially engage our attention in the 29th Āhnika specially from verses 29 to 95. Thus it may be contended that under the overall Sthānaprakalpa-scheme Āhnikas from 6 to 12 are linked with various phases of Ṣaḍadhva and Āṇava Upāya, 15 to 27 are connected with Nityakarma (daily rites) and 28 to 29[3] deal with Naimittikakarma (occasional rites).

Sometimes Jayaratha does not envisage an overall schematisation, but organises the different Āhnikas, devoted to a continued or connected theme, into a loose whole. He, accordingly, unearths an under-

1. स्थानकल्पने इति षष्ठादाह्निकात् प्रभृति वक्ष्यमाणे ।
T.A.V., III, p. 469

2. ध्याने तदपि चोच्चारे करणे सोऽपि तद्ध्वनौ ।
स स्थानकल्पने बाह्यमिति क्रममुपाश्रयेत् ॥

3. Cf. यागादौ यागमध्ये च यागान्ते गुरुपूजने ।
नैमित्तिकेषु प्रोक्तेषु शिष्यः कुर्यादिमं विधिम् ॥ T.A. 29.291

lying relationship between the 6th, 13th and 14th Āhnikas from the point of view of the five Godly functions. Jayaratha points out that in the course of Saṁhāracitratānirūpaṇa (lit., discussion on the variety of withdrawal or dissolution—3rd ancillary topic in the 6th Āhnika) Abhinava takes up Sṛṣṭi, Sthiti and Saṁhāra (creation, sustenance and withdrawal); in the course of Śaktipāta (descent of grace—13th Āhnika) he deals with Anugraha (grace); and in the course of Dīkṣopakrama (commencement of initiation—14th Āhnika) Abhinavagupta undertakes to discuss Tirobhāva (disappearance).[1]

Likewise Jayaratha once again discovers the thematic unity characterising the four Āhnikas from 29th to 32nd. In the Kula system, according to Jayaratha, a scripture consists of four seats e.g., Vidyā, Mantra, Mudrā and Maṇḍala.[2] He no doubt bases his stand on Abhinavagupta's authority. According to Jayaratha, while the 29th deals summarily with all the four seats, the 30th deals with Vidyā alias Brahmavidyā and Mantra,[3] the 31st with Maṇḍala[4] and 32nd with Mudrā.[5] Together they constitute worship according to the Kula process or Kula system.[6]

1. इह तावत्परमेश्वरः पञ्चविधकृत्यकारीति सर्वत्रोक्तम्। तत्रास्य पूर्वं संहारचित्रतानिरूपणावसरे सृष्ट्यादित्रयं दर्शितं समनन्तराह्निके चानुग्रह इति संप्रत्यवशिष्टं तिरोभावाख्यं पञ्चमं कृत्यं द्वितीयार्धेन प्रतिपादयितुमाह।
T.A.V., VIII, p. 215

2. इह विद्यामन्त्रमुद्रामण्डलात्मतया चतुष्पीठं तावच्छास्त्रम्। तत्र मन्त्रमुद्रात्मनः पीठद्वयस्य संप्रदाय उक्तः। इदानीमत्रैव अवशिष्टस्य विद्यामण्डलात्मनोऽपि अस्य संप्रदायं निरूपयति। Ibid., XI, p. 114 (29th Āhnika)

3. इत्येवं मन्त्रविद्यादिस्वरूपमुपवर्णितम्॥ T.A. 30.123

4. अथ मण्डलसद्भावः संक्षेपेणाभिधीयते। Ibid. 31.1

5. अथ कथये मुद्राणां गुर्वागमगीतमत्र विधिम्। Ibid., introductory verse, 22nd Āhnika (T.A.V., XII, p. 303)

6. अथ सर्वाप्युपासेयं कुलप्रक्रिययोच्यते। Ibid. 29.1

(g) NON-ORGANISATION OF THE TANTRĀLOKA INTO JÑĀNA, YOGA, KRIYĀ AND CARYĀ

A striking feature one is not likely to miss is the absence of any division or organisation of the *Tantrāloka's* subject matter on the traditional tantric pattern of Jñāna, Yoga, Kriyā and Caryā. In the opinion of B.V. Dwivedi (as per one of our conversations) Jñāna-Yoga-Kriyā-Caryā division seems to be an old-time phenomenon losing considerable ground in the later era. Even in the later tantric texts proper there are broadly two divisions—Jñāna and Kriyā, the latter incorporating Yoga and Caryā as well. The problem constitutes an important facet of the tantric historiology, but we refrain from delving deep into it for the time being. It must, however, be said that Abhinavagupta seems to be quite conversant with this division and his occasional references will bear ample testimony to it. For example, in the 16th Āhnika he examines the role of Jñāna vis-á-vis Yoga and Dīkṣā and explores their *inter se* relationship.[1] Ābhinavagupta has devoted one of the several chapters dwelling upon Naimittika vidhi i.e., the 25th Āhnika, to the theme of Śrāddha (post-funeral rites performed in honour of the departed) as leading to enjoyment and emancipation both. Now this Śrāddha is essentially a Caryā phenomenon whose efficacy has been established on the basis of its deriving sustenance from Bhakti.[2] One of the apparent rea-

1. न चाधिकारितां दीक्षां विना योगेऽस्ति शाङ्करे ।
क्रियाज्ञानविभेदेन सा च द्वेधा निगद्यते ॥ T.A. 16.291

2. ननु दीक्षैव भोगमोक्षसाधिकेत्युक्तं तत् कथं श्राद्धाद्यात्मनः चर्यामात्रादपि एतत्स्यादित्याशंक्याह .... अतः श्राद्धाद्यात्मनः चर्यामात्रादेव कथं मुक्तिः स्यादिति न संशयितव्यम् । किंतु अत्र भक्तिरेव दार्ढ्येन आश्रयणीया येनैवं स्यात् ।
T.A.V., X, pp. 323-26

sons for not adopting the Jñāna-yoga-kriyā-caryā pattern lies in the synthetic approach of Abhinavagupta which is manifested in two ways. In one, all the four form a harmonious whole that culminates into Jñāna. It is why Abhinavagupta devotes his opening Āhnika to Jñāna and its varieties. In other, all the three except Jñāna originate from the relatively weeker and feebler descent of grace leading[1] to the rise of different Sādhakas.

IV *Cross-references: a collateral source of thematic organisation*

As already advised earlier in this chapter[2], one very rich source of our understanding the contents of the *Tantrāloka* consists in the cross-references to various Āhnikas and their subjectmatter as appearing in both Abhinavagupta and Jayaratha. This also constitutes a fair basis for the cross-checking of the contents as furnished by Abhinavagupta in his enumeration. A note of caution, however, must be sounded here. Major and minor or primary and secondary items do not indicate the primary and secondary issues as such in the respective Āhnikas. They have been so termed on the basis of their direct and indirect allusions respectively. But on the whole they subscribe to the original scheme of Abhinavagupta. By collating and collecting such references we get the

1. किरणायां तथोक्तं च गुरुतः शास्त्रतः स्वतः ॥
ज्ञानयोग्यास्तथा केचिच्चर्यायोग्यास्तथापरे । T.A. 13.161-62
Cp. ज्ञानयोग्यास्तथा केचिच्चर्यायोग्यास्तथापरे ।
दीक्षायोग्या योगयोग्या इति श्रीकैरणविधौ । Ibid. 15.18

2. Cf. pp. 169-170 supra.

following picture about the contents of various Āhnikas.[1]

(a) First Āhnika

The issues discussed are—

(i) Free will leads to manifold manifestation of the unitary principle without, while retaining its unitary character.[2]

(ii) Variety of Upāyas (redemptive knowledge as a means).[3] It includes the discussion on hierarchical gradation in between Upāyas where out of the four Upāyas (namely Āṇava, Śākta, Śāmbhava and Anupāya) each preceding leads to and culminates into each succeeding.[4]

> This view has been echoed in the 4th Āhnika as is clear from the footnote 4 below. In the 13th Āhnika also the view is reiterated.[5]

1. Our interference has been minimal in the matter. We have taken the liberty of stepping in only when the original author appeared to be mute or vague on certain reference and we found ourselves reasonably sure about the precise whereabouts of the relative reference.

2. एतच्च निर्णीतपूर्वं इति पुनरिह नायस्तम् । यथोक्तम् "बहुशक्तित्वमप्यस्य तच्छक्त्यैवावियुक्तता ।" (T.A. 1.68) T.A.V., I, p. 196

3. उपायस्यापि इति अपिशब्दो भिन्नक्रमः तेन नो वार्या तदन्यत्वादपि इति व्याख्येयम् । एतच्च प्रथमाह्निक एव वितत्य निर्णीतम् इति नेह पुनरायस्तम् । (Jayaratha on T.A. 2.6) Ibid., I, p. 7

4. अनन्तराह्निकोक्तेऽस्मिन्स्वभावे पारमेश्वरे ।
प्रविविक्षुर्विकल्पस्य कुर्यात्संस्कारमञ्जसा ।। T.A. 4.2
अनन्तराह्निक here refers to the Ist Āhnika.
Cp. यद्वक्ष्यति "अनन्तराह्निकोक्तेऽस्मिन् . . . . अञ्जसा"(T.A.4.2)
इत्याद्युपक्रम्य "ततः स्फुटतमोदारताद्रूप्यपरिबृंहिता ।
संविदभ्येति विमलामविकल्पस्वरूपताम् ।।" (T.A. 4.6) इति ।
अतएव हि शाक्तोपायस्य उपायोपायत्वमुक्तम् ।
T.A.V., I, pp. 238-39

5. उपाययोगक्रमतो निरुपायमथाक्रमम् ।
यद्रूपं तत्परं तत्त्वं तत्र तत्र सुनिश्चितम् ।। T.A. 13.157

(iii) The summing up of the theory of bondage and salvation.[1]

(iv) Fifty varieties of Samāveśa (complete immersion).[2]

This aspect has a special bearing on the 3rd and 9th Āhnikas, as we shall see in their respective places.

(v) Theory of ignorance (Mala).[3] Ignorance is nothing but a phase of self-dynamism.

The doctrine of Mala forms a special feature of the 9th and 13th Āhnikas, as we shall see later.

(vi) The ultimate is of the nature of self-luminosity and so is ensuing plurality.[4]

(vii) Means of cognition derive their subsistence from cognizer.[5]

1. इह अस्मिन्नाह्निके (Jayaratha on T.A. 1.330) ।
ययोर्बन्धमोक्षयोः संग्रहेण संक्षेपेण एषोऽर्थः प्रकटितः इत्यनेनैव संबंधः ।
T.A.V., I, p.303

2. निर्विकल्पे परामर्शे शाम्भवोपायनामनि ।
पञ्चाशद्भेदतां पूर्वसूत्रितां योजयेद्बुधः ॥ T.A. 3.274

Jayaratha observes पूर्वेति प्रथमाह्निके । यदुक्तम्—
"पञ्चाशद्विधता चास्य समावेशस्य वर्णिता ।
तत्त्वषट्त्रिंशकैतत्स्थस्फुटभेदाभिसन्धितः ॥ (T.A. 1.186-187)
T.A.V., II, p. 250

3. तेन स्वरूपस्वातन्त्र्यमात्रं मलविजृम्भितम् ॥
निर्णीतं विततं चैतन्मयान्यत्रेत्यलं पुनः । T.A. 9.83-84

Jayaratha explains अन्यत्रेति प्रथमाह्निकादौ, अतएव पुनरित्युक्तम् ।
T.A.V., VI, p. 73

4. तस्मात् प्रकाश एवायं पूर्वोक्तः परमः शिवः ॥ T.A. 10.55

Comments Jayaratha पूर्वोक्त इति प्रथमाह्निकादौ । यदुक्तम् "ज्ञेयस्य च परं तत्त्वं यः प्रकाशात्मकः शिवः" (T.A. 1.52) इत्याद्यनन्तप्रकारम् ।
T.A.V., VII, p. 44

5. इत्यस्य स्वप्रकाशत्वे किमन्यैर्युक्तिडम्बरैः ॥
मानानां हि परो जीवः स एवेत्युक्तमादितः । T.A. 10.116-17

(viii) Plurality of Dīkṣā is due to gradual unfoldment of self-consciousness with the necessary implication that even the most inert is essentially divine.[1]

This view has been enlarged upon in the 16th Āhnika.

(ix) As against the popular notion that Siddhi is attained through observance of time, place and vows etc., it is the feeling of identity with the external objects and reflecting upon them as essentially one with I-consciousness that leads to self-realization. This phenomenon has been termed as Grāmadharmavṛtti.[2]

The 29th Āhnika makes special use of this view in identifying the spritual seat and its presiding powers with I-consciousness.

(x) The entire variety of spiritual cycles (Cakras)

Jayaratha adds प्रत्युत प्रमाणानां तदधीना सिद्धिरित्यादितः प्रथमाह्निक एवोपपादितमित्यर्थः । यदुक्तं तत्र "प्रकाशो नाम . . . . . स एव परमेश्वरः" (T.A. 1.54-55) T.A.V., VII, p. 86

1. इत्थं क्रमसंवित्तौ मूढोऽपि शिवात्मक भवति ।
   यद्यपि विकल्पवृत्तेरपि मोक्षं दीक्षयैव देहान्ते ॥
   शास्त्रे प्रोवाच विभुस्तथापि दृढवासनायुक्ता । (T.A. 198-200)

Jayaratha supplements शास्त्रे इति निशाटनादौ। तच्च प्रथमाह्निकादौ बहूक्तम् । T.A.V., X, p. 76

2. न तिथिर्नच नक्षत्रं नोपवासो विधीयते ।
   ग्राम्यधर्मरतः सिध्येत्सर्वदा स्मरणेन हि ॥ T.A. 29.65

Jayaratha remarks ग्राम्यधर्मरतः इति तद्वृत्तिरित्यर्थः । एतच्च प्रथमाह्निके एव उक्तमिति तत एवावधार्यम् ।

T.A.V., XI, p. 45 (29th Āhnika)

This, in all probability, has reference to—

प्रकाशावस्थितं ज्ञानं भावाभावादिमध्यतः ॥
स्वस्थाने वर्तनं ज्ञेयं दृष्टृत्वं विगतावृति ।
विविक्तवस्तुकथितशुद्धविज्ञाननिर्मलः ॥
ग्रामधर्मवृत्तिरुक्तस्तस्य सर्वं प्रसिध्यति । T.A. 1.84-86

is inform in the sense that they display the aspects of cosmic dynamism.[1]

The 33rd Āhnika is devoted to the development of this theme.

(b) SECOND ĀHNIKA

(i) There is no Upāyopeyabhāva in Anupāya.[2] Hence the problem of bondage and freedom therefrom has no room here.

(ii) Compassion for others is the sole motive force behind the activity of a Sāṁsiddhika (self-accomplished) teacher.[3]

(iii) Dīkṣā (initiation) practically has no role in the context of Anupāya because of the speediest descent of grace.[4]

1. यदुक्तं चक्रभेदेन सार्धं पूज्यमिति त्रिकम् ।
तत्रैव चक्रभेदानामेकीकारो दिशानया ॥ T.A. 33.1

Observers Jayaratha उक्तमिति प्रथमाह्निकादौ । तथा च तत्र "एकवीरो यामलोऽथ त्रिशक्तिश्चतुरात्मकः" (T.A. 1.110) इत्यादि "विश्वचक्रे महेशानो विश्वशक्तिर्विजृम्भते" (T.A. 1.112) इत्यन्तं बहु । T.A.V., XII, p. 337

2. प्राक्तने त्वाह्निके काचिद्भेदस्य कलनापि नो ।
तेनानुपाये तस्मिन् को मुच्यते वा कथं कुतः ॥ T.A. 3.272-273

Also Cp. उच्यते स्वात्मसंवित्तिः स्वभावादेव निर्भरा ।
नास्यामपास्यं नाधेयं किंचिदित्युदितं पुरा ॥ T.A. 4.9

Jayaratha clarifies पुरा अनुपायाह्निके "अत्र तावत्क्रियायोगो नाभ्युपायत्वमर्हति" (T.A. 2.8) इत्यादिनोक्तम् । T.A.V., III, p. 9

3. सांसिद्धिकस्य गुरोः स्वात्मनि कृतकृत्यत्वात् शेषवृत्तौ परानुग्रह एव प्रयोजनम् । यदुक्तं प्राक् "समस्तयन्त्रणातन्त्र .... प्रयोजनम्" (T.A. 2.38) इति । तथा "स्वं कर्तव्यं किमपि ....लोककर्तव्यमात्रम् ॥ (T.A. 2.39)
Ibid, III, pp. 53-56

4. ये तु तीव्रतमोद्रिक्तशक्तिनिर्मलताजुषः ॥
न ते दीक्षामनुन्यासकारिणश्चेति वर्णितम् । T.A. 15.275-76

Jayaratha adds वर्णितमिति द्वितीयाह्निके । T.A.V., IX, p. 136

(iv) Likewise, in Turyātīta (i.e., beyond the fourth) state (which is identical with Anupāya state) there is complete absence of Yoga.[1]

(c) THIRD ĀHNIKA

(i) The notion of Jīvanmukti (emancipation during life-time) becomes meaningful only in relation to Upāyas beginning with Śāmbhava to Āṇava.[2]

(ii) Śāmbhava marks the culminating point of the hierarchy of Upāyas characterized by the vibration of consciousness emanating from object (Artha) up to Prāṇa.[3]

(iii) Twofold purity of consciousness—primary and secondary.[4]

(iv) The three short vowels A, I, U represent three powers of Bhairava e.g., Parā, Parāparā and Aparā that constitute the primary triad (Trika).[5]

1. योगाद्यभावतस्तेन नास्मिन्नादिशद्विभुः । T.A. 10.280

Jayaratha explains तेनेति योगादेरसद्भावेन । यथा चैतत्तथा द्वितीयाह्निकादौ उक्तम् । T.A.V., VII, p. 189

2. इत एव प्रभृत्येषा जीवन्मुक्तिर्विचार्यते ।
यत्र सूत्रणयापीयमुपायोपेयकल्पना ।। T.A. 3.272

Jayaratha remarks सूत्रणयाऽपि इति आह्निकान्तरेषु पुनः स्फुटैव भविष्यतीति भावः । T.A.V., II, p. 249

3. बीजपिण्डात्मकं सर्वं संविदः स्पन्दनात्मताम् ।।
विदधत्परसंवित्तावुपाय इति वर्णितम् । T.A. 7.2-3

Jayaratha observes सर्वमिदं बीजपिण्डात्मकं मन्त्रजातम् अर्थात् प्राणान्तरुदयत् संविदः स्पन्दनात्मतां शाक्तस्वरूपावेशं विदधत् परसंवित्तावुपायः पारम्पर्येण शाम्भवमपि रूपमाविशेत् । T.A.V., IV, p. 2 (7th Āhnika)

4. अनेनैव चाभिप्रायेण पूर्वं "नैर्मल्यं मुख्यमेतस्य संविन्नाथस्य सर्वतः । अंशांशिकातः क्वाप्यन्यत् . . . ." (T.A. 3.9) इत्यादिना बोधस्य तदितरेषां केषांचन भावानां च स्वच्छत्वस्य मुख्यामुख्यतया द्वैविध्यमुक्तम् । Ibid., II, p. 59

5. ह्रस्वत्रयमेव च भैरवात्मनः परस्य तत्त्वस्य शक्तिरूपतया पूर्वं निर्णीतम्,

(v) Mantra, Mudrā, Kriyā, and Upāsanā—all these aspects of worship are simply superfluous in Śāmbhava Upāya.[1]

(vi) A as Visarga and Aṁ as Vindu together constitute Kuleśa and Kuleśvarī (male and female presiding authority of Kula).[2]

These and other allied ideas are again discussed in the 5th Āhnika.

(vii) Rāva (sound) is tenfold.[3]

(viii) Concept of Visarga (emission, discharge) in the esoteric context of Caryākrama i.e., sex-union.[4]

Again this is taken up in the 5th Āhnika.

तदुक्तम् "अतः षण्णां त्रिकं सारं चिदिष्युन्मेषणात्मकम् ।
तदेव त्रितयं प्राहुः भैरवस्य परं महः ॥' (T.A. 3.192)

Ibid., II, p. 233

1. अत्र शांभवोपाये काश्चन मन्त्रमुद्राक्रियोपासा न ततः पूर्णाहन्तापरामर्शादन्याः .... । वक्ष्यति च "स्नानं व्रतं ... कापि नात्र भेदेन युज्यते ।" (T.A. 3.289-90) T.A.V., II, p. 247

2. अं अ इति कुलेश्वर्या सहितो हि कुलेशिता । T.A. 5.68

Jayaratha adds यदुक्तम्

"अत्र प्रकाशमात्रं यत्स्थिते धामत्रये सति ।
उक्तं बिन्दुतया शास्त्रे शिवबिन्दुरसौ मतः ॥" (T.A. 3.134)

इति । "अस्यान्तर्विसिसृक्षासौ या प्रोक्ता कौलिकी परा ।
सैव क्षोभवशादेति विसर्गात्मकतां ध्रुवम् ॥" (T.A. 3.137)

इति च । T.A.V., V, pp. 373-74

3. श्रीब्रह्मयामले चोक्तं श्रीमान् रावो दशात्मकः ॥ T.A. 5.97

Jayaratha explains एतच्च प्राक् "तस्य प्रत्यवमर्शो...स्थूलसूक्ष्मपरत्वतः (T.A. 2.235-37) इत्यादिना "तत्परं त्रितयं...परचिदात्मकः । (T.A. 3.248) इत्यन्तेन निर्णीतप्रायम् इति तत एवैतत्सतत्त्वमवधारणीयम् ।

T.A.V., III, p. 409

4. The T.A. 5.124 and 142 refer to the T.A. 3.144 and 167 respectively. See T.A.V., III, pp. 433 and 458.

(ix) The wordy flow of consciousness consists of 81 letters.[1]

> This is also taken up in detail in the 6th and 33rd Āhnikas.

The subordinate topics, which otherwise constitute major topics in the other Āhnikas, discussed here include—

(1) Twelve Kālikās (IVth Āhnika),
(2) inclusion of 81 letters in 50 letters (6th Āhnika),
(3) absence of the hierarchy of Upāyas in Anupāya (2nd Āh.), and
(4) 50 varieties of Samāveśa (9th Āhnika).

(d) Fourth Āhnika

(i) Twelvefold rise of the ultimate principle called Parama Śiva and manifold appurtenant doctrines.[2] These twelve manifestations technically go by the name of twelve Kālīs.[3-4]

1. ननु अखण्डैकघनाकारे अत्र कुतस्त्यम् आनन्त्यम् इत्याशंक्याह—
विश्वमेकपरामर्शसहत्वात्प्रभृति स्फुटम् ।
अंशांशिकापरामर्शान् पर्यन्ते सहते यतः ॥
अतः पञ्चाशदैकात्म्यं स्वरव्यक्तिविरूपता ।
वर्गाष्टकं वर्णभेद एकाशीति कलोदयः ॥
इति प्रदर्शितं पूर्वम् . . . . । T.A. 33.25-27

Explains Jayaratha पूर्वमिति तृतीयषष्ठाह्निकादौ । T.A.V., XII, p. 348

2. एतच्च (परमशिवस्य द्वादशधा उदयः) बहुप्रघट्टकवक्तव्यम् इति शाक्तोपायाह्निक एव वितत्य विचारयिष्यते इति नेहायस्तम् । T.A.V., I, p. 152

3. एतच्च (द्वादश काल्यः) शाक्तोपायाह्निक एव वितत्य विचारयिष्यते इति नेहायस्तम् । Ibid., II, p. 236

4. एतच्च (द्वादश देव्यः) अनन्तराह्निक एव वितत्य निर्णीतम्—इति न पुनरिहायस्तम् । Ibid., III, p. 336

This issue has been discussed in the Ist, IIIrd and Vth Āhnikas also.

(ii) Akalpitakalpaka type occupies the place of supreme importance amongst all the teachers.[1] Sāṁsiddhika is the chief[2] among Akalpitakalpakas and is identical with Svayambhū type.[3] Sāṁsiddhika is Bhairava personified.[4]

This views is elaborately echoed in the 13th Āhnika also.

(iii) The entire variety of spiritual cycle ranging from trident or the three-spoked to the countless-spoked one.[5]

(iv) Sṛṣṭibīja and Saṁhārabīja (seeds of creation and dissolution), though discussed under Varṇa (un-

1. सर्वाचार्याणां वक्ष्यमाणानाम् अकल्पितकल्पकादीनां मुख्यत्वादेव च तत्संनिधावन्येषां न परानुग्रहादौ अधिकारः इत्युक्तं "तत्संनिधाने न" इत्यादि यद्वक्ष्यति । (Reference is to the T.A. 4.74-76) T.A.V., III, p. 48

2. इति श्रीमालिनीनीत्या यः सांसिद्धिकसंविदः ।
स उत्तमाधिकारी स्याज्ज्ञानवान् हि गुरुर्मतः ॥ T.A. 15.16

Jayaratha adds सांसिद्धिकसंविद इति स्वतःप्रवृत्तसत्तर्क इति इत्यर्थः। यदुक्तं प्राक् यस्य स्वतोऽयं . . . . मध्ये मुख्यः प्रकीर्तितः । (T.A. 4.42-43) T.A.V., IX, p. 11

3. उक्तः स्वयंभूः शास्त्रार्थप्रतिभापरिनिष्ठितः । T.A. 13.135

Jayaratha adds तदुक्तं प्राक् and refers to the T.A. 4.40. T.A.V., VIII, p. 88

4. उक्तोऽनन्योपकार्यत्वात्स साक्षाद्वरदो गुरुः । T.A. 13.158

Jayaratha elucidates यदुक्तम्

यस्त्वकल्पितरूपोऽपि संवाददृढताकृते ।
अन्यतो लब्धसंस्कारः स साक्षाद् भैरवायते ॥ (T.A. 4.77)

T.A.V., VIII, p. 101

5. On T.A. 5.37-38 (एवं त्रिशूलात् प्रभृति . . . . असंख्यारसहस्रं वा चक्रं ध्यायेदनन्यधीः) Jayaratha comments

एतच्च पुरस्तादेव गतार्थं इति न पुनरिहायस्तम् । Ibid., III, p. 346

der Āṇavopāya), are essentially integral to Saṁvitkrama, an aspect of Krama system or Śāktopāya.[1]

The preceding item and the present one incidentally figure in the 5 Āhnika also.

(v) Parity between negation and injunction.[2]

The idea is briefly taken up in the 12th Āhnika also.

(vi) Homa and Laya as part of worship culminate into the supreme subject.[3]

This point has been taken up in the 29th Āhnika also as part of Arcāvidhi in Kulayāga.

(vii) An aspirant of the Samayī variety attains unity with the Godhead if he is steady with his practice of knowledge in tune with his intellectual equipment.[4]

This has specific relevance to Samayidīkṣā in the 15th Āhnika.

(viii) When it is Āgama versus Śruti on a common issue, it is Āgama that may sublate the Vedic injunction.[5]

1. "स्वरूपे निर्वृतिं प्राप्य" (T.A. 5.75) इत्यादिना संवित्क्रमेण प्रागुच्चारः उक्तः सोऽप्यत्रानुसंधेयः, संवित्क्रमस्य सर्वत्रैव भावात् ॥ T.A.V., III, p. 461

2. एतच्च प्रागेव विधिनिषेधतुल्यत्वाभिधानसमये निरूपितमित्यत एवावधार्यम् । Ibid., VII, p. 104 (12th Āhnika)

3. तदुपायायेति मेयमानादिसोपानक्रमेण परप्रमातरि विश्रान्तेरुक्तत्वात् । एतच्च शाक्तोपायाह्निक एव विभज्य उक्तमिति तत एव अवधार्यम् ।
Ibid., XI, p. 63

4. स्वविज्ञानोचितमिति अकृतशिवतत्त्वयोजनिकोऽपि हि समयी तथा तथा ज्ञानमभ्यस्यंस्तदैकात्म्यं यायादित्याशयः । पुरा इति चतुर्थाह्निकादौ ।
Ibid., IX, p. 9

5. क्वचिद्विषयतुल्यत्वाद् बाध्यबाधकता यदि ।
तद्बाध्या श्रुतिरेवेति प्रागेवैतन्निरूपितम् ॥ T.A. 15.178

Jayaratha explains प्रागिति चतुर्थाह्निके । T.A.V., IX, p. 90

Besides, the minor issues, though forming major topics elsewhere, discussed in the 4th Āhnika, include—

(1) The rise of intuitive knowledge (Prātibhajñāna) due to Śuddhā Vidyā (13th Āhnika),

(2) *inter se* relationship between the Upāyas (in the first seven Āhnikas),

(3) Anupāya lacking the Upāya character (2nd Āhnika),

(4) among Pralayākala subjects some become Mantra subjects by transcending the impure order and some continue to remain transmigratory (9th Āhnika),

(5) Pallī, Ghara, Chummā etc. (29th Āhnika), and

(6) observance of Samayācāra (15th Āhnika).

(e) FIFTH ĀHNIKA

(i) Because of subsidiary divisions there are infinite modes of Āṇavopāya.[1]

(ii) The host of practices like initiation etc., are subsumed under Āṇavopāya.[2]

> Initiatory practices are specially dealt with in the 15th Āhnika.

(iii) Expansion and contraction constitute the es-

1. क्रियोपायेऽभ्युपायानां ग्राह्यबाह्यविभेदिनाम् ।
भेदोपभेदवैविध्यान्निःसंख्यत्वमवान्तरात् ॥ T.A. 1.164

2. दीक्षादिर्विचित्रः कर्मकलापः भावी वक्ष्यमाणः आणवेऽन्तर्भविष्यति ।
T.A.V., I, p. 249

The above-noted statement is a remark by Jayaratha on T.A. 1.231—

........भेदोपायं तदाणवम् ॥
अन्ते ज्ञानेऽत्र सोपायं समस्तः कर्मविस्तरः ॥
प्रस्फुटेनैव रूपेण भावी सोऽन्तर्भविष्यति ॥

sence of dynamic principle called Mahāpīṭha (great seat) manifesting as creation and withdrawal.[1]

The subordinate items discussed include—

(1) The notion of Kuleśī (3rd Āhnika),
(2) sound (Rāva) is tenfold (3rd Āhnika),
(3) concept of Visarga (emission) as linked with Liṅgasamāpatti (grasp of phallus or sign)—(3rd Āhnika),
(4) ecstatic murmur or sigh also marks the initial stage of meditational trance[2] (3rd Āhnika),
(5) the virility of Mantra finally rests in the principle of consciousness (8th Āhnika),
(6) *inter se* hierarchy of Upāyas (3rd-5th Āhnikas), and
(7) Karaṇas (11th, 15th, 16th, 29th and 32nd Āhnikas).

(f) Sixth Āhnika

(i) The ultimate power, which is one with Śiva,

1. Vide मूलाभिधमहापीठसंकोचप्रविकासयोः ॥
ब्रह्माद्यनाश्रितान्तानां चिनुते सृष्टिसंहृती । T.A. 6.186-7
Jayaratha adds "रासभी बडवा यद्वत्" (T.A. 5.58) इत्यादिप्रागुक्तयुक्त्या
जन्माधारोदितायाः शक्तेयौं संकोचविकासौ तौ. . ।
T.A.V., I, p. 151
The verses under reference read—
रासभी बडवा यद्वत्स्वधामानन्दमन्दिरम् ॥
विकाससंकोचमयं प्रविश्य हृदि हृष्यति ।
तद्वन्मुहुर्लीनसृष्टभावव्रातसुनिर्भराम् ॥
श्रयेद्विकाससंकोचरूढभैरवयामलाम् । T.A. 5.58-60

2. सुखसीत्कारसत्सम्यक्साम्यप्रथमसंविदः ।
संवेदनं हि प्रथमं स्पर्शोऽनुत्तरसंविदः ॥ T.A. 5.142
Jayaratha connects it with the 3rd Āhnika. Says he यदुक्तं प्राक्
क्षोभाद्यन्तविरामेषु तदेव परमामृतम् ।
सीत्कारसुखसद्भावसमावेशसमाधिषु ॥ (T.A. 3.167)
T.A.V., III, pp. 457-58

consists of eightyone letters when reckoned by half Mātrās.[1] The determinate thought marked by contemplation of 81 letters is conducive to the attainment of one's ultimate essence called Śiva.[2]

These eightyone letter are included within standard fifty letters of Nāgarī alphabet. This is dealt with in the 3rd and 7th Āhnikas. In fact this is a common theme of the 3rd and 6th Āhnikas.[3]

(ii) The sixfold division of the root passage (Ṣaḍadhva) is nothing but a vibration of the Godly dynamism.[4]

This has reference to the 7th and 11th Āhnikas as well.

1. अतएव चार्धमात्रागणनाक्रमेण एकाशीतिपदापि देवी वर्णपञ्चाशत्येवान्तर्भावयिष्यते, इत्याह—

एकाशीतिपदा देवी ह्यत्रान्तर्भावयिष्यते ॥' (T.A. 3.197)

अत्रान्तर्भावयिष्यते इति—एतन्निष्ठतयैव पर्यवसाययिष्यते, यद्वक्ष्यति—

"कालोऽर्धमात्राः. . . . . . . .तु लॄ ॥

एकाशीतिमिमामर्धमात्राणामाह नो गुरुः ॥

यद्वशाद्भगवानेकाशीतिकमन्त्रमभ्यधात् ॥

. . . . .शिवात्मिका । (T.A. 6.225-27)

T.A.V., II, p. 190

2. एकाशीतिपदोदारशक्त्यामर्शात्मकस्ततः ॥

विकल्पः शिवतादायी पूर्वमेव निरूपितः । T.A. 7.37-38

Although Jayaratha is silent here, Abhinava's 'पूर्वमेव' obviously refers to T.A. 6.228-230 which reads—

तथा तथा परामर्शशक्तिचक्रेश्वरः प्रभुः । . . . . . .

एकाशीतिपदोदारविमर्शक्रमबृंहित : ॥

3. . . . .एकाशीतिकलोदयः । इति प्रदर्शितपूर्वम् . . . . . . ।

T.A. 33.27

Jayaratha adds पूर्वमिति तृतीयषष्ठाह्निकादौ । T.A.V., XII, p. 348

4. तत्र शक्तिपरिस्पन्दस्तावान् प्राक् च निरूपितः ॥ T.A. 11.50

Jayaratha adds यश्चायं षोढाध्वविभागः स पूर्वस्तच्छक्तिपरिस्पन्द एवेत्युक्तं प्राग्बहुशः । T.A.V., VIII, p. 41 (11th Āhnika). Jayaratha's 'बहुशः' implies the 6th and 7th Āhnikas also in addition to the 11th.

(iii) All these passages find their final repose in consciousness[1] or Prāṇa (breath).[2]

This view is echoed in the 7th, 8th and 10th Āhnikas.

(iv) Tuṭi has four parts.[3]

(v) First three phases of cosmic functionalism known as creation, sustenance and withdrawal.[4]

This is in contrast with the 14th and 13th Āhnikas dealing respectively with the fourth and fifth function i.e., Tirobhāva and Anugraha.

(vi) The great creation of Śākta order, and the three eggs as compared to the great creation.[5]

1. अध्वा समस्त एवायं चिन्मात्रे संप्रतिष्ठितः । T.A. 8.4

2. सर्वाध्वनः पदं प्राणः संकल्पोऽवगमात्मकः । T.A. 10.254

Jayaratha comments सर्वाध्वनः पदमिति स्थानम् यथा चैतत्तथा षष्ठाह्निक एव निर्णीतम् । T.A.V., VII, p. 173. Also vide—ननु प्राक् 'अन्तः संविदि सर्वोऽयमध्वा विश्रम्य तिष्ठति' (T.A. 6.28) इति प्रतिज्ञातं तत्कथमिह कालाध्वनः प्राण एवैवं प्रतिष्ठितत्वमुच्यते इत्याशंक्याह—'इत्येष कालविभवः प्राण एव प्रतिष्ठितः ॥' (T.A. 7.62)

T.A.V., IV, p. 49 (7th Āh.)

3. समस्तेऽर्थे निर्ग्राह्ये तुटयः षोडश क्षणाः ॥
षट्त्रिंशदङ्गुले चारे सांशद्व्यङ्गुलकल्पिताः । T.A. 10.187-88

Jayaratha adds सांशेति सचतुर्भागेत्यर्थः । यदुक्तम्,
"तुटिः सपादाङ्गुलयुक्प्राणः . . . . । (T.A., 6.64)
T.A.V., V, pp. 129-30

4. तत्रास्य पूर्वं संहारचित्रतानिरूपणावसरे सृष्ट्यादित्रयं दर्शितं समनन्तराह्निके चानुग्रह इति संप्रत्यवशिष्टं तिरोभावाख्यं पंचमं कृत्यं द्वितीयार्धेन प्रतिपादयितुमाह । T.A.V., VIII, p. 215

5. सृष्टिसंस्थितिसंहारान्विधत्तेऽवान्तरस्थितीन् ।
महासर्गे पुनः सृष्टिसंहारानन्त्यशालिनि ॥ T.A. 14.3

Jayaratha explains अवान्तरस्थितीन् इति शाक्तमहासृष्ट्याद्यपेक्षया । यदुक्तं प्राक् (and refers to कालाग्निर्भुवि . . . . . तस्मा T.A. 6.171-72) महत्त्वमेवास्य दर्शयति सृष्टिसंहारानन्त्यशालिनीति । यदुक्तं प्राक् (and again refers to श्रीमानघोरः . . . . . महासृष्टिरुदाहृता ।" T.A. 6.172-73).
T.A.V., VIII, pp. 216-17

(vii) Kāla as based on Prāṇa is the general theme.[1]

This also forms an important topic of the 7th Āhnika and 28th Āhnika (as identical with Kulaparva as part of Parvabheda under Bhairavakula).

(viii) The rise of Prāṇa.[2]

This has again been discussed in the 28th Āhnika under the ancillary topic called Mṛti.

(ix) The notion of the movement of Prāṇa (Prāṇacāra).[3] Once a Mantra has been identified with either Prāṇa or self there remains no difference between Mantra and its contemplator.

This has been discussed in the 29th Āhnika also.

The minor items include—

(1) Dynamicity is characterized by expansion and contraction (5th Āhnika),
(2) several Aṣṭakas (8th Āhnika), and
(3) twelve Rudras (33rd Āhnika).

1. कुलपर्वेति तद्ब्रूमो यथोक्तं भैरवे कुले ।।
हैडरे त्रिकसद्भावे त्रिककालीकुलादिके ।
योऽयं प्राणाश्रितः पूर्वं कालः प्रोक्तः सुविस्तरात् ।। T.A. 28.14-15

Jayaratha clarifies पूर्वमिति षष्ठाह्निके सप्तमाह्निके च ।
T.A.V., XI, p. 9

2. स इति प्रथमः प्राणोदयः । . . . . . तदुक्तं प्राक्—
सा प्राणवृत्तिः प्राणाद्यै रूपैः पञ्चभिरात्मसात् ।
देहं यत्कुरुते संवित्पूर्णस्तेनैव भासते ।। (T.A. 6.14)
T.A.V., XI, p. 87

3. यो विकल्पयते तस्य सिद्धिमुक्ती सुदूरतः ।
अथ षोडशलक्षादि प्राणचारे पुरोक्तवत् ।। T.A. 29.91

Though Jayaratha is silent, "पुरोक्तवत्" obviously refers to the notion of Prāṇacāra whose treatment commences with the T.A. 6.23 onwards.

(g) SEVENTH ĀHNIKA

(i) It is the power of pure awareness that assumes the form of a Nāḍī.[1]

(ii) In common with the sixth Āhnika it propounds the theme of Kāla as dependent upon Prāṇa.[2]

(iii) The kindling of rise of cycles means the kindling of uttered Mantras.[3]

This forms the special feature of the 32nd Āhnika.

The minor issues involve—

(1) *Inter se* relationship of Upāyas (3rd, 4th and 5th Āhnikas),

(2) propounding 81 letters in the sound-system (6th Āhnika),

(3) final rest of all the passages in consciousness (6th and 8th Āhnikas), and

(4) sixfold division of the cosmic passage (6th and 11th Āhnikas).

(h) EIGHTH ĀHNIKA

(i) Regions falling under Deśādhvan are innumerable and varied which constitute the world.[4] Lack-

1. Commenting on the T.A. 8.283 (पुंसि नादमयी शक्तिः प्रसराख्या च यत्स्थिता) Jayaratha observes यदुक्तं प्राक्

"चित्स्पन्दप्राणवृत्तीनामन्त्या या स्थूलता सुषिः ।
सा नाडीरूपतामेत्य देहं सन्तानयेदिदम् ॥" (T.A. 7.66)

T.A.V., V, P. 194

2. See item (vii) supra under sixth Āhnika.

3. बोधावेशः सन्निधिरैक्येन विसर्जनं स्वरूपगतिः ।
शङ्कादलनं चक्रोदयदीप्तिरिति क्रमात्कृत्यम् ॥ T.A. 32.67

While explaining Abhinava's above verse Jayaratha comes out with the following observation—

चक्रोदयदीप्तिरिति सप्तमाह्निकनिरूपितस्थित्या उदितानां मन्त्राणां दीप्तिर्दीपनमित्यर्थः । T.A.V., XII, p. 335

4. देशाध्ववक्ष्यमाणनीत्या निःसंख्याकत्वादनन्ता नानासंनिवेशात्मकत्वाच्च

ing as it does in essence, it is as good as a dream-abode.

(ii) The virility of Mantra basically rests on consciousness.[1]

This is taken up in the 5th Āhnika as well.

(iii) All the octads (Aṣṭakas) such as eight parts of a day etc., eight deities, eight powers etc. etc.[2]

This is again dealt with in the 9th Āhnika.

(iv) Treatment of the passage called Deśa.[3]

(v) The heterogeneous effects such as intelligence (Mahat) etc., are caused by inequilibrium of Guṇas.[4]

(vi) Not only 'spatial passage' but its subdivisions also[5] owing to difference in Guṇas.

चित्राः अतएव सन्तः शोभना गर्भा भुवना नियस्यैवंविधो यः संसारस्तत्तत्तत्त्वात्मा विश्वस्फारः स एवासारत्वात् स्वप्नसद्म । Ibid., II, p. 257

1. तत्र विश्रान्तिमागच्छेद्यद्वीर्यं मन्त्रमण्डले ।
शान्त्यादिसिद्धयस्तत्तद्रूपतादात्म्यतो यतः ॥ T.A. 5.82

Jayaratha observes संविद्विश्रान्तिमन्तरेण हि न किंचिदेव भवेदिति भावः । यद्वक्ष्यति—'यत्तत्र नहि विश्रान्तं तन्नभः कुसुमायते ।' (T.A. 8.3)
T.A.V., II, p. 393

2. एते च सर्वं एवाष्टका भुवनाध्वनि वक्ष्यन्ते इति तत एवावधार्याः इति किं तद्व्यावर्णनग्रन्थविस्तरेण । Ibid., IV, p. 62

3. तत्पदमन्त्रवर्णात्मना त्रिप्रकारः कालाध्वा विचारितः इति तदानन्तर्येण युक्तं देशाध्वनोऽत्र निरूपणम् इत्यत एव क्रमेण भुवनतत्त्वकलाप्रतिपादकं वक्ष्यमाणमाह्निकचतुष्टयम् । Ibid., V, p. 2

According to this, the 8th Āh. will deal with regions of space, the 9th and 10th with categories and the 11th with Kalās.

4. कार्यमिति महदादि विजातीयमिति गुणानां वैषम्यात् । इत्येतच्च पुरा भुवनाध्वनिरूपणावसरे एवोक्तम् इति न पुनरिहायस्तम् । Ibid., VI, p. 179

5. भुवनं पृगथेवात्र दर्शितं गुणभेदतः । T.A. 9.224

Jayaratha remarks अत्र च ग्रन्थिवत् भुवनविभागोऽपि पूर्वमेव दर्शितः . . . . तदुक्तं प्राक्—

'क्रमात् तमोरजःसत्त्वे गुरूणां पङक्तयः स्थिताः ।
तिस्रो द्वात्रिंशदेकातस्त्रिंशदप्येकविंशतिः ॥' (T.A. 8.260-261)
T.A.V., VI, p. 180

This issue is relevant to the 9th Āhnika also.

(vii) The theme of Deśa, together with that of categories and Kalās, is objective in character.[1]

Tattva and Kalā discussed respectively in the 9-10th and 11th Āhnikas share the objective character of Deśa while the passages of Pada, Mantra and Varṇa partake of the subjective character and are treated in the later part of the 11th Ahnika.

(viii) The concept of Vidyāpadma[2] (lotus consisting of Śuddhavidyā—pure knowledge) which is below Brahmarandhra and also the trans-Māyā region of Brahmā.[3]

These types have been dealt with again in the 15th Āhnika.

(ix) Under the nine types of 'piercing' (Vedha), the 'piercing' relating to regions.[4]

This is in fact one of the major constituents of the last ancillary topic under Rahasyaprakriyā in the 29th Āhnika.

The minor items include—

(1) Incidental discussion of the 'passage of time'

1. मेयभागगतः प्रोक्तः पुरतत्त्वकलात्मकः ।
अधुना मातृभागस्थं रूपं त्रेधा निरूप्यते ॥ T.A. 11.431

Jayaratha explains प्रोक्तः प्रोक्त इत्यष्टमाह्निकात् प्रभृति ।
T.A.V., VII, p. 36

2. विद्यापद्मेऽत्र तच्चोक्तमपि प्राग्दर्श्यते पुनः ॥ T.A. 15.304

Jayaratha adds प्रागिति भुवनाध्वनि । पुनर्दर्श्यते इति प्रतीतिदार्ढ्याय ।
T.A.V., IX, p. 153

3. मायोत्तीर्णं हि यद्रूपं ब्रह्मादीनां पुरोदितम् । T.A. 15.308

Jayaratha has the same explanation पुरेति भुवनाध्वनि ।
T.A.V., IX, p. 154

4. देहं स्वच्छीकृत्य क्षादीनान्तान् स्मरन्पुरोक्तपुर्योघान् ।
निजमण्डनिध्यानात् प्रतिबिम्बयते भुवनवेधः ॥ T.A. 29.260

Jayaratha comments पुरेति अष्टमाह्निकादौ ।
T.A.V., XI, p. 161 (29th Āh.)

(Kālādhvan) consisting of Pada, Mantra and Varṇa (11th Āhnika),

(2) individual's power (which is) of the nature of sound designated as Prasarā (7th Āhnika), and

(3) agency as belonging to Puruṣa and not to inert Prakṛti (9th Āhnika).

(i) NINTH ĀHNIKA

(i) All the categories within the fold of Māyā are known through inference from their effects.[1]

(ii) The two types of Pralayākala subjects—some belonging to Mantra cadre beyond the realm of Māyā and others continuing as empirical subjects glued to transmigration—are due to variety of Kārma Mala.[2]

(iii) Kārma Mala is absent in Vijñānākala subject.[3]

(iv) Vijñānākala acts as a ladder to the attainment of Śivahood.[4]

1. इत्याद्युक्तेः तन्मात्राणि इति, स्वकार्येभ्यो भूतेभ्य एषाम् अनुमेयत्वम्। एवम् अनेनैव अनुमानेन मायान्तः सकलतत्त्ववर्गोऽनुमातव्यः। एतच्च तत्त्वाध्वनि भविष्यति इति नेहायस्तम्। T.A.V., I,p. 219

2. ननु समानेऽपि प्रलयाकलत्वेकेषांचिन्मन्त्रत्वम् केषांचित् संसारित्वम् इत्यत्र किं निमित्तम् इत्याशंक्याह—

"एतच्चाग्रे तनिष्याम इत्यास्तां तावदत्र तत्।" (T.A. 4.32)

अग्र इति नवमाह्निकादौ यद्वक्ष्यति "एतत्कार्ममलं प्रोक्तं.....चित्रं कर्मतः चित्राच्च।" (T.A. 9.138-141) T.A.V., III, p. 37

3. प्रकृतं ज्ञानाकलस्योक्तचरस्य यत्। T.A. 9.117

Jayaratha comments उक्तचरस्य इत्यनेन प्रागुक्तं कार्ममलाभावोपपादकं निखिलमेव प्रमेयमनुस्मारितम् अतश्च विज्ञानाकलस्य कार्ममलो नास्ति।

T.A.V., VI, p. 95

4. ननु विज्ञानाकलस्य "निष्कर्मा हि स्थिते .... याति शिवात्मताम्" (T.A. 9.90-93) इत्यादिप्रागुक्तयुक्त्या मन्त्रमन्त्रेश्वरमन्त्रमहेश्वरत्वाय अभिधीयतां प्रबोधः..... । T.A.V., VII, p. 98

Vide also—

(v) The rise of Vijñānākala subject is consequent upon the differentiation between Puruṣa and Prakṛti in the wake of exhaustion of all the deeds.[1]

This is briefly taken up in the 10th and 13th Āhnikas.

(vi) Within the realm of Māyā all the categories from Kalā down to earth differ from self to self.[2]

(vii) Śakti category is the instrument of Śiva category.[3]

This concept has been discussed in the 10th Āhnika in detail.

(viii) Concept of ignorance called Mala.[4]

विज्ञानाकलतां प्राप्तः केवलादधिकारतः ।।
मलान्मुक्ततदीशादिभावमेति सदा शिवात् । T.A. 13.275

Jayaratha connects it with the 9th Āhnika—

यदुक्तं प्राक् "स पुनः . . . . याति शिवात्मताम् ।"

T.A.V., X, p. 169

1. ज्ञानाकलः प्राक्तनस्तु कर्मी तस्याश्रयसंस्थितेः । T.A. 13.274

Jayaratha adds तदुक्तं प्राक् "तदा मायापुंविवेकः . . . . यात्यतः पुमान् ।।" (T.A. 9.185) T.A.V., VII, p. 168

2. कलादिवसुधान्तं यन्मायान्तः संप्रचक्षते ।।
प्रत्यात्मभिन्नमिवैतत् सुखदुःखादिभेदतः । T.A. 9.187-88

Jayaratha adds संप्रचक्षते इत्यग्रे । T.A.V., VI, p. 130

अग्रे would mean 'later in the 9th Āhnika itself'.

3. स्वातन्त्र्यमात्रसद्भावा या त्विच्छा शक्तिरैश्वरी ।
शिवस्य सैव करणं तथा वेत्ति करोति च । T.A. 10.17

Jayaratha connects it with the 9th Āhnika उक्तं च प्राक् इति
"तेनाशुद्धैव विद्यास्य सामान्यं करणं पुरा ।
ज्ञप्तौ कृतौ तु सामान्यं कला करणमुच्यते ।।" (T.A. 9.244)

T.A.V., VII, p. 12

4. अत्रोच्यते मलस्तावदित्थमेष न युज्यते ।
इति पूर्वाह्निके प्रोक्तं पुनरुक्तौ तु किं फलम् ।। T.A. 13.53

Jayaratha identifies the Āhnika पूर्वाह्निक इति नवमाह्निकादौ ।

T.A.V., VIII, p. 37

This has been discussed in the 1st Āhnika also, primarily as an offshoot of freedom.

(ix) Concept of specific type of ignorance called Kārma Mala which is relied upon by the self as an instrument to bind itself owing to its intrinsic freedom.[1]

Both of these items vide serial No. (viii) and (ix) figure in the 13th Āhnika as well.

(x) Both, the pentadic system of categories and the triadic system thereof (Pañcatattvavidhi and Tritattvavidhi), originate from the variation in primary categories.[2]

This view is held in common with the 10th Āhnika and is incidentally discussed in the 11th Āhnika.

(xi) Agency belongs to conscious principle called Puruṣa and not to inert Prakṛti.[3]

(xii) Initiation of the dying due to inherent potency of Mantra.[4]

1. स स्वयं कल्पिताकारविकल्पात्मककर्मभिः ।
बध्नात्यात्मानमेवेह स्वातन्त्र्यादिति ॥ T.A. 13.104

Observes Jayaratha कार्मेण मलेन स्वस्वातन्त्र्यादात्मानं बध्नाति तत्तज्जात्यायुर्भोगवैचित्र्येण संसरति—इति नवमाह्निकादौ उक्तप्रायम् । T.A.V., VIII, p. 70

2. इमौ भेदावुभौ तत्त्वभेदमात्रकृताविति ।
तत्त्वाध्वैवायमित्थं च न षडध्वस्थितेः क्षतिः ॥ T.A. 11.36

Jayaratha's remarks अयमिति समनन्तराह्निकद्वयोक्तः । [T.A.V., VII, p. 32 (11th Āhnika)] precisely implies immediately preceding 9th and 10th Āhnikas.

3. एतच्च समनन्तराह्निके एव साधयिष्यते तत एवावधार्यम् । T.A.V., V, p. 195

4. तत्र त्वेषोऽस्ति नियम आसन्ने मरणक्षणे ।
तां कुर्यान्नान्यथारब्ध कर्म यस्मान्न शुध्यति ॥
उक्तं च पूर्वमेवैतन्मंत्रसामर्थ्ययोगतः ।
प्राणैर्वियोजितोऽप्येष भुङ्क्ते शेषफलं यतः ॥ T.A. 13.236-37

This is discussed briefly in the 13th Āhnika and specially in the 19th Āhnika.

(xiii) There is gradual hierarchy amongst the Vaiṣṇavas, Mantra subjects, Mantreśa subjects etc. Although they all are under the spell of ignorance they mark out the stages of gradual awakening.[1]

This is discussed again in the 10th Āhnika and also in the 35 th Āhnika from a different point of view.

(xiv) That form of deity alone which is dense or compact with awareness and bliss is worthy of being adored.[2]

This theme is shared by the 9th Āhnika in common with the 13th. This again figures in the 26th Āhnika as a part of the residual daily routine (Seṣavṛtti under Nityakarmavidhi).

Among the auxiliary items covered are the following—

(1) Fifty varieties of immersion (3rd and 9th Āhnikas),

Jayaratha comments on उक्तं च पूर्वमेवैतद् as पूर्वमिति नवमाह्निके। (T.A. 9.130-31) यदुक्तं तत्र

"आरब्धकार्यं देहेऽस्मिन्यत्पुनः कर्म तत्कथम् ॥
उच्छिद्यतामन्त्यदशं निरोद्धुं न हि शक्यते ॥"

इत्यादि। T.A.V., VIII, p. 147

1. भावनादिबलादन्यवैष्णवादिनयोदितात् ॥
यथास्वमाधरौत्तर्यविचित्रात्संस्कृतस्तथा।
लीनः प्रबुद्धो मन्त्रत्वं तदीशत्वमथैति वा। T.A. 10.135-36

Jayaratha explains तथेति यथास्वमाधरौत्तर्येणैवेत्यर्थः। वैष्णवादिनयानां च यथास्वमाधरौत्तर्यं पूर्वमेव वितत्य निर्णीतमिति नेहायस्तम्। तदुक्तं प्राक् "ये पुनः . . . . . . च कर्मतः" (T.A. 9.140-41)

T.A.V., VII, p. 97

2. कृत्वा जपं ततः एवं देवतायै समर्पयेत्।
तच्चोक्तं कर्तृतातत्त्वनिरूपणविधौ पुरा ॥ T.A. 26.68

Jayaratha suggests पुरेति नवमत्रयोदशाह्निकादौ। T.A.V., X, p. 352

(2) non-reversal of the deed that has commenced giving fruits (19th Āhnika), and

(3) ineffectiveness of the principle of Kalā (limited action) in the initiation relating to immediate salvation (19th Āhnika).

(j) Tenth Āhnika

(i) The macrocosmic character of the categories beginning with earth etc. due to internal sub-division such as fifteen etc.[1]

This is briefly discussed in the 1st Āhnika.

(ii) Five stages, beginning with waking or Piṇḍastha as the object of Yogins and Jñānins.[2]

This idea is extended to Kulayāga in the 29th Āhnika as well.

(iii) It is through identification with the self that the subject is able to cognize all the objects.[3]

The ancillary issues discussed are—

(1) Absence of Kārma impurity in the Vijñānākala subject (9th and 13th Āhnikas),

(2) graded hierarchy among the subjects such as Vaiṣṇavas, Mantra, Mantreśa etc., (9th Āhnika),

(3) final repose of all the passages (Adhvan) in Prāṇa (6th Āhnika),

1. धरादेर्विश्वरूपत्वं पाञ्चदश्यादिभेदतः । T.A. 1.196

Jayaratha adds एतच्च तत्त्वभेदने भविष्यति इति ग्रन्थविस्तरभयात् नेह आयस्तम् । T.A.V., I, p. 223

2. पिण्डस्थादि च पूर्वोक्तं सर्वातीतावसानकम् ।
अवस्थापञ्चकं प्रोक्तभेदं तस्मै निरूपयेत् ॥ T.A. 29.224

Jayaratha makes the suggestion explicit पूर्वेति दशमाह्निके प्रोक्तभेदमिति योगिज्ञानिविषयतया । T.A.V., XI, p. 143 (29th Āhnika)

3. प्रमाता स्वकतादात्म्यभासिताखिलवेद्यकः । T.A. 10.112

Jayaratha adds स्वकतादात्म्येति न तु मन्त्रमन्त्रेश्वरादिवद्भेदाभेदादिरूपतयेत्यभिप्रायः । एतच्चाह्निकारम्भ एव निर्णीतप्रायमिति नेह पुनरायस्तम् । T.A.V., VII, p. 83

(4) four parts of Tuṭi (6th Āhnika),
(5) success of a means of knowledge as depending on subject (1st Āhnika), and
(6) absence of Yoga in the fifth--Turyātīta—stage (2nd Āhnika).

(k) ELEVENTH ĀHNIKA

(i) The Karaṇa (i.e., instrument, techincally 'conscious practice') of pure awareness.[1] This forms the 6th Upāya under Āṇava-upāya.

This is partly discussed in the 5th Āhnika.

(ii) Comprehensive treatment of Kālādhvan as one of the three sub-passages under Deśādhavan.[2]

The topic has been introduced in the 8th Āhnika.

(iii) Discussion on the three sub-passages e.g., Pada, Mantra and Varṇa, as constituting Kālādhvan (i.e., passage of time or dynamicity) and as being subjective is character.[3]

The idea is initially mooted out in the 8th and subsequent Āhnikas.

(iv) The assignment of Padādhvan (word-passage) in Putrakadīkṣā as ancillary to Śodhyavaicitrya (variety of the items subject to refinement).[4]

1. तथाहि . . . "यत्तु सर्वाविभागात्म स्वतंत्रं बोधसुन्दरम् ।।
सप्तत्रिंशं तु तत्प्राहुस्तत्त्वं परशिवाभिधम् ।" (T.A. 11.21-22)
इत्यादिनैकादशाह्निके संवित्तेः । T.A.V., III, p. 442

2. . . . . इत्यत एव क्रमेण भुवनतत्त्वकलाप्रतिपादकं वक्ष्यमाणमाह्निकचतुष्टयम् । T.A.V., V, p. 2

3. मेयभागगतः प्रोक्तः पुरतत्त्वकलात्मकः ।
अधुना मातृभागस्थं रूपं त्रेधा निरूप्यते ।। T.A. 11.43
Jayaratha supplements प्रोक्त इत्यष्टमाह्निकात्प्रभृति ।
T.A.V., VII, p. 36

4. अपरादिविधित्रैतादथ न्यासः पदाध्वनः ।
पूर्वं दशपदी चोक्ता स्वतन्त्रा न्यस्यते यदा ।। T.A. 16.132

(v) Same is the case with the assignment of Mantrādhvan (Mantra-passage).[1]

> These two items figure in the 16th Āhnika as well.

(vi) Sixfold division of the passages is nothing but the vibration of power.[2]

> This is mainly discussed in the 6th and 7th Āhnikas.

(vii) The notion of gradual purification of the passages (Adhvaśuddhi) as derived from the *Svacchandatantra*.[3]

> Its non-sequential counterpart is taken up in the 18th Āhnika.

The ancillary issues treated include the pentadic and the triadic systems of categories (9th and 10th Āhnikas).

(1) TWELFTH ĀHNIKA

The Āhnika primarily aims at bringing out the utility of Adhvans. However, during discussions no major item has been pointed out either by Abhinava-

---

Jayaratha explains पूर्वमिति as एकादशाह्निकादौ । T.A.V., X, p. 55

1. मन्त्राध्वनोऽप्येष एव विधिर्विन्यासयोजने ॥
व्याप्तिमात्रं हि भिद्येतेत्युक्तं प्रागेव तत्तथा । T.A. 16.138-39

Jayaratha's explains प्रागिति एकादशाह्निकादौ । T.A.V., X, p. 57

2. तत्र शक्तिपरिस्पन्दस्तावान् प्राक् च निरूपितः । T.A. 11.50

Jayaratha's following comment does not explain प्राक् but reference is obvious—यश्चायं षोढाध्वविभागः स पूर्वस्तच्छक्तिपरिस्पन्द एवेत्युक्तं प्राग्बहुशः । T.A.V., VII, p. 41

3. ननु शोध्यस्य षड्विधस्याप्यध्वनः का नाम शुद्धिरित्याशंक्याह । अत्र च . . . तदेतत् . . . सर्वं शोधनमाख्यातं संस्कारजातं श्रीमत्स्वच्छन्दशास्त्राद्युक्तरूपात क्रमाद् भवेत् ।

T.A.V., VII, p. 68

gupta or by Jayaratha. Among the ancillary topics covered is the parity between injunction and prohibition (Niṣedhavidhitulyatva—T.A. 12.14-22) which forms an important topic in the fourth Āhnika.

(m) THIRTEENTH ĀHNIKA

(i) Gradual loss of innate impurity (Āṇava Mala) as invariably linked up with variation in the descent of divine grace.[1]

This is one of the main themes in 1st Āhnika.

(ii) Variation in the descent of divine grace.[2]

The 4th Āhnika too discusses this issue in detail.

(iii) Grace (Anugraha) as the sole cause behind the removal of ignorance i.e., delimitation, and its twofold division into (a) quick and (b) gradual.[3] The entire creation ensues from the principle of delimitation or contraction.

1. तथाप्यावृतिनिर्ह्रासतारतम्यात्स लक्ष्यते ॥
तद्विस्तरेण वक्ष्यामः शक्तिपातविनिर्णये ।
समाप्य परतां स्थौल्यप्रसंगे चर्चयिष्यते ॥ T.A. 1.138-39

Jayaratha remarks वक्ष्यामः । यद्वक्ष्यति—
'तारतम्यप्रकाशो यस्तीव्रमध्यममन्दताः ॥
ता एव शक्तिपातस्य प्रत्येकं त्रैधमास्थिताः ॥'
(T.A. 13.129-30) इत्यादि बहुप्रकारम् । T.A.V., I, p. 179

2. गुरुशास्त्रगते सत्त्वेऽसत्त्वे चात्र विभेदकम् ।
शक्तिपातस्य वैचित्र्यं पुरस्तात्प्रविविच्यते ॥ T.A. 4.37

Jayaratha explains अत्रेति समनन्तरोक्ते, पुरस्तादिति शक्तिपाताह्निकादौ ।
T.A.V., III, p. 41

3. संकोचहानिरूपेऽस्मिन्कथं हेतुरनुग्रहे ।
अनुग्रहश्च क्रमिकस्तीव्रश्चेति विभिद्यते ॥
प्राक् चैष विस्तरात्प्रोक्त इति किं पुनरुक्तिभिः । T.A. 28.235-36

Jayaratha adds प्रागिति शक्तिपातपरीक्षाह्निके । T.A.V., XI, p. 93

The exact reference is to the T.A. 13.114-116.

This point is briefly touched in the 28th Āhnika.

(iv) Two types of descent of grace, namely primary and secondary. The primary is characterised by complete devotion to the Godhead without any desire for fruit, while the secondary is marked by desire for fruit necessarily involving deeds etc.[1]

(v) Due to the unrestricted Godly will the purity of consciousness may be inherited from previous birth.[2]

(vi) The intuitional wisdom, having an all-encompassing scope, arises from the principle of pure knowledge (Śuddhavidyā) alone and does not depend either on guide or on scripture.[3]

This is discussed in the 1st, 2nd and 4th Āhnikas as well.

(vii) Refutation of dualists' position in treating ignorance or impurity as a substance and initiation as an activity and consequent depiction of the pre-

1. अनपेक्ष्य शिवे भक्तिः शक्तिपातोऽफलार्थिनाम् ।
या फलार्थितया भक्तिः सा कर्माद्यमपेक्षते ॥ T.A. 13.118

Jayaratha adds एवमाद्यः परः शक्तिपातो, द्वितीयस्त्वपर इति सिद्धम् । यद्वक्ष्यति—"इदं सारमिह. . . .पर्यन्ते शिवताप्रदः ॥" (T.A. (13.254-256) इति ।
T.A.V., VIII, p. 80

2. नैर्मल्यं संविदश्चेदं पूर्वाभ्यासवशादथो ॥
अनियन्त्रेश्वरेच्छात इत्येतच्चर्चयिष्यते । T.A. 186-87

Jayaratha explains पूर्वाभ्यासो जन्मान्तरीयः इति अतएव चर्चयिष्यते त्रयोदशाह्निकादौ । T.A.V., I, p. 215

3. यद् (शुद्धविद्या)वशादेव अस्य गुरुशास्त्रानपेक्षं सर्वविषयं
प्रातिभं महाज्ञानमुदियात् यद्वक्ष्यति—
मध्यतीव्रात्पुनः सर्वमज्ञानं विनिवर्तते ।
अयमेव यतो याति बन्धमोक्षतथात्मताम् ॥
तत्प्रातिभं महाज्ञानं शास्त्राचार्यानपेक्षि यत् । (T.A. 13.131-32)
T.A.V., III, p. 51

cise role of all the three impurities—Āṇava, Kārma and Māyīya.[1]

(viii) Individuation stems from the Godly freedom which alone, in the final analysis, is the ultimate residue.[2]

(ix) A teacher/guide is to be initiated at the time of the descent of grace.[3]

The method of such initiation has been outlined in the 16th Āhnika.

(x) Introduction of the idea of Liṅgoddhāradīkṣā.[4]

This is the main them of the 22nd Āhnika.

(xi) Modality of Anuttara Dīkṣā as enjoined in different tantric systems.[5]

1. मलो नाम किल द्रव्यं चक्षुःस्थपटलादिवत् ।
तद्विहन्त्री क्रिया दीक्षा त्वञ्जनादिकर्मवत् ॥
तत्पुरस्तान्निषेत्स्यामो युक्त्यागमविगर्हितम् ।
मलमायाकर्मणां च दर्शयिष्यामहे स्थितिम् ॥ T.A. 1.239-40

Although Jayaratha does not offer any clue with regard to पुरस्तात् and दर्शयिष्यामहे, the reference is obviously to the 9th and 13th Āhnikas.

2. स्वातन्त्र्यात्तु तिरोभावबन्धो भोगेऽस्य भोक्तृताम् ।
पुष्णन्स्वरूपमेव स्यान्मलकर्मादिवर्जितम् ॥ T.A. 13.265

Jayaratha observes यदुक्तं प्राक्—
"देवः स्वतन्त्रश्चिद्रूपः . . . . अप्यणुतामयः ॥ (T.A. 13.103-05)
इति । T.A.V., VIII, p. 163

3. इति प्रमेयं कथितं दीक्षाकाले गुरोर्यथा ॥ T.A. 16.311

Comments Jayaratha इतीत्थमेतत्प्रमेयमिहोक्तं यथा येन प्रकारेण काले शक्तिपातावसरे गुरोर्दीक्षा कार्या भवेदिति । T.A.V., X, p. 127

4. लिङ्गोद्धाराख्यामथ वच्मः शिवशासनैकनिर्दिष्टाम् । T.A. 22.1

Jayaratha explains एकेति as यदुक्तं प्राक् and quotes T.A. 13.357-359 vide T.A.V., X, p. 244.

5. सिद्धान्ते दीक्षितास्तन्त्रे दशाष्टादशभेदिनि ॥
भैरवीये चतुःषष्टौ तान्पशून्दीक्षयेत्त्रिके ।
सिद्धवीरावलिसारे भैरवीये कुलेऽपि च ॥
पञ्चदीक्षाक्रमोपात्ता दीक्षानुत्तरसंज्ञिता । T.A. 22.40-42

(xii) The method behind attainment of salvation, even without support from a teacher, by an aspirant who rejoins the system after drifting away under the spell of ignorance.[1]

> Although it is the prime concern of the 23rd Āhnika, the procedure has been detailed in the 13th Āhnika.

(xiii) Principle of agency which also includes total surrender of all Japa to the Godhead which is compact with consciousness and bliss.[2]

> This is held in common with the 9th Āhnika. Incidentally the 26th Āhnika also pays attention to it.

Among the ancillary items the following find special mention—

(1) The hierarchical relationship among the means of redemptive knowledge (Upāyas) (Ist Āhnika),

(2) the great creation of Śakta class (6th and 14th Āhnikas),

(3) absence of Kārma Mala in Vijñānākala subjects (9th Āhnika),

---

Jayaratha says all this has been duly considered in the 13th Āhnika एतच्च त्रयोदशाह्निक एव विचारितमिति तत एव अवधार्यम् ।
T.A.V., XI, p. 252

1. भवेत्कोऽपि तिरोभूतः पुनरुन्मुखितोऽपि सन् ।
विनापि दैशिकात् प्राग्वत् स्वयमेव विभुरुच्यते ॥ T.A. 23.94

Jayaratha adds सन्नपीति प्रागपि योज्यम् । प्राग्वदिति त्रयोदशाह्निकादौ प्रोक्तक्रमेण इत्यर्थः । T.A.V., X, p. 300

2. Jayaratha explains पुरा as नवमत्रयोदशाह्निकादौ (T.A.V., X, p.352) while commenting upon the following verse—

कृत्वा जपं ततः सर्वं देवतायै समर्पयेत् ।
तच्चोक्तं कर्तृतातत्त्वनिरूपणविधौ पुरा ॥ T.A. 26.68

(4) pre-eminent position of the teacher of Akalpitakalpaka, specially Sāṁsiddhika, type and identity of Svayambhū with Sāṁsiddhika (4th Āhnika),

(5) initiation of the dying (Maraṇāsannadīkṣā) (9th Āhnika),

(6) primary ignorance and Kārma ignorance (9th Āhnika) and

(7) Liṅgoddhārādidīkṣā's irrelevance to the seeker of Trika principle (Trikārthin) (9th Āhnika).

(n) FOURTEENTH ĀHNIKA

(i) Initiatory activity is mainly addressed to those who are devoid of knowledge.[1]

The idea finds its echo in the 15th and 16th Āhnikas as well.

(ii) The fourth phase of Godly functionalism namely, disappearance (Tirobhāva).[2]

(o) FIFTEENTH ĀHNIKA

(i) Inclusion of the host of activities represented by initiation etc., in Āṇava Upāya.[3]

This is also a prominent point of discussion in the 5th Āhnika.

1. ज्ञानोपायस्तु दीक्षादिक्रिया ज्ञानवियोगिनाम् ।
इत्यधुनैवास्तां स्वप्रस्तावे भविष्यति ।। T.A. 13.155

Jayaratha adds अधुना आस्तामेवेति शक्तिपातविचित्रतानिरूपणावसरे तत्प्रसंगाभावात् । अतएवोक्तं स्वप्रस्तावे भविष्यति । स्वप्रस्ताव इति दीक्षाप्रकरणे ।
T.A.V., VIII, p. 99

2. इति संप्रत्यवशिष्टं तिरोभावाख्यं पञ्चमं कृत्यं द्वितीयार्धेन प्रतिपादयितुमाह–'तिरोभावस्वरूपं तु कथ्यमानं विविच्यताम् ।' (T.A. 14.1)
Ibid., VIII, p. 215

3. दीक्षादिर्विचित्रकर्मकलापः भावी वक्ष्यमाणः आणवेऽन्तर्भविष्यति ।
Ibid., I, p. 249

(ii) Initiation liberates even those who are neither proficient in knowledge, nor in Yoga.[1]

> This issue has incidentally figured in the 14th and 16th Āhnikas also.

(iii) One of the seven Karaṇas (i.e., conscious practice) under Āṇava Upāya called Vyāpti (permeation).[2]

> The issue has been raised in the 5th Āhnika with reference to other Karaṇas finding expression in the other Āhnikas e.g., 11th, 16th, 29th, and 32nd etc.

(iv) Virility in a Mantra arises not from book but from teacher. Mantra, therefore, has to be well-guarded and discreetly transmitted.[3]

(v) The process of unification (Yojanikā) behind the fetter-burning (Pāśa-dāha).[4]

1. ननु ज्ञानयोगादिवन्ध्यस्य दैशिकोऽपि किं कुर्यात् इत्याशंक्याह
'दीक्षा च केवला ज्ञानं निजापि निजमान्तरम् ॥
मोचिकेवैति कथितं युक्त्या चागमतः पुरा ।' (T.A. 16.299-300)
पुरा इति पंचदशाह्निकादौ । T.A.V., X, p. 122
2. "इह किल दृक्कर्मेच्छाः शिव उक्तास्तास्तु वेद्यखण्डनके ।" (T.A. 15.339)
इत्यादिना पञ्चदशाह्निके व्याप्तेः । T.A.V. III, p. 442
3. ततः सुशिक्षितां स्थानदेहान्तःशोधनत्रयीम् ॥
न्यासं ध्यानं जपं मुद्रां पूजां कुर्यात्प्रयत्नतः । T.A. 26.28-29
Jayaratha explains सुशिक्षितामिति as पंचदशाह्निकोक्तयुक्त्या ।
T.A.V., X, p. 339
4. ततः प्रागुक्तसकलप्रमेयं परिचिन्तयन् ॥
शिष्यदेहादिमात्मीयदेहप्राणादियोजितम् ।
कृत्वात्मदेहप्राणादिर्विश्वमन्तरनुस्मरेत् ॥
उक्तप्रक्रियया चैवं दृढबुद्धिरनन्यधीः ।
प्राणस्थं देशकालाध्वयुगं प्राणं च शक्तिगम् ॥
तां च संविद्गतां शुद्धां संविदं शिवरूपिणीम् ।
शिष्यसंविदभिन्नां च मन्त्रवह्न्याद्यभेदिनीम् ॥
ध्यायन् प्राग्वत् प्रयोगेण शिवं सकलनिष्कलम् ।

According to the original index of the ancillary items of Abhinavagupta this ought to be the proper topic of the 17th Āhnika. However, the relative procedure is detailed in the 15th and 16th Āhnikas. Jayaratha's statement below further implies that the 17th Āhnika is, in a sense, continuation of the 15th and 16th.

(vi) Daily worship of the sacred ground (Sthaṇḍila) as part of the residual or subsidiary functions (Śeṣavṛtti).[1]

Daily worship on the ground is one of the main themes in the 26th Āhnika.

(vii) Method of holding and abandoning the tooth-twig (used as tooth-brush, lit. Dantakāṣṭha)[2] as part of the daily routine.

This method is re-employed in the context of Śivahastavidhi representing other (than one's own) system in the 29th Āhnika.

(viii) Variety of special assignment.[3] This also

द्वयात्मकं व क्षिपेत्पूर्णां प्रशान्तकरणेन तु ॥ T.A. 17.78-82

Observes Jayaratha प्रागुक्तेति उक्तप्रक्रिययेति प्राग्वदिति च अनेन षोडशपञ्चदशाह्निकादौएतद्विस्तरेणोक्तमिति स्मारितम् अतएव एतदस्माभिरपि ग्रन्थविस्तरभयान्नेह वितानितम् ।

T.A.V., X, p. 161

1. अर्घपात्रं पुरा यद्वद्विधाय स्वेष्टमन्त्रतः ।
तेन स्थण्डिलपुष्पादि सर्वं संप्रोक्षयेद् बुधः ॥ T.A. 26.39

Jayaratha supplements पुरा पञ्चदशाह्निकादौ । T.A.V., X, p. 343

2. अनेनैव प्रयोगेण चरुकं ग्राहयेद् गुरुः ।
शिष्येण दन्तकाष्ठं च तत्पातः प्राग्वदेव तु ॥ T.A. 29.195

Jayaratha explains प्राग्वदेवेति पञ्चदशाह्निकोक्तवत् ।

T.A.V., XI, p. 128

3. सामान्यमर्घमात्राम्भो विप्रुड्भिः प्रोक्ष्य चाखिलम् ।
योगोपकरणं पश्चाद् बाह्ययागं समाचरेत् ॥ T.A. 15.180

Jayaratha observes सामान्यमिति विशिष्टस्य वक्ष्यमाणत्वात् ।

T.A.V., IX, p. 91

covers the sixfold assignment (Soḍhānyāsa).[1]

> This is in fact the 13th ancillary item as per Abhinavan scheme.

(ix) Variety of consecrations[2] in the overall context of the assignment of the eligibility of the prospective initiate.

> This constitutes the Ist ancillary topic in the 15th Āhnika (beginning at the T.A. 15.30) according to the original scheme of Abhinavagupta.

(x) External means constitute the gradual process specially for those whose consciousness is not fully awake.[3]

Among the minor issues occur the following—

(1) Initiation's role in Anupāya is insignificant (2nd Āhnika),

(2) procedure for the adoration of preceptorial lineage (16th Āhnika),

---

Obviously the reference is to the T.A. 15.239 where the Viśeṣanyāsa begins.

1. पूर्वेण विधिनास्त्रं च कर्कर्यां विघ्ननुद्यजेत् । T.A. 15.387

According to Jayaratha पूर्वेण विधिना means षोढान्यासादिना which again brings us to the T.A. 15.239.

2. निरीक्षणं प्रोक्षणं च ताडनाप्यायने तथा ।
विगुण्ठनं च संस्काराः साधारास्त्रिशिरोमते ॥ T.A. 15.370

Jayaratha is quite clear साधारा इति सर्वकर्मसु । संवादितं च एतत् स्नानप्रकरणे । T.A.V., IX, p. 188

3. तादृशीं ये तु नो रूढां संवित्तिमधिशेरते ।
अक्रमात्तत्तत्प्रसिध्यर्थं क्रमिको विधिरुच्यते ॥. . . . .
अतएव हि तत्रापि दार्ढ्यादार्ढ्यविलोकनात् ।
क्रियमाणे कृते वापि संस्क्रियाल्पेतरापि वा ॥ T.A. 15.394, 396

Jayaratha adds तत्रापीति क्रमिके विधौ । अल्पतरेति । उक्तं च एतत् प्राक् "क्रियया सिद्धिकामो यः स क्रियां भूयसीं चरेत्" (T.A. 15.143) इत्यादि बहुप्रकारम् । T.A.V., IX, p. 198

(3) single articulation (Ekoccāra) connected with summary initiation (18th Āhnika),
(4) occasional rites (28th Āhnika),
(5) fifty Rudras in the assignment of matrices (Mātṛkānyāsa) (33rd Āhnika),
(6) reconciliation with Brahmavidyā method (19th and 30th Āhnikas) and
(7) Śivahastavidhi (29th Āhnika).

(p) SIXTEENTH ĀHNIKA

(i) One of the seven Karaṇas (i.e., conscious practice) under Āṇava Upāya relating to the cognizer and the cognizable.[1]

(ii) Procedure for veneration of the preceptorial lineage.[2]

(iii) The process of unification (Yojanikā) behind the fetter-burning (Pāśa-dāha) in common with the 15th and 17th Āhnikas.

(iv) The alternative course of the assignment of dagger etc. (Kṣurikādinyāsa) in the allied view where the offering of oblation is permissible (as against the regular course under initiation pertaining to the instantaneous passing away—Sadya Utkrānti—which has no room for oblation).[3]

1. तथाहि ''अर्थस्य प्रतिपत्तिः . . . . मंत्रसन्ततौ ॥'' (T.A. 16.253)
इत्यादिना षोडशाह्निके ग्राह्यग्राहकयोः । T.A.V., III, p. 442

2. अर्चयित्वासनं पूज्या गुरुपंक्तिस्तु भाविवत् । T.A. 15.320
Jayaratha adds भाविवदिति । यद्वक्ष्यति—
''गणपतिगुरुपरमाख्या परमेष्ठी पूर्वसिद्धवाक्क्षेत्रपतिः ।
इति सप्तकमाख्यातं गुरुपंक्तिविधौ प्रपूज्यमस्मद्गुरुभिः ।'' (T.A. 16.10)
T.A.V., IX, p. 161

3. षोडशाधारषट्चक्रलक्ष्मत्रयखपञ्चकात् ।
क्वचिदन्यतरत्राथ प्रागुक्तपशुकर्मवत् ॥ (T.A. 19.15)

The ancillary items include—

(1) Initiation's effectiveness in occasioning release of the one who is devoid of both knowledge and Yoga (15th Āhnika),

(2) the assignment of Padādhvan and Mantrādhvan (word-, Mantra-passage) (11th Āhnika),

(3) initiation of a teacher at the time of the descent of grace (13th Āhnika),

(4) due to gradual unfoldment of self-consciousness even the inert becomes divine (1st Āhnika), and

(5) the trident constitutes a ring in a collective rite (31st Āhnika).

(q) Seventeenth Āhnika

(i) Assignment of 15 letters in the garland of letters (Akṣasūtra) comprising 115 letters to be followed by assignment of Mātṛkā and Mālinī.[1]

(ii) Modality for refinement of the purifiable categories.[2]

(iii) This, as we have seen, is an extension of the 15th and 16th Āhnikas, so far as unificatory process behind the burning of fetters is concerned.

Jayarath explains प्रागिति षोडशांह्निके। T.A.V., X, p. 189

1. उत्तमे तु द्वयीं न्यस्येत् न्यस्य पूर्वं प्रचोदितान् ॥ T.A. 27.35
Jayaratha explains पूर्वमिति सप्तदशाह्निके। यदुक्तं तत्र
"पिबन्याद्यष्टकं चास्त्रादिकं षट्कं परा तथा।" (T.A. 17.39) इति,
पञ्चदश एते स्युरिति। T.A.V., X, p. 372

2. एवं सर्वाणि शोध्यानि तत्त्वादीनि पुरोक्तवत्। T.A. 29.205
Jayaratha adds पुरेति तत्त्वदीक्षाप्रकरणे T.A.V., XI, p. 133 (29th Āh.). Perhaps it refers to the T.A. 17.7 onwards.

(r) EIGHTEENTH ĀḤNIKA

(i) Single articulation (Ekoccāra) as an ingredient of the summary initiation (Saṁkṣiptadīkṣā)[1].

(ii) The trans-gradual process of pruification of the sixfold cosmic passage.[2]

> In fact out of the twofold refinement, gradual and trans-gradual, the first one adopts the procedure as laid down in the *Svacchanda Tantra*, while the latter follows the course as laid down in the 18th Āhnika.

(s) NINETEENTH ĀHNIKA

(i) Fruition of Ārabdha Karma (deeds whose fruition has already begun) cannot be reversed even with reference to the initiation embarked upon for securing release of the dying.[3]

1. एकोच्चारेण वा बाह्यपरिवारेति शब्दिताः ।   T.A. 15.182

Jayaratha clarifies एकोच्चारेण इति संक्षिप्तदीक्षादौ ।

T.A.V., IX, p. 92

2. शोधनं बहुधा तत्तत्भोगप्राप्त्येकतानता ॥
तदाधिपत्यं तत्त्यागस्तच्छिवात्मत्ववेदनम् ।
तल्लीनता तन्निरासः सर्वं चैतत्क्रमाक्रमात् ॥   T.A. 11.85-86

Jayaratha's observation is significant अत्र च शुद्धिस्वरूपमात्राभिधित्सया क्रमो न विवक्षितः इत्येवमेषामभिधानम् । तदेतज्जन्माधिकारभोगलयनिष्कृतिविशे(श्ले)षोद्धारादिलक्षणं सर्वं शोधनसमाख्यातं संस्कारजातं श्रीमत्स्वचच्छन्दशास्त्राद्युक्तरूपात् क्रमाद्भवेत् । तीव्रतीव्रशक्तिपातवतां च "जननादिविहीनां तु येन येनाध्वना गुरुः । कुर्यात्स एकतत्त्वान्तां . . . . ॥" (T.A. 18.2) इत्यादिवक्ष्यमाणस्वरूपादक्रमाद्वेति ।   T.A.V., VII, p. 68 (11th Āhnika)

3. अन्त्यदशं निरोद्धुं नहि शक्यते इति . . . . सद्योनिर्वाणदीक्षादि पुनरासन्नमरणादेरेव भवेदिति तत्रापि दत्तप्रायफलत्वात् ततः पराङमुखमेव कर्म शोध्यमिति न कश्चिद्दोषः, तदुक्तम्,

"दृष्ट्वा शिष्यं जराग्रस्तं व्याधिना परिपीडितम् ।
उत्क्रमय्य ततस्त्वेनं परतत्त्वे नियोजयेत् ॥" (T.A. 19.8) इति ।

T.A.V., VI, pp. 103-4

(ii) Kalā, the principle of limited agency, fails to produce its fruit in the form of limited doership while maintaing its association with the individual self who has become isolated due to the initiation for instantaneous release (Sadyonirvāṇadīkṣā).[1]

Among the minor issue the following have been referred to—

(1) Two optional views regarding the assignment of dagger—gradual (30th Āhnika) and non-gradual (16th Āhnika),
(2) ineligibility of a non-yogin in respect of physical movement or articulation (30th Āhnika) in the context of the initiation for the instantaneous passing away, and
(3) Brahmavidyā (30 Āhnika).

(t) Twentieth Āhnika

No major issue has been indicated. Only one minor item i.e., 2nd stage of Śakti called Udbhava, which is synonymous with Laghubhāva (lightness), has been alluded to in the context of Tulādīkṣā (the proper theme of the 20th Āhnika) as an item to be discussed in detail in the 30th Āhnika.

(u) Twentyfirst Āhnika

(i) The indirect initiation (Parokṣadīkśā) relating to the dead, termed as redemptive initiation of the dead (Mṛtoddhāradīkṣā).[2]

1. सद्योनिर्वाणदीक्षोत्थपुंविश्लेषे हि सा सती ।
शिलष्यन्त्यपि च नो सूते तथापि स्वफले क्वचित् ॥ T.A. 9.177
2. सर्वेषामधरस्थानां गुर्वन्तानामपि स्फुटम् ।
शक्तिपातात्पुरा प्रोक्तात् कुर्यादन्त्येष्टिदीक्षणम् ।

In fact indirect initiation is of two kinds. One relates to the dead and is an extension of the instantaneous passing away (19th Āhnika) and the other relates to the alive (though dying) and is associated with the ground-rite (Sthaṇḍila Yāga) in the 26th Āhnika. This has a special bearing on the funeral rite (24th Āhnika).

(v) TWENTYSECOND ĀHNIKA

(i) Necessity of an additional course called Liṅgoddhāra (elevation of phallus or sign) for the heterodox who ultimately turn to the fold of monistic Śaivism.[1]

Incidentally this issue figures in the 13th and 35th Āhnikas.

Among the ancillary items Anuttaradīkṣā in Kula (13th Āhnika) has also been briefly touched upon.

(w) TWENTYTHIRD ĀHNIKA

(i) Aspirants of the 'reborn' (Punarbhū) variety[2] i.e., those who though ineligible for Liṅgoddhāradīkṣā are eager to rejoin Śaiva fold.

यत्किंचित्कथितं पूर्वं मृतोद्धाराभिधे विधौ ।
प्रतिमायां तदेवात्र सर्वं शवतनौ चरेत् ॥ T.A. 24.2/5

Comments Jayaratha पुरा इति मृतोद्धारदीक्षायाम् । T.A.V., X, p. 307. मृतोद्धारदीक्षा possibly refers to जालविधि under परोक्षदीक्षा in the 21st Āhnika.

1. ननु यदि एवं शैवबौद्धादिरेव आगमः तत् बौद्धादिशास्त्रवर्तिनां शिवशास्त्रौन्मुख्ये कस्मात् लिङ्गोद्धारादिसंस्कारान्तरमपि उक्तमित्याशंकां दृष्टान्तोपदर्शनेन उपशमयति

यथैकत्रापि वेदादौ तत्तदाश्रयगामिनः ।
संस्कारान्तरमत्रापि तथा लिङ्गोद्धृतादिकम् ॥ (T.A. 35.28)
T.A.V., XII, p. 372

2. साधकाचार्यतामार्गे न योग्यास्ते पुनर्भवः ।
पुनर्भवोऽपि ज्ञानेद्धा भवन्ति गुरुतास्पदम् ॥ T.A. 22.29

It is however closely connected with Liṅgoddhāradīkṣā in the previous Āhnika.

Among the ancillary items is included the method of achieving salvation without preceptorial assistance by one who returns to the fold after having been led astray (13th Āhnika).

(x) TWENTYFOURTH ĀHNIKA

No major or minor theme has been referred to.

(y) TWENTYFIFTH ĀHNIKA

No major or minor issue is found to have been referred to.

(z) TWENTYSIXTH ĀHNIKA

(i) Method or procedure pertaining to Anuyāga (i.e., subsequent or subordinate rite) or subordinate or residual issue.[1]

This is an important item under Kula system (29th Āhnika) and has been discussed under Maṇḍala—one of the four limbs of a Kula treatise i.e., Vidyā, Mantra, Mudrā and Maṇḍala.

(ii) Like body, as above, one should visualize circularity (Maṇḍalātmatva) in breath also. This is again a part of Anuyāga.[2]

Jayaratha adds ते च "पुनर्भूश्चान्यलिङ्गो यः पुनः शैवे प्रतिष्ठितः" (T.A. 23.10) इति लक्षयिष्यमाणाः । T.A.V., X, p. 254

1. अनुयागोक्तविधिना द्रव्यैर्हृदयहारिभिः ।
तथैव स्वस्वकामर्शयोगादन्तः प्रतर्पयेत् ॥ T.A. 29.175

Jayaratha clarifies अनुयागोक्तविधिनेति यदुक्तं प्राक् "यद्यदेवास्य .... शम्भोर्विनिश्चयः ॥ (T.A. 26.55) इत्यादि उपक्रम्य "शिवाभेदभराद्भाव .... अर्पयेद्बुधः ॥" (T.A. 26.61) इति ।
T.A.V., XI, p. 118

2. अथवा प्राणवृत्तिस्थं समस्तं देवतागणम् ।
पश्येत्पूर्वोक्तयुक्त्यैव तत्रैवाभ्यर्चयेद्गुरुः ॥ T.A. 27.178

(iii) Conception of the deities presiding over cycles in relation to those who are given to action.[1]

Among the minor themes the following are alluded to—

(1) Virility of a Mantra solely depends upon its being received from a teacher (15th Āhnika),
(2) daily worship of ground as part of residual activities (15th Āhnika) and
(3) esoteric or mystic rite consisting of throwing away into deep waters (29th Āhnika).

(aa) Twentyseventh Āhnika

No topic, either primary or ancillary, has been taken note of.

(bb) Twentyeighth Āhnika

(i) Samayin's entitlement to the occasional rites (Naimittika Karma).[2] Occasional rites are the dominant theme of the 28th Āhnika.[3]

Though Jayarath does not explain पूर्वोक्तयुक्त्यैव, context makes it abundantly clear that Abhinavagupta is referring to Anuyāga-vidhi.

1. ते तत्र शक्तिचक्रे तेनैवानन्दरसमयेन बहिः ॥
दिक्षु चतसृषु प्रोक्तक्रमेण गणनाथतः प्रभृति सर्वम् । T.A. 29.130-31

Jayaratha adds तेनैवेति अभ्युदितरूपेण । प्रोक्तेति नित्यार्चाभिधानावसरे । T.A.V., XI, p. 94 (29th. Āhnika). नित्यार्चाभिधानावसरे refers to the T.A. 26.38 onwards.

2. समय्यधिकृतोऽन्यत्र गुरुणा विभुमर्चयेत् ॥ T.A. 15.521

Jayaratha explains अन्यत्र इति नैमित्तिकादौ । T.A.V., IX, p. 258.

It may be noted that the 15th Āhnika deals with Nitya Karma while the 28th with Naimittika Karma.

3. यागादौ यागमध्ये च यागान्ते गुरुपूजने ।
नैमित्तिकेषु प्रोक्तेषु शिष्यः कुर्यादिमं विधिम् ॥ T.A. 29.291

Jayaratha adds प्रोक्तेष्विति अष्टाविंशाह्निके । T.A.V., XI, p. 171

This has been incidentally dealt with in the 15th Āhnika and also in the context of Vedhadīkṣā in the 29th Āhnika.

(ii) Kulaparva as part of the variety of Parvans in the *Bhairavakula*.[1]

This is especially connected with the doctrine of Kula as based on Prāṇa in the 6th and 7th Āhnikas.

The ancillary topics include—

(1) Rise of Prāṇa especially under the sub-topic Mṛti (6th Āhnika),

(2) atonement for the violation of rules (Samaya-niṣkṛti) (29th Āhnika) and

(3) congregation or union of Yoginīs (Yoginīme-laka—9th Anuja in this Āhnika and one of the 23 occasionals) (30th Āhnika).

(cc) Twentyninth Āhnika

(i) Supreme utility of semen and blood.[2]

This is discussed briefly in the 3rd Āhnika also.

(ii) Preceptorial identificatory distinctions such as Ghara, Pallī, Mudrā and Chummā etc.[3]

1. कुलपर्वेति तद्ब्रूमो यथोक्तं भैरवे कुले । T.A. 28.14

2. यल्लोहितं तदग्निर्यद्वीर्यं सूयन्दुविग्रहम् ।
अ इति ब्रह्म परमं तत्संघट्टोदयात्मकम् ॥ T.A. 23.227

According to Jayaratha it refers to the 29th Āhnika. Says he
अतएव धामत्रयात्मकत्वादेतदुभयमपि कुण्डगोलकादिशब्दव्यपदेश्यं परं पावनं, येनास्य "....तत्रार्घः शक्तिसंगमात् ।" (T.A. 29.15)
इत्यादिवक्ष्यमाणनीत्या परमोपादेयत्वमुक्तम् । T.A.V., II, p. 216

3. आदिशब्देन च घरं पल्ली पीठोपपीठकम् ॥
मुद्रा छुम्मेति तेषां च विधानं स्वपरस्थितम् । T.A. 4.267-68

Jayaratha adds "घरम्" इति षण्णां साधिकाराणां राजपुत्राणां भिन्नं भिन्नमाश्रमस्थानम् । "पल्ली" भिक्षास्थानम् । यद्वक्ष्यति—"एते हि साधिकाराः ....षट्कं घरपल्लिपीठगं क्रमशः ॥" (T.A. 29.35-39)
T.A.V., III, pp. 297-98

These items have also been enjoined upon for the benefit of the aspirant towards the end of the 4th Āhnika.

(iii) Two Karaṇas (i.e., conscious practice) of relinquishment and projection (Tyāga and Ākṣepa)[1].

These find place in the 5th Āhnika in an overall general context.

(iv) The method of entry into deep waters as part of the ground-rite (Sthaṇḍila Yāga).[2]

(v) The technique of Śiva's hand (Śivahastavidhi) where atonement for breach of rules is also provided for.[3]

(vi) In Kulayāga one should aim at realizing the Absolutic character in oneself by unification of both seat and power in one's body.[4]

1. "एवं त्रिविधविसर्गावेश. . . . मंत्रवीर्यं स्यात् ॥" (T.A. 29.147) इत्यादिना, "यत्र सर्वे लयं यान्ति . . . कालानलसमप्रभाम् ॥" (T.A. 29.182) इत्यादिना चैकान्नत्रिंशाह्निके त्यागस्याक्षेपस्य च . . . .स्वरूपं वक्ष्यति । T.A.V., III, p. 443

2. प्राणिनो जलजाः पूर्वदीक्षिताः शम्भुना स्वयम् ।
विधिना भाविना श्रीमन्मीननाथावतारिणा ॥ T.A. 26.71

Jayaratha explains भाविना इति एकोनत्रिंशाह्निकादौ वक्ष्यमाणेन । T.A.V., X, p. 353

3. समयनिष्कृतिमेव उदाहरणदिशा उपदर्शयति—
यत्स्वयं शिवहस्ताख्ये विधौ संचोदितं पुरा । (T.A. 28.415)
एतच्च समनन्तराह्निके शिवहस्तप्रकरणे एव संवादयिष्यते इति नेह लिखितम् । T.A.V., XI, p. 178

Although Śivahastavidhi is also found in the T.A. 15.456, the present reference is to the 29th Āhnika (T.A. 29.186 onwards) because of the suggestion implied in समनन्तराह्निके.

4. तत्रोक्तमन्त्रतादात्म्याद्भैरवात्मत्वमानयेत् ॥ T.A. 29.22

Jayaratha adds उक्ता मातृसद्भावादयः । वक्ष्यति हि—

(vii) Four Āhnikas from 29th to 32nd constitute the four-seated Kula scripture consisting of Mantra, Mudrā, Vidyā and Maṇḍala. The 29th Āhnika pertains to Vidyā.[1]

These four are the extension of the mode of worship (Upāsanāvidhi) according to Kulaprakriyā.

The ancillary items referred to include—

(1) Movement of breath under 'mode of worship' in Kulayāga (6th Āhnika),
(2) nine divisions of Vedha (8th Āhnika),
(3) method of picking and abandoning the tooth-twig (15th Āhnika),
(4) refinement of categories as per Putraka initiation (17th Āhnika),
(5) method of worship as enjoined in Anuyāga (26th Āhnika),
(6) subdivisions of categories in terms of pentadic states forming objects of Jñānins' and Yogins' experience (10th Āhnika),
(7) Homa and Laya (oblation and repose) as part of worship culminating into supreme subjectivity (4th Āhnika) and
(8) mode of occasional functionalism (28th Āhnika).

"नाहमस्मि न चान्योऽस्ति केवलाः शक्तयस्त्वहम्।
इत्येवं वासनां कुर्यात्सर्वदा समृतिमात्रतः ॥" (T.A. 29.64)

T.A.V., XI, p. 19 (29th Āhnika)

1. इह विद्यामन्त्रमुद्रामण्डलात्मतया चतुष्पीठं तावच्छास्त्रम्। तत्र मन्त्रमुद्रात्मनः पीठद्वयस्य संप्रदाय उक्तः। इदानीमत्रैव अविशिष्टस्य विद्यामण्डलात्मनोऽपि अस्य संप्रदायं निरूपयति ॥

T.A.V. XI, p. 114 (29th Āhnika)

(dd) THIRTIETH ĀHNIKA

(i) The mode of assignment of the dagger etc.[1]

This is especially discussed as the 2nd ancillary item in the 19th Āhnika according to the original Abhinavan scheme. This is again discussed in the 16th Āhnika. In the former oblation is prohibited, while in the latter it is enjoined full scale.

(ii) Brahmavidyā[2]—a special type of Mantra propagated by Bhūtirāja and invoked to secure instant release.

This finds a sepcial mention in the 19th Āhnika.

(iii) Udbhava (rise) as the 2nd of the five stages of power under Tulādīkṣā (20th Āhnika) means lightness (Laghubhāva) consequent upon the disappearance of body.[3]

(iv) Redemption of Mantras which includes two types of the union of Yoginīs[4], one forcibly and the other willingly.

(v) As a constituent of Catuṣpīṭhaśāstra the present Āhnika represents Mantra.

1. तामुत्कृष्य ततोऽङ्गुष्ठादूर्ध्वान्तं वक्ष्यमाणया । T.A. 19.13
Jayaratha explains वक्ष्यमाणया इति त्रिंशाह्निके । T.A.V., X, p. 187

2. अनभ्यस्तप्राणचारः कथमेनां करिष्यति ।
वक्ष्यमाणां ब्रह्मविद्यां सकलां निष्कलोम्भिताम् ।। T.A. 19.24
Jayaratha remarks वक्ष्यमाणाम् इति त्रिंशे । T.A.V., X, p. 192

3. भाविलाघवमन्त्रेण शिष्यं ध्यात्वा समुत्प्लुतम् । T.A. 20.14
Jayaratha observes भावीति त्रिंशे । T.A.V., X, p. 211
The reference is to the T.A. 30.93

4. योगिनीमेलको द्वेधा हठतः प्रियस्तथा ।
प्राच्ये च्छिद्राणि संरक्षेत्कामचारित्वमुत्तरे ।।
स च द्वयोऽपि मंत्रोद्धृतप्रसङ्गे दर्शयिष्यते । T.A. 28.371-73
Jayaratha adds मंत्रोद्धृतप्रसंगे इति त्रिंशाह्निके । T.A.V., XI, p. 157

(ee) THIRTYFIRST ĀHNIKA

(i) Cycle or ring constituted by a trident is necessary[1] according to the *Trikasadbhāva*. Similarly assignment of the trident-lotus[2] is approved by Abhinavagupta following the *Triśirobhairava*.

(ii) In a collective rite the trident-lotus itself constitutes the ring or circumference.[3]

(iii) As a part of the four seated system this Āhnika represents Maṇḍala.

(ff) THIRTYSECOND ĀHNIKA

(i) Description of the seventh Karaṇa (i.e., conscious practice) called Sanniveśa (form, arrangement or deep entry) through unravelling of the notion of Mudrā.[4]

(ii) As a part of the four-seated system it represents the item Mudrā (posture).

Among the ancillary issues the kindling of the

1. मध्यश्रृङ्गं वर्तयित्वा सर्वः पूर्वोदितो विधिः ।
ततो यदुन्मुखं खण्डचन्द्रयुग्मं पुरोदितम् ॥ T.A. 31.24
Jayaratha explains पुरेति पूर्वशूलवर्तनावसरे । T.A.V., XII, p. 235
This has reference to the earlier portion of the 31st Āhnika itself.

2. रक्तैः रजोभिर्मध्यं तु यथाशोभं तु पूरयेत् ।
अस्या व्याप्तौ पुरा चोक्तं तत्रैवानुसरेच्च तत् ॥ T.A. 31.123
Jayaratha adds पुरेति त्रिशूलाभिधानावसरे । T.A.V., XII, p. 281
The reference is to the 31st Āhnika itself.

3. वर्तना मण्डलस्याग्रे संक्षेपादुपदेक्ष्यते ।
आलिख्य मण्डलं गन्धवस्त्रेणैवास्य मार्जनम् ॥ T.A. 16.7
Jayaratha explains अग्र इति एकत्रिंशाह्निके । T.A.V., X, p. 4

4. ....तत्तन्मुद्रास्वरूपनिरूपणद्वारेण द्वात्रिंशाह्निके सन्निवेशस्य स्वरूपं वक्ष्यति इति तत एवैतत्सतत्त्वं स्वयमेवावधारणीयम् । T.A.V., III, p. 443
This probably refers to the T.A. 32.10 onwards.

recited Mantras (7th Āhnika) is the only item that has been referred to.

(gg) THIRTYTHIRD ĀHNIKA

(i) The number of deities in a cycle may vary from those in the other due to intrinsic Godly freedom. In this Āhnika the six-spoked cycle representing six divinities has been discussed.[1]

(ii) Fifty Rudras, the assignment (Nyāsa) on whom helps accomplishment of external worship (Bahiryāga) known as Mātṛkānyāsa. These Rudras are syllabic embodiments of power.[2]

(iii) Similarly, the twelve Rudras from Dakṣa to Pitāmaha have also been discussed.[3]

Among the ancillary items the following have been referred to—

1. षडात्मा इति, यद्वक्ष्यति—
"विश्वा तदीशिका रौद्री वीरका त्र्यम्बिका तथा ।
गुर्वीति षडरे देव्य ..... ॥" ((T.A. 33.2)) T.A.V., I, p. 153

The reading in the relevant printed portion, however, slightly differs as under—

विश्वा तदीशा हारौद्री वीरनेत्र्यम्बिका तथा ।
गुर्वीति षडरे देव्यः श्रीसिद्धावीरदर्शिताः ॥ T.A. 33.2

2. ललाटवक्त्रे दृक्कर्णनासागण्डरदौष्ठगे ॥ ....
इत्येष मातृकान्यासो मालिन्यास्तु निरूप्यते ॥ T.A. 15.117-120

Jayaratha adds एतद्वाच्याश्च पञ्चाशद्रुद्रा एकीकाराह्निके वक्ष्यन्ते इति तत एव ग्रवधार्याः । T.A.V., IX, p. 61

3. प्राणीये वर्षं एतस्मिन्कार्तिकादिषु दक्षतः ॥
पितामहान्तं रुद्राः स्युर्द्वादशाग्रेऽत्र भाविनः । T.A. 6.122-23

Jayaratha explains अग्र इत्येकीकारप्रकाशनाह्निके । T.A.V., IV, p. 106

The reference is to the T.A. 33.8-9 which reads

दक्षश्चण्डो हरः शौण्डी प्रमथो भीममन्मथौ ॥
शकुनिः सुमतिर्नन्दो गोपालश्च पितामहः ।

(1) The alleged division of various cycles is basically one and culminates into Trika (1st Āhnika), and
(2) the infinite ,variety of cycles represented by 81 letters (3rd and 6th Āhnikas).

(hh) Thirtyfourth Āhnika

No major or minor issue is noticed to have been referred to.

(ii) Thirtyfifth Āhnika

(i) All the Āgamas share one essential character that their strength is derived from convention or general consensus (Prasiddhi).[1] This is the reason behind compulsive acceptability of the Āgamas.

Among the ancillary issues the necessity of an additional course called Liṅgoddhāra (22nd Āhnika) has been alluded to.

(jj) Thirtysixth & Thirtyseventh Āhnikas

No issue, whether minor or major, has been found referred to.

From the above account we may conveniently conclude that the Āhnikas 1, 4, 8, 9, 11, 13, 15 and 29 have caught the fancy of Abhinava and Jayaratha

1. उक्तनीत्यैव सर्वत्र व्यवहारे प्रवर्तिते ।
प्रसिद्धावुपजीव्यायामवश्यग्राह्य आगमः ॥ T.A. 37.1

Jayaratha by way of explanation adds इह सार्वत्रिके व्यवहारे प्रवर्तिते पञ्चत्रिंशाह्निकोक्तनीत्या समस्तशास्त्रमेलनेन प्रसिद्धावुपजीव्यायाम् आगम एव अवश्यग्राह्यो न अन्यथा किंचिद् सिध्येत् ।

T.A.V., XII, p. 390

more as compared to the other Āhnikas presumably because of greater importance of their subject matter. Likewise the Āhnikas 27, 34, 36 and 37 have not arrested their attention at all while making internal cross-references.

CHAPTER FIVE

AGENDA FOR FUTURE RESEARCH

At the very outset we pointed out the limitations of the present 'Introduction'. It is at the most an elementary attempt to understand the technique of the *Tantrāloka* by piecing together obvious but scattered indications about its contents, their organic treatment and the guiding norms that characterised the approach of two master minds. An attempt has also been made to enlarge and deepen our familiarity with the environ, contributions, and personal details of the author and the commentator of the *Tantrāloka*. In Indian parlance it offers a Bahiraṅga treatment. It covers only two steps of the ladder—where to study and how to study, leaving the third—what to study—for future. Our conclusions are approximations in the present state of our knowledge. This 'Introduction', therefore, does not go beyond this point and is not intended to be a substitute for a 'research work' or 'study'. Its purpose will be amply realised if it arouses interest of the scholarly world to undertake deeper and meaningful studies in future.

While working on the Introduction it was our intention to include a few pages on the agamic and tantric sources of the *Tantrāloka* and to undertake a division of its contents on such a basis. But as we proceeded on, it occurred to us that in view of the complex and encyclopaedic character of the text and our elementary knowledge we could not possibly touch all the aspects and it would be much better to leave it for future study. It, however, appeared proper to us to share our thinking with the scholars about the lines on which future studies may proceed. Knowing full well there would be many more fruitful ways of doing so, devised by scholarly ingenuity, we venture to set out the following agenda for future attention of the scholars.

1. Our most urgent task is to have a critically edited text of the *Tantrāloka* and the *Viveka*. In the foregoing pages we visualised its necessity several times. By the time of Jayaratha the text of the *T.A.* was eclipsed by corruptions and he gives ample testimony of his having edited and restored the text (e.g., the *Viveka* on

the *T.A.* 23.23, 23.25, 29.265-66 and 37.4-5 etc.). The printed KSTS edition is in dire need of the same type of approach. An effort is to be made to locate as many MSS as possible and to collate and compare them. This may help settle many such problems as we have seen with regard to the difference in readings between Pandey's MS and the KSTS edition and resulting complications or with regard to several variants given by Jayaratha which are traceable to none of the MSS on which the KSTS edition is based. As a first step, an internal comparative study may be undertaken as we notice variations in the portions referred to or cross-referred to. As a second step, citations appearing in the *T.A.* and the *Viveka* may be compared with their original sources wherever available either in print or in MS. This may be done with an historical overview since even some apparently correct readings give rise to historical absurdities (e.g., Bhrātā'pi for Bhartā'pi in the *T.A.* 37.75). As a third step, a track has to be kept of the situations where Jayaratha, though seldom, is at variance with his master. For example the *T.A.* 8.406 says something, but it means something else from Jayaratha's comments.

2. As an essential corollary and supplement to the above a comparative study of the cognate but external sources with an appeal to their contents is another primary necessity. To explicate. Abhinavagupta on the one hand conceives, as we have already seen, the *Tantrāloka* as a logical extension of the *M.V.T.* and *P.T.V.*, and on the other composes the *T.S.* and *T.V.D.* as representative summaries of his *magnum opus*. By a comprehensive comparison between the contents of the three texts—*M.V.T.*, *P.T.V.* and *T.A*—keeping in view their successively progressive character, a fairly compact text of the *T.A.* may be resurrected. If one more text i.e., the *Sv.T.*, is also added to this list alongwith its commentary *Uddyota* by Kṣemarāja we may get practically an unassailable text which will ward off many anomalies arising from the textual readings of the existing edition giving us an additional opportunity to take stock of the scholastic bias or over-enthusiasm, if any, of the commentators, be he Jayaratha or Kṣemarāja. In the next stage, a comparision with the *T.S.* and *T.V.D.* will bring into focus the relative importance of the issues. The *T.S.* has 22 Āhnikas and the *T.V.D.* only 3 as against 37 of the *T.A.* In the first instance, while it underlines the importance of purely metaphysical theses, it also projects subtle difference between the

approaches underlined at the two places. For example, the discussion on Vyākhyāvidhi under Śrutavidhi in both the texts (*T.A.* and *T.S.*) may be looked into. In the third stage, once again the internal comparative study ought to be resorted to—this time with reference to the contents and with an intent to loosen the knots. For example, the riddle of Ādi (etc.), Prāk and Purastād (earlier), Vakṣyāmaḥ (will propound later), Agre (later) etc., as appearing in Abhinava and Jayaratha, appears to be quite enigmatic as and when the authors choose to keep mum about their specific places or meanings. This can be resolved by a close comparative investigation alone. Such a study will further take care of other gaps in our understanding. Jayaratha, for instance, explains Anyatra (elsewhere) in the *T.A.*15.521 as Naimittikādau (in the occasionals etc.) and quotes a verse. While Naimittikādau should have immediate reference to the 28th Āhnika, the verse quoted is neither found in the 28th nor in the 15th Āhnika. Similarly, as we have already seen, Jayaratha suggests inclusion of the occasional rite (Naimittika) among the daily rites (Nityakarma) in the 15th Āhnika notwithstanding its apparent misplacement. These two types of complementary enterprises, as outlined in columns 1 and 2, will go a long way in offering a faithful text of the *Tantrāloka* particularly in view of Abhinava's own admission that his treatment is staggered—i.e, he does not give all information at one place.

3. The *Tantrāloka* offers magnificent scope for a philosophical study of its thought contents. It is a true reflection of Abhinava's encyclopaedic genius and keen historical sense. It is a complete digest of Śaivism, specially Kashmir Śaivism in all its variety and splendour. Together with the *Viveka* it serves as a storehouse of knowledge on tantricism and other systems—both speculative and ritualistic. It not only furnishes the reasoned out philosophical theories but also underscores the evolutionary phases through which the major concepts and schools of Śaivism have passed. The theories of freedom (Mokṣa) and ignorance (Mala), cosmological theory of reflection (Bimbapratibimbavāda), tools of freedom—initiation and redemptive knowledge (Dīkṣā and Upāyacatuṣṭaya), cosmic ontology of six passages (Ṣaḍadhva) including Śaiva categoriology of 36 principles (Tattvas), theory of causation (Kartṛkarmabhāva) and trans-causation called manifestation(Ābhāsavāda), its attendant principle of determinism (Niyati) and bearing thereof on freedom of action and fruition of action (Karma-phala-

vyavasthā), monism through Absolutic dynamism, descent of grace, culmination of determinate thought construct into indeterminate pure thought, theory of knowledge famed as re-cognition, ensuing means of knowledge, parallelism as well as synthesis between Jñāna and Yoga, concept of reality as pure verbum and awareness or theory of reality as meaning which is an aspect of self-transcendence of the word— all these and many more issues provoke a very thorough, lively and intense deliberation. While other works on Kashmir Śaivism like the *I.P.K.*, *I.P.V.* etc. also discuss the similar issues, the *T.A.* is distinguished in its treatment by its tantric orientation. The *T.A.* provides a comprehensive backdrop setting against which philosophical problems are dealt with not in isolation from but as complement to the tantric, esoteric and ritualistic issues. The *T.A.* excels in tantric symbolism offering a rich insight into tantric esotericism which has been variously styled as Caryākrama, Rahasyaprakriyā, Ādiyāga etc. It is from this point of view that the tantric esotericism is said to have emanated from the sixth source or face known as Yoginīvaktra in contrast (*T.A.* 6.193) to all the Śaiva systems which are portrayed as proceeding from five faces of Śiva or five sources (Pañcasrotorūpa Bhairava). Thus in order to have a complete philosophical understanding it must combine and synthesize metaphysical, ritualistic, symbolic and esoteric aspects as all of them, both jointly and severally, lead to the attainment of the self-divine. This study will *ipso facto* concentrate on a comprehensive inventory of all the places where a particular topic has been discussed and also on all its phases through which it has passed in course of evolution to its present state. Besides, Abhinava's aesthetic theory presents a brilliant example of applied metaphysics. The 3rd, 4th and 28th Āhnikas are replete with such references, specially the 3rd is very rich in its observations on aesthetics of music. Any philosophical study worth the name is bound to take all this into account.

4. An historical study is necessitated by the very handling of the source material in the *T.A.* and *Viveka.* As we have seen, both Abhinava and Jayaratha display a tremendous historical sense. In the first place, they furnish significant informations about themselves and their ancestral and preceptorial origins. In the second, as observed by Goudriaan,[1] the *T.A.* comes up as one of the three

1. H.T.S.L., p. 20

concrete sources for dating the tantras. Same is the case, we may add, with Jayaratha also. In the third, their contribution in restoring several missing links in the tradition is invaluable. In the fourth, they furnish and handle enormous tantric source material from various periods of history which must be subjected to rigorous historical, chronological and evolutionary scrutiny so that the entire tantric edifice as dwelt upon by Abhinava and Jayaratha may be restored to its original grandeur and authenticity. In so doing we may profitably fall back upon all the available sources of contemporary history of that age—literary, architectural, epigraphical and internal i.e., other works of Abhinava and Jayaratha as well as those of their precursors and successors. Another rich source is provided by the texts from other branches of tantricism spread throughout the country. For instance, the omissions in the *Śrīkaṇṭhī's* list of the 64 Bhairava Tantras are removed only with reference to the contents of the *Pratiṣṭhā-lakṣaṇasāra-samuccaya*, a text brought out from Nepal. Even a preliminary study on these lines is bound to yield substantial results. With gaps removed in our understanding we would be better poised for a fuller appreciation of the philosophical content.

5. Another interesting and enlightening field of study may be offered by its evaluation as a source book of new information. Abhinava offers many insights into the history of Indian thought and the then culture of Kashmir. His references to some Naiyāyikas (Keṣāṁcana Naiyāyikānāṁ *T.A.* 2.12-44), Vairiñca Brahmavādins (*T.A.V.*, III, p. 25), Nāstika philosophers subscribing to the negation of soul and not to the denial of the authority of the Veda (*T.A.* 6.19-20) invite us to explore this unexplored area. Similarly his presentation of the Kaumārila view on Vedyatā and its lengthy masterly refutation (*T.A.* 10.21-57) adds new dimensions to our understanding of Kumārila. Abhinava's presentation of Siddhānta Śaivism in the 4th Āhnika in contrast to the sister systems opens a new vista of information throwing new light on the evolution of the dualistic Śaivism in Kashmir. He is an invaluable source of information on Buddhism. He practically refers to all sects of Buddhism so much so that he remains the only source of many exclusive theories of Buddhists. For example "Abhinavagupta, contemporary of Nāropā," observes Naudou[1], "devoted a whole

1. Buddhists of Kashmir, p. 180

chapter of the *Tantrāloka*, chapter XXV, to study of the imagination during sleep...." Presentation and criticism of the doctrine of Kālacakra by Abhinavagupta in the 16th Āhnika has elicited the following praise from Naudou[1], "...such criticism constitutes one of the principal sources for knowledge of that Tantric cycle, side by side with the Buddhistic texts themselves, in the front rank of which it is fitting to place the *Sekoddeśaṭīkā* of Nāropā (perhaps a Kashmīri), the only text of the system at this time."

Jayaratha closely follows his illustrious master both in spirit and approach. His references to Mausula, Kāruka (*T.A.V.*, I, p. 70), and Pāśupata equip us with new insight into the history of Śaivism. Similarly his references to Ṣaḍaṅga Yoga (4th Āhnika) reflect the continuity of the Buddhist thesis and its assimilation into the Śaiva fold.

Moreover, Abhinava furnishes a lot of geographical data in the 8th Āhnika and subtle cultural information throughout the *T.A.* These are but a few glimpses. A study fathoming all the new material contained in the pages of this vast text will, indeed, be rewarding.

6. The 35th Āhnika termed as Samastaśāstramelana reminds us of the synthetic Vedāntic effort represented by the phenomenon of Vedāntavākyasamanvaya (synthetic unity of all Vedāntic propositions). It underlies Abhinavagupta's synthetic approach which seeks to view the *T.A.* as an eclectical organism where one system culminates into the other and so on ultimately culminating into Trika system. Thus Tārkika, Śrauta, Bauddha, Ārhata, Vaiṣṇava, Siddhānta, Vāmaka, Dakṣa, Mata, Kula, Kaula, and Trika move in a hierarchical order. It will be interesting and significant to unearth as to how Abhinava propounds their synthetic progression.[2]

7. The meaning of 'Tantra' as understood by Abhinava is to be investigated. In his *T.A.* he quotes and alludes to even Śruti (*T.A.* 3.226) which is an external authority (Bāhya Śāstra) as Tantra. Jayaratha, following his master, even refers to Paurāṇika Prakriyā (Jayaratha on the *T.A.* 8.58). Abhinava goes on invoking his teachers, scriptures and even secular texts as authority. Now if

1. Buddhists of Kashmir, p. 150

२. अशेषतन्त्रसारं तु नामदक्षिणमाश्रितम् ।
एकत्र मिलितं कौलं श्रीषडर्धशासने ॥ T.A. 37.2

all these constitute authority what is the precise implication of the word Tantra in Abhinavagupta. He himself distinguishes Tantra from Āgama.[1] His use of the word Tantra in the *Tantrāloka* and 'Tantra-prakriyā' must of necessity be in two different senses. Because, while Tantra-prakriyā has been distinguished from Kulaprakriyā on all the three counts namely, Mantra, Ādhāra and Itikartavyatā (*T.A.* 29.5-8)., both have been subsumed under *Tantrāloka*. If the meaning were identical at both the places, Kulaprakriyā would have remained outside the domain of the *Tantrāloka*.

Such study will bring Abhinava's attitude towards tantra and several tantric systems into bold relief. In this connection one more topical issue may be raised. As we have pointed out elsewhere[2], there was an acute controversy with regard to the exact status of Spanda system i.e., whether it was an independent system or a part of Trika system. Abhinava obviously joins the second group because while paying glowing tributes to Kallaṭa, the author of the *Sp.K.*, he does not accord a separate status to Spanda system. Now under Kula-prakriyā only one system i.e., Kula system, finds mention, whereas Tantraprakriyā subsumes Krama, Trika and Pratyabhijñā within itself. What is then the locus standi of Spanda according to Abhinavagupta?

Even though we are not sure of the meaning of the term 'Tantra' in the *Tantrāloka*, there is no doubt that all the three classified authoritative sources—experience, scripture and reason—have been frequently drawn upon.[3] The entire subject matter of the *T.A.* is somehow based on at least one of these sources. Sometimes a particular point is based on more than one authority also. Abhinavagupta has exploited every opportunity to tell or point out his source of authority. For instance, the treatment of Kāla

1. स तन्निबन्धं विदधे महार्थं
युक्त्यागमोदीरिततन्त्रतत्त्वम् ।
आलोकमासाद्य यदीयमेष
लोकः सुखं संचरिता क्रियासु ॥ T.A. 37.83
2. K.T. pp. 113-118
3. इति यज्ज्ञेयसतत्त्वं दर्श्यते मया तच्छिवाज्ञया ।
मया स्वसंवित्सत्तर्कपतिशास्त्रत्रिकक्रमात् ॥ T.A. 1.106

(time) is based on all the three sources.[1] Rise of Cakra is based on experience and scripture (*T.A.* 7.71), while the pure universality of the divine on experience and reason (*T.A.* 3.44). Similarly Abhiṣekavidhi is an exclusively agamic phenomenon (*T.A.* 23.1 & 23.103). Abhinava does not remain content with general description of the source. He even prefers to identify the source. For instance, his theory of scriptural unity (Śāstramelana) is ascribed to Śambhunātha (*T.A.* 35.44), the brief procedure (Saṁkṣiptavidhi) is traced to the *Dīkṣottara* and *Kiraṇā* (*T.A.* 18.11). Abhinavagupta thus affords us a clear peep into his sources of topicwise treatment. A complete chart drawn on these lines will enable us to know Abhinavan mind and appreciate the thematic unity of apparently divergent sources much better.

8. Jayaratha throws some esoteric hints in all his benedictory verses in each Āhnika. A clear understanding of the same will help us understand Jayaratha better.

9. Abhinavagupta has employed about 76 illustrations (Dṛṣṭānta) to exemplify his stand on various matters. These illustrations are interspread throughout the *Tantrāloka*. A complete estimate of these illustrative instances will present Abhinavan thinking in a much more lucid way.

10. On the strength of the material provided by Abhinava and Jayaratha, critical studies of the *Śrīpūrvaśāstra* alias *Mālinīvijayottaratantra* (vide *T.A.* 13.212-253, 15.4-7, 21.2-5 etc.), *Svaccandatantra* and *Parātriṁśikā* may be undertaken. Such studies will indeed further our understanding of the *T.A.* and vice versa.

The agenda, as outlined above, do not exhaust the areas or directions of research. They simply underline the beginning of our quest to understand Abhinava and his celebrated text.

१. इति कालतत्त्वमुदितं शास्त्रमुखागमनिजानुभवसिद्धम् । T.A. 7.1

APPENDICES

1. TEXTS REFERRED TO BY NAME IN THE TANTRĀLOKA

Texts	*Āhnika/Verse*
Aghoreśa-tantra[1]	27.58
Aitareya Vedānta[2]	3.226
Amaryāda	29.177
Ānanda/-śāstra/-śāsana[3]	13.354; 15.45, 282, 590, 601; 16.65; 37.10, 18
Ānandādhika-śāsana	8.40
Ānanda-gahvara	14.18
Ānandeśvara	29.200
Ananta-kārikā[4]	28.313

1. An incomplete manuscript titled *Aghoratantra* (No. C91) is available in the Āryabhāṣā Pustakālaya, Varanasi. Brij Vallabh Dvivedi, on the authority of the T.A. 25.58, finds it to be identical with the *Svacchanda Tantra*. If it is so, it has been published in KSTS in six volumes (Vol. V in two parts) with the *Uddyota* by Kṣemarāja.

2. Identical with the *Aitareyopaniṣad*. Brought out with Śaṁkara's commentary by Gita Press, Gorakhpur alongwith 10 other principal Upaniṣads in 3 volumes.

3. Eight MSS of one *Ānandatantra*—five complete, one incomplete and two with the commentary of Navasiṁhācārya—are available in the Government Oriental Manuscript Library, Madras. The MSS are numbered as D5562-69 and R-5314. The India Office Library Catalogue lists a complete MS bearing No. 2541 (Tā. Sā. p. 45). One *Ānandaśāsana* is noticed as referred to in the New Cat. Cat., II, p. 118 (Upodghāta., p. 20).

4. The *Anantakārikā* is *Ādhārakārikā*, published in KSTS as the *Paramārthasāra* with Yogarāja's commentary. It is a Śaivite adaptation of the Vaiṣaṇava/Yoga original which has been published along with the commentary of Rāghavānanda in Acyutagranthamālā.

Anuttara-prakriyā[5]	9.313
Arṇava	29.165
Bhairavāgama[6]	29.251
Bhairava-/Bhairavīya-/kula	13. 302; 22.41; 27.45; 28.14, 51, 59, 388
Bhairava Tantra[7]	13.304
Bhargaśikhā/-śāstra	4.255; 12.20; 15.280
Bhargāṣṭaka-śikhākula	32.62
Bharuṇa Tantra	25.14
Bhaṭṭāraka	16.19
Bhogahastaka	29.198
Brahmayāmala[8]	4.54, 60; 5.97; 13.145; 15.44; 18.9; 23.43; 27.29; 28.419, 423; 29.11
Caryākula	29.166
Catuṣkapañcāśikā	26.44
Cintāmaṇi[9]	16.51

5. Published in KSTS under the title *Parātrīśikāvivaraṇa* comprising the *Parātriśikā* and Abhinavagupta's *Vivaraṇa* commentary, later crically edited with an annotated Italian translation by R. Gnoli (Rome). Also published in KSTS with Rājānaka Lāsaka's commentary called *Lāsakī* or *Laghuvṛtti.*

6-7. Four incomplete MSS of the *Bhairava Tantra* are reported to be extant—one, at the Āryabhāṣā Pustakālaya, Varanasi (No. C2927), second at B.H.U. (No. 5446), third at the K.S. Sanskrit University, Darbhanga (No. 296 [12]) and fourth at Bhārata Itihāsa Saṁśodhaka Maṇḍala, Poona (No. BL 12165). The Tā. Sā. (p. 449) lists one MS at the Royal Asiatic Society of Bengal (No. 6041).

8. By now we know of seven MSS viz.,—the Royal Asiatic Society of Bengal (6392), the Curator's Office Library, Trivendram (T982) and the Darbar Library, Nepal (3/370, 1/296, 1/1160, 1/1557 and 1/147). According to the Tā.Sā. (p. 429), the Trivendrum catalogue lists one more MS as 1103 B and that of the Royal Asiatic Society of Bengal lists one at No. 5892. All are incomplete but two are quite large. Mark Dyczkowski is presently working on its critical edition.

9. One MS named *Cintāmaṇi* is listed at Trivendrum (COL 6888) but, perhaps it is not the one in question, since Jayaratha

Ḍāmara-yāga/-mahāyāga[10]	3.70; 15.335; 30.55
Devī-/Devyā-yāmala/-śāstra	3.70; 8.16, 212; 15.253, 335, 460, 522; 22.31; 23.10, 14, 15, 39; 28.386, 390; 31.60, 85; 32.1
Devyāmala	31.60
Dīkṣottara(rā)/-śāstra/-śāsana	1.62; 2.9; 5.148; 8.9; 15.458; 17.97; 18.11; 19.21; 21.61; 24.4, 17; 28.65; 29.243
Gahvara[11]	13.319; 16.181; 19.7, 20; 28. 224, 227; 29.240; 32.53
Gama/-śāstra/-śāsana	1.150; 13.230, 232; 15.280, 424, 531, 553; 16.286; 29.142
Gītā[12]	1.124-125, 129; 28.324
Haiḍara	28.15, 18
Hārdeśa	29.165
Hṛd-/Hṛdya-śāstra	3.69; 13.303
Iśānaśivapaddhati[13]	22.30
Jñānottara(rā)[14]	4.248; 9.45; 23.20; 27.6
Kacabhārgava	23.6
Kālīkula[15]	28.15; 29.43; 35.33

interprets *Cintāmaṇi* as the *Tattvārthacintāmaṇi*, a non-extant work by Kallaṭa.

10. We learn of one *Ḍāmaraka Tantra* at Adyar (No. 6041). But we are not sure if it is the one we are looking for. One *Ḍāmaratantra* is also listed in the catalogue of the Sanskrit University, Varanasi (No. 24385). Vide Tā.Sā., p. 227

11 & 19. The Nepal Darbar Library, according to Dvivedi (Upodghāta., p. 28), stores a MS of some *Matagahvarpañcāśītikā*. It is, however, open to doubt if it is one with the *Kulagahvara*.

12. Published in numerous editions.

13. The *Īśānaśivapaddhati* is not to be confused with the *Īśānaśivagurudevapaddhati* which has been edited and published by T. Ganapati Shastri in two volumes. (Upodghāta., p. 209, fn. 3).

14. See fn. 45 below.

15. MSS available in the Darbar Library, Nepal (Vide Tantra Catalogue, Vol. I, pp. 37-42). For other references see New Cat. Cat., Vol. IV, pp. 48-49, 72-73 (Upodghāta., p. 26). It appears identical with the *Kālikākulakramasadbhāva* (I16) or the *Kālikākulasadbhāva* (I/686) at the Darbar Library, Nepal. We are told

Kālīmukha	27.44
Kālīvidhi	13.306
Kālottara[16]	11.19
Kāmika(kā)[17]	1.59, 66; 4.25; 6.94, 190; 8.213; 22.32; 23.4; 32.48
Khamata	29.165
Kiraṇa(ṇā)/Kairaṇa/-āgama/-vidhi[18]	1.75; 4.41, 78; 9.47; 13.162, 284; 15.18; 18.11
Krama	12.23
Krama-pūjana	29.2
Kramarahasya	29.14
Kula-gahavara/-guhkara[19] (? Kulaguhvara)	3.146, 168; 15.598; 24.16
Kulavidhi	13.306
Mādhavakula[20]	15.533, 571; 24.22; 29.56

A. Sanderson (Oxford) is working on a critical edition of this text.

16. According to Dvivedi (Upodghāta., pp. 217-18), the *Kālottara* is *Triṁśikākālottara* which is another name of the *Mataṅgapārameśvara*. The latter with Rāmakaṇṭha's commentary has been brought out by the French Institute of Indology, Pondichery. We gather that R. Torrella (Rome) is bringing out a critical edition of the same. One *Devīkālottarāgama* has been included in the 2nd volume of the *Tantrasaṁgraha* published from the Sanskrit University, Varanasi. However, two MSS, one named as *Kalottara-mahātantra* and the other as *Kalottaratantra*, have been noticed in Jodhpur collection (No. 290) and the Oriental Research Institute, Baroda (No. 791).

17. Previously the *Kāmikāgama* was published in two volumes in Grantha script from Madras. It was reprinted in Nāgarī script as *Pūrvakāmika* (Part I, ed. Svaminā thaśīvācārya) by Dakṣiṇabhāratārcakasaṅgha and as *Uttarakāmika* (Part II) by Civaña Napotayantraśālai, Cintatripeṭṭai, Madras.

18. First published from Devakoṭṭai, Tirupati in 1932 in Grantha script. One MS has been listed at the French Institute of Indology, Pondichery (MS No. 290).

19. See Fn. 11 above.

20. According to Jayaratha (on T.A. 29.56) it is a section of the *Tantrarāja-bhaṭṭāraka* which, according to A. Padoux, is

identical with the *Jayadrathayāmala* and is being brought out by A. Sanderson, Oxford University (Upodghāta., p. 219). It is perhaps identical with the *Śiraścheda*.

21-22. Published in KSTS as *Mālinīvijayottara-tantra*.

23. Published in KSTS.

24-26. Published in KSTS as *Mālinīvijayottara-tantra*.

27. Several MSS of *Śrīmatasāra* are listed in the MSS collection of the Darbar Library, Nepal (3/275; 2/219; 5/4849).

28-29. Published with Rāmakaṇṭha's commentary by the French Institute of Indology, Pondichery as *Mātaṅgapārameśvarāgama* (Kriyāpāda, Yogapāda and Caryāpāda).

30. One MS (R5126) of the *Mātṛsadbhāvatantra* is recorded in the catalogues of the Oriental Manuscript Library, Madras and

two (COL1642/A and -/B) in those of the Curator's Library, Trivendrum. The Tā.Sā (P. 512) notes two MSS in the Trivendrum collection at 1017A and -B. It also talks of one more MS, complete whereabouts of which have not been furnished.

31-32. An incomplete MS of the *Maukuṭāgama* is found in BORI, Poona (BL 11428) and that of the *Makuṭāgama* at Baroda (6827/C). The Tā.Sā. (p. 517) notices one *Mukuṭasaṁhitā* in the India Office Catalogue on page 840.

33. Jñāna and Yoga Pādas with Nārāyaṇakaṇṭha's commentary published from Kashmir in KSTS as *Mṛgendra-tantram* and Caryā and Kriyā Pādas from Pondichery as well as from Devakoṭṭai as *Mṛgendra-āgama.*

34. Gonda (Medieval Religious Literature, p. 206, fn. 165) identifies it with the *Netratantra* which is published in KSTS. If so it is one with the *Amṛteśa* (Upodghāta, p. 14), (Tā.Sā. p. 16-17).

35. Available in the MS form under several titles e.g., *Niḥśvāsa-tattvasaṁhitā* (I/277), *Niḥśvāsatantra* (I/279) and *Niḥśvāsākhya-mahātantra.* The first two are listed in the Darbar Library, Nepal. See Tā.Sā. p. 342; Upodghāta, p. 45; New Cat. Cat. III, p. 64. A MS of the *Pratiṣṭhātantra*, being a part of the *Niḥśvāsamahā-tantra*, is listed in the Darbar Library, Nepal catalogue (I/1003). We learn from Dvivedi, T. Goudriaan from Holland is

Niśāṭana[36]	1.50; 4.79; 13.197; 28.72
Niśā-/Niśi-/Naiśa-/saṁca (cā)ra/cā(ca)ra[37]	4.178; 6.31; 12.23; 13.241; 14.43; 15.83, 105, 596
Nityā-tantra[38]	28.123
Paddhati (of Īśānaśiva)	22.30
Pārameśvara Lakṣaṇa	27.17
Pauṣkara[39]	16.254
Picumata	28.383
Picuśāstra	27.21, 24; 28.409
Pramāṇastutidarśana	13.128; 17.115
Pratiṣṭhā(?)	27.41
Pūjanastotra	15.152
Purāṇa	13.285; 28.266, 344
Ratnamālākulāgama[40]	28.128
Ratnamālā/-śāstra	1.274; 13.230; 28.112, 256, 309, 416; 29.55, 192, 201, 283; 37.25
Rātrikula	15.593
Rauravamata[41]	6.142
Raurava/-śāsana[42]	8.32, 101, 168; 9.217; 13.355
Rauravasaṅgraha	9.40
Raurava(sva)vṛtti	6.134
Rauravavārtika	8.92, 183
Ruru/-śāsana[43]	1.46; 8.87, 162

critically editing the *Niḥśvāsamahātantra* (Upodghāta, p. 47).

36-37. Listed in the Tantra catalogue of the Darbar Library, Nepal (Vol. I, p. 227). Its number is 1/1606.

38. See Tā.Sā. p. 335. It appears to be a generic name. But if it is identical with the *Nityāṣoḍaśikārṇava*, it is published with the *Setubandha* of Bhāskararāya in Ānandāśrama Series and with the *Artharatnāvalī* and *Ṛjuvimarśinī* by the S.S. University, Varanasi.

39. We know of three MSS, all named *Pauṣkarāgama*—one at Baroda (6827 a), second at the Punjab University Library, Lahore (number not available) and third, with a commentary by Jñānaprakāśācārya (4395) at VVRI, Hoshiarpur. According to the Tā.Sā. (p. 388) one more MS (2606) is listed in the India Office Library catalogue and one (6827C) in the Oriental Institute, Baroda.

40. H.P. Shastri records in his Notices (2nd Series) a MS at No. 1/306 (Tā.Sā., p. 548).

41-43. Published in two volumes by the French Institute of Indology, Pondichery as *Rauravāgama*.

Ṣaḍardhahṛdaya	13.301; 31.54
Ṣaḍardhasāra	37.32
Sadbhāvakrama	31.10
Sadbhāvaśāsana	29.212
Santatyāgama[44]	30.101
Sāra/-śāsana/-śāstra	3.353; 8.321; 13.121; 14.33; 15.112, 253, 546; 16.158, 252; 23.96; 31.61
Sarvācāra	12.23; 13.303
Sarvācārahṛdaya	13.303; 29.103
Sarvajñāna	28.251
Sarvajñānottara[45]	4.248
Sarvavīra	4.54; 13.145
Siddhā	4.54; 16.4; 29.166; 31.155; 36.1
Siddhāmata[46]	7.40; 15.157; 20.11; 26.23; 28.94
Siddhā/-śāsana/-tantra	1.243; 8.41, 115, 184; 15.332; 23.28; 24.6; 25.2; 27.25; 31.8, 58, 60, 155
Siddhānta	22.40; 28.266
Siddhasantāna-rūpaka	2.48
Siddhasantāna-ūrmimahākula	14.31
Siddhāṭanasadbhāva	28.113
Siddhāvīra	33.2
Siddhavīrāvalīsāra	22.41
Siddhayogīśvarīmata[47]	2.41; 3.220; 9.7; 11.81; 15.321;

44. One incomplete but large MS titled *Santānasaṁhitā* is said to be available in the Palace Library of Tanjore and is listed at No. 11408 (Tā.Sā., p. 673).

45. See fn. 14 above also. Identical with *Jñānottara*. Published by Muttaiya Pillai from Devakoṭṭai, Tirupati in 1923 (Upodghāta, p. 74). The Tā.Sā. (pp. 685-686) refers to a MS of Aghoraśivācārya's commentary on it. A MS of the *Jñānottarayogaśāstra* (C 99) is reported to be available in the BHU collection (Upodghāta, p. 35).

46. A MS called *Siddhāmata* is listed in the catalogue of the Punjab University, Lahore (1643).

47. According to the Tā.Sā. (p. 697) its MSS are available in the Royal Asiatic Society of Bengal (5948) and also in the Darbar Library (2/32). The India Office Library also lists one MS in the catalogue. Mark Dyczkowski records two MSS at the Royal Asiatic Society of Bengal (3917 and 5465) and one at Nepal National Archives (5/2403).

48. Published in KSTS with the *Padasaṅgati* or *Ālocana* commentary by Utpala.

49. Published in KSTS in separate volumes with the *Vārtikas* of Bhāskara as well as Kṛṣṇadāsa alias Varadarāja and the *Vimarśinī* of Kṣemarāja.

50. Published as the *Spanda-kārikā* in KSTS with the commentaries of Kallaṭa and Rāmakaṇṭha. Also published with the *Pradīpikā* of Utpala by Vamanaśāstri Islampurkar in 1898 and later included in the *Tantrasaṁgraha,* Part I published from the S.S. University, Varanasi. Also published with the *Nirṇaya* of Kṣemarāja in KSTS. The Ist Sūtra of the *Spanda-kārikā* with the *Sandoha* commentary by Kṣemarāja published in KSTS.

51. Published in KSTS as *Mālinīvijayottara-tantra.*

52. Available in several printed editions.

Svacchanda/-śāsana/-śāstra/-[53] tantra	1.37; 4.38; 6.50, 136, 137; 7.67; 8.11, 191, 237; 13.278, 307, 316; 15.21, 421; 16.174; 17.18; 27.58; 28.293; 35.27, 36
Svaśāstra (Ādhārakārikā)	28.309
Svāyambhuva[54]	1.46; 15.3; 28.263
Svāyambhuva-vṛtti[55]	16.210
Tantrāloka[56]	1.245, 286, 334; 36.15; 37.83
Tantraguhya	31.61
Tantra-sadbhāva/-śāsana[57]	20.12; 29.212; 30.59, 99; 31.61
Tantrasāra[58]	28.9
Tattvarakṣaṇa	29.141
Tattvarakṣā-vidhāna	3.112, 215
Trika	22.41
Trika-kula	28.15, 51; 30.1; 31.60
Trika-sadbhāva	28.15
Trika/-śāsana/-śāstra	1.18, 106; 4.50, 274; 10.1, 2, 277; 28.51; 30.24; 31.51
Trika-sūtra	12.15
Triṁśaka/Traīśika/Trīśikā/-śāstra[59]	3.206; 4.50; 13.154; 15.15; 16.17
Trīśikāśāstra-vivṛti	13.150

53. Published in KSTS in six volumes (Volume V has two parts) with Kṣemarāja's *Uddyota*. See fn. 1 above.

54. Dvivedi informs us about the availability of one incomplete MS at the French Institute, Pondichery (Upodghāta., p. 83).

55. One incomplete MS is reported to be present at Pondichery (Upodghāta., p. 82).

56. Published in 12 Volumes in KSTS with Jayaratha's commentary, now being reprinted by Motilal Banarsidass.

57. A MS is said to be available in the Darbar Library, Nepal as per the Tantra catalogue, Vol. II, p. 204. Its photo-transcript is available with Mark Dyczkowski (1/363 at Nepal National Archives).

58. For details see Ist chapter of the present work. It is different from Abhinava's text of the same name published in KSTS. According to the Tā.Sā. (p. 246) there is one MS in the S.S. University, Varanasi (25452), ascribed to one Siddhanātha.

59. Published in KSTS with Abhinavagupta's *Vivaraṇa* and Lāsaka's *Lāsaki*. Also see fn. 5 above.

Triśirobhairava	5.86; 31.10
Tri (Trai) śi-ra/-rasa/-mata	1.82, 114; 5.20; 15.370; 29.9, 141; 30.12; 31.60
Tri (Trai) śi-raḥ/-rasa/-śāsana/-śāstra/-tantra	1.136; 2.32; 3.137, 256; 5.9, 36, 112, 128, 136; 6.22; 8.12, 15,184; 15.69, 184, 436, 540; 16.4, 110; 17.83; 28.63, 112, 146, 320; 29.110; 30.27, 120; 31.100
Ūrmi/-āgama/-śāsana/-śāstra	15.563, 573, 588; 23.43; 28.53, 59
Ūrmimahāśāstra	2.48
Ūrmimahākula	14.31
Utfulla	29.166
Vairiñca	9.46
Vaiyākaraṇa-darśana	9.259
Vājasa (si) neya	4.54; 13.143
Veda	4.252; 15.176, 597
Vijayottara[60]	10.104
Viṁśatika-trika	7.56
Vīra[61]	4.54
Vīrālī	12.23
Virāvalī/-śāstra[62]	4.89, 241; 29.163, 165, 177, 186
Virāvalībhairava	29.235
Vīrāvalīhṛdaya	15.102
Vīrāvalīkula	6.74; 29.272

60. Identical with the *Mālinīvijayottara*. Published in KSTS.

61. Two MSS of the *Vīra-tantra* are found listed in the Royal Asiatic Society collection (3161 and 9347) and six MSS entitled *Vīrāgama* are found in the Madras collection (R 1761, D5502-4, D5498-99). According to the Tā.Sā (pp. 602-603), the Royal Asiatic Society has two MSS of the *Vīratantra* (5925, 6146), the Nepal Darbar Library has two (2/246 Ca and 2/125) and the Baṅgīya Sāhitya Pariṣad has one (1409). According to the same source (Tā.Sā. p. 604) Rajendra Lal Mitra records in his Notices two MSS at Sl. No. 229 and 268. Similarly one *Vīrāgama* is taken note of in the Palace Library of Tanjore (6721).

62. According to Dvivedi he sighted one of its MSS in a list in the possession of late Prof. V.S. Agrawal. There is one more MS (C776) in the B.H.U. collection.

63. One MS captioned *Yoginīsañcāra* is included in the catalogue of the Darbar Library, Nepal (4/78).

2. PERSONS* REFERRED TO BY NAME IN THE TANTRĀLOKA

Abhinanda	37.62
Abhinavagupta	1.1, 16, 20, 21; 2.1; 4.278; 11.53; 16.195, 274; 37.56, 67, 80, 86
Abhinavaguptaguru	16.195
Abjaja	36.2
Agastya	37.38
Ahīndra	29.41
Ahīśāna	28.309
Ajaramekhalā	29.32
Ali	29.33
Amara	29.33
Ambā	37.79
Amardaka	4.266; 36.12
Ānanda	37.60
Ānandamekhalā	29.31
Anantamekhalā	29.30
Aniruddha	13.293-94
Antaka	28.391
Aṇurāṭ	36.1
Aparamekhalā	29.34
Ardhatryambaka	36.13
Attrigupta	37.38
Avijita	29.31
Bhagavatī	1.13
Bālamitra	37.66
Bali	36.4
Bhairava-nātha	36.1
Bhairavī	36.1
Bhaktivilāsa	37.62
Bhārgava	23.6; 36.4
Bhāskara	1.21; 37.62
Bhava	37.62

*The list includes certain mythical names as well.

3. SYSTEMS/MAJOR DOCTRINES REFERRED TO BY NAME IN THE TANTRĀLOKA

A-dhaḥ(dhara)/-darśana/-dṛṣṭi/-śāsana/-śāstra/-tantra	13.346; 21.7; 22.35; 23.70, 71, 76; 24.2; 28.269, 395; 35.9; 37.7, 8, 9, 13
Adhyātma	13.346
Abheda	See Advaita
Advaita/Advaya	2.16, 18; 3.288; 4.106, 214; 9.198; 10.225, 283-284; 29.74; 36.12
Anuttaraṣaḍardhārthakrama	1.14
Anuttaratrika	11.88
Ārhata	4.27; 6.152, 153; 13.305, 346; 35.26
Atimārga	13.346; 15.467
Bāhya	4.27; 6.10
Bhairava/-tantra	13.304; 37.17
Bauddha	1.180-81; 4.27; 7.32, 33, 35; 13.346; 15.471; 22.12; 35.26, 30
— (Saugata)	4.22; 13.348
— (Śūnyadṛṣṭyavalambin)	11.114
— (Sarvāpahnavahevāka-dharmā)	1.56
— (Vikalpāpekṣanirvikalpa-prāmāṇyavādin)	1.228, 180-181
Bhedavāda	
— (Dvaita Śāstra)	1.194, 224; 2.18; 4.12, 106, 254; 9.198; 10.225, 283-84; 29.74
— (Dvaitin)	6.30, 193
Bhedābheda/-vāda	4.255; 36.12
Cārvāka	6.16
Dakṣa	11.87; 13.301, 320
Dakṣiṇa-śāstra	15.319; 37.18, 26, 27
Dvaita Śāstra	See under Bhedavāda
Dvaitin	See under Bhedavāda

4. IMPLIED OR INCOMPLETE TEXTUAL REFERENCES IN THE TANTRĀLOKA AS IDENTIFIED AND/OR COMPLETED BY JAYARATHA

*Text**	*Volume/Page* (KSTS Edition)	*Volume/Page* (MLBD Edition)
Āgama		
(Kila, 9.307)	VI/246	IV/1880
Ādhārakārikā		
(Śvaśāstra, 28.309)	XI/122	VII/3228
Bhairavakula		
(Atra, 28.18)	XI/8	VII/3115
Bhargaśikhā		
(2.28-29)	I/22 (2nd Āh.)	II/332
Brahma-yāmala		
(Tatra, 4.60)	III/67	III/683
(Anena, 4.62)	III/68	III/685
(Tatra, 4.63)	III/70	III/686
Chāndogyopaniṣad		
(Śrutyanta, 17.7)	X/132	VI/2858
Cillācakreśvarīmata		
(Ādi, 1.46)	I/85	I/85
Devyāyāmala		
(Yāmalādau, 23.15)	X/268	VI/2994
Gamaśāstra		
(Ādi, 12.23)	VII/106 (12th Āh.)	V/2198
(Nirūpitam, 13.232)	VIII/144	V/2344
(Nigama, 29.141)	XI/99 (29th Āh.)	VII/3389
Gītā		
(Gururāha, 3.115)	II/121	II/473
Haiḍara		
(Tatra, 28.25)	XI/13	VII/3119
Hṛdayabhaṭṭāraka		

*The name of the identified text is followed by the relative description as appearing in the T.A. followed by Āhnika/Kārikā number within brackets.

(Hārdeśa, 29.165)	XI/113	VII/3403
Hṛdayanayarahasya		
(Hṛdaya, 3.69)	II/82	II/434
Kālottara		
(Tatra tatra, 11.20)	VII/12 (11th Āh.)	V/2104
Khecarīmata		
(Khamata, 29.165)	XI/113 (29th Āh.)	VII/3403
(Khecarī, 32.6)	XII/307	VII/3597
Kiraṇā-Saṁhitā		
(Tatra, 4.42)	III/45	III/661
(Tatra tatra, 18.6)	X/179	VI/2905
Kramabhaṭṭāraka		
(Nirucyate, 4.150)	III/163	III/779
Kramadarśana		
(Kramaḥ, 12.23)	VII/106 (12th Āh.)	V/2198
Kulagahvara		
(Gahvara, 32.53)	XII/326	VII/3616
Kularatnamālā		
(Ratnamālā, 1.274)	I/281	II/281
Malinīvijaya		
(Aṣṭādaśa-paṭala, 4.213)	III/241	III/857
(Srīpūrva, 9.40)	VI/41	IV/1675
Mālinīvijayottara		
(Trikābhidha, 10.2)	VII/2	V/1886
(Vijayottara, 10.104)	VII/78	V/1962
Ma(Mā)taṇga/-śāstra		
(Proktā, 6.227)	IV/185	III/1273
(Atra, 8.380)	V/248	IV/1598
(Tatra, 15.10)	IX/7	VI/2447
(Uktyā, 17.77)	X/159	VI/2885
Mṛgendra		
(Ādi, 9.190)	VI/149	IV/1783
Mṛtuñjaya		
(Anyatra, 27.8)	X/360	VI/3086
Nandiśikhā		
(Ādi, 15.279)	IX/138	VI/2578
Nirmaryāda Śāstra		
(Maryādāhīna, 29.166)	XI/113 (29th Āh.)	VII/3403
Niśāṭana		
(Niśisañcāra, 4.178)	III/207	III/823

(Śāstra, 16.200)	X/76	VI/2802
Pañcaśatika		
(Āgama, 4.148)	III/158	III/774
(Tatra, 4.152)	III/166	III/782
Pañcikā		
(Nirūpitā, 23.75)	X/292	VI/3018
Parātriṁśikā		
(Pracakṣate, 3.167)	II/166	II/518
(Trīśikā-śāstra, 3.206)	II/198	II/550
(Trikaśūtra, 12.15)	VII/101 (12th Āh.)	V/2193
Parātriṁṣikā-vivaraṇa		
(Anuttara, 9.313)	VI/249	IV/1883
Prajñālaṅkāra		
(Uktam, 3.55)	II/62-64	II/416
Prakīrṇaka-vivaraṇa		
(Anyatra, 10.44)	VII/33	V/1917
Pramāṇaśtotra		
(Mānastuti, 9.173)	VI/138	IV/1769
Raurava-Saṅgraha		
(Raurava, 9.40)	VI/41	IV/1675
Ruru-śāstra		
(Śāstra, 9.220)	VI/176	IV/1810
Ruru-vārtika		
(Ādi, 8.345)	V/230	IV/1580
Ruruvṛtti		
(Ādi, 6.137)	IV/119	III/1207
Saṁvitprakāśa		
(Bhāṣitam, 5.155)	III/467	III/1083
Sārabhaṭṭāraka		
(Sāraṁ, 3.69)	II/82	II/434
Sarvavīra		
(Tatra, 12.24)	VII/106	V/2198
Siddhāmata		
(Mate, 4.66)	III/72	III/668
(Matādiṣu, 15.157)	IX/80	VI/2520
Siddha-yogīśvarīmata		
(Tadetat, 7.40)	IV/32 (7th Āh.)	III/1324
Śivadṛṣṭi		
(Uktaṁ, 2.48)	I/40 (2nd Āh.)	II/350
Śivāgama		

(Tat, 1.75)	I/116	II/116
Śiva-/Śaivī-tanu/-śāstra		
(Uktaṁ, 8.303)	V/209	IV/1559
(8.323)	V/220	IV/1570
Spanda-śāstra		
(Śāstra, 4.183)	III/213	III/829
Śrīpūrvaśāstra		
(Varṇitā, 1.186)	I/215	II/215
(1.192)	I/220-221	II/220-221
(Advayaśāstra, 1.194)	I/222	II/222
(Asmin, 1.196)	I/223	II/223
(Tattatsiddhi, 10.212)	VII/144	V/2028
(Uktamiti, 10.239)	VII/164	V/2048
(Bhaṇyate, 10.272)	VII/184	V/2068
(Trikaśāsana, 10.277)	VII/187	V/2071
(Nirūpitāḥ, 11.72)	VII/57 (11th Āh.)	V/2149
(Samupāsyatā, 11.80)	VII/63 (11th Āh.)	V/2155
(Uktaḥ, 13.214)	VIII/136	V/2336
(Atraiva, 13.219)	VIII/138	V/2338
(Na coditam, 30.18)	XII/185	VII/3475
Śrīpūrvavivaraṇa		
(Nirūpitaḥ, 23.75)	X/292	VI/3018
Śrīsvāyambhuva		
(Vairiñca, 9.46)	VI/45	IV/1680
(Śāstra, 9.67)	VI/60-61	IV/1694
(Anyatra, 28.264)	XI/103	VII/3209
Svacchanda-śāstra		
(Uktaḥ, 4.19)	III/22-23	III/638
(Gurūttamaiḥ, 8.357)	V/237	IV/1587
Tantrāloka		
(Iti, 1.245)	I/258	II/258
(Uktam, 9.224)	VI/179-180	IV/1813
(Śāstramasmatkṛtam, 13.160)	VIII/102	V/2302
Tantrarāja		
(Mādhavakula, 29.56)	XI/40	VII/3330
Tantrasadbhāva		
(Sadbhāvaśāsana, 29.212)	XI/136	VII/3426
Tattvārthacintāmaṇi		
(Cintāmaṇi, 16.51).	X/19	VI/2745

Trikahṛdaya		
(Ṣaḍardhahṛdaya, 31.54)	XII/250-251	VII/3542
Trikakula		
(Ūrdhvaśāsana, 26.20)	X/336	VI/3062
(Advaye, 36.12)	XII/389	VIII/3679
Trikasāra		
(Sāraśāstra, 3.253)	II/236	II/588
Trikaśāstra		
(Tatsāram, 1.18)	I/49	II/49
Triśirobhairava		
(Sahasrāra, 1.112)	I/154	II/154
(Triśiraḥśāstra, 1.136)	I/177	II/177
(Proktam, 5.94)	III/405	III/1021
Ūrmikaula-siddhasantānarū-		
paka (Ūrmimahāśāstra, 2.48)	I/59 (2nd Āh.)	II/349
Utphullakamata		
(Utphulla, 29.166)	XI/113	VII/3403
Vijñānabhairava		
(Uktaṁ, 5.135)	III/448	III/1064
(Tatra tatra, 10.204)	VII/140	V/2024
Yonyarṇava		
(Arṇava, 29.165)	XI/113	VII/3403

5. TEXTS NAMED AND ALSO QUOTED AND SOMETIMES EXPLAINED BY ABHINAVAGUPTA

(a) *Directly quoted* (शब्दशः)

Text	*Āhnika/Verse*
Āgama	35.23
Ānandeśvara	29.200
Bhairavāgama	29.251-252
Devīyāmala	15.336-338
Kāmikā	4.25-28; 6.190-191; 8.213-215; 22.32
Kulaguhkara (? Kulaguhvara)	3.146-148
Paddhati (of Īśānadeva)	22.29-30
Ratnamālā	13.230-231
Śāra	16.252-253
Śrīpūrva	10.284
Svacchanda	13.307
Tattvarakṣāvidhāna	3.215-219
Triśirastantra	16.110-112
Triśirobhairavāgama	5.86
Triśiromata	1.87-88
Ūrmimahāśāstra	14.31
Yoginīkaula	7.41

(b) *Indirectly cited* (अर्थतः, तात्पर्यतः)

Text	*Āhnika/Verse*
Āgama	37.1
Aitareyavedānta	3.326-327
Ānanda	13.354
Anandādhikaśāsana	8.36-40
Ānandagahvara	14.19
Ānanda-śāstra	15.45, 59, 601; 16.65; 37.10, 18
Anuttara-prakriyā	9.313
Bhairavakula	13.302; 28.59, 388
Bhairava Tantra	13.304

Vijñānabhairava	15.480-489
Viṁśatika	7.56
Vīrāvalī	4.89, 241; 29.163, 243; 32.32-47
Vīrāvalībhairava	29.235
Vīrāvalīhṛdaya	15.102-103
Vīrāvalīkula	6.74-76; 29.272-273
Vīrāvalīpāda	29. 186-191
Yogā(ga)-/cā(ca)ra/saṁcā(ca)ra	6.58; 13.242; 15.65, 391-393; 23.12; 28.10; 29.83-88, 97, 150; 32.12-31
Yogasūtra	3.92-95

(c) *Quoted partly directly and partly indirectly* (उभयत:)

Gahvara	29.240-241
Gītā	1.124-125
Mālinīvijayottara	17.112-113
Triśiromata	1.82-86

(d) *Quoted and explained*

Ādhārakārikā/Anantakārikā	28.309, 312-315
Brahmayāmala	4.60-64
Gamaśāsana	1.150-155
Mālinī/-mata	10.199-122; 16.288-295; 21.2-5
Mataśāstra	4.69
Raurava	8.168-179
Sāra	23.96-99
Śrīpūrva/-śāstra	1.167-175; 23.67, 73-74
Yoga-sañcāra/cāra	4.120, 125-146; 29.82-89

6. PERSONS NAMED AND ALSO QUOTED BY ABHINAVAGUPTA

Person	*Āhnika/Verse*
Aniruddha	13.293-295
Bālamitra	37.66
Bhavabhūti	13.150-151
Dharmaśiva	21.50-53
Kalyāṇa	13.149-151
Kallaṭa/-nātha	10.208; 13.344-345; 29.123-124
Kheṭapāla	9.275-276
Śaṁbhunātha	5.52; 9.264; 10.187, 230; 13.254, 333-335; 15.133; 28.35; 35.44, 37.61
Śeṣamahāmuni	13.146
Somānanda	13.149-151
Śrīkaṇṭha	5.40; 6.171; 8.241
Utpala	12.25; 13.290-291
Vidyā(dhi)pati	1.201; 14.9-12
Vidyāguru	13.128

7. SYSTEMS IMPLIEDLY REFERRED TO IN THE TANTRĀLOKA AND IDENTIFIED BY JAYARATHA

System	*Āhnika/Verse*	*Volume/Page* (KSTS Ed.)	*Volume/Page* (MLBD Ed.)
Advaitavādin	1.223	(I/244)	II/244
Bauddha	1.56	(I/95)	II/95
– (Vaibhāṣika)	1.228	(I/247)	II/247
	4.30	(III/33)	III/649
– (Vijñānavādin)	4.30	(III/32)	III/648
	35.37	(XII/376)	VIII/3665
Bhedavādin	1.165	(I/200)	II/200
	1.237	(I/254)	II/254
	9.153	(VI/120)	IV/1754
Brahmavādin	3.282	(II/255)	II/607
	4.29	(III/32)	III/648
– (Vairinca)	4.22	(III/25)	III/641
Kāṇāda	9.290	(VI/233)	IV/1867
Kaula	4.259	(III/290)	III/906
Kaumārila	See Mīmāṁsā		
Kula	36.12	(XII/389)	VIII/3679
Mīmāṁsā	1.127-128	(I/166-168)	II/166-168
	1.134	(I/174)	II/174
	4.228-240	(III/250-266)	III/866-881
– (Kaumārila)	10.21	(VII/16)	V/1900
	10.52-57	(VII/42-45)	V/1926-1929
– (Prābhākara)	10.57	(VII/45)	V/1929
Naiyāyika	9.258	(VI/207)	IV/1842
	9.273-74	(VI/220)	IV/1854
Nyāya	9.257-258	(VI/207-208)	IV/1841-1842
	9.268-270	(VI/215-217)	IV/1849-1851
	9.285-290	(VI/229-234)	IV/1863-1868
	10.71-75	(VII/57-61)	V/1941-1945
Pātañjala	13.346	(VIII/207)	V/2407
	28.301	(XI/119)	VII/3225
Pātañjalasūtra	13.146	(VIII/95)	V/2295

Picuvaktra-saṁ-pradāya	29.124-125	(XI/89, 29th Āh.)	VII/3379
Prācya	27.23	(X/365)	VI/3091
Prābhākara	See Mīmaṁsā		
Sāṁkhya	6.18	(IV/17)	III/1105
	8.247	(V/170)	IV/1520
	8.253-259	(V/173-179)	IV/1523-1529
	9.14-21	(VI/25-29)	IV/1659-1663
	9.220-225	(VI/175-180)	IV/1811-1815
	9.239	(VI/192)	IV/1826
	9.271-274	(VI/217-221)	IV/1851-1855
	13.32-40	(VIII/22-28)	V/2221-2227
	13.271-272	(VIII/167)	V/2367
– (Kāpila/Kapila)	8.279-285	(V/189-196)	IV/1539-1546
	35.37	(XII/376)	VIII/3636
Siddhānta	4.258	(III/290)	III/903
	22.12	(X/248)	VI/2975
Śivāgama	1.75	(I/116)	II/116
Smṛti	13.346	(VIII/207)	V/2407
Trikakula	36.12	(XII/389)	VIII/3679
Vaibhāṣika	See Bauddha		
Vaiśeṣika	9.305	(VI/243-244)	IV/1877-1878
	10.71-75	(VII/57-61)	V/1941-1945
	13.345	(VIII/206)	V/2406
Veda	4.28	(III/30)	III/646
Vijñānavādin	See Bauddha		

8. IMPLIED PERSONAL REFERENCES IN THE TANTRĀLOKA AS IDENTIFIED BY JAYARATHA

Person	*Phrase/Āhnika/Kārika*	*Volume/Page* (KSTS edition)	*Volume/Page* (MLBD edition)
Amaranātha	(Svasantāna, 4.268)	III/299	III/915
Aniruddha	(Guravaḥ, 9.261)	VI/210	IV/1844
Bhagavatī	(Bhaṭṭārikā, 1.16)	I/34	II/34
Bhairava	(Etaiḥ, 36.3)	XII/363	VIII/3673
Bṛhaspati	(Gurubhiḥ, 8.101)	V/76	IV/1426
Bhūtirāja(?)	(Maheśvareṇa guruṇā, 3.90)	II/100	II/452
Jyotsnākāra	(Anyaiḥ, 9.305)	VI/243	IV/1877
Kallaṭa	(Āhuḥ, 6.12)	IV/11	III/1099
Kalyapāla	(Vikoṣi, 29.66)	XI/46 (29th Āh.)	VII/3336
Kāpālika	(Dhātuvibheda, 29.66)	XI/46 (29th Āh.)	VII/3336
Kapila	(Anye, 8.151)	V/113	IV/1463
	(Vyapodhṛtāḥ, 35.37)	XII/376	VIII/3666
Khagendra Nātha	(Kūrmādyā, 4.267)	III/297	III/913

Kheṭapāla	(Paribhāṣyate, 13.52)	VIII/36	V/2236
Kṛṣṇa	(37.65)	XII/423	VIII/3713
Lakṣamaṇagupta	(15.246-247)	IX/122	VI/2562
	(30.16)	XII/184	VII/3474
Līlākāra	(Kecit, 8.108)	V/81	IV/1431
Nṛsiṁhagupta	(Pañcamukhagupta, 1.1)	I/13-14	II/13-14
Pratyabhijñākāra	(Guruṇā, 9.278)	VI/224	IV/1858
	(Anye, 10.288)	VII/194	V/2078
Ruruvṛttikāra	(Ādi, 6.137)	IV/119	III/1207
Sadyojyoti	(Kheṭapālādyaiḥ, 9.262)	VI/211	IV/1845
Śambhunātha	(Bhaṭṭanātha, 1.16)	I/34	II/34
Somadeva	(Sumatyantenivāsinaḥ, 1.213)	I/235-236	II/235-236
Somānanda	(Sampradāyadhanā janāḥ, 10.217)	VII/147	V/2031
Śrīkaṇṭha	(Guruḥ, 8.9)	V/7	IV/1357
	(Tanmaṇḍalaṁ, 8.247)	V/170	IV/1520
	(9.225)	VI/180	IV/1814
	(Purāguravaḥ, 12.13)	VII/100	V/2192
	(Matsama, 13.220)	VIII/139	V/2329
	(Prakīrtitā, 15.253)	IX/125	VI/2565
Śrīvaradeva	(Paraḥ, 4.269)	III/299	III/915
Sugata	(Vyapodhṛtāḥ, 35.37)	XII/376	VIII/3666
Svatantreśa	(Viduḥ, 9.224)	VI/179	IV/1813

Utpala	(Gurūditam, 3.8)	II/9-10	II/362
	(Somānandaputrakāḥ, 3.85)	II/95	II/447
Vāmanadatta	(Gurubhiḥ, 5.155)	III/467	III/1083
Vāsudeva	(Guruḥ, 1.124)	I/162-163	II/162-163
Vidyādhipati	(Guruḥ, 9.173)	VI/135	IV/1769
Vimalakalā	(Vimalakalā, 1.1)	I/13-14	II/13-14

9. TEXTUAL REFERENCES IN THE TANTRĀLOKA—CITATIONS TRACED/IDENTIFIED BY JAYARATHA

Textual source	*Āhnika/Kārikā*	*Volume/Page* (KSTS edition)	*Volume/Page* (MLBD edition)
Ādhārakārikā	28.309	XI/122	VII/3228
Aitareyopaniṣad (Aitareyākhyavedānta)	3.226-231	II/216-221	II/568-573
Amākhyakalāsvarūpa-sphārasiddhānta (Kalāvyāptyanta)	3.137	II/141-143	II/493-495
Ānandādhikaśāsana	8.40	V/34-35	IV/1384-1385
Bhairavakula	13.302	VIII/182	V/2382
Bhairava Tantra	13.305	VIII/184	V/2384
Bhargaśikhā	4.255	III/284	III/900
	12.20	VII/103 (12th Āh.)	V/2195
	15.280-281	IX/138-139	VI/2578-2579
Brahmayāmala	28.418-419	XI/178-179	VII/3284-3285
Ḍāmarayāga	15.335-338	IX/169-170	VI/2609-2610
Devīyāmala/-śāstra (Mahāḍāmarakayāga)	3.70	II/82	II/434
	8.16	V/12	IV/1362

	8.212	V/149	IV/1499
	15.335-338	IX/169-170	VI/2609-2610
	15.460-463	IX/233-234	VI/2673-2674
	28.386-387	XI/164	VII/3270
	28.390-403	XI/166-172	VII/3272-3278
	31.85, 97	XII/265, 271	VII/3555, 3561
	32.1	XII/304	VII/3594
Gahvara	28.224-227	XI/89-90	VII/3195-3196
	32.50-53	XII/328	VII/3618
Gamaśāstra	13.232-233	VIII/144-145	V/2344-2345
Gītā	3.115	II/121	II/473
	28.326	XI/130	VII/3236
	37.65	XII/423	VIII/3713
Īśvarapratyabhijñākārikā	10.288-291	VII/194-198	V/2078-2082
Kiraṇaśāstra	1.75-77	I/116-121	II/116-121
	4.41	III/45-46	III/661-662
	9.47	VI/46-47	IV/1680-1681
	15.18	IX/12-13	VI/2452-2453
Kramarahasya	29.14-17	XI/14-16 (29th Āh.)	VII/3305-3306
Kramasadbhāva	12.23-24	VII/107 (12th Āh.)	V/2199
Kulagahvara	3.146-148	II/148-149 (29th Āh.)	II/500-501
	3.168-174	II/167-173	II/519-525
	24.13-16	X/310-311	VI/3036-3037
	32.49-53	XII/326-328	VII/3616-3618

Kularatnamālā (Ratnamālā)	1.274-283	I/281-287	II/281-287
Mādhavakula	29.56-67	XI/40-47(29th Āh.)	VII/3330-3337
Mālinīmata	8.300	V/206	IV/1556
	13.199-206	VIII/127-131	V/2327-2331
	15.3-4	IX/3	VI/2442
	19.54-55	X/204	VI/2930
Mālinī/-śāstra	15.15-17	IX/11	VI/2451
	28.293	XI/116	VII/3222
Mālinī-tantra	14.41-42	VIII/236	V/2436
	16.233-236	X/90-92	VI/2816-2818
Mālinī-vijaya/-vijayottara	1.243-245	I/257	II/257
	10.104	VII/78-80	V/1962-1964
	27.32-38	X/369-371	VI/3097-3099
Mataṇga-pārameśvara	8.379-380	V/247-249	IV/1597-1599
Ma(ā)taṅga/-śāstra	1.224	I/245	II/245
	6.228	IV/185	III/1273
	8.320	V/217-218	IV/1567-1568
	8.428-433	V/272-274	IV/1622-1624
	9.6	VI/6	IV/1640
	13.294	VIII/179	V/2379
	15.9-10	IX/5-7	V/2445-2447
	15.279	IX/138	V/2578
	25.24-29	X/324-327	VI/3050-3053
Mataṅgaśāstra-vṛtti	8.428-434	V/274-275	IV/1624-1625

	23.89	X/298	VI/3024
Mata/-śāstra	4.66-69	III/72-75	III/688-691
	4.262-270	III/292-299	III/908-915
Mokṣadharma	15.514	IX/254-255	VI/2694-2695
Mṛgendra-śāstra	9.190	VI/149	IV/1783
Mṛtyuñjaya	16.59-62	X/24-25	VI/2750-2751
Mṛtyuñjaya-siddha	21.11-15	X/221-222	VI/2947-2948
Mukuṭa-śāstra	15.514	IX/255	VI/2695
Nandiśikhā/-tantra	12.12	VII/99(12th Āh.)	V/2191
	13.163-195	VIII/104-125	V/2304-2325
Niśā-/Niśi-/Naiśa-/saṁca (cā)ra/cā(ca)ra	6.31-32	IV/32-33	III/1120-1121
	13.241-242	VIII/149	V/2349
	15.83-97	IX/47-50	VI/2487-2490
	15.105-107	IX/55	VI/2495
Niśākula	13.126-127	VIII/84-85	V/2284-2285
Niśāṭana	4.79	III/84	III/700
	4.177	III/207	III/823
Nityātantra	28.123-124	XI/51	VII/3157
Parātriṁśikā (Trīśikā)	3.206	II/198	II/550
(Trikasūtra)	12.15-16	VII/101(12thĀh.)	V/2193
Prajñālaṅkāra	3.54	II/62	II/414
	3.55	II/64	II/416
Ratnamālā/-śāstra	28.415-416	XI/178	VII/3284

	29.55	XI/40(29th Āh.)	VII/3330
	29.192-195	XI/127(29th Āh.)	VII/3417
	29.201	XI/132(29th Āh.)	VII/3422
	29.283	XI/168(29th Āh.)	VII/3458
Rauravamata	6.142	IV/123	III/1211
Raurava/-śāsana	8.32	V/30	III/1380
	9.217	VI/174	IV/1808
Rauravasaṅgraha	9.40	VI/41	IV/1675
Rauravavārtika	8.92	V/70	IV/1420
	8.183	V/132	IV/1482
Ruru/-śāsana	8.87	V/66	IV/1416
Ruru-vārtika	8.345-352	V/230-232	IV/1580-1582
Sāra-śāstra/-śāsana	8.321	V/218	IV/1568
	14.33-35	VIII/232-233	V/2432-2433
Sarvajñānottara (Jñānottara)	4.248-251	III/275-279	III/891-895
	9.45	VI/45	IV/1679
Sarvavīra	4.55-57	III/61-63	III/677-678
	12.23-24	VII/106-107 (12th Āh.)	V/2198-2199
Siddhāmata (Mata)	4.66	III/72	III/688
Siddhā/-tantra	8.41-42	V/34-36	IV/1384-1386
	8.115-117	V/89-90	IV/1439-1440
	8.184-185	V/133-134	IV/1483-1484
	15.333-334	IX/166-167	VI/2606-2607
	25.2	X/315	VI/3041

	27.25-28	X/367	VI/3093
	31.8-9	XII/227-228	VII/3517-3518
Siddhayogīśvarīmata	3.220-225	II/207-214	II/559-566
	9.7	VI/7	IV/1641
	11.81	VII/64-65(11th Āh.)	V/2156-2157
	15.321-323	IX/162-163	VI/2601-2602
	17.113-114	X/172-173	VI/2898-2899
Śivadṛṣṭi(Saṁpradāyadhanāḥ)	10.216-217	VII/147	V/2031
Śiva-/Śaivī-tanu/-śāstra	8.299	V/205	IV/1555
	8.301	V/207	IV/1557
	8.345-351	V/233	IV/1583
	9.206-207	VI/166-167	IV/1800-1801
Spanda/-śāsana	3.281	II/254	II/606
	11.32	VII/29(11th Āh.)	V/2121
	15.113-114	IX/58	VI/2498
Śrīpūrva/-śāsana/-śāstra/-tantra			
(Varṇitā)	1.186-187	I/215	II/215
	1.196	I/223	II/223
	4.106-108	III/112-114	III/728-730
	8.300	V/207	IV/1557
	8.325	V/221	IV/1571
	8.436	V/277	IV/1627
	9.120-121	VI/96-97	IV/1730-1731
	9.147-149	VI/115	IV/1749

	11.72	VII/57	V/2149
	11.80	VII/63	V/2115
	11.89	VII/71-72(11th Āh.)	V/2163-2164
	10.301-309	VII/206-207	V/2090-2091
	15.135-137	IX/72	VI/2512
	16.211-212	X/81	VI/2807
	16.278	X/113	VI/2839
	23.11-12	X/266	VI/2992
Svacchanda/-śāsana/-śāstra/-tantra	6.50	IV/43-44	III/1131-1132
	6.136-137	IV/118	III/1206
	7.67	IV/54 (7th Āh.)	III/1346
	8.11	V/8	IV/1358
	8.191-193	V/137-138	IV/1487-1488
	15.21-26	IX/16-17	VI/2456-2457
	35.26-27	XII/370-371	VIII/3660-3661
Svāyambhuva (Vairiñca)	9.46	VI/46	IV/1680
	9.67	VI/60	IV/1694
Tantrasadbhāva (Sadbhāva-śāsana)	29.211-216	XI/136-139(29th Āh.)	VII/3426-3429
Tattvārthacintāmaṇi (Kallaṭa)	10.208	VII/142	V/2026
Traiśika	15.15	IX/10	VI/2450
Trikasāra (Sāraśāstra)	3.253	II/236	II/588
	23.96-97	X/302	VI/3028

Tri(Trai)śi-ro/-rasa/-mata	1.114-115	I/156-157	II/156-157
	30.12-14	XII/179-180	VII/3469-3470
Tri(Trai)śi-raḥ/-rasa/-śāsana/-śāstra/-tantra	2.32	I/26(2nd Āh.)	II/336
	3.137	II/141	II/493
	3.256	II/237	II/589
	5.128-130	III/439-441	III/1055-1057
	8.12	V/9-11	IV/1359-1361
	15.69-70	IX/39	VI/2479
	15.184-193	IX/95	VI/2535
Triśirobhairava	1.86-90	I/131-136	II/131-136
Ūrmikaulasiddhasantānarūpaka (Ūrmimahāśāstra) (Ūrmimahākula)	2.48	I/39-40(2nd Āh.)	II/349-350
	14.31-36	IX/230-233	V/2430-2433
Vājasaneya	13.143-144	VIII/94	V/2294
Vijñānabhairava	5.71	III/377-380	III/993-996
	5.135	III/448	III/1064
	10.204	VII/140	V/2024
Vīrāvalī	4.241-243	III/268	III/884
Vīrāvalīkula	6.74-75	IV/65-66	III/1153-1154
Yogacāra	23.12-13	X/266	VI/2992
Yogasūtra	28.285	XI/113	VII/3219
Yoginīkaula	7.40	IV/32(7th Āh.)	III/1324

10. PERSONAL REFERENCES IN THE TANTRĀLOKA— CITATIONS TRACED/IDENTIFIED BY JAYARATHA

Person	*Āhnika/Kārikā*	*Volume/Page* (KSTS edition)	*Volume/Page* (MLBD edition)
Aniruddha	13.293-295	VIII/179	V/2379
Bhagavān Vāsudeva (Guruḥ)	1.324	I/162	II/162
Bṛhaspati (Gurubhiḥ)	1.104	I/146	II/146
Kallaṭa	10.208	VII/142	V/2026
	28.338-340	XI/138	VII/3244
Pratyabhijñākāra	9.278	VI/224	IV/1858
	10.289-291	VII/194-195	V/2078-2079
Sadyojyoti (Kheṭapāla)	9.262	VI/211	IV/1845
Śeṣamahāmuni	13.146	VIII/95	V/2295
Somānanda (Śivadṛṣṭi)	2.48	I/40 (2nd Āh.)	II/350
Śrīkaṇṭha	8.9-10	V/7	IV/1357
	8.247	V/170	IV/1520
(Viduḥ)	9.224	VI/179	IV/1813
(Svatantreśa)	9.225	VI/180	IV/1814
Utpala (Gurūditam, Pratyabhijñākārikā	3.8	II/10	II/362

11. FIRST PERSONAL REFERENCES IN THE TANTRĀLOKA

मम	1.1	मम	6.91
नौमि	1.2, 1.3	नो गुरुः	6.226
मे	1.5	संप्रचक्ष्महे	6.249
मम	1.6	नः	8.230
मे	1.7	मह्यम्, निजैः	8.406
नुमः	1.11	ब्रूमः	9.24
मे	1.12	नः	9.32
मे	1.13	अस्मदुक्ते	9.42
रचये	1.15	मया	9.84
प्रकटीकुर्मो	1.19	ब्रूमहे	9.117
मया	1.106	संप्रचक्ष्महे	9.167
वक्ष्यामः	1.139	अस्माभिः	9.219
अस्माकं	1.193	मम	9.261
निषेत्स्यामो/दर्शयिष्यामहे	1.240	अस्मत्	9.263
मया	1.245	मम	9.264
मन्ये	1.332	नः	9.276
ब्रूमः	2.3	अस्मन्मते	9.299
मया	3.90	ब्रूमः	10.28
ब्रूमहे	3.91	नरीनृत्यामहे	10.34
नः	3.111	मया	10.44
नः गुरवः	3.173	अस्माकं	10.62
कथयामः	4.1	मन्ये	10.68
तनिष्यामः	4.32	उपलभामहे	10.148
अस्मद्दृशि	4.98	मया	10.227
मे	5.41	मया	10.230
ब्रूमो	5.43	अस्माभिः	11.1
अस्मभ्यम्	5.52	अस्मद्गुरवः	11.15
मम	5.97	अस्मद्गुरुः	11.59
मे	6.89	मन्महे	11.113

अस्मत्प्रभुः	11.115
अस्मद्गुरोर्गुरुः	12.25
स्वमतं	13.2
न मन्महे	13.60
न मन्महे	13.101
अस्मत्परमेष्ठी	13.108
अस्मत्कृतम्	13.160
नो भरः	13.263
अस्माकं	13.290
मे	13.333
अहम्	13.345
असेविषि	13.346
अस्माकं	15.152
ब्रूमहे	15.179
मे	15.245
मम	15.352
मे	15.408
मयापि	15.409
अस्मद्गुरुभिः	16.11
अस्मद्हृदयेश्वरे	16.145
मया	16.197
अस्मद्गुरवो जगुः	17.19
मया	17.47
अस्माकं गुरुणा	19.3
मे	20.6
मया	21.26
वच्मः	22.1
अस्मद्गुर्वागमः	23.65
वच्मः	25.19
मया प्रोक्तम्	26.62
अस्मद्गुरवः	28.48
अस्मद्गुरुक्रमः	28.92
मया	28.186
ब्रूमहे	28.217
अस्मत्संतानगुरुणा	28.338
वच्मि	28.385
मया	29.169
अर्चये	29.176
मे	29.243
अस्मभ्यम्	30.63
अस्मभ्यम्	30.123
कथये	32.1
नास्माभिः	32.9
मम	35.44
मया	37.30
वयं नाद्रियामहे	37.31
मन्ये	37.40
मन्ये	37.57

12. ĀGAMAS FORMING ONE GROUP ON SPECIFIC ISSUES IN THE TANTRĀLOKA

Āgamas	*Āhnika/ kārikā*
Āgama and Ratnamālā	13.230
Aghoreśa Tantra and Svacchanda	27.58
Ānanda-śāsana and Nandiśikhā	15.282
Bhairavakula and Trikaśāstra	28.51
Bhairavakula and Ūrmiśāstra	28.59
Bhairavīyakula and Siddhavīrāvalīsāra	22.41
Bhargaśikhā-śāstra and Gamaśāsana	15.280
Brahmayāmala, Vājasaneya, Vīra and Siddhā	4.54
Brahmayāmala and Sarvavīra	13.145
Ḍamarayāga, Mastaka, Śrīpūrvaśāstra and Devīyā-mala	3.70-71
Devīyāmala, Ḍāmarayāga, Mastaka and Śrīpūrvaśāstra	3.70-71
Devī-yāmala and Sāraśāstra	15.253
Devīyāmala, Śrīpūrva, Siddhātantra, Trikakula and Triśiromata	31.60
Dīkṣottara and Kairaṇa	18.11
Gama-śāsana and Bhrgaśikhā-śāstra	15.280
Gama-śāsana, Sarvācāra, Virāvalī, Niśācara and Krama	12.23
Haiḍara, Kālīkula, Trikakula and Trikasadbhāva	28.15
Kālikula, Trikakula, Trikasadbhāva and Haiḍara	28.15
Kairaṇa and Dīkṣottara	18.11
Kaula and Ṣaḍardhaka-śāsana	37.26
Khecarīmata and Mālinīmata	32.6
Kiraṇa and Mataṅga	13.284
Krama, Sarvācāra, Vīrāvalī, Niśācara and Gamaśāstra	12.23
Mālā, Mālinisāraśāsana and Siddhāṭana-sadbhāva	28.113
Mālinīmata and Khecarīmata	32.6
Mālinīsāraśāsana, Mālā and Siddhāṭana-sadbhāva	28.113
Mastaka, Ḍāmarayāga, Devīyāmala and Śrīpūrva śāstra	3.70-71

13(A). TEXTS NAMED AND/OR QUOTED BY NAME BY JAYARATHA IN THE TANTRĀLOKA-VIVEKA

Text	*Volume/Page* (KSTS edition)	*Volume/Page* (MLBD edition)
(I) Ādhārakārikā[1]	XI/122	VII/3228
Āgama	I/46, 175, 256; III/95, 132, 154, 160, 161, 162, 188, 200, 218, 317; IV/203; IV/51 (7th Āh.), 53; V/142; VI/167, 246; VII/19 (11th Āh.), 24, 73; VII/105 (12th Āh.); VIII/33, 57, 75, 81, 109, 110, 174, 176; IX/27, 210-211; X/22, 23, 24, 26, 33, 37, 38, 50, 132, 137, 140, 186, 259, 270, 276, 284, 302, 308, 324, 368; XI/24, 98, 104, 115, 122; XI/12 (29th Āh.),	II/46, 175, 256; III/711, 748, 770, 776, 777, 778, 804, 816, 834, 933, 1291, 1343, 1345; IV/1492, 1880, 1801; V/2111, 2116, 2165, 2197, 2233, 2257, 2275, 2281, 2309, 2310, 2374, 2376; VI/2467, 2650-2651, 2748, 2749, 2750, 2752, 2759, 2763, 2764, 2776, 2858, 2863, 2866, 2912, 2985, 2996, 3002, 3010, 3028, 3034, 3050, 3094; VII/3130, 3204, 3210, 3221, 3228, 3302, 3304, 3369, 3382, 3403, 3438, 3452, 3474, 3623; VIII/3645, 3646, 3651, 3654,

* '(A)' after a title indicates a fresh reference by Jayaratha.

** '(I)' in the beginning of the word indicates that this has already been taken care of in Appendix I.

*** 'S1' to 'S63' denote the 64 tantras as enumerated in the *Śrīkaṇṭhī* as quoted in the *Viveka*. See the following index—13(B).

1. See under *Anantakārikā* (Appendix I).

(I)	Bhairavatantra	I/153; VIII/183	II/153, V/2383
	Bhairavī[2] (A)[s7]	I/43	II/43
	Bhairavī (-śikhā)[s8] (A)	I/42	II/43
	Bhārata (A)	V/61	IV/1411
	Bharga (-śikhā)	I/22 (2nd Āh.)	II/332
	Bhargaśikhākula	XII/333	VII/3623
	Bhogakārikā (A)	VI/195, 250	IV/1829, 1884
	Bhūṣaṇa (A)	II/14	II/366
	Bhūtakṣobha (A)	IX/140	VI/2580
(I)	Brahmayāmala[s9]	I/42;III/64, 67, 69, 70; XI/179	II/42, III/680, 683, 685, 686; VII/3285
	Brāhmīkalā[s10]	I/42	II/42
	Cālikā(mata) (A)[s11]	I/42	II/42
	Caṇḍa(-bhairava) (A)[s12]	I/42	II/42
	Candrākhyā (A)[s13]	I/43	II/43
	Candralekhā (A)[s14]	I/43	II/43
	Candrāṅśu (A)	I/40	II/40
	Catuṣkapañcāśikā	X/344	VI/3070
	Chāndogyopaniṣad (A)	X/132	VI/2858
	Cillācakreśvarīmata (A)	I/85-86	II/85-86
(I)	Cintāmaṇī	X/19	VI/2745
	Cintya (A)	I/40	II/40

2. The Tā.Sā. mentions one *Bhairavīkavaca* abstracted from the *Rudrayāmalatantra*. This is listed at No. 8071 (C) in the Baroda Collection. Jayaratha, however, refers to it as an independent Āgama.

	Citrikā (A)[s15]	I/43	II/40
	Dakṣa (A)	I/41; VIII/181, 212	II/41; V/2381, 2412
(I)	Ḍāmara(-śikhā)[s16]	I/43	II/43
	Devīpañcā(ca)-śata/-śatika(A)	XI/31 (29th Āh.); XII/197	VII/3321; VII/3487
	Devī-/-Devyā-/yāmala	IX/125; X/254, 268; XI/164, 166; XI/40(29th Āh.), 41, 49; XII/198, 200, 265, 304	VI/2565, 2980, 2994; VII/3270, 3272, 3330, 3331, 3339, 3488, 3490, 3555, 3594
	Dharamālaṅkāra(A)	VI/18, 20	IV/1652, 1654
	Dīkṣottara	III/462	III/1078
	Dīpta (A)	I/40	II/40
(I)	Gahvara	X/185	VI/2911
	Gama/-śāsana/-śāstra	I/189; VII/106 (12th Āh.); VIII/144, 145; XI/99 (29th Ah.), 100	II/189; V/2198; V/2344, 2345; VII/3389, 3390
(I)	Gītā	I/162, 172, 197; I/33, 38-39 (2nd Āh.); II/121, 166, 216, 220, 221; III/438; VI/76-77, 89, 109; VII/82 (11th Āh.); VIII/231; XI/130; XII/423	II/162, 172, 197, 343, 348-349, 473, 518, 568, 572, 573; III/1054; IV/1710-1711, 1723, 1743; V/2174, 2431; VII/3236; VIII/3713
	Guhyacakra (A)[s17]	I/43	II/43
	Haiḍara	XI/9, 13	VII/3115, 3119
	Haṁsa (A)[s18]	I/43	II/43
	Hārdeśa	XI/113 (29th Āh.)	VII/3403
	Hastanaya (A)	III/200	III/816

Hṛdayabhaṭṭāraka	XI/113 (29th Āh.)	VII/3403
Hṛdayanayarahasya (A)	II/82	II/434
Hṛllekhā (A)[s19]	I/43	II/43
Jvālina (A)[s20]	I/43	II/43
(I) Jñānottara	See Sarvajñānottara	
Jyotsnā	VI/243	IV/1877
Kabandha (A)[s21]	I/43	II/43
Kadambikā A)[s22]	I/43	II/43
Kalācakra (A)[s23]	I/43	II/43
Kālikākrama[3] (A)	III/390	III/1006
(I) Kālottara	VII/12 (11th Āh.)	V/2104
Kāmaja (A)	I/40	II/40
(I) Kāmikā	X/255; XII/325	VI/2981; VII/3615
Kapālīśa (-bhairava)[4] (A)[s24]	I/42	II/42
Khacakra[s25] (A)	I/43	II/43
Khemata	XI/113 (29th Āh.)	VII/3403

3. There are two works referred to in the Darbar Library, Nepal. One is the *Kālikākulakramasadbhāva* (I/76) and the other is the *Kālikākulapañcakramārcana* by Vimalaprabodha whose two MSS are listed, one incomplete (I/169) and the other complete (3/314). We are told A. Sanderson (Oxford) is working on these texts. The *Kālikākrama*, also known as *Devikākrama* in other sources (see our K.T., p. 235-36), is perhaps an abridged version of either of these two texts.

4. In the Curator's Office Library we find a MS entitled *Kāpālikatantra* numbered as 7475 and listed under Śāktatantra.

	Khecarīmata (A)	XI/113 (29th Āh.)	VII/3403
(I)	Kiraṇa/-śāstra/-saṁhitā	I/40; III/45, 84; V/41; VIII/173; X/179	II/40; III/661, 700; V/2373; IV/1391; VI/2905
	Krama	VII/106 (12th Āh.)	V/2198
	Kramabhaṭṭāraka (A)	III/163	III/779
	Kramakamala (A)	III/196, 197	III/812, 813
	Kramakeli (A)	III/191	III/807
	Kramasadbhāva/-bhaṭṭāraka[5](A)	III/136, 172, 190, 191; VII/107 (12th Āh.)	III/752, 788, 806, 807; V/2199
	Kṛṣṇavākya (A)	XII/423	VIII/3713
	Kramastotra[6] (A)	III/158, 160, 162, 165, 166, 169, 173, 178, 181, 183, 185, 187, 201	III/774, 776, 778, 781, 782, 785, 789, 794, 797, 799, 801, 803, 817
	Krodha(-bhairava) (A)[s26]	I/42	II/42
(I)	Kulaguhvara	II/148, 168, 173; XII/326	II/500, 520, 525; VII/3616
	Kulakrīḍāvatāra (A)	XI/28 (29th Āh.)	VII/3318
	Kulakramodaya (A)	XI/44 (29th Āh.)	VII/3334
	Kularatnamālā (A)	I/281; VII/20 (11th Āh.)	II/281; V/2112

5. There is a reference to the MS of one *Kālikā-kulakramasadbhāva* (I/76) in the Darbar Library, Nepal in the Tantra catalogue, Vol. I, p. 37. This needs be compared.

6. The *Kramastotra*, as available in the pages of the *Viveka*, with Hindi translation and commentary has been published by Sri Lakṣmaṇa Joo, Srinagar, under the title *Krama-naya-pradīpikā*. It has also been printed by Silburn with translation into French.

	— (Ratnamālā)	I/281; XI/59; XI/131(29th Āh.), 168	II/281; VII/3165, 3421, 3458
	Lakṣmīmata[7] (A)[s27]	I/42	II/42
	Lampaṭākhya (-mata) (A)[s28]	I/42	II/42
	Lalitā (A)	I/40	II/40
	Līlā (A)	V/81	IV/1431
	Madgīta (A)	I/40	II/40
(I)	Mādhavakula (A)	XI/40 (29th Āh.), 49	VII/3330, 3339
	Mahocchuṣma-bhairava(A)[s29]	I/42	II/42
	Mālinī (A)	I/49; VII/70 (11th Āh.)	II/49; V/2162
(I)	Mālinīmata	I/49; V/206; VIII/127; IX/3; XII/307	II/49; IV/1556; V/2327; VI/2443; VII/3597
(I)	Mālinīślokavārtika	I/49	II/49
(I)	Mālinī-vijaya/-vijayottara/-tantra/-satka	I/55; III/241; VI/7, 41, 96; VII/2, 78; VIII/234	II/55; III/857; 1641, 1675, 1730; V/1886, 1962, 2434
	Maṅgalā[s30]	I/43	II/43
	Mantracakra (A)[s31]	I/43	II/43
	Manvādiśāstra (A)	XII/395	VIII/3685
	Maryādāhīna	XI/113 (29th Āh.)	VII/3403
	Mata (-mata)[s32]	I/42	II/42

7. We do not know if it is identical with the *Lakṣmītantra* belonging to the Nāradapāñcarātra, which has been published by V. Krishnamacharya from Adyar, Madras.

	Matabhaṭṭāraka	IX/65	VI/2505
(I)	Mata/-śāstra	I/49; III/293; IX/80	II/49; III/909; VI/2520
(I)	Mataṅgapārmeśvara	V/247	IV/1597
(I)	Mātaṅga/-śāstra	I/85; IV/185; V/233, 234, 248; VI/148, 149, 210; VIII/173; IX/5, 7; X/159	II/85; III/1273; IV/1583, 1584, 1598, 1782, 1783, 1844; V/2373; VI/2445, 2447; VI/2885
	Mātṛrodana (A)[s33]	I/43	II/43
(I)	Maukuṭa	I/40	II/40
(I)	Mṛgendra	V/62; VI/149, 165	IV/1412, 1783, 1799
	Mṛgendrā (A)	IX/19	VI/2459
	Mṛgendrottara	V/51	IV/1401
(I)	Mṛtuñjaya	X/360	VI/3086
	Mukhabimba (A)	I/40	II/40
	Mūlasañjñaka (A)[s34]	I/43	II/43
	Nāda(-cakra) (A)[s35]	I/43	II/43
	Nāmaka	I/49; VII/70 (11th Āh.)	II/49; V/2162
	Nandiśikhā	V/14-15; V/186, 237, 241, 243, 256; VIII/127; IX/138	IV/1364-1365, 1536, 1587, 1591, 1593, 1606; V/2327; VI/2578
	Nārasiṁhaka (A)	I/40	II/40
	Navanityāvidhāna (A)	IX/139	VI/2579
	Nighaṇṭu (A)	II/145	II/497
(I)	Niḥśvāsa/-śāsana	I/40; XII/210	II/40; VII/3500
	Nijastotraikadeśa	XI/118 (29th Āh.)	VII/3408
	Nirmaryādaśāstra	XI/113 (29th Āh.)	VI/3403

(I) Niśā-/ca(cā)ra	I/49; VII/106 (12th Ah.)	II/49; V/2198
(I) Niśāṭana	I/89; III/207; X/76	II/89; III/823; VI/2802
Pañcāmṛta (A)	IX/140	VI/2580
Pañcikā (A)	X/56, 292	VI/2782, 3018
Pañcāśikā (A)	XI/129 (29th Āh.)	VII/3419
Pañcaśatika (A)	III/158, 160, 161, 163, 165, 166, 169, 173, 178, 181, 183, 185-186, 187, 189, 194	III/774, 776, 777, 779, 781, 782, 785, 789, 794, 797, 799, 801-802, 803, 805, 810
Pārameśvara (A)	I/40	II/40
Parātriṁśikā[8] (A)	II/166, 198;	II/518, 550
— (-Triśikā)	VII/101 (12th Āh.)	V/2193
Pātañjalasūtra	VIII/95	V/2295
Parātriṁśikā-vivaraṇa[9] (A)	VI/249	IV/1883
Picu(-bhairavī) (A)[s36]	I/42	II/42
Picuvaktra	XI/59	VII/3165
Piṅglā(-mata) (A)[s37]	I/42	II/42
Prajñālaṅkāra (A)	II/54, 62, 64	II/406, 414, 416
Prakīrṇakavivaraṇa (A)	VII/33	V/1917
Pramāṇastotra	VI/135	IV/1769

8. Published in KSTS alongwith Abhinavagupta's *Vivaraṇa* commentary. Also published with Lāsaka's commentary in a separate volume in KSTS.

9. Published in KSTS. Another edition with annotated translation into English by Jaidev Singh is shortly coming out. See Appendix I also.

	Pratyabhijñā-/kārikā[10] (A)	II/84; VI/178; VII/67	II/436; IV/1812; V/1951
	Purāṇa	III/43; V/61, 114, VIII/174	III/659; IV/1411, 1464; V/2374
(I)	Pūrvaśāstra[11] (A)	V/145; VII/19 (11th Āh.)	IV/1495; V/2111
	Raktākhya(-mata) (A)[s38]	I/42	II/42
	Rāmāyaṇa (A)	V/61	IV/1411
(I)	Ratnamāla	See Kularatnamālā	
(I)	Raurava	VIII/211	V/2411
(I)	Rauravamata	IV/123	III/1211
	Rauravasaṁgraha	VI/41	IV/1675
	Rauravavārtika	V/70, 132	IV/1420, 1482
	Ṛgveda (A)	V/114, 180	IV/1464, 1530
	Rudrayāmala (A)[s39]	I/42	II/42
(I)	Ruruśāsana	V/66	IV/1416
	Ruru(-bheda) (A)[s40]	I/43	II/43

10. Published in KSTS with Utpala's own *Vṛtti* alongwith *Saṁbandhasiddhi*, *Ajaḍapramātṛsiddhi* and *Īśvarasiddhi* under the title *Siddhitrayī*. Critical editions of the complete *Vṛtti* by Utpala is under preparation of HP Alper (Dallas) and R. Torrella (Rome). Also published in KSTS with Abhinavagupta's *Vimarśinī* (two volumes) and *Vivṛtivimarśinī* (three volumes) entitled respectively as *Īśvarapratyabhijñāvimarśinī* and *Īśvarapratyābhijñāvivṛtivimarśinī*. Later published by KC Pandey under the title *Bhāskarī* (two volumes) alongwith Abhinava's *Vimarśinī* and Bhāskarakaṇṭha's *Bhāskarī*. The same with a large commentary by an anonymous author edited by Pandey and the present author is shortly coming out from Motilal Banarsidass.

11. It seems to be a scribal mistake for the *Śrīpūrvaśāstra* which is none other than the *Mālinīvijayottara*. See Appendix I.

	Ruru (-yāmala) (A)[s41]	I/42	II/42
(I)	Ruru/-śāstra	I/84; V/117, 186; VI/174, 176.	II/84; IV/1467, 1536, 1808, 1810
	Ruruvārtika	V/230	IV/1580
	Ruruvṛtti	VI/169	IV/1803
	Sadbhāvaśāsana	XI/136 (29th Āh.)	VII/3426
	Ṣaḍardhahṛdaya	VIII/181	V/2381
	Śaiva	I/48, 72; III/278; VIII/212	II/48, 72; III/894; V/2412
	Śakticakra (A)[s42]	I/43	II/43
	Sāmaveda (A)	I/43	II/43
	Saṁmoha-(-śikhā) (A)[s43]	V/114, 180	IV/1464, 1530
	Saṁvitprakāśa (A)	V/186	IV/1536
	Saṅgraha (A)	III/467	III/1083 (Vth Āh.)
	Saṅkarṣaṇayāmala (A)	IX/139	VI/2579
(I)	Santānagama[12]	I/40	II/40
	Sārabhaṭṭāraka	II/82	II/434
	Sāraśāstra	II/236; VIII/231	II/588; V/2431
	Sārdhaśatika (A)	III/161, 189	III/777, 805
(I)	Sarvajñānottara	VI/45, 46	IV/1679, 1680
	Śātātapa	VIII/11	V/2211
	Sarvamaṅgalā (A)[s44]	I/43	II/43
(I)	Sarvavīra	III/61; VII/106 (12th Āh.)	III/677; V/2198
	Saurabheya	I/40	II/40

12. See fn. 44 under Santatyāgama (Appendix I).

	Siddha (A)	I/40	II/40
	Siddhā/-tantra	I/49; V/16, 20, 35; VII/70 (11th Āh.); IX/74, 163	II/49; IV/1366, 1370, 1385; V/2162; VI/2514, 2603
(I)	Siddhāmata	III/72; IX/80	III/688; VI/2520
	Siddhānta/-śāstra	III/280	III/896
	Siddhāvīra	XII/341	VII3631
(I)	Siddhayogīśvarīmata	IV/32 (7th Āh.); V/35, 88; XII/384	III/1324; IV/1385, 1438; VIII/3674
	Siddhayogīśvarītantra[13] (A)	VI/7	IV/1641
	Śiraścheda(-śikhā) (A)[s45]	I/43	II/43
(I)	Śivadṛṣṭi	I/40 (2nd Āh.)	II/350
	Śivadharmottara[14] (A)	V/115	IV/1465
	Śivāgama	I/116	II/116
	Śivāśāstropaniṣad (A)	XII/434	VIII/3724
(I)	Śivasūtra	I/18, 58; VII/163	II/18, 58; V/2047
	Śiva-/Śaivī-tanu/-śāstra	V/186, 205, 209, 220	IV/1536, 1555, 1559, 1570
	Skandayāmalatantra	X/302	VI/3028
	Smṛti	IX/88, 255; X/23, 279; XI/25, 77; XI/73 (29th Āh.)	VI/2528, 2695, 2749, 3005; VII/3131, 3183, 3363
(I)	Spanda-śāstra	III/213; VII/29 (11th Āh.); VIII/165	III/829; V/2121, 2365

13. Perhaps identical with the *Siddhayogīśvaramata*. See Appendix I.
14. All India Kashiraj Trust is bringing out a critical edition based on the available MSS.

Śrīkaṇṭhī (A)	I/39-40, 41-44	II/39-40, 41-44
Srīpara	VII/12 (11th Ah.)	V/2104
(I) Śrīpūrva/-śāstra	I/215, 220-222, 223; II/223; III/29, 112, 279; V/130, 206; VI/7, 41, 48, 111, 148, 149, 161, 165, 179, 186, 219, 222, 223, 247; VII/80, 117, 127, 144, 164, 184, 187, 190; VII/39 (11th Āh.), 43, 57, 63, 71; VIII/127, 136, 137, 138, 153; IX/125, 210, 230; X/59, 269; XI/14, 116; XII/185, 187, 198, 253, 309	II/215, 220-222, 223, 575; III/645, 728, 895; IV/1480, 1596, 1641, 1675, 1682, 1745, 1782, 1783, 1795, 1799, 1813, 1820, 1853, 1856, 1857, 1881; V/1964, 2001, 2011; 2028, 2048, 2068, 2071, 2074, 2131, 2135, 2149 2155, 2163, 2327, 2336, 2337, 2338, 2353; VI/2565, 2650, 2670, 2785, 2995; VII/3120, 3222, 3475, 3477, 3488, 3543, 3599
Śruti	IX/87, 88; X/23, 279; XI/52	VI/2527, 2528, 2749, 3005; VII/3158
Stotra	III/191; VIII/85	III/807; V/2285
Stotrabhaṭṭāraka (A)	III/223	III/839
Subodhamañjarī[15] (A)	II/4	II/356
Sūkṣmasvāyambhuva(A)	IX/3	VI/2443
Sūtravimarśinī (A)	III/449	III/1065
Svacchanda (-bhairava) (A)[s46]	I/42	II/42

15. A MS of the *Subodhamañjarī* ascribed to Vāmanadatta is said to be available in B.H.U. (C4255). Another text going by the name of *Svabodhodayamañjarī* is also reported in the same collection (C100), vide Upodghāta, pp. 78, 83. The latter text is also ascribed to Vāmanadatta.

(I) Svacchanda/-śāstra	I/71; III/22, 280; IV/41, 43, 170; V/8, 64, 104, 144, 145, 146, 147, 158, 199, 237, 272; VI/129, 161, 165; VII/68 (11th Āh.); VIII/191; IX/14, 23; XII/371	II/71; III/638, 896, 1129, 1131, 1258; IV/1358, 1414, 1454, 1494, 1495, 1496, 1497, 1508, 1549, 1587, 1622, 1763, 1795, 1799; V/2160, 2391, 2454, 2463; VIII/3661
Svacchanda (-yāmala)[s47]	I/42	II/42
(I) Svā(va)yambhuva	I/40, 84; VI/46, 60; XI/103	II/40, 84; IV/1680, 1694; VII/3209
(I) Tantrāloka	I/4, 6, 13-14, 19, 22, 27, 29-30, 34, 53, 54, 55, 62, 71, 74-75, 153, 162, 179, 180, 236, 238, 258, 287, 309; I/5 (2nd Āh.); II/88, 92, 102, 114, 117-118, 190, 194, 212, 233, 247, 250, 264; III/37, 48, 51, 53-55, 72-73, 126, 131, 138-139, 219-220, 231, 289, 293, 297, 298, 313, 393, 442-444, 457-458; IV/4, 17, 21-22, 156, 169, 177, 203; IV/49 (7th Āh.), 50; V/19, 22, 188; VI/7, 203, 204; VII/3, 4, 44, 128, 137; VII/68 (11th Āh.); VIII/80, 102, 134, 147, 152, 218; IX/	II/4, 6, 13-14, 19, 22, 27, 29-30, 34, 53, 54, 55, 62, 71, 74-75, 153, 162, 179, 180, 236, 238, 258, 287, 309, 315, 440, 444, 454, 466, 469-470, 542, 546, 564, 585, 599, 602, 616; III/653, 664, 667, 669-671, 688-689, 742, 747, 754-755, 835-836, 847, 905, 909, 913, 914, 929, 1009, 1058-1060, 1073-1074, 1092, 1105, 1109-1110, 1244, 1257, 1265, 1291, 1341, 1342; IV/1369, 1372, 1538, 1641, 1837, 1838; V/1887, 1888, 1928, 2012, 2021, 2160, 2280, 2302, 2334, 2347, 2352, 2418; VI/2565 2686-2687, 2837, 2904, 2925, 2937, 2982, 3056; VII/3121, 3142-3143, 3309, 3324, 3407, 3421, 3437, 3438; VIII/3722, 3723, 3724

	125, 246-247; X/111, 178, 199, 211, 256, 330; XI/15, 36-37; XI/19 (29th Āh.), 34, 117, 131, 147, 148; XII/432, 433, 434	
Tantrālokaviveka[16] (A)	XII/434	VIII/3724
Tantrabhairavī (A)[s48]	I/42	II/42
Tantrarāja	X/211	VI/2937
Tantrarājabhaṭṭāraka (A)	II/145; III/189; V/17, 20, 22, 63; XI/40 (29th Āh.), 69	II/497; III/805; IV/1367, 1370, 1372, 1413; VII/3330, 3359
(I) Tantrasadbhāva	II/77; XI/136 (29th Āh.)	II/429; VII/3426
Tatabhairavī (A)[s49]	I/42	II/42
Tattvarakṣāvidhāna	XI/99 (29th Āh.)	VII/3389
Tattvārthacintāmaṇi (A)	VII/142; X/19	V/2026; VI/2745
Traikālyaparīkṣā	VI/18	IV/1652
Traiśirasamata	I/156; II/237; III/399; XI/7 (29th Āh.)	II/156, 589; III/1015; VII/3297
Trikahṛdaya (A)	XII/252	VII/3542
Trikakula	X/336; XI/25; XII/389	VI/3062; VII/3131; VIII/3679
Trikasadbhāva	XII/227	VII/3517
Trikasāra (A)	II/236; X/302	II/588; VI/3028
Trikśāsana	III/303	III/919
Trikasūtra	VII/101 (12th Āh.)	V/2193

16. Published in KSTS in 12 volumes. See Appendix I.

(I) Triṁśikāśāstra	III/57-58	III/673-674
Triśikā/-grantha	II/198; X/8	III/550; VI/2734
Triśirobhairava	I/131-132, 136, 154, 156, 157, 177; II/142-143; III/279-80, 402, 405; V/9, 15; IX/64, 221; X/47; XI/59; XI/70 (29th Āh.), 100; XII/186, 198, 297, 341	II/131-132, 136, 154, 156, 157, 177, 494-495; III/895-896, 1018, 1021; IV/1359, 1365; VI/2504, 2661, 2773; VII/3165, 3360, 3390, 3476, 3488, 3587, 3631
Uddyota (A)	IX/19, 231	VI/2459, 2671
Unmatta (-bhairava)[17] (A)[s50]	I/42	II/42
Unmeṣa (A)	X/221	VI/2947
Upaniṣad	V/114	IV/1464
Ūrdhva[18]	I/46	II/46
Ūrmikaula-siddhasantāna-rūpaka	I/39 (2nd Āh.)	II/349
Ūrmikīlu (?) (A)	III/214	III/830
Ūrmikula (A)	X1/26	VII/3132
Uttaphulla	XI/113 (29th Āh.)	VII/3403

17. C. Elizabeth has procured MS of this text as well as that of the *Unmatta-bhairava Pañcāṅga* and has been awarded doctorate for her excellent work thereon by the University of Paris.

18. This is a doubtful reference. If, however, it stands for the *Ūrdhvatantra*, our attention is caught by one *Ūrdhvāmnāyatantra* whose several incomplete MSS have been listed in several collections (5962 at Royal Asiatic Society of Bengal; 923 at Bangīya Sāhitya Parisad, Calcutta; 4894 at Raghunātha Temple Library, Jammu; 24719, 24733 and 24779 at S. Sanskrit University, Varanasi). See Tā.Sā. p. 84.

Uttaphullaka(-mata)[19] (A)[s51]	I/42	II/42
Uttaphullakamata (A)	XI/113 (29th Āh.)	VII/3403
Uttaragrantha (Kiraṇa)	I/119	II/119
Vairiñca	III/25; VI/46	III/641; IV/1680
Vāma	I/38, 39	II/38, 39
Vāmakeśvarīmata[20] (A)	II/78	II/430
Varṇabhaṇṭha (A)[s52]	I/43	II/43
Varṇa(-cakra) (A)[s53]	I/43	II/43
Vārtika (A)	XI/2 (29th Āh.)	VII/3292
Veda	I/48, 49, 71; V/114; X/53, 56	II/48, 49, 71; IV/1464; VI/2779, 2782
Vetāla(-yāmala) (A)[s54]	I/42	II/42
Viḍaṅga (A)[s55]	I/43	II/43
Vidyullekhā (A)[s56]	I/43	II/43
Vidyumān (A)[s57]	I/43	II/43

19. The Tā. Sā. refers to certain *Utphullikāmata* (p. 77).

20. Published with Jayaratha's commentary in KSTS captioned as the *Vāmakaśvarīmatavivaraṇa*. This is identical with the *Vāmakeśvaratantra* and has two parts, namely—*Yoginīhṛdaya* and *Nityāṣoḍaśikārṇava*. The *Yoginīhṛdaya* has been brought out in Prince of Wales, Saraswati Bhawan Series with Amṛtānanda's *Dīpikā* and the *Nityāṣoḍaśikārṇava* in Anandāśrama Sanskrit Series alongwith Bhāskararāya's *Setubandha*. The *Nityāṣoḍaśikārṇava* has been again brought out by S. Sanskrit University, Varanasi together with the *Ṛjuvimarśinī* by Śivānanda and the *Artharatnāvalī* by Vidyānanda. B.V. Dvivedi, Varanasi and Andre Padoux, Paris are engaged in bringing out a critical edition of the *Yoginīhṛdaya* with *Dīpikā* togetherwith its translation into French.

	Vijaya (A)	I/40	II/40
	Vijayākhya (A)[s58]	I/42	II/42
	Vijñānabhairava[21] (A)	III/448; VII/140; IX/243	III/1064; V/2024; VI/2683
	Vimala (A)	I/40	II/40
	Vīṇāmaṇi (śikhā) (A)[s59]	I/43	II/43
	Vīṇā(-śikhā)[22] (A)[s60]	I/43	II/43
	Vinducakra (A)[s61]	I/43	II/43
	Vīrabhadra (A)	I/40	II/40
(I)	Vīrāvalī	VII/106 (12th Āh.); XII/318	V/2198; VII/3608
	Visara	I/40	II/40
	Viṣṇupūrāṇa (A)	XI/141	VII/3247
	Viṣṇuyāmala[23] (A) [s62]	I/42	II/42
	Viśvādya(-mata)[s63]	I/42	II/42
	Vivaraṇa (Śrīpūrvavivaraṇa)	X/292	VI/3018

21. Published in KSTS with the commentaries of Kṣemarāja (partly) and Śivopādhyāya in one volume and with that of Bhaṭṭa Ānanda in an other volume, bound in one. Later published by L. Silburn under the title *Le Vijñāna Bhairava*, text and commentary translated into French under the Institute of Indian Civilization Series. Text with English translation by Jaidev Singh and Hindi/Sanskrit Commentaries by B.V. Dvivedi both published by Motilal Banarsidass.

22. T. Goudriaan has recently brought out a critical edition and English translation under the title *Vīṇāsikhātantra: A Śaiva Tantra Of The Left Current* (Delhi, 1985).

23. Two MSS are listed in the catalogue of the Palace Library of Tanjore (650A, 651B). The Tā. Sā. lists some MSS with the *jyotsnā* commentary (p. 60).

— (Tantrāloka-)	III/471; XII/433	III/1087; VIII/3723
Vivṛtti	I/32	II/32
Yajurveda (A)	V/114, 180	IV/1464, 1530
Yogaja (A)	I/40	II/40
(I) Yoga/-śañcara/-sañcāra	III/135; XI/57 (29th Āh.); XII/310	III/751; VII/3347, 3600
Yogaśāstra (A)	I/70	II/70
Yoginīkaula	IV/11 (7th Āh.), 32	III/1303, 1324
Yogīśvarīmata	XII/385	VIII/3675
Yonyarṇava (A)*	XI/113 (29th Āh.)	VII/3403

*Of late we learn from Mark Dyczkowski that one MS of the *Śivadharmottara* is deposited in the Nepal National Archives (4/531). From him we also learn that the *Devipañcaśatika*, *Sārdhaśatika* and *Kramasadbhāva* have been edited by Sanderson from Nepali MSS but are awaiting publication. The *Śīraścheda* is identical with the *Jayadrathayāmala* and *Tantrarāja-bhaṭṭāraka* which are preserved in Nepalese MSS. See Appendix I also.

13(B). SIXTYFOUR BHAIRAVA TANTRAS AND THEIR EIGHTFOLD CLASSIFICATION IN THE GROUPS OF 8 EACH IN THE ŚRĪKAṆṬHĪ AS REFERRED TO BY JAYARATHA.*

(I) *Bhairavāṣṭaka*

1. Svacchanda
2. Caṇḍa
3. Bhairava
4. Krodha
5. Unamattabhairāva
6. Asitāṅga
7. Mahocchuṣma
8. Kapālīśa

(II) *Yāmalāṣṭaka*

1. Brahmayāmala
2. Visnuyāmala
3. Svacchanda
4. Ruru
5. Ātharvaṇa
6. Rudra
7. Vetāla

(III) *Matāṣṭaka*

1. Rakta
2. Lampaṭa
3. Mata
4. Lakṣmī
5. Cālikā
6. Piṅgalā
7. Utphullaka
8. Viśvādya

(IV) *Maṅgalāṣṭaka*

1. Picubhairavī
2. Tantrabhairavī
3. Tatabhairavī
4. Brāhmīkalā
5. Vijayā
6. Candrākhyā
7. Maṅgalā
8. Sarvamaṅgalā

(V) *Cakrāṣṭaka*

1. Mantracakra

(VI) *Bahurūpāṣṭaka*

1. Andhaka

* Going by the assertion of Jayaratha there are sixty four tantras as enumerated in the *Śrīkaṇṭhī*. But, a perusal of the relevant extracts shows only 63 Āgamas, omitting one in the Yāmala group (there are only 7 Yāmalas named). Dvivedi omits one Tantra namely Bhairava (under Bhairavāṣṭaka) and adds four more e.g., Uḍḍīśa, Kukkuṭākhya, Kubjikā and Rurubhairava (Upodghāta, pp. 94-111) admittedly as per *Śrīkaṇṭhī*. His total comes to 66 instead of 63 or 64. We have, however, not been able to trace the textual support from the extracts of the *Śrīkaṇṭhī* as cited by Jayaratha (T.A.V., I, pp. 39-44) either for these omissions or additions. Also see Abhi., pp. 141-143.

2. Varṇacakra
3. Śakticakra
4. Kalācakra
5. Vinducakra
6. Nādacakra
7. Guhyacakra
8. Khacakra

2. Rurubheda
3. Aja
4. Mūla
5. Varṇabhaṇṭha
6. Viḍaṅga
7. Jvālina
8. Mātṛrodana

(VII) *Vāgīśāṣṭaka*

1. Bhairavī
2. Citrikā
3. Haṁsa
4. Kadambikā
5. Hṛllekhā
6. Candralekhā
7. Vidyullekhā
8. Vidumat

(VIII) *Śikhāṣṭaka*

1. Bhairavīśikhā
2. Vīṇā
3. Vīṇāmaṇi
4. Sammoha
5. Ḍāmara
6. Atharvaka
7. Kabandha
8. Śiraścheda

14. PERSONS* NAMED AND/OR QUOTED BY JAYARATHA IN THE TANTRĀLOKAVIVEKA

Name	*Volume/Page* (KSTS edition)	*Volume/Page* (MLBD edition)
Abhinavagupta	I/13, 34; III/193, 443; VII/44 (11th Āh.); X/111; XII/427, 428	II/13, 34; III/809, 1059; V/2136; VI/2837; VIII/3717, 3718
— (Anenaiva)	I/32, 305; II/73; III/134, 443; VI/175; VII/30 (11th Āh.); VIII/81, 150, 152, 171; IX/129	II/32, 305, 425; III/750, 1059; IV/1809; V/2112, 2281, 2350, 2352, 2371; VI/2569
Āgamavid (A)**	III/279	III/895
Agastya	V/192	IV/1542
Alinātha	XI/29 (29th Āh.)	VII/3319
Amara	XI/29, (29th Āh.)	VII/3319
Amaranātha	III/299	III/915
Ambā	XII/341	VII/3631
Amareśa	V/193	IV/1543
Amṛtaratha (A)	XII/430	VIII/3720
Aṅgirā (A)	V/109, 193	IV/1459, 1543
Ananta(kṣitīndra) (A)	XII/430	VIII/3720
Anantanātha	I/283	II/283

*Includes mythical figures as well.

**'(A)' against a name indicates a fresh reference by Jayaratha.

Anantesa (A)	I/283	II/283
Aniruddha	VI/210; VIII/179	IV/1844; V/2379
Ardhanārīśvara (A)	V/193	IV/1543
Ardhatrayambaka	I/26, 27	II/26, 27
Asmadādiguru	See under Guru	
Asmadguravaḥ	See under Guru	
Asmadguru	See under Guru	
Asmadgurubhiḥ	See under Guru	
Asmākaṁ Gurubhiḥ	See under Guru	
Asmatparamagurubhiḥ (A)	See under Guru	
Avatārakanātha (A)	III/195, 197	III/811, 812
Atri (A)	V/109	IV/1459
Babhru (A)	V/204	IV/1554
Baka (A)	XII/343	VII/3633
Balabhadra (A)	V/29; X/1; XII/344	IV/1379; VI/2727; VII/3634
Bali	XII/343	VII/3633
Bālakhilya (A)	V/193	IV/1543
Baleśvara (A)	XII/344	VII/3434
Bhadantaka (A)	V/192	IV/1542
Bhagavān	I/6, 132; I/39 (2nd Āh.); II/100, 141, 168, 204, 215; III/18, 68, 72, 74, 97, 279; 449; VIII/120; X/110; XI/142, 151, 156, 178	II/6, 132, 349, 452, 493, 520, 556, 567; III/634, 684, 688, 690, 713, 895, 1065; V/2320; VI/2836; VII/3248, 3257, 3262, 3284
Bhagavatī	I/34, 131; I/39 (2nd Āh.); II/141,	II/34, 131, 349, 493, 495; III/684, 713,

Caṇḍī (A)	XII/385	VIII/3675
Caṇḍikā (A)	III/70	III/686
Cārmika	XI/37	VII/3143
Chagalāṇḍa (A)	XII/343	VII/3633
Citra	XI/29 (29th Āh.)	VII/3319
Citrabhānu (A)	V/44	IV/1394
Citraratha (A)	V/45, 144	IV/1395, 1494
Cukhulaka	I/13, 31	II/13, 31
Cūrṇikākāra (A)	III/254	III/870
Dakṣa	IV/106; V/180; XII/385	III/1194; IV/1530; VIII/3675
Dāruka (A)	XII/343	VII/3633
Darśanāntarīyaguru	See under Guru	
Dāśarathī (A)	XII/290, 385	VII/3580; VIII/3675
Devabala (A)	VI/250	IV/1884
Devaratha (A)	XII/431	VIII/3721
Devī	I/257	II/257
Dharmaratha (A)	XII/430	VIII/3720
Dhruva (A)	V/193	IV/1543
Durvāsā (A)	I/28; V/192	II/28; IV/1542
Dviraṇḍa (A)	XII/343	VII/3633
Eraka	III/192-193	III/808, 809
Gahanādhipati (A)	XII/383	VIII/3673
Gālava (A)	V/192	IV/1542
Gaṇapati	I/22; IX/161	II/22; VI/2601

	Āh.); X/92; XII/197, 317, 414, 433	3607; VIII/3704, 3723
— āmnāya	VIII/112	V/2312
— paṅkti	IX/161	VI/2601
— paramparā	I/33, 52; VII/129	II/33, 52; V/2013
— pāramparya	I/34, 46	II/34, 46
— santati	I/34; XI/81	II/34; VII/3187
— uttamaḥ	I/83; III/67	II/83; III/683
— vara	III/197; XI/167; XII/429	III/813; VIII/3719
— (Asmadguru)	II/46; VII/147; VII/11 (11th Āh.); IX/161; XI/137; XII/198	II/46; V/2031, 2103; VI/2601; VII/3243; XII/3488
— (Asmadādiguru)	XI/21 (29th Āh.); XII/198	VII/3311, 3488
— (Asmākaṁ Gurubhiḥ)	XII/221	VII/3511
— (Asmatparamagurubhiḥ)	III/203	III/819
— (Darśanāntarīyaguru)	III/41	III/657
— (Mahāguru)	I/15, 47, 48; III/161, 192	II/15, 47, 48; III/777, 808
— (Paramaguru)	I/236; II/10; III/197; XI/57	II/236, 362, 813; VII/3163
— (Parameṣṭhīguru)	I/11, 30; XI/23 (29th Āh.)	II/11, 30; VII/3313
— (Purā/Pūrva-guru)	VII/100 (12th Āh.); XI/33 (29th Āh.)	V/2192; VII/3323
— (Śāstrajñaguru)	III/83	III/699
— (Svaguru)	I/24	II/24
Gurunātha	I/50	II/50
Hara (A)	V/193	IV/1543

Hrasvanātha (A)	III/196, 202	III/812, 818
Hulahula	V/34	IV/1384
Indra	IV/121; V/43, 65, 71, 92, 108, 159; XII/383	III/1209; IV/1393, 1415, 1421, 1442, 1458, 1509; VIII/3673
Indrajit (A)	V/193	IV/1543
Īśarāja (A)	V/44	IV/1394
Īśvarakṛṣṇa (A)	V/191	IV/1541
Jahnu (A)	V/192	IV/1542, 1543
Jamadagni-suta (A)	V/193	IV/1543
Jaṇṭhī (A)	V/193	IV/1543
Jaya (A)	XII/344	VII/3634
Jayakīrti (A)	XII/344	VII/3634
Jayamūrti (A)	XII/344	VII/3634
Jayanta (A)	XII/344	VII/3634
Jayaratha (A)	I/310; II/264; III/307; IV/203; IV/57 (7th Āh.); V/283; VI/250; VII/208; VII/91 (11th Āh.); VIII/214, 239; IX/285; X/305, 327, 356, 380; XI/184; XI/172 (29th Āh.); XII/222, 302, 335, 351, 354, 380, 390, 428, 434, 435	II/310, 316; III/923, 1291, 1349; IV/1633, 1884; V/2092, 2183, 2414, 2439; VI/2725, 3031, 3053, 3082, 3106; VII/3290, 3462, 3513, 3592, 3625, 3641, 3644; VIII/3670, 3680, 3718, 3724, 3725
Jayarudra (A)	XII/344	VII/3634
Jayavardhana (A)	XII/344	VII/3634
Jyeṣṭharatha (A)	XII/430	VIII/3720

Jyotsnākāra	VI/243	IV/1877
Kakāradevī (A)	III/195	III/811
Kallaṭa/-nātha	IV/11; XI/138; XI/88 (29th Āh.)	III/1099; VII/3244, 3378
Kalyāṇa (A)	I/2; 310; V/204; VIII/205; XII/433	II/2, 310; IV/1554; V/2405; VIII/3723
Kalyāṇikā (A)	III/192, 195,	III/808, 811
Kalyapāla	XI/46 (29th Āh.)	VII/3336
Kamaladatta (A)	XII/430	VIII/3720
Kaṇabhuk	VI/250	IV/1884
Kaṇāda	I/194	II/194
Kanakadatta (A)	XII/431	VIII/3721
Kaṅkāla (A)	V/34	IV/1384
Kapālī (A)	V/181	IV/1531
Kāpālika (A)	V/34, 108; XI/46 (29th Āh.)	IV/1384, 1458; VII/3336
Kapālīśa (A)	V/120, 193	IV/1470, 1543
Kapila	V/78, 113, 192; XII/376	IV/1428, 1463, 1542, VIII/3666
Kāśa (A)	V/192	IV/1542
Kārtikeya (A)	V/199	IV/1549
Kaṣṭaśrīdhara (A)	XII/245	VII/3535
Kāśyapa (A)	V/192	IV/1542
Kaunteya (A)	I/163; VI/109	II/163; IV/1743
Kauśika (A)	XII/223, 344	VII/3513, 3634
Ketumāla (A)	V/72	IV/1422
Keyūra/-vatī (A)	III/192, 195, 196	III/808, 811, 812

Khagendranātha	III/297; XI/3 (29thĀ h.)	III/913; VII/3293
Kheṭapāla	VI/211; VIII/36	IV/1845; V/2236
Krodheśa (A)	V/186	IV/1536
Kṛṣṇa	V/193; XI/37; XII/423	IV/1543, VII/3143; VIII/3713
Kṛtsna (A)	V/192	IV/1542
Krūra (A)	V/193; XII/342	IV/1543; VII/3632
Kṣemaka (A)	V/78	IV/1428
Kṣemarāja (A)	II/178	II/530
Kūrmanātha	III/297	III/913
Kuru (A)	V/72	IV/1422
Kurunandana (A)	XII/423	VIII/3712
Lakṣmaṇa	XII/388	VIII/3678
Lakṣmaṇagupta	IX/122; XII/184	VI/2562; VII/3474
Lakṣmīdatta (A)	XII/430	VIII/3720
Lakule (lī)śa	V/181; XII/343, 383	IV/1531; VII/3633; VIII/3673
Lāṅgalī (A)	XII/343	VII/3673
Lāṅguli (A)	V/181	IV/1531
Laṅkaratha (A)	XII/431	VIII/3721
Līlākāra (A)	V/81	IV/1431
Lokākṣa (A)	V/180	IV/1530
Macchanda	I/24, 25	II/24, 25
Madanikā (A)	III/192, 195	III/808, 811
Mahābhāṣyakāra (A)	II/90	II/442
Mahāguru (A)	See under Guru	

Mahānanda (A)	XII/433	VIII/3723
Mahocchuṣma (A)	V/34	IV/1384
Manmatha (A)	IV/106	III/1194
Manoratha (A)	XII/430	VIII/3720
Maskarī (A)	V/192	IV/1542
Medhātithi (A)	V/72, 77, 204	IV/1422, 1427, 1554
Meṣa	XII/343	VII/3633
Mīna	I/24; XII/343	II/24; VII/3633
Mātaṅga	V/34; XI/37	IV/1384; VII/3143
Nanda (A)	IV/106; XII/385	III/1194; VIII/3675
Nandā (A)	XII/342	VII/3632
Nandī (A)	V/199	IV/1549
Nandikumāra	I/283	II/283
Nandiratha (A)	XII/431	VIII/3721
Nārada	V/144	IV/1494
Narasiṁha	see Nṛsiṁha-gupta	
Nāsiketu (A)	V/192	IV/1542
Navera/Naverakanātha (A)	III/196	III/812
Nṛsiṁha-gupta	I/13-14, 34	III/13-14, 34
Ojarāja (A)	XII/197	VII/3487
Pañcāntaka (A)	V/186	IV/1536
Pāṇini (A)	II/196; XII/349	II/548; VII/3639
Para (A)	V/193	IV/1543
Parameṣṭhīguru	See under Guru	

Parameṣṭhin	I/41, 207; III/212; IX/161	II/41, 207; III/828; VI/2601
Parāśara (A)	V/192	IV/1542
Patañjali (A)	III/102	III/718
Piṅgala (A)	V/193	IV/1543
Piṅgeśa		
Pippalāda (A)	V/192	IV/1542
Pitāmaha (A)	V/32; XII/383, 385	IV/1382; VIII/3673, 3675
Pratoda (A)	V/193	IV/1543
Prakāśaratha (A)	XII/430	VIII/3720
Pratyabhijñākāra	VI/224; VII/26, 194-195	IV/1858; V/2118
Pravara(nṛpati)	XII/429	VIII/3719
Pūraṇa (A)	V/192	IV/1542
Pūrṇamanoratha (A)	XII/430	VIII3720
Purā/Pūrva-guru	See under Guru	
Rāma	V/193; XII/290, 388	IV/1543; VII/3580; VIII/3678
Rāvaṇa	XII/384, 385	VIII/3674, 3675
Ṛṣabha (A)	V/72, 180	IV/1422. 1530
Ruruvṛttikāra (A)	IV/119	III/1207
Sadyojyoti	VI/211, 250	IV/1845, 1884
Śākalya (A)	V/192	IV/1542
Śakra (A)	XII/383	VIII/3673
Śakraratha (A)	XII/431	VIII/3721
Śakuni (A)	IV/106; XII/385	IV/1194; VIII/3675
Śambhunātha	I/34, 53, 236; III/356; V/283;	II/34, 53, 236; III/972; IV/1633;

	VII/129, 193; IX/122; X/186, XII/380	V/2013, 2077; VI/2562; VIII/3670
Sammaratha (A)	XII/431	VIII/3721
Saṁvarta	V/193; XII/343, 385	IV/1543; VII/3633; VIII/3675
Sanaka (A)	V/114	IV/1464
Sananda (A)	V/114	IV/1464
Sanatkumāra	I/283; V/114, 192	II/283; IV/1464 1552
Saṅgrahakāra (A)	V/19	IV/1369
Śaṅkara	I/257; V/193	II/257; IV/1453
Śaṅkaranandana (A)	VI/250	V/1884
Śaṅkha-dhara (A)	I/310; VIII/205	II/310; V/2405
Śaṅku (A)	V/114	IV/1464
Śāradā	XII/429	VIII/3719
Śarbilla	XI/29 (29th Āh.)	VII/3319
Śāstrajñaguru	See under Guru	
Śāstrāvatāraka	I/139, 143	II/139, 143
Saumitra (A)	V/192	IV/1542
Saunika	XI/37	VII/3143
Siddha/-pāda	I/85; I/2 (2nd Āh.), 34; III/199; VIII/238; XI/2 (29th Āh.)	II/85, 344; IV/1395; V/2438; VII/3292
Śiva	I/149; V/32, 180, 193	II/149; IV/1352, 1530, 1543
Śivānandanātha (A)	III/192	III/808
Śivaratha (A)	XII/431	VIII/3721
Soma	V/108	IV/1452

Somadeva	I/235-236	II/235-336
Somānanda/-pāda	I/40 (2nd Āh.); II/95, 136; III/192, 194; XII/429	II/350, 441, 488; III/808, 810; VIII/3719
Somarāja (A)	III/196	III/812
Somaśarmā (A)	XII/343	VII/3633
Śrīcakra (A)	XII/431	VIII/3721
Śrīkaṇṭhanātha	I/26, 28, 34, 71, 129, 283; IV/17, 130, 146; V/7, 30, 165, 166, 170, 173, 188, 199; VI/179, 180; VIII/139; IX/125	II/26, 28, 34, 71, 129, 283; III/1105 1218, 1234; IV/1357, 1380, 1515, 1516, 1520, 1523, 1538, 1549, 1813, 1814; V/2329; VI/2565.
Śrīnātha	I/26	II/26
Śrīrājarāja (A)	I/310; XII/432	II/310; VIII/3722
Śṛṅgāra (A)	XII/433	VIII/3723
Śṛṅgāraratha (A)	XII/432	VIII/3722
Stotrakāra	VIII/85	V/2285
— (Krama-)Stotrakāra (A)	III/191	
Subhaṭa-datta/-pāda (A)	XII/433	
Sugata	XII/376	
Śukra (A)	V/193; XII/385	
Sumati	I/236; IV/106; VII/193; XII/385	
Sūryaratha (A)	XII/430	
Sūtrakāra	II/13	
Svacchanda	XII/383	
Svaguru	See under Guru	

Svatantreśa	VI/180; VIII/139; IX/125
Svāyambhuva Manu	V/72
Śvetaketu (A)	X/132
Tākṣyamuni (A)	V/192
Tapasvin (A)	III/131
Trayambaka	I/26, 27, 28
Tribhuvanadatta (A)	XII/433
Triśaṅku (A)	V/114
Tṛṇavindu (A)	V/192
Turyanātha (A)	I/24
Udbhaṭṭa	III/192
Udyota/-kṛt/-kāra (A)	V/102, 104, 142, 241, 243; IX/19, 231
Ujjaṭa (A)	III/192
Unmeṣakṛt (A)	X/221
Utpala	II/9-10, 95; VIII/177; XII/430
Utpalaratha (A)	XII/430
Vajrātreya (A)	V/193
Vālmīki (A)	V/192
Vāmanabhānu (A)	III/196; XII/385
Vāmadeva (A)	I/44; IV/134; V/180
Vāmanadatta	III/467
Vāmanātha	XII/414
Varadeva	III/299; XI/29 (29th Āh.)

Vyāsa	IX/256	VI/2696
Yama (A)	V/193	IV/1543
Yaśaskara (A)	XII/430	VIII/3720
Yogeśa (A)	I/257	II/257
Yudhiṣṭhira (A)	IX/255	VI/2695

15. SYSTEMS/MAJOR DOCTRINES REFERRED TO BY NAME BY JAYARATHA IN THE TANTRĀLOKAVIVEKA

System/Doctrine	*Volume/Page* (KSTS edition)	*Volume/Page* (MLBD edition)
Ābhāsavāda	I/213	II/213
Abheda/-daśā	I/36	II/36
— (Abhedākhyāti)	VI/11	IV/1645
Adhara (Adho)-darśana/-śāsana/-śāstra	I/302; VIII/183, 207; X/247, 255, 256; XII/394	II/302; V/2383, 2407; VI/2973, 2981, 2982; VIII/3684
Adhyātma/Ādhyātmika	VIII/207; XII/371	V/2407; VI/3661
Advaita/Advaya/-vāda/-vādin	I/26, 106, 112, 196, 244; III/283; IV/160; V/114; XII/389	II/26, 106, 112, 196, 244; III/899; IV/1464; VIII/3679
— āgama	I/41 (2nd Āh.)	II/41
— arthopadeśin	IV/160	III/1248
— darśana	III/286	III/902
— naya	I/266; VII/73 (11th Āh.)	II/266; V/2165
Akṣapādamata	See under Nyāya	
Amākhyakalāsvarūpasphāra-siddhānta	II/141	II/493
Anuttaraṣaḍrthakrama	I/52	II/52
Anuttaratrika	VII/70 (11th Āh.)	V/2162
Anya	III/127; V/114; VI/6, 86, 220;	III/743; IV/1464, 1640, 1720, 1854;

	VII/22; XI/33; XI/32 (29th Āh.)	V/1906; VII/3138, 3322
— śāstra	III/43; XI/70	III/659; VII/3176
Ārhata	IV/131; XII/370, 371	III/1219; VIII/3660, 3661
Arvāgdarśin	I/4 (2nd Āh.); VI/118, 123	II/314; IV/1752, 1757
Asaṁvedyabuddhivāda	See under Sāṁkhya	
Asmad-darśana	III/31, 44; V/177; VI/29, 55-56, 146; VII/7, 98, 124; VIII/71, 207; IX/210, 256; X/133; XI/4, 72 (29th Āh.); XII/341	III/647, 660; IV/1527, 1663, 1689-1690, 1780; V/1891, 1982, 2008, 2271, 2407; VI/2652, 2696 2859; VII/3110, 3362, 3631
— mata	VII/52	V/1936
— pakṣa	VII/50, 54	V/1934, 1938
— śāstra	III/59; X/118, 164, 190, 210, 213, 245, 267	III/675; VI/2844, 2890, 2916, 2936, 2939, 2971, 2993
— (Asmindarśana)	VII/96; IX/124	V/1980; VI/2564
— (Ātmīyaśāstra)	III/278	III/894
— (Svadarśana)	II/86; VI/247; VII/184; IX/170; X/255	II/438; IV/1881; V/2068; VI/2610, 2981
— (Svamata)	VII/52	V/1936
— (Svaśāstra)	III/293; XI/122	III/909; VII/3228
— (Svasiddhānta)	III/16; VIII/2	III/632; V/2202
Asmindarśane	See under Asmaddarśana	
Āstika-darśana (Āstikyavāsanā)	IV/19-22	III/1107-1108
Ātmadṛṣṭi	I/69	II/69
Ātmīyaśāstra	See under Asmaddarśana	

Ati-mārga	I/236; VIII/207; XI/68 (29th Āh.); XII/371	II/236; V/2407; VII/3358, VIII/3661
— naya	III/195	III/811
Āyātikramavid	I/236	II/236
Āyurvedavid	IX/39	VI/2479
Bāhya	III/9	III/625
Bāhyārthavādin	II/32	II/384
Bauddha	I/64, 69, 70, 71, 72, 95, 96; IV/131; IV/25 (7th Āh.); VI/30, 31; VIII/68; XI/52 (29th Āh.); XII/368, 370, 375	II/64, 69, 70, 71, 72, 95, 96; III/1219, 1317; IV/1664, 1665; V/2268; VII/3342; VIII/3658, 3662, 3665
— (Kṣaṇikavādin)	I/66	II/66
— (Mādhyamika)	I/66, 95	II/66, 95
— (Nairātmyadṛṣṭi)	I/69	II/69
— (Saugatamata)	VI/34, 90	
— (Sugata)	VIII/189; XII/376	V/2389; VIII/3666
— (Svābhāvyavādin)	I/66	II/66
— (Vaibhāṣika)	I/95, 247; III/33	II/95, 247; III/649
— (Vijñānanayavādin)	VII/89 (11tn Āh.)	V/2181
— (Vijñānavāda)	I/67	II/67
— (Vijñānavādin)	III/32	III/648
— (Vikalpāpekṣanirvikalpa-prāmāṇyavādin)	I/247	II/247
— (Yogācāra)	I/64, 95	II/64, 95

Bhairava-āgama	XI/9 (29th Āh.), 79	VII/3299, 3369
— tantra	VIII/182, 184	V/2382, 2384
— srotas	X/256	VI/2982
Bhairavīya-darśana	X/304	VI/3030
Bhāvadharmavedyatāpakṣa	VII/56	V/1940
Bhāvasvabhāvādhikadikkālāpahnavavādin	IX/97	VI/2537
Bhāṭṭa	See under Mīmāṁsā	
Bhedābheda/-vāda/-daśā	I/36, 45, 242, 248; II/199; IV/37; VI/225; VII/83; VIII/205; X/138	II/36, 45, 242, 248, 551; III/1125; IV/1859; V/1967, 2405; VI/2864
— (Bhedādvaitavādin)	VI/50	IV/1684
— (Dvaitādvaya)	XII/428	VIII/3718
Bheda-vāda	I/254; VI/112	II/254; IV/1746
— vādin	IV/141, VII/70; VIII/65, 71, 75, 85	III/1229; V/1954, 2265, 2271, 2275, 2285
— (Dvaita/-śāstra)	I/244; III/112	II/244; III/728
— (Dvaitin)	XI/113, 114 (29th Āh.)	VII/3403, 3404
— (Dvaya)	I/26	II/26
Bhedeśvara/-vāda	III/81	III/697
— vādin	I/254	II/254
Brahmav ādin	II/255; III/25, 32; IV/130	II/607; III/641, 648, 1218
Caryākrama	II/95, 97, 99, 104, 105, 216; III/430	II/447, 449, 451, 456, 457, 568; III/1046

Cārvāka	IV/15, 17	III/1103, 1105
Dakṣa	I/49; III/56; VIII/181, 182, 212	II/49; III/672; V/2381, 2382, 2412
Dakṣiṇa-śāstra	I/48	II/48
Devītantra	XI/12 (29th Āh.)	VII/3302
Dvaitādvaya	See under Bhedābhedavāda	
Dvaita/-śāstra	See under Bhedavāda	
Dvaitin	See under Bhedavāda	
Dvaya	See under Bhedavāda	
Ekapramātṛsatatvava-stuvāda	VII/50	V/1934
Guṇaguṇidvaitavādin	See under Nyāya	
Guṇatattvavādin	V/176	IV/1257
Guru/-śāstra/-śāsana	III/51, 84; VIII/208; IX/177; XI/72 (29th Āh.)	III/667, 700; V/2408; VI/2617; VII/3362
— āgama	VIII/109; XII/214	V/2309; VII/3504
— āmnāya	VIII/112	V/2312
— antaramata	VII/194	V/2078
— paramparā	IX/206	VI/2646
— vākya	I/3 (2nd Āh.), 41	II/313
Hetuśāstra	III/118	III/634
Īśvarādvaitavāda	XII/429	VIII/3719
Īśvarādvayavāda	I/109, 111	II/109, 111
Jaminivākya	See under Mīmāṁsā	
Jñātrabhāvavādin	I/95	II/95

Jñātṛ-jñeyābhāvavādin	I/95	II/95
Jyotiḥ-śāstra	IV/112; XI/23	III/1200; VII/3129
Kāṇāda	I/194; VI/233, 240	II/194; IV/1867, 1876
— ādidarśana	I/195	II/195
— ādidṛṣṭi	VI/67	IV/1701
— (Vaiśeṣika)	VIII/43, 206	V/2243, 2406
Kāpālika	V/34	IV/1384
Kapila	See under Sāṁkhya	
Kāpila	See under Sāṁkhya	
Karmavādin	VIII/11	V/2211
Kāruka	I/70	II/70
Kaula	I/48, 49; III/27, 278, 288; VIII/181, 182, 184	II/48, 49; III/643, 894, 904; V/2381, 2382, 2384
Kaulika	XI/3 (29th Āh.), 113	VII/3293, 3403
Kaumārilamata	See under Mīmāṁsā	
Kheṭapāla	See under Siddhānta	
Krama	II/235; III/189, 190; VII/106 (12th Āh.)	II/587; III/805, 806; V/2198
— naya	III/157, 189	III/773, 805
Kṣaṇikavādin	See under Bauddha	
Kula	I/46, 49; III/56, 286, 288; VIII/181, 182, 184; X/336; XI/25; XI/3, 4, 92 (29th Āh.)	II/46, 49; III/672, 902, 904; V/2381, 2382, 2384; VI/3062; VII/3131, 3382
— āgama	I/24; XII/333	II/24; VII/3623

— āmnāya	XI/66 (29th Āh.)	VII/3356
— prakriyā	I/24, 31, 32, 35, 153; X/237; XI/1 (29th Āh.), 2, 3	II/24, 31, 32, 35, 153; VI/2963; VII/3291, 3292, 3293
Loka/Laukika	I/72, II/41, 243; III/41, 269, 277; VI/31, 40, 42, 43; VIII/206, 207; XI/119; XII/364, 371, 373, 378	II/72, 393, 595; III/657, 885, 893; IV/1665, 1674, 1676, 1677; V/2407; VII/3225; VIII/3654, 3661, 3663, 3668
Mādhyamika	See under Bauddha	
Mahāmārga	XI/68 (29th Āh.)	VII/3358
Mahānaya	III/195	III/811
Mahāyogin	See under Yogin	
Mata	I/49; III/56; VIII/181	II/49; III/672; V/2381
Mausula	I/70	II/70
Māyīyaśāstra	III/30	III/646
Mīmāṁsā	V/114	IV/1464
— (Bhāṭṭa)	I/167	II/267
— (Jaiminivākya)	XII/433	VIII/3723
— (Kaumārilamata)	VII/16, 45	V/1900, 1929
— (Mīmāṁsaka)	V/114; XI/25	IV/1464; VII/3131
— (Prābhākara)	I/167; VII/45	II/267; V/1929
— (Śābara)	VII/40, 45	V/1924, 1929
Mokṣavādin	III/43	III/659
Nairātmyadṛṣṭi	See under Bauddha	
Nāstika/-darśana (Nāstikya-vāsanā)	IV/18-19, 20	III/1106-1107

Nigama	III/258	III/874
Nyāya		
— (Akṣapādamata)	III/34	III/650
— (Naiyāyika)	II/13, 33, 44; III/262; VI/197; VII/54; VII/3 (11th Āh.); VIII/28, 206	II/365, 385, 396; IV/1731; V/1938, 2095, 2228, 2406
— (Tārkika)	III/18, 19; VIII/206	III/634, 635; V/2406
Pāñcarā-tra/-trika	IV/131; XII/371, 372	III/1219; VIII/3661, 3662
Paradarśana	IV/20	III/1108
Parādvayadarśana	III/105	III/721
Paraprakāśavāda	VII/181	V/2065
Pa(Pā)rameśvara-darśana/-śās-ana/-śāstra	See under Śiva-śāsana	
Pāśupata	See under Śiva-śāsana	
Pātañjala	See under Yoga	
Pati-śāsana/-śāstra	See under Śiva-śāsana	
Picuvaktra	XI/59; XI/89 (29th Āh.)	VII/3165, 3379
Piṭharapākapakṣa	VI/243	IV/1877
Prābhākara	See under Mīmāṁsā	
Prācya	IV/78; X/365; XII/184	III/1166; VI/3091; VIII/3474
Purāṇa/-jña	III/43; V/61; VIII/174	III/650; IV/1411; V/2374
Rahasya-prakriyā	II/94, 96	II/446, 448
— śāstra	IV/160; XII/252, 364	III/1248; VII/3542; VIII/3654
— śāstravid	III/295	III/911

Seśvaramīmāṁsā	VIII/8	V/2208
Siddhadarśana	I/2 (2nd Āh.)	II/312
Siddānta/-darśana	III/285; VII/7-8; VII/69 (11th Āh.); XI/108; XIII/52 (29th Āh.)	III/901; V/1891, 1892, 2161; VII/3214, 3342
— (Kheṭapāla)	VI/211	IV/1845
— (Saiddhāntika)	III/295; VIII/209; X/256	III/911; V/2409; VI/2982
Śiva-śaiva-śāsana/-śāstra	I/26, 27, 73, III/25, 26; IV/33; V/34, 150; VIII/93; X/287; XII/372, 397, 433, 434	II/26, 27, 73; III/641, 642, 1121; IV/1384, 1500; V/2293; VI/3013; VIII/3662, 3687, 3723, 3724
— (Pa/pā-rameśvara-darśana/-śāsana/-śāstra)	I/73; VI/2, 67	II/73; IV/1636, 1701
—(Parameśvarādvayavāda)	I/83	II/83
— (Pāśupata)	I/70; XI/52 (29th Āh.)	II/70
— (Pati-śāsana/-śāstra)	I/150; III/283; VIII/189	II/150; III/899; V/2389
— (Śivādvaita)	XII/433	VIII/3723
— (Śivaśāstropaniṣad)	XII/434	VIII/3724
— (Vrata)	I/70	II/70
Śivādvaita	See under Śivaśāsana	
Śivasiddhānta	XI/108	VII/3214
Smārta-darśana	XI/52 (29th Āh.)	VII/3342
Smṛti	VIII/207; IX/88, 255, 256, 257; XI/176	V/2407; VI/2528, 2695, 2696, 2697; VII/3282
Śrauta	VIII/189	V/2389
Śruti	See under Veda	

16. UNSPECIFIED CITATIONS/ REFERENCES IN JAYARATHA*

	Volume/Page (KSTS edition)	*Volume/Page* (MLBD edition)
अकस्मात्सर्वशास्त्रार्थं....अदृश्यत जनैः स्फुटम् ॥	VIII/137	V/2337
अकारः सर्ववर्णानामन्तर्यामितया स्थितः ॥	II/120	II/472
अकारश्च हकारश्च....मारुताम्बरयोरिव ॥	II/80	II/432
अकारश्च हकारश्च द्वावेतावेकतः स्थितौ ।	II/139, 193	II/491, 545
अकारस्य शिरो रौद्री....ज्येष्ठा चैवायुधं स्मृता ॥	II/80	II/432
अकुलस्यास्य देवस्य.... ।	II/146	II/498
अकुलात्पञ्चशक्त्यात्मा....स्पर्शाः प्रकीर्तिताः ॥	II/154	II/506
अकृतार्थो नरस्तावद्यावद्हंसं न विन्दति ।	III/147	III/763
अक्के चेन्मधु विन्देत किमर्थं पर्वतं व्रजेत् ।	VII/35 (11th Āh.); VIII/ 62, 124	V/2127, 2262, 2324
अङ्गुष्ठाग्रसमासक्ते....मृगीनाममहामुद्रा ।	IX/212	VI/2652
अङ्गुलीन्यासभेदेन....मानसी परिकीर्तिता ।	XII/308	VII/3598
अजवीथी दक्षिणं तु....कथितोऽनुक्रमेण तु ।	V/83	IV/1433

* The list does not take into account those unidentified references in Jayaratha which have been traced or identified by the editor of the KSTS edition. It also excludes two other types of references—one, which are from the *Tantrāloka* and are cited with the note "Vakṣyati" or "Vakṣyamāṇanītyā" or some such similar expression and two, which are connected with certain previously quoted/named text and are covered by the remark 'Yaduktaṁ tatra' or 'Tatraiva'.

अज्ञो जन्तुरनीशो....स्वर्गमेव वा ॥	VIII/166	V/2366
अत ऊर्ध्वं तथा तिर्यग्दातव्या विप्रुषः प्रिये ।	XI/20(29th Āh.)	VII/3310
अतएव....कलात्मकः ।	I/4	II/4
अत एव स्पर्श एव वायुः....भूतं कारणमाहुः ।	VI/230	IV/1864
अतिसौख्यसमावेश....दृप्तामपि वरस्त्रियम् ॥	II/151	II/503
अतीन्द्रियं न यद्वस्तु....प्रसिद्धः क्षुद्यथा च तृट् ॥	I/116	II/116
अतः कंचित्प्रमातारं....कंचिदंशांशिकाक्रमात् ॥	I/303	II/303
अतः परं भवेन्माया....ह्यमोक्षे मोक्षलिप्सया ।	III/42	III/658
अथ चेत्सविकल्पा तद्विकल्पाः शब्दयोनयः ।	VII/56 (11th Āh.)	V/2148
अथ पात्रविधिर्नास्ति....कृत्वा पानं प्रसिद्ध्यति ॥	XI/43	VII/3149
अथ ब्रह्म परं शुद्धमादिवर्णत्वमागतम् ।	III/200	III/816
अथ वेदाश्रिता शैवं....प्रायश्चित्तं परस्परम् ॥	VIII/190-91	V/2390-91
अथ हूहुककालाग्निरुद्रौ....कटाहस्यान्तरे स्थिताः ॥	V/19	IV/1369
अथानादिर्मलः पुंसां पशुत्वं परिकीर्तितम् ।	VI/60	IV/1694
अथान्यत्संप्रवक्ष्यामि....युञ्जतो यस्य सुव्रते ।	IX/66	VI/2506
अदाम्भिको गुरौ भक्तौ....मद्यमासपराङ्मुखः ॥	XI/64 (29th Āh.)	VII/3354
अदीक्षितानां पुरतो नोच्चरेच्छास्त्रपद्धतिम् ।	X/197	VI/2923
अदीक्षितानां पुरतो नोच्चरेच्छिवपद्धतिम् ।	I/82; III/77; IX/9; X/197	II/82; VI/2449; 2923
अदूतिको वरं यागो न तु दुर्दूतिदूषितः ।	XI/70 (29th Āh.)	VII/3360
अद्यास्मान्सतः....दुःखेन तैः स्थीयते ॥	I/306	II/306

अधमा वश्यदा सिद्धिः. . . .सिद्धिरुत्तमा ॥	X/118	VI/2844
अधमस्तु जपः प्रोक्तः प्राणसंख्याविवर्जितः ।	IV/40 (7th Āh.)	III/1332
अधराधरतत्त्वेषु स्थिता. . . .भवेत्पूर्वहानितः ॥	VII/134	V/2018
अधर्मं धर्ममित या बुद्ध्यते तमसावृता ।	III/170	III/786
अधिकारार्थमाचार्यं परापरपदे. . . .समयिन्यैश्वरे तथा ।	IX/236	VI/2676
अधिकारं न चेत्कुर्याद्विघ्नेशः स्यात्तनुक्षये ।	X/203, 303	VI/2929, 3029
अधिष्ठाता च कर्त्ता च सर्वस्याहमवस्थितः ।	X/37-38	VI/2764
अधुना मण्डलं पीठं. . . .शतं यावदनुक्रमात् ॥	XII/228	VII/3517-18
अधुना श्रोतुमिच्छामि मन्त्रोद्धारस्य लक्षणम् ।	III/449	III/1065
अधो ब्रह्मबिलं देवि. . . .प्रक्रियाण्डैर्युतः प्रिये ।	V/260	IV/1610
अध्यवसायो बुद्धिः ।	I/76	II/76
अध्यर्धानि सहस्राणि द्वादशार्युहिरण्मये ।	V/58	IV/1408
. . . .अध्वा बन्धस्य कारणम् ।	I/71; X/79	II/71; VI/2805
अनधिगतविषयं प्रमाणमज्ञातार्थप्रकाशो वा ।	I/92; III/89	II/92; III/705
अनन्तशक्तिचन्द्रांशु. . . .पद्मषण्डसरः सदा ।	V/18	IV/1368
अनन्तो भैरवोच्छ्रायो. . . .अणुत्वं प्रविलीयते ॥	IX/119	VI/2559
अनपेक्षानुवृत्तेश्च. . . .मृदः कुण्डादिके यथा ॥	VI/31	IV/1665
अनयोः कथयेज्ज्ञानं. . . .स्वक्रियाकरणं प्रति ॥	X/305	VI/3031
अनाथलुप्तपिण्डानां. . . .दीक्षा मृतवती भवेत् ॥	X/218	VI/2944
अनादिमलसम्बन्धाद्. . . . ।	VIII/33	V/2233

अनाद्यनादि सम्बन्धो मलः. . . . ।	VIII/33	V/2233
अनाश्रितं तु व्यापारे निमित्तं हेतुरिष्यते ।	V/262	IV/1612
अनाश्रितः कर्मफलं कार्यं कर्म करोति यः ।	VI/89	IV/1723
अनाहतहतोत्तीर्णो. . . .रावो देव्या विजृम्भते ॥	II/76	II/428
अनुभावो विकल्पोत्थो. . . .ज्ञेयो नैव सर्वथा ॥	I/117	II/117
अनेन क्रमयोगेन. . . .दीक्षोक्तं फलमश्नुते ॥	X/204	VI/2930
अनेन लक्षयेद्योगी. . . .बहुधा संव्यवस्थितम् ॥	III/111	III/727
अन्तः कौलो बहिः शैवो लोकाचारे तु वैदिकः ।	III/27, 278	III/643, 894
. . . .अन्तर्भुवनानि विशोधयेत् ॥	V/18	IV/1368
अन्तर्मुखगतानां. . . .स्युरिच्छादिकाः क्रियाः ॥	VI/190	IV/1824
अन्तर्लक्ष्यो बहिर्दृष्टिः परमं पदमश्नुते ।	III/435	III/1051
अन्तःसारविबोधैक. . . .सप्तत्रिंशे परे विभौ ।	XII/378	VIII/3668
अन्तः संविदि. . . .विदधतामित्यत्र संदिह्महे ॥	III/104	III/720
. . . .अन्धात्तैमिरिको वरः ।	III/35	III/651
अन्येऽन्तःकरणं. . . .सिद्धौ करणं तु किम् ॥	VI/191	IV/1825
अन्योऽन्यमिथुनाः सर्वे सर्वे सर्वत्रगामिनः ॥	VI/188	IV/1822
अणवश्चिदचिद्रूपाः. . . . ।	VI/114	IV/1748
अणुं स्वरूपदृश्वानं. . . .तनुते ज्ञानकर्मणोः ।	IV/50	III/1138
अपरं मानमिदं स्यात्केवलशोधकमनुन्यासे ।	X/91	VI/2817
अपरः षोडशो यावत्कालः. . . .कृत्वा चैव त्यजेत्पुनः ।	I/127	II/127

अपरोक्षे भवत्तत्त्वे....न विन्दन्ति ते ॥	I/184; I/12 (2nd Āh.)	II/184, 322
अपरिच्युतस्वरूपैरपृथग्भूतापि....तद्ब्रह्मणः समाख्यातम् ॥	XI/67-68 (29th Āh.)	VII/3357-3358
अपानस्यापि संचारे....वायुरधस्तादुपयाति हि ॥	IV/155	III/1243
अप्रत्यक्षोपलम्भस्य नार्थदृष्टिः प्रसिद्ध्यति ।	VII/74-75	V/1959
अबोधोऽपि बुद्ध्यमानो बोधात्मभूत ईश्वर एव ।	I/91	II/91
अभावान्नित्यपूजाया अवश्यं ह्येषु पूजयेत् ।	XI/58	VII/3164
....अभिलाषो मलोऽत्र तु ।	I/32 (2nd Āh.)	II/342
अमन्त्रका तावत्पूजा न स्यात् ।	III/211	III/827
अमूर्ता मूर्तिमाश्रित्य....उत्तमद्रव्यलिप्सया ॥	XI/19 (29th Āh.)	VII/3309
अश्वमेधसमायुक्तं मण्डलानां शतं मतम् ।	XII/228	VII/3518
अम्बिकाधस्ततस्तिस्रो....जयाद्या गुह्यशक्तयः ॥	III/200	III/816
अम्बुवाहा वहेद्वामा....दक्षस्था रक्तवाहा च.... ॥	III/148; XI/106(29th Āh.)	III/764; VII/3396
अयं रसो येन....जपादिचर्याविषवद्विभाति ॥	II/247	II/599
अयमेव भेदो भेदहेतुः....अध्यासः कारणभेदो वा ।	VII/78 (11th Āh.)	V/2170
अयष्ट्वा भैरवं....नरकं व्रजेत् ॥	XI/11 (29th Āh.)	VII/3301
अर्थातिशये पक्षे च सर्वसर्वज्ञता भवेत् ।	VII/36	V/1920
अललाटे द्वितीयं....प्राणकोशेषु पञ्चकम् ॥	IX/61	VI/2501
अव्यक्तं चतुरष्टाश्रयवृत्तभागोपलक्षितम् ।	V/38	IV/1388
अव्ययमकुलममेयं....काल्याः परं धाम ॥	III/185	III/801
....अशिवा भेदप्रथाप्रदा ।	VI/118	IV/1752

अशुद्धं नास्ति तत्किंचित्....अशुद्धं तेन जायते ॥	III/121	III/737
अष्टकसप्तकस्य तु....नामानीति तत्त ॥	XI/38 (29th Āh.)	VII/3328
अष्टौ सिद्धा....सुतेजसः ।	I/25	II/25
असूत सा कलातत्त्वं....तुट्यादिभिरवस्थितः ॥	I/75	II/75
अस्य प्राणव्याप्तिः....निर्दिशन्ति गुरवः ।	I/23	II/23
अस्मिंश्चतुर्दशे धाम्नि स्फुटीभूतत्रिशक्तिके ।	III/218	III/834
अहंप्रत्यवमर्शो यः....द्वयापेक्षी विनिश्चयः ॥	II/130	II/482
अहमेव परो हंसः.... ।	III/59	III/675
अहमेव सर्वत्र स्थितः ।	I/238	II/238
आगतस्य तु मन्त्रस्य....हरत्यर्धशरीरं ।	XI/20 (29th Āh.)	VII/3310
आगन्तु सहजं शाक्तं....त्रिवृत्त्रिगुणतन्तुना ॥	X/130	VI/2856
आचार्यः स्वजनानां....संतारयिष्यति ॥	I/253	II/253
आज्ञाविलङ्घनाद्देवि क्रव्यादत्वं शतं समाः ।	IX/22	VI/2462
आ तन्मयत्वसंसिद्धेरा चाभीष्टफलोदयात् ।	X/364	VI/3090
आत्मा चतुर्विधो ह्येषः ।	I/216	II/216
आत्मा ज्ञातव्यो मन्तव्यः ।	XII/394	VIII/3684
आत्मानं मणिमाश्रित्य....वेध इत्यभिसंज्ञितम् ॥	XI/148 (29th Āh.)	VII/3438
आत्मा श्रोतव्यो मन्तव्यो निदिध्यासितव्यः ।	III/32	III/648
आदिमध्यावसानानि चिन्त्यानि क्षणवत्पुनः ।	IV/18 (7th Āh.)	III/1310
आदिमान्त्यविहीनास्तु मन्त्राः स्युः शरदभ्रवत् ।	III/226	III/842

आदौ स्नानं प्रकुर्वीत सर्वकिल्विषनाशनम् ।	IX/40	VI/2480
आधानमिच्छासंयोग....भावानां चापि संभवे ॥	IV/102	III/1190
आनन्दजननं पूजायोग्यं हृदयहारि यत् ।	XI/76 (29th Āh.)	VII/3366
आनन्दशक्तिविश्रान्तो योगी समरसो भवेत् ।	I/29 (2nd Āh.)	II/339
आनन्दस्यन्दि यद्गीतं....सौषुम्नं रूपमुच्यते ॥	III/430	III/1046
आनन्देनैव सम्पन्ने ब्रह्मावस्थः स्वयं स्थितः ।	XI/36 (29th Āh.)	VII/3326
आनन्दो ब्रह्मणो रूपम्....। I/256; III/150; XI/133;	XI/64 (29th Āh);	II/256; III/766; VII/3239,
	XI/91 (29th Āh.)	3354, 3381
आप्तं तमेव भगवन्तं ....मतिमानिति वर्णितं प्राक् ॥	III/258-59	III/874-875
आप्याश्चरुपुरोडाशाः....होमस्त्वावाहिते शिवः ॥	IX/223	VI/2663
आ महाप्रलयस्थायि....शरीरघटाद्यतः ॥	VI/6	IV/1640
आयुष्यं प्राङ्मुखो भुङ्क्ते....ऋतं भुङ्क्ते पराङ्मुखः ॥	IX/108	VI/2548
आवाहिते मन्त्रगणे....पश्चात्पुष्पधूपादिविस्तरः ॥	XI/39 (29th Āh.)	VII/3329
आवृत्याण्डं स्थिता ह्येते....केसरैः परिवारितम् ॥	V/132	IV/1482
आश्यानं चिद्रसस्यौघं....प्रत्यक्षं भैरवं वपुः ।	V/2	IV/1352
इच्छाज्ञानक्रियापूर्वा....।	XII/327	VII/3617
इच्छात्वं तस्य....प्रतिपद्यते ।	I/17	II/17
इच्छाद्यन्तः प्रवेशेन तेऽन्तस्था इति कीर्तिताः ।	II/159	II/511
इच्छासंरम्भबोधाख्या....त्वन्तर्मनोऽहंकारबुद्धयः ॥	VI/189	IV/1823
इच्छैव स्वोष्मणाक्रान्ता कलात्रयसमाश्रिता ।	II/163	II/515

इत्थं गुणवतः....अधस्ताद्व्यापकं महत् ॥	I/245	II/245
इत्थं नानाविधैः रूपैः....एक एव शिवः प्रभुः ॥	I/195	II/195
इत्थमत्यर्थ....व्यवहारोऽनुभूयते ॥	I/280	II/280
इत्थं मध्ये विभिन्नं....सम्प्रदायक्रमात्स्थितम् ॥	I/46	II/46
इत्थं यथोक्त....प्रत्यक्षसिद्धा लोकस्य ॥	VI/232	IV/1866
इत्यन्तःकरणस्यैव....विस्फूर्जितमिदं जगत् ॥	I/67	II/67
इत्यर्थवादा....प्रमाणत्वममी भजन्ते ॥	III/261	III/877
इत्याशयेन मुद्रा मोचयते....मुद्रयति तदेकरूपतया ॥	XII/305	VII/3595
इत्येतदुभयं विप्र....निजगुः कर्तृकारकम् ॥	VI/143	IV/1777
इत्येवं देवदेवेशि आदियागस्त्वोदितः ।	XI/112 (29th Āh.)	VII/3402
इनस्त्वनन्त इत्युक्तः....राहुः क्रूरग्रहो भवेत् ।	IV/62	III/1150
इन्द्रियत्वं मनोबुद्ध्योः....परता परिकीर्तिता ।	VIII/121	V/2321
इयं सा खेचरी....भेदस्तैस्तैरवस्थितम् ॥	XII/306	VII/3596
इष्टेन शिवलिङ्गेन विश्वं समर्पितं भवेत् ।	III/286	III/902
ईशकोणादितः क्रमात्....पूर्वदक्षिणवारुण्यः ॥	XI/51 (29th Āh.)	VII/3341
ईशतत्पुरुषाजातैः....दशानामभवत्स्थितिः ।	I/37	II/37
ईश्वरेच्छावशक्षुब्धभोगलोलिका.... ।	VI/112	IV/1746
ईश्वरेच्छावशादस्य....मायामाविश्यशक्तिभिः ॥	VI/56	IV/1690
उत्क्षेपणावक्षेपण....पञ्चैव कर्माणि ।	VI/208	IV/1842
उत्तमं तु सदा पानं मासादूर्ध्वं पशुर्भवेत् ॥	XI/11 (29th Āh.)	VII/3301

उदगयने शुभवारे स्थिरलग्ने स्थापनाधिवासः स्यात् ॥	XI/55 (29th Āh.)	VII/3345
उदये सङ्क्रमे शान्तौ त्रिलक्षो जप उच्यते ।	XI/104 (29th Āh.)	VII/3394
उन्मनातः परं तत्त्वमनाख्यं यत्प्रकाशते ।	IX/158	VI/2598
उन्मना तु ततोऽतीता तदतीतं निरामयम् ।	I/128	II/128
उन्मना तु परो भावः....कारणा भुवनानि च ।	I/101	II/101
....उन्मन्यन्ते परः शिवः ।	V/259; X/277	IV/1609; VI/3003
उपादायापि ये हेयास्तानुपायान्प्रचक्षते ।	III/46	III/662
उपाध्यायाद्दशाचार्य....शतं पिता ।	I/31	II/31
उपायभेदे तद्भाति यदि बुद्धिभिदा कुतः ।	VI/235	IV/1869
उपायैर्न शिवो भाति....संविन्मया स्थिताः ॥	I/3 (2nd Āh.)	II/313
उपायो नापरः....स सुखी भवेत् ॥	I/29 (2nd Āh.)	II/339
उभयोत्थेन वीर्येण मन्त्रविद्या यजेत्तथा ।	XI/93 (29th Āh.)	VII/3383
उभयोर्भावयोर्ज्ञाने....विकसत्यति भावना ॥	I/127	II/127
उमा दुर्गा भद्रकाली....वागीशी दशमी स्मृता ।	I/154	II/154
उष्णीशमुकुटाद्यांश्च....कर्तव्येत्यधिकारः शिवाज्ञया ।	X/271	VI/2997
ऊनाधिकं यद्विपरीतचेष्टं....पुनरागमनाय ॥	XI/71	VII/3177
ऊर्ध्वं तु भवति रुद्रो....ब्रह्माद्यं सचराचरम् ॥	V/41	IV/1391
ऊर्ध्वं नाभेर्यानि....देहाच्चैव मलाश्च्युताः ॥	III/250	III/866
ऊर्ध्वबाहुर्महाकायो....धारयित्वा जगत्स्थितः ॥	V/22	IV/1372
ऊर्ध्वे तु संस्थिता....बैन्दवी परमा कला ।	I/10	II/10

ऊर्ध्वे बिन्दू रविः....सिद्धसेव्यो लयात्मकः ॥	II/169	II/521
ऊर्ध्वे स्थिता....पूर्णामृतानन्दरसेन देवी ।	I/10	II/10
ऊहोऽन्तरङ्गं योगस्य....मुक्तेर्भूयसोपकरोति हि ॥	III/15	III/631
ऋक्षपक्षितरक्ष्वादीन् स्थावराण्यपि मोचयेत् ।	X/208	VI/2934
ऋतुमुनिसंख्यं रूपं....जगत्तारिणी जननी ॥	III/201	III/817
एकान्ते विजने रम्ये.... ।	IX/57	VI/2497
एकाराकृति यद्दिव्यं....बोधरत्नकरण्डकम् ॥	II/104	II/456
एकैकं पञ्चवक्त्रं....ततो भेदेष्वसंख्यता ॥	I/44	II/44
एकैकस्यापि तत्त्वस्य षट्त्रिंशत्तत्त्वरूपता ।	II/56	II/408
एकैकापि च चिद्वृत्तिः....पुर्यष्टकदेवताः ॥	III/341	III/957
एकं दशगुणं पूर्वं....स्थानानि गणितस्य तु ।	IV/144	III/1232
एकं सृष्टिमयं बीजमेका....पूज्यः कुलागमे ॥	XII/333	VII/3623
एकं स्वरूपरूपं....जयति ते रूपम् ॥	III/197	III/813
एकं स्वरूपरूपं हि....पूजनीयतया स्थिताः ।	III/128, 199	III/744, 815
एक एव स आकारः....तद्वैचित्र्यं सर्वमश्नुते ॥	VI/27	IV/1661
एक एवास्य धर्मोऽसौ सर्वाक्षेपेण वर्तते ।	I/113	II/113
एकजन्मा द्विजन्मा वा सप्तजन्मा समुद्भवेत् ।	X/25	VI/2751
एकमात्रो भवेद्ह्रस्वो....व्यञ्जनं त्वर्धमात्रिकम् ॥	XII/348	VII/3638
एकमेवाद्वितीयं ब्रह्म ।	III/31	III/647
एकमेवेदं संविद्रूपं....विवर्तं पश्यामः ॥	I/69	II/69

एकमेवेदं संविद्रूपं....यथेष्टं संज्ञाः क्रियन्ताम् ।	II/109	II/461
एकस्यार्थस्वभावस्य....प्रमाणैः परीक्ष्यते ॥	III/90	III/706
एकवृक्षः शिवः प्रोक्तः.... ।	IX/54	VI/2494
....एकाकी न रमाम्यहम् ।	I/131	II/131
....एकान्ते जपमारभेत् ।	XI/61 (29th Āh.)	VII/3351
एतदभावे मोक्षमब्रवीत् ।	I/56, 57	II/56, 57
एतदेवान्यथाभूतं दुःस्वप्न....गर्तादिपतनादिकम् ॥	IX/243	VI/2683
एतद्देवि परं गुह्यं....कर्त्तव्यं चुम्बकादिभिः ॥	XI/72	VII/3178
एता मुद्रा महादेवि....तथा चैव विसर्जने ॥	IX/127	VI/2567
एतेषां चलनान्मन्त्री....मन्दतीव्रादिकं बुधः ॥	XI/128 (29th Āh.)	VII/3418
एतेषां तु अधस्ताद्वै....ब्रह्माण्डोदरवर्तिनः ॥	V/19	IV/1369
एवं कालः प्रसर्तव्यस्तच्च तत्त्वमनिन्दितम् ।	IV/37	III/1125
एवं चक्रोदयं ज्ञात्वा....सा तु संकर्षिणी स्मृता ॥	XI/49 (29th Āh.)	VII/3339
एवं च पुद्गलस्यान्तर्मलः....तुषवत् कञ्चुकानि स्युः ।	VI/170	IV/1804
एवं ते भाषितं लिङ्गं त्रिषु लोकेषु पूजितम् ।	V/41	IV/1391
एवं पञ्चफणा देवी निर्गताधरमण्डलात् ।	XI/153 (29th Āh.)	VII/3443
एवं भूतमिदं वस्तु....कुर्वत्यत्र क्रियोच्यते ॥	I/18	II/18
एवं मध्ये सदा पूजां शूलपद्मस्य कारयेत् ।	IX/165	VI/2605
एवंविधं प्रधानं....व्यक्तिमायाति तत्क्षणात् ॥	VI/180	IV/1814
एवं व्याप्तिं....साक्षाच्छिवः परमकारणम् ॥	I/252	II/252

एवमस्य त्रिहस्तस्य. . . . ।	X/380	VI/3106
एवमेतदिदं. . . .ज्ञानशक्तिर्निगद्यते ।	I/19	II/19
एवमेषां स्वरूपांशस्पर्शे. . . .भिन्नसंसारस्थितिवर्तनम् ॥	III/466	III/1082
एवमेषा द्विरूपापि . . . . चिन्तामणिरिवेश्वरी	I/109	II/109
एष ते कौलिको यागः. . . .नानृतं प्रवदाम्यहम् ॥	XI/113-14 (29th Āh.)	VII/3403-3404
ऐन्द्रजालिकवृत्तान्ते न रज्येत कदाचन ।	VIII/230	V/2430
ऐन्द्राग्नमेकादशकपालं निर्वपेत् ।	I/168	II/168
कथितं गोपितं तेभ्यः. . . .अन्यथा न कदाचन ॥	III/73	III/689
कदम्बगोलकाकारः स्फुरत्तारकसन्निभः ।	I/100	II/100
कदम्बो मन्दरे ज्ञेयो. . . .पितृसंज्ञं क्रमात्स्थितम् ।	V/48	IV/1398
. . . .कन्दे षड्सलम्पटाः ।	XII/320	VII/3610
कन्याख्ये यत्कृतं कर्म. . . .तद्बीजं फलभोगदम् ॥	V/67	IV/1417
करकायविलाप. . . .मुद्रा चतुर्विधा ज्ञेया ॥	XII/308	VII/3598
करणमरीचिचक्रमुदयं. . . .केवलतया विलसत्यमला ॥	II/165	II/517
करणेन येन भोग्यं. . . .तत् परं करणं ।	VI/142	IV/1776
कर्तव्या सर्वतो दूतिर्दूतिहीनो न सिद्धिभाक् ।	XI/63 (29th Āh.)	VII/3353
कर्तृशक्तिं व्यनक्त्यस्य. . . .भोगेऽणुः कर्तृकारकम् ॥	VI/143	IV/1777
कर्म तल्लोकरूढं हि. . . .तिरोधत्ते भोक्तृरूपं ।	VIII/164	V/2364
कर्मेन्द्रियाणां पतयो. . . .मित्रश्च ।	V/155	IV/1505
कलविङ्कं प्लवं हंसं चक्राह्वं ग्रामकुक्कुटम् ।	IX/88	VI/2528

कलशं नेत्रबन्धं च....मध्ये पूज्या कृशोदरी ।	XI/53 (29th Āh.)	VII/3343
कलातत्त्वं पवित्राणु....बध्नीयाच्छिवतेजसा ।	III/288	III/904
कलाशुद्ध्यवसाने....शब्दस्पर्शौं त्यजेदस्मिन् ।	X/313	VI/3039
कला सप्तदशी यासावमृताकाररूपिणी ।	I/5	II/5
कवलीकृतनिःशेषतत्त्वग्रामस्वरूपकम् ।	I/124	II/124
कां कां सिद्धिं न वितरेत्किं वा न्यूनं न पूरयेत् ।	IX/70	VI/2510
काञ्चिकोसलकर्णाटाः....राष्ट्रियान्परिवर्जयेत् ।	X/267	VI/2993
काणो विद्वेषजननः खल्वाटश्चार्यनाशनः ।	X/267	VI/2993
कादिभिश्च स्मृता योनिः.... ।	II/177	II/529
कामशोकभय....पुरतोऽवस्थितानिव ॥	I/77; VII/170; X/115	II/77; V/2054; VI/2841
कारणमापूरकं च तस्यैव ।	V/214	IV/1564
कार्यं चेदुपलभ्येत किं कारणपरीक्षया ।	VIII/67	V/2267
कार्यहेतु सहोत्थत्वात्त्रैधं साक्षादथान्यथा ॥	XI/72 (29th Āh.)	VII/3362
कार्ये विशेषमाधित्सुः....विचित्राः कर्मसंगताः ॥	VIII/80	V/2280
कालं सर्वगतं चैव....नववर्णा कुलेश्वरी ।	XII/202	VII/3492
कालस्य कालि देहं....तद्रूपं कुर्वती जयसि ॥	III/198	III/814
कालाग्निरुद्रात्प्रसृतं....युक्त्यात्मचिदर्करूपम् ॥	II/79	II/431
किंतु कारणवक्त्राब्ज....स्वस्थो निर्वात्यसंशयः ॥	VI/144	IV/1778
किंतु गुर्वाज्ञया गच्छेत्तं....कोटिजापाद् भवेदपि ॥	X/260	VI/2986
किं पूज्यं पूजकः....ब्रूहि त्रिलोचन ॥	XI/78 (29th Āh.)	VII/3368

कुमार्याख्यस्य निकटे मध्यस्था....वराहश्चैव षष्ठः स्यात् ॥	V/65	IV/1415
कुम्भमण्डलवह्निस्थः....अध्वसन्धिः प्रकीर्तितः ॥	VII/94 (12th Āh.)	V/2186
कुलं पदमनामाख्यं.... ।	I/9	II/9
कुलं शरीरमित्युक्तं.... ।	XI/4 (29th Āh.)	VII/3294
कुलं स परमानन्दः.... ।	XI/4 (29th Āh.)	VII/3294
कुलं हि परमा शक्तिः.... ।	XI/3 (29th Āh.)	VII/3293
....कुलमुत्पत्तिगोचरः ।	I/12; III/64	II/12; III/680
कुलाचारसमायुक्तो....प्रायश्चित्तं तदा चरेत् ॥	XI/11 (29th Āh.)	VII/3301
कुलात्मस्वरूपं तु.... ।	XI/4 (29th Āh.)	VII/3294
कुलाम्नायेषु ये सक्ता....तैस्तु सह वर्तनम् ॥	XI/66 (29th Āh.)	VII/3356
कूष्माण्डहाटकाद्यास्तु क्रीडन्ति महदाह्वये ।	V/113	IV/1463
कृच्छ्रचान्द्रायणेनैव....पवित्रारोहणे कृते ।	XI/72	VII/3178
कृष्णविषाणया कण्डूयतीति....हृदयस्याग्रेऽवद्यतीति च ॥	IX/87	VI/2527
कृष्णायां मार्गशीर्षस्य....द्वादशं पर्व कीर्तितम् ।	XI/17-18	VII/3123-3124
क्लृप्तकलप्यविरोधे च क्लृप्तः क्लृप्तपरिग्रहः ।	VI/206	IV/1840
क्लपिर्मतिः स्यतिश्चैव....तेनान्तःकरणं त्रिधा ॥	VI/192	IV/1826
केन्द्रायाष्टधनेषु....ब्राह्मणः ।	XI/46	VII/3152
कोटिद्वयं त्रिपञ्चाशल्लक्षाणि....सप्तद्वीपाः ससागराः ॥	V/80	IV/1430
कौलिकी सा परा शक्तिरवियुक्तो यया प्रभुः ॥	II/139	II/491
क्रमकुलचतुष्टयाश्रय....चक्रे सवंशनिर्वंशान् ॥	III/195	III/811

क्रमेण सर्वभोगाप्त....मोक्षैकपद्धतिः ।	VIII/131	V/2331
क्रियादिभेदभेदेन....तत्कार्यं नान्यतन्त्रतः ॥	III/279; V/16; X/266	III/895; IV/1366; VI/2[illegible] 2
क्रियाधिकाः शक्तयस्ताः संविद्रूपाधिका नहि ।	VI/67	IV/1701
क्रिया कुण्डलिनी कुण्डं.... ।	IX/195	VI/2635
क्रीडन्ति विविधैर्भावैर्देव्यः पिण्डान्तरस्थिताः ।	XI/122 (29th Āh.)	VII/3412
क्रीडाकर्माण्यथोक्तानि...पुराणि नगनन्दिनि ॥	VIII/114	V/2314
क्रूरकर्माणि तत्रैव....न च सिद्ध्यन्ति सुव्रते ॥	IV/67	III/1155
क्रोधो वह्निपुटान्तस्थः....क्रोधकर्षणे क्षुरिका मता ॥	X/18	VI/2744
क्षुधाद्यनुभवो यत्र विकल्पः....विभुरप्येकधर्मतः ॥	I/119	II/119
क्षुभिताच्छब्दतन्मात्रात्....भूमिःसर्वदैव विभज्यते ॥	VI/231	IV/1865
क्षेत्रेऽष्टधा विभक्ते मध्ये....कुलक्रमे मण्डलं सचतुरस्रम ।	XI /38 (29th Āh.)	VII/3328
क्षेत्रोपक्षेत्रसंदोहाद्याश्रयान्निर्मलो भवेत् ॥	III/291	III/907
खण्डैरेकोनविंशैस्तु....यावत्सिद्धयोगीश्वरीमतम् ॥	XII/385	VIII/3675
खमनन्तं तु जन्माख्ये....मध्यलक्ष्यं तृतीयकम् ।	X/189	VI/2915
खमनन्तं तु मायाख्यं.... ।	XII/331	VII/3621
खमात्मा केवलं विद्यात्....खमभूत्तत्त्वलक्षणम् ।	III/405	III/1021
खेचर्याः परिवारस्तु अष्टौ....तदशेषं व्यवस्थितम् ।	XII/328	VII/3618
गता सा परमाकाशं परं निर्वाणमण्डलम् ॥	XI/153 (29th Āh.)	VII/3443
गन्धाद्यपलब्धिक्रिया....छिदिक्रियावत् ।	VI/207	IV/1841
गणेशं पूजयित्वा....पूजयेद्गुरुपद्धतिम् ॥	XI/23 (29th Āh.)	VII/3313
गणेशं वटुकं सिद्धान् गुरुपङक्तिं तथैव च ।	XI/24 (29th Āh.)	VII/3314

गणेशाधस्ततः सर्वं. . . . वर्गं तत्रैव परिपूजयेत् ॥	XI/24 (29th Āh.)	VII/3314
गणेशो विघ्नहर्तासौ देवीपुत्रः. . . . ।	I/23	II/23
गरीयान्कर्मिणो योगी स च ज्ञानवतः शिशुः ।	IX/13	VI/2453
गुणतत्त्वोर्ध्वभोग्यस्य. . . . नैव युक्तमसंक्षयात् ॥	VI/145	IV/1779
गुरुं संपूजयेच्छिष्यो यथाविभवविस्तरैः ।	X/271	VI/2997
गुरुणैव यदा काले. . . . यन्त्रं तिष्ठति केवलम् ॥	I/82	II/82
गुरुदेवाग्निशास्त्रस्य. . . . ह्यमोक्षे मोक्षलिप्सया ॥	III/18	III/634
गुरुभक्तस्य दान्तस्य. . . . दीक्षाकर्म विधीयते ॥	X/217	VI/2943
गुरुभ्योऽपि. . . . चुखुलाभिधम् ।	I/31	II/31
गुरोरप्यवलिप्तस्य. . . . परित्यागो विधीयते ॥	X/297	VI/3023
गुरोरवज्ञया मृत्युर्दारिद्र्यं. . . . सिद्धोऽपि नरकं व्रजेत् ।	X/259	VI/2985
गुर्वन्तररते मूढे. . . . सम्पर्कं नैव कारयेत् ॥	VIII/208	V/2408
गुरुशास्त्रानपेक्षं. . . . तत्त्वनिष्ठो महामुनिः ॥	III/45	III/661
गुरुशिष्यपदे स्थित्वा. . . . तन्त्रं समवतारयत् ॥	I/268	II/268
गृहस्थानां जलेनैव नैष्ठिकानां तु भस्मना ।	X/159	VI/2885
गृहे गृहोद्भवैर्द्रव्यैः. . . . शवलं न समाचरेत् ॥	X/375	VI/3101
गोघ्नश्चैव कृतघ्नश्च. . . . मुच्यन्ते सर्वपातकैः ॥	X/196	VI/2922
गोपनात्सिद्धिमायाति. . . . ।	X/339	VI/3065
गौडी माध्वी तथा पैष्टी ऊर्ध्वे आनन्दभैरवः ।	XI/10 (29th Āh.)	VII/3300
ग्राह्यग्राहकभावो हि सामान्यः सर्वदेहिनाम् ।	III/240	III/856
घटो मदात्मना. . . . घटात्मना ।	I/15 (2nd Āh.)	II/325

घृतेनाभ्यज्य गात्राणि....भ्रातुर्भार्यां यवीयसः ॥	XI/73 (29th Āh.)	VII/3363
घ्राणादिश्रोत्रपर्यन्ता....बुद्धीन्द्रियेषु ते ॥	V/156	IV/1506
चक्रद्वयेऽन्तः....परा स्थितिः ।	I/9	II/9
चक्राधाराटव्यां भ्रमन्त्यसत्यां परिच्युतविवेकाः ।	III/357	III/973
चतुरश्रमघो ब्रह्मा.... ।	V/40	IV/1390
चतुरस्रस्त्वयं धर्मः....शान्तितत्परः ॥	XI/10 (29th Āh.)	VII/3300
चतुर्दशविधं ....संसारमण्डलम् ।	I/63	II/63
चतुर्विंशतिदीपांश्च....रक्तवर्त्यपरिस्थिताः ॥	XI/51 (29th Āh.)	VII/3341
चतुर्वेदार्थविदुषां....कोटिर्भवति भोजिता ॥	XI/33	VII/3139
चन्द्ररूपेण तपति क्रियाशक्तिः शिवस्य तु ॥	II/125	II/477
चरुकः सम्प्रदायश्च विज्ञानं....योगिनीनां मुखे स्थितम् ॥	XI/19 (29th Āh.)	VII/3309
चितिः प्रत्यवमर्शात्मा....प्रोक्ता हृदयं परमेष्ठिनः ॥	III/212	III/828
चित्तभेदान्मनुष्याणां....न सर्वत्र गुरुर्भवेत् ॥	III/55	III/671
चित्तमात्रमिदं....चित्तमात्रव्यवस्थितिः ।	I/66	II/66
चित्रस्वभावकाः प्रोक्ता....पटे रूपं तु वेष्टिते ॥	VI/234	IV/1868
चिदात्मैव हि देवः....अर्थजातं प्रकाशयेत् ॥	II/96	II/448
चिदानन्देषणाज्ञान....तत्त्ववर्णेषु पञ्चधा ॥	VI/49	IV/1683
चैतन्यखचितात्कायान्नात्मान्योऽस्तीति मन्वते ।	IV/14	III/1102
चोदनेति क्रियायाः प्रवर्तकं वचनम् ।	I/168; III/250	II/168; III/866
छायात्मा स पराङ्मुख आदर्शादौ च संमुखो ज्ञेयः ।	XI/161 (29th Āh.)	VII/3451
जटाभस्मादिचिह्नं....कुर्यात्कर्मणा मनसा गिरा ।	III/288	III/904

ज्ञेयरूपमिदं पंचविंशत्यन्तं यतः स्फुटम् ।	II/178	II/530
तच्च साक्षादुपायेन. . . . . ।	I/201	II/201
तच्छत्रं कुक्कुटाण्डं च. . . . . ।	V/38	IV/1388
तत ऊर्ध्वं सूर्यसंज्ञं. . . . कल्पे कल्पे ह्यसंख्याताः ।	V/154-55	IV/1504-1505
. . . . ततः पूर्णां विनिक्षिपेत्. . . . सत्यं सत्यं न संशयः ॥	X/235	VI/2961
ततः सर्गो बुद्बुदत्वेनाभिव्यज्यते ।	III/32	III/648
. . . . ततः पुंसां मलः स्मृतः ।	VI/61	IV/1695
ततोऽपि संहृताशेषभाव. . . . प्रापयाभेदभूमिकाम् ॥	I/46	II/46
ततोऽस्वरोऽर्क. . . . प्रमाणार्थप्रमातृदः ॥	II/79	II/431
ततोऽस्य मस्तके चक्रं. . . . सद्यः प्रत्ययकारकः ।	XI/126 (29th Āh.)	VII/3416
ततोऽस्य याजयेच्छक्तिं सोऽहमित्यपराजिताम् ।	IX/119	VI/2559
ततो दूतीं क्षोभयित्वा. . . . प्राशयेच्च परस्परम् ॥	XI/93 (29th Āh.)	VII/3383
ततो वीराष्टकं पश्चाच्छक्त्युक्तविधिना यजेत् ॥	XI/38 (29th Āh.)	VII/3328
ततो हूहुकरुद्रस्य. . . . पुरं वीरगणाकुलम् ॥	V/18	IV/1368
. . . . तत्क्षणाद्वा शिवं व्रजेत् ।	VIII/141	V/2341
तत्तद्रूपतया ज्ञानं . . . . प्राप्तमेतस्मादवसीयते ॥	II/66	II/478
तत्त्वं त्रिविधमाख्यातं. . . . देवदेव विविच्यते ॥	VIII/109	V/2309
तत्त्वज्ञस्य तृणं शास्त्रं . . . . ।	I/4 (2nd Āh.)	II/314
तत्त्वैः षट्त्रिंशतार्धेन. . . . परापरविभूतये ॥	VII/34 (11th Āh.)	V/2126
तत्पीठं शाकिनीचक्रे. . . . लीनमद्वैतं परमं शिवं ॥	XI/106 (29th Āh.)	VII/3396
तत्र च पञ्च अवस्था जाग्रदाद्याः. . . . न्यासे पूर्णत्वात् भैरवीभावः ।	IX/129	VI/2569

तदेवमागतं मर्त्ये....तस्माद्दाशरथिं गतम् ।	XII/385	VIII/3675
तद्वन्नासापयोभ्यां....वाचकौ पद्मचक्रयोः ॥	XII/201	VII/3491
तन्त्रं जज्ञे....तथैवाभेदभागिना ।	I/45	II/45
तन्मात्रेभ्यश्च भूतानि.... ।	I/218	II/218
तमनित्येषु भोगेषु योजयन्ति विनायकाः ।	I/53	II/53
तमाराध्य ततस्तुष्टाद्दीक्षतामासाद्य शांकरीम् ।	III/76	III/692
....तर्को योगाङ्गमुत्तमम् ।	I/30	II/30
तस्मात्प्रविततात्....शैवं धाम नयत्यपि ॥	I/80	II/80
तस्मात्सत्यपि बाह्यार्थे....नानेकेव प्रसज्येत ॥	IV/16 (7th Āh.)	III/1308
तस्मात्संपूर्णसंबोध....स पर आगमः ॥	XII/365	VIII/365
तस्मादकृतविघातात्....व्रजति च समतां परेशेन ॥	IX/214	VI/2654
तस्मादेको महादेवः....बिम्बप्रतिबिम्बोदयात्मना ॥	II/13	II/365
तस्माद् गुरुक्रमायातं दिशन्नेति परं शिवम् ।	I/52	II/52
तस्माद्यत्संविदो नातिदूरे तच्छुद्धमाहरेत् ।	XI/91 (29th Āh.)	VII/3381
तस्य दीक्षां विनैव....सर्वशास्त्रेषु परिनिष्ठितम् ॥	I/81	II/81
तस्य देवातिदेवस्य....सर्वज्ञज्ञानशालिनी ॥	III/187, 387	III/803, 1003
तस्य मे....नोपदेशदरिद्रता ।	I/29	II/29
तस्य शक्तय एताश्च....तेनैता द्वादशोदिताः ॥	III/134	III/750
तस्यां....दशायामैश्वरो भावः पशोरपि ।	I/239; III/324	II/239; III/940
तस्यान्तर्भासते भानुर्न बहिः सुरसुन्दरि ।	V/82	IV/1432
तस्यैव तु प्रसादेन भक्तिरुत्पद्यते नृणाम् ।	VIII/174; X/12	V/2374; VI/2738

तस्योर्ध्वं नरका घोरा एकविंशतिकोटयः ।	V/16	IV/1366
ता एताश्चतस्रः. . . .द्वादश भवन्ति ।	III/134	III/750
तादृङ्मेलककलिका. . . .ज्ञानभाजनं भक्तः ।	I/14	II/14
तार्किकं न गुरुं कुर्यात्. . . . ।	III/18	III/634
. . . .तार्किके वधबन्धनम् ।	III/19	III/635
तिथिच्छेदस्तथा वृद्धिः. . . .प्राणवृत्तिनिरोधतः ॥	IV/94	III/1182
. . . .तिथिं यत्नेन याजयेत् ।	XI/25	VII/3131
तिला लाजा यवाश्चैव. . . .मिश्रोऽयं विकिरः शुभः ।	IX/187	VI/2627
तिष्ठेत्संवत्सरं पूर्णं. . . .सा दिनैकेन योषिताम् ॥	XI/87 (29th Āh.)	VII/3377
तुटिपाते सर्वज्ञतादयः ।	VII/142	V/2026
तुल्ये गुणान्वितत्वे. . . .धन्या तार्किकता तव ।	VI/192	IV/1826
तृणात्पर्णाच्च पाषाणात्. . . .विभो क्व नु ते स्थितिः ॥	VII/89	V/1973
तेन निर्भरमात्मानं. . . .प्रीत्या च तर्पयेत् ॥	XI/77 (29th Āh.)	VII/3367
तेन स्वातन्त्र्यशक्त्यैव. . . .शक्त्यैवावियुक्तता ॥	I/27 (2nd Āh.)	II/337
तेनाजडस्य भागस्य. . . .वैचित्र्यं बहुधा स्थितम् ।	I/303	II/303
तेनास्म्याराधितो देवि पवित्रेण महात्मना ।	XI/49	VII/3155
तेषां ज्ञानी नित्ययुक्त. . . .स च मम प्रियः ॥	I/197	II/197
तेषामपि परो जीवः स एव परमेश्वरः ।	I/95	II/95
तेषु मध्ये शतं श्रेष्ठं. . . .राजराजेश्वरास्त्रीणि . . . .॥	V/26	IV/1376
तैजसानां मणीनां च. . . .शुद्धिरुक्ता मनीषिभिः ॥	III/244	III/860
त्रिकोणं भगमित्युक्तं. . . .तन्मध्ये चिञ्चिनीक्रमम् ॥	II/104	II/456

त्रिकोणमण्डलं पूज्यं. . . .लिङ्गं व पश्चिमामुखम् ॥	III/430	III/1046
त्रिकोणे देवताः सर्वा ब्रह्मविष्णुमहेश्वराः ।	III/431	III/1047
त्रिदलं भगपद्मं तु. . . . ।	XI/105 (29th Āh.)	VII/3395
त्रिनेत्रः स चतुर्वक्त्रो वह्निज्वालावलीधरः ।	V/22	IV/1372
त्रिपदार्थकारी सत्ता. . . . ।	VII/60	V/1944
त्रिप्रत्ययमिदं ज्ञानं. . . . ।	X/331	VI/3057
त्रिबद्धचित्कलायोगा. . . . ।	VI/168	IV/1802
त्रिषु स्थानगतो विन्दुमेकत्रैव विभावयेत् ।	II/118	II/470
त्रिष्वेव संस्थितो रुद्रः कालरूपी महेश्वरः ।	IV/146	III/1234
त्रीणि मूलानि सूत्राणि. . . .वदन्विघ्नैर्हि बाध्यते ॥	XI/174	VII/3280
त्रैगुण्यात्मा विवेकेन शक्ता. . . .अविविक्ता यतःस्वयम् ॥	VI/152	IV/1786
त्वच्छक्तिचक्रात्मकमेव. . . .भवतोऽस्ति किंचित् ॥	I/223	II/223
दक्षनामा तु यो रुद्रः. . . .मासस्याश्वयुजस्य च ॥	IV/106	III/1194
दक्षश्चण्डो हरिश्चण्डी. . . .रावणो दैवकण्टकः ॥	XII/385	VIII/3675
दधि होमात्परा पुष्टिः. . . . ।	I/161	II/161
दन्तकाष्ठं तथा देवि. . . .दापयेच्चुम्बकोत्तमः ।	XI/71	VII/3177
दन्तपक्त्यां द्वितीयं. . . .सर्वसिद्धिप्रदायकम् ।	XII/201	VII/3491
दर्भाणां तालमानेन कृता. . . .वेणी बोधासिरुत्तमः ॥	IX/217	VI/2657
दश पञ्च च शोध्यानि भुवनान्यैश्वरे क्रमात् ।	V/237	IV/1587
दशानां तु परं देवि. . . .मध्ये शक्त्यात्मिका स्मृता ॥	IV/165	III/1253
दशावस्थाश्चिनोत्यन्तः. . . .तावन्मुक्तो भवार्णवात् ।	III/415	III/1031

दार्शपौर्णमासाभ्यां यजेत स्वर्गकामः ।	I/167	II/167
दिनकरसममहद्....यो नमस्तस्मै ।	I/22	II/22
दिनमेकं दिनार्धं....प्रायश्चित्ती भवेन्नरः ॥	XI/11 (29th Āh.)	VII/3301
दीक्षाकाले तु ....शूद्रस्यान्त्येष्टिकर्मणि ॥	XI/11 (29th Āh.)	VII/3301
दीक्षाज्ञानविशुद्धानाम....श्राद्धं वै विधिपूरणम् ॥	X/318	VI/3044
दीक्षितः शिवसिद्धान्ते....तीर्थमात्रफलेप्सुना ॥	XI/108	VII/3214
दीक्षैव मोचयत्यूर्ध्वं शैवं धाम नयत्यपि ।	I/192; X/328	II/192; VI/3054
....दीक्षोक्तं फलमश्नुते ।	VIII/236	V/2436
दीपपर्वणि कर्त्तव्यं....सा च नित्या प्रकीर्तिता ॥	XI/51	VII/3157
....दीपाद्दीपमिवोदितम् ।	III/234	III/850
दीपाद्दीपमिवोद्यतम् ।	II/261	II/613
दीपान्कुर्याद्रक्तवर्तीन्घृततैलप्रपूरितान् ।	XI/15 (29th Āh.)	VII/3305
दीपो यथा निर्वृतिम्....केवलमेति शान्तिम् ।	III/33	III/649
दीयते ज्ञानसद्भावः....दीक्षा तेनेह कीर्तिता ।	I/80	II/80
दूतीं कुर्यात्तु कार्यार्थी न पुनः काममोहितः ।	XI/73 (29th Āh.)	VII/3363
दूरान्तिकतयार्थानां....एकत्वमनिवारितम् ॥	VI/44	IV/1678
दृष्टमपि अविमृष्टमदृष्टमेव ।	III/325	III/941
दृष्ट्वा शिष्यं जराग्रस्तं....परतत्त्वे नियोजयेत् ॥	VI/104; VIII/147	IV/1738; V/2347
देवादीनां च सर्वेषां....मुख्यं संसारकारणम् ॥	VI/56	IV/1690
देवीपञ्चशताशयमाश्रित्य च भूतिराजपूर्वाणाम् ।	III/194	III/810
देवीपुत्रोऽत्र बटुकः स्वशक्तिपरिवारितः ।	I/23	II/23

...देहपाते शिवं व्रजेत् ।	I/80	II/80
देहस्थं तु चरुं वक्ष्ये....देहस्थं ग्राह्योच्चरुम् ।	XI/130 (29th Āh.)	VII/3420
द्रव्यैश्च लोकविद्विष्टैः....पूजनीयस्त्वयं क्रमः ॥	XI/8 (29th Āh.)	VII/3298
द्राघीयसी वेदवृत्तिः....स्याद्रात्रिविस्तरः ॥	IV/76	III/1164
द्वादशारावियोगेन देवीं द्वादशधा यजेत् ।	III/188	III/804
द्वादशैव स्वराः प्रोक्ता....कलाद्वादशसंज्ञिताः ।	III/156	III/772
द्वावेव मोक्षदौ प्रोक्तौ ज्ञानी योगी च शाङ्कर ।	VIII/197	V/2397
द्वासप्ततिसहस्राणि नाडीनां नाभिचक्रके ।	XI/101 (29thĀh.)	VII/3391
द्विकरं पञ्च तद्भागाः....पृथुत्वाद्भागसंमितम् ॥	XII/261	VII/3551
द्वितीयः सूत्रदेहस्तु....सूत्रस्थाने न विग्रहे ॥	X/132	VI/2858
धर्मादयोऽप्यभिष्वङ्ग....बुद्धिधर्मत्वेन गणिताः ॥	VI/158	IV/1792
धर्मान्तरप्रतिक्षेपाप्रतिक्षेपौ....द्रव्यभावाभिधायिनोः ।	I/60	II/60
धाम्नां त्रयाणामप्येषां....प्रकाशवपुरव्ययः ।	I/151	II/151
धीवरी चक्रपूजा....मातङ्गीकुलसंभवम् ॥	XI/18	VII/3124
ध्रुवेण कुण्डबाह्ये तु त्रिधा भ्राम्यावतारयेत् ।	IX/202	VI/2642
ध्यानं या निश्चला बुद्धिः....मुखहस्तादिकल्पना ॥	I/134	II/134
न कुर्यादधिकारं....शाकिन्यो वै शपन्ति तम् ॥	VIII/195	V/2395
न क्रियारहितं ज्ञानं न ज्ञानरहिता क्रिया ।	VIII/228	V/2428
न क्वापि गत्वा....भव्यास्तेभ्यो नमो नमः ॥	III/287	III/903
न गच्छेत्पटलादूर्ध्वं.... ।	XI/174	VII/3280
न चर्या भोगतः....किं वा चलं मनः ।	III/269; XI/74 (29th Āh.)	III/885; VII/3364

न च शास्त्रान्तरे कर्तुं....नान्यत्स्यादनवस्थितेः ।	IX/211	VI/2651
न चाधिकारिता दीक्षां विना योगेऽस्ति शाङ्करे ।	I/250; III/47	II/250; III/663
न चाप्यहंकृतो जन्म नियमे कारणं मम ।	VI/193	IV/1827
न चावज्ञा क्रियाकाले....शिष्यधुङ्नारकी भवेत् ॥	IX/24	VI/2464
न चावज्ञा क्रियाकाले संसारोद्धरणं प्रति ।	II/262	II/614
....न ज्ञानरहिता क्रिया ।	I/198	II/198
न तु मामभिजानन्ति तत्त्वेनातश्च्यवन्ति ते ।	I/170	II/170
न ते मन्त्रप्रयोक्तारः पुनर्भवतया स्थिताः ॥	X/254	VI/2980
नदते दशधा सा तु....व्याहरेद्दशधा रवम् ॥	III/410	III/1026
न दिवा पूजयेत् देवं....दिनरात्रिपरिक्षये ॥	IV/85	III/1173
न नद्यो मधुवाहिन्यो....कुतः सिद्धिः कुलागमे ॥	IX/86	VI/2526
नन्दन्ति पितरस्तस्य....सोऽस्मान्संतारयिष्यति ॥	I/13	II/13
नन्वदिव्येन देहेन....सर्वं भवति निष्फलम् ॥	XI/19 (29th Āh.)	VII/3309
न पुंभिरार्षवाक्यं....बाध्यते तु कदाचन ।	III/276	III/892
न पुंसि न परे तत्त्वे....नियुक्तस्तु सर्वकर्मफलप्रदः ।	III/425	III/1041
न पुंसि न परे तत्त्वे शक्तौ मन्त्रान्नियोजयेत् ।	X/136	VI/2862
न प्राप्तोऽपि परां दीक्षां....कर्म यन्मोक्षसाधनम् ॥	X/216	VI/2942
नभः स्थिता यथा....नान्यत्संसारोद्धरणं प्रति ।	I/24	II/24
नभस्थे च तेजसि रूपप्रतिबिम्बयोगः ।	II/5	II/357
नभस्यनभसोर्मध्ये पक्षयोः कृष्णशुक्लयोः ।	XI/53	VII/3159
न भावो नापि चाभावो मध्यमाप्रतिपत्तितः ।	IV/9	III/1097

न मे प्रियश्चतुर्वेदो....पूज्यो यथाह्यहम् ॥	III/234	III/850
न मे बन्धो....जलेष्विव विवस्वतः ॥	II/27	II/379
नमः शिवायेति पदं षडर्णं प्रणवादिकम् ।	IV/187	III/1275
....नवतत्त्वीं प्रचक्ष्महे ।	VII/33 (11th Āh.)	V/2125
नवधा वर्गभेदतः....शतार्धकिरणोज्ज्वला ॥	II/192	II/544
नवमी चक्रिणी या सा....कन्दवेष्टविनिर्गता ॥	XI/48 (29th Āh.)	VII/3338
नवमी रोहिणीयोगे पुष्ये....कर्त्तव्यं वारगणनम् ....॥	XI/46-47	VII/3152-3153
न विन्दति यदा मन्त्री....शिवाज्ञासंप्रचोदिताः ॥	IV/35 (7th Āh.)	III/1327
न विवाहे पशुं हन्यात्....पशुयागे कृते सति ।	X/22-23	VI/2748-2749
न वै युगपदाकारद्वितयं....भेदानुपग्रहात् ॥	VII/24	V/1908
न शण्ठं च पशुं....स्त्रीपशुं नैव भैरवि ॥	X/28	VI/2754
न शान्तमुदितं....यन्न केनचिदुच्यते ॥	I/25 (2nd Āh.)	II/335
न शिवः शक्तिरहितो....यामलं प्रसरं सर्वं ....॥	II/80	II/432
न हठेन पशुं हन्यात्....यागपूर्वं विधानवित् ॥	X/22	VI/2748
न हि भेदात्परं दुःखं तमो नाद्वयसंवृतेः ।	XI/167 (29th Āh.)	VII/3457
नागाग्राल्लुठिता ये च....संख्या न विद्यते ॥	X/217-18	VI/2943-2944
नागृहीतैस्तु गन्धाद्यैः....जलादिभ्यः पृथक्च भूः ।	VI/233	IV/1867
नह्यग्निष्टोमीयहिंसा हिंसैव भवति	X/22	VI/2748
नातः किंचिदपास्यं....क्षेत्रादिपर्यटनैः ॥	III/291	III/907
नातितीव्रमदा लघ्वी पथ्या बैभीतकी सुरा ॥	IX/39	VI/2479
नातिरहस्यमेकत्र....गोप्यम् इति हि अस्मद्गुरवः ।	III/443	III/1059

नात्र शुद्धिर्न चाशुद्धिः. . . . ।	III/256	III/872
नादं दीर्घं समुच्चार्य. . . .नादवेध उदाहृतः ।	XI/152 (29th Āh.)	VII/3442
नादाख्यं यत्परं बीजं सर्वभूतेष्ववस्थितम् ।	II/149	II/501
नादो मन्त्रः स्थितिर्मुद्रा. . . . ।	III/232	III/848
नानेन रहितो मोक्षो. . . .सिद्धिर्विशेषाद् भैरवागमे ॥	XI/9 (29th Āh.)	VII/3299
नापनेयमतः. . . .भूतदर्शी विमुच्यते ॥	III/9	III/625
नाभिदेशे त्वलिपुरं कन्दोर्ध्वे परमेश्वरि ।	XI/43 (29th Āh.)	VII/3333
नाभिस्थाने स्रुचो. . . .कृत्वा चैवमधोमुखम् ॥	IX/216	VI/2656
. . . .नार्थवादः शिवागमः ।	III/257; XII/378	III/873
नावश्यं कारणानि कार्यवन्ति भवन्ति ।	III/66	III/682
नावेदनमतो वेद्यम्. . . . ।	II/126	II/478
नासमीहितं फलं भवति ।	VI/87	IV/1721
नासिद्धे भावधर्मोऽस्ति. . . .सत्ता साध्यते कथम् ॥	VI/124	IV/1758
नास्य मण्डलकुण्डादि. . . .स्नानादि च यथेच्छया ।	I/35 (2nd Āh.); XI/6 (29th Āh.)	II/345; VII/3296
नास्योच्चारयिता. . . .प्राणिनामुरसि स्थितः ॥	II/76, 149; III/211	II/428, 501; III/827
नाहं प्राणो नैव शरीरं. . . .सोऽस्म्यहमेव . . . .॥	I/304	II/304
निःशङ्कः सिद्धिमायाति. . . .अवीरो हि विनश्यति ॥	X/19	VI/2745
नित्यादित्रितयं कुर्याद्गुरुः. . . .यावज्जीवं शिवाज्ञया ॥	IX/258; XI/3	VI/2698; VII/3109
नित्यानन्दरसास्वादात्. . . .कामतत्त्वस्य वेदकः ॥ II/151;	XI/110 (29th Āh.)	II/503; VII/3400
नित्याह्निके समाप्ते तु कुर्यान्नैमित्तिकं बुधः ।	IX/1	VI/2441
नित्योदिता पराशक्तिः. . . .दुर्लभा कौलिकी स्थितिः ॥	VII/101 (12th Āh.)XI/63 (29th Āh.)	V/2193; VII/3353

निन्द्यमानमहामन्त्र....यात्नाधाम्नि सर्वथा ॥	VIII/222	V/2422
निमित्तमभिलाषाख्यम्....।	VI/57, 75	IV/1691, 1709
निमित्तमभिलाषाख्यं नैमित्तिकमतः परम् ।	VIII/57	V/2257
नियतोभयांशावलम्बी विमर्शः संशयः ।	I/261	II/261
....निरालम्बः परः शिवः ॥	XI/95 (29th Āh.)	VII/3385
निराशंसात्पूर्णादहमिति....परमशिवशक्त्यात्मनिखिलम् ।	VI/51	IV/1685
निर्भर्त्स्यैवं विधानेन अभिषेकं प्रदापयेत् ।	X/271	VI/2997
निर्वात्यनन्तनाथस्तद्धामाविशति सूक्ष्मरुद्रस्तु ।	IX/155	VI/2595
निर्विकल्पकदशायां हि सोऽयमैश्वरो भावः पशोरपि ।	VI/225	IV/1859
निर्विशेषं हि सामान्यं भवेच्छशविषाणवत् ।	I/270	II/270
निविडजडिमबन्धात्....तादृशेनैव नाम्ना ॥	VII/30 (11th Āh.)	V/2122
....निश्चयो नैव जायते ।	III/20	III/636
निष्कम्पः सकलः शान्तो...बीजाभिख्यासमन्वितम् ॥	X/227	VI/2953
नीलोत्पलदलाभास....स्थापयेत्कुण्डमध्यतः ॥	IX/202	VI/2642
....नेदं बीजं च कस्यचित् ।	II/173	II/525
नैर्मल्यं मुखमेतस्य....श्रंशांशिकातः क्वाप्यन्यत्.... ॥	II/58	II/410
नैवाधिकपरिच्छेदः....कोऽधिकोऽर्थः प्रकाशते ॥	III/90	III/706
नोर्ध्वं निरीक्षते देवो मेदं भूद्भस्मसाज्जगत् ।	V/22	IV/1372
नौम्यनुत्तरनाथस्य....परापरफलप्रदम् ॥	II/75	II/427
पक्षद्वयं परित्यज्य....अन्यथा सिद्धिभाग्भवेत् ॥	IV/93	III/1181
पञ्चकर्मकृतो वायोः....संरम्भोऽहंकृतो वृत्तिः.... ॥	VI/185	IV/1819

....पञ्चतद्भागाः पद्मपीठतिरोहिताः ।	XII/236	VII/3526
पञ्चत्रिंशत्तत्त्वी शिवनाथस्यैव शक्तिरुक्तेयम् ।	VI/3	IV/1637
पत्युर्धर्माः शक्तयः स्युः.... ।	I/193	II/193
पदं पदवतां श्रेष्ठं....स्वोपकाराय चेष्टते ।	III/93-94	III/709-710
पदानि मन्त्रारब्धानि....स्थूलसूक्ष्मपरात्मता ॥	IV/34	III/1122
पदैकादशिका सा....समनैकादशी स्मृता ॥	I/128	II/128
पद्मस्याष्टदलस्येत्थं....हृदयेनैव भाव्यते ।	IV/164	III/1252
पद्मं हृत्पद्मेवात्र....मानसी परिपठ्यते ।	XII/328	VII/3618
....परं त्विच्छात्मकं मतम् ।	I/235	II/235
परभावात्तु तत्सूक्ष्मं शक्तितत्त्वं निगद्यते ।	VIII/122	V/2322
परमात्मा शिवो हंसः.... ।	III/147	III/763
परमार्थतः सा शाक्ती तनुः ।	IX/70	VI/2510
परमार्थविकल्पेऽपि....शुभे वाऽप्यथ वाऽशुभे ॥	I/57; III/7	II/57; III/623
परां काष्ठामनुप्राप्तो....ब्रह्महत्याफलं लभेत् ।	V/98	IV/1448
....परावस्था हि भासनम् ।	VII/22	V/1906
परासम्पुटमध्यस्थां....परां वा केवलां प्रिये ॥	XI/18 (29th Āh.)	VII/3308
....परेह शिवसमता ।	III/81	III/697
परो महानन्तरालो....सम्बन्धः षड्विधस्तन्त्रे.... ॥	I/280	II/280
पवित्रो नाम नागेन्द्रो ज्येष्ठो भ्रातास्ति वासुकेः ॥	XI/50	VII/3156
पर्शुर्नित्यो ह्यमूर्तोऽज्ञो....भोगोपायविचिन्तकः ॥	VI/114	IV/1748
पशुर्वै नीयमानः स मृत्युं....त्वा लोकं गमयिष्यामः ।	X/24	VI/2750

....पशूंश्च प्रोक्षयेद्बहून् ।	X/25	VI/2751
पश्चात् स्रुचं....उत्थितां समपादस्थः ....॥	X/235	VI/2961
पश्चिमं विवृतं कार्यम्.... ।	XII/252	VII/3542
पश्येन्नेकमदृष्टस्य....विनाप्याख्यातृभिर्जनः ।	XII/356	VIII/3646
पादाङ्गुष्ठाग्रतो व्यक्ता....निर्मिता परमेष्ठिना ॥	IV/53 (7th Āh.)	IV/1345
पादोऽस्य विश्वा भूतानि त्रिपादस्यामृतं दिवि ।	III/32	III/648
पादो मूलं तथोद्धार....मया ख्यातः सुविस्तरात् ।	XII/387	VIII/3677
पापं कृत्वा तु संतप्य....निवृत्त्या तु स पूयते ॥	VI/86	IV/1720
पाशं विना न शम्भुः....मुक्ताणुगकर्तृ शक्तिमिव ॥	VI/141	IV/1775
पाशवं ज्ञानमुज्झित्वा पतिशास्त्रं समाश्रयेत् ।	III/283	III/899
पाशाश्च पौरुषाः....दीक्षा न निष्फला ॥	I/57	II/57
....पीठाधः पद्ममालिखेत् ।	XI/170	VII/3276
पीत्वा कुलामृतं दिव्यं....तन्त्रेऽस्मिन्पारमेश्वरे ।	III/397	III/1013
....पुंसः प्रादुर्भवत्परम् ।	I/74	II/74
पुरुषः पञ्चविंशकः ।	II/155; V/178	II/507; IV/1528
पुरुषे षोडशकले .... ।	X/311	XI/3037
पुरुषे षोडशकले तामाहुरमृतां कलाम् ।	III/370	III/986
पुर्वोऽष्टभागो....होरां निशि पञ्चमेन ॥	IV/59	III/1147
पुष्टावाप्यायने वर्गैः.... ।	I/160	II/160
पुष्पे गन्धस्तिले....कुलमन्तः प्रतिष्ठितम् ॥	I/45	II/45
पूजकाः शतशः सन्ति....प्रभोर्द्वित्रा न पञ्चषा ॥	II/260	II/612
पूजयेद्बिम्बवद्देवीः करणत्वेन दीधितीः ।	II/26	II/378

प्रजाः प्रजानां पतयः....सर्वे परमेशस्य धीमतः ॥	IV/130	III/1218
प्रजानां पतयस्तत्र मानसा ब्रह्मणः.... ।	V/114	IV/1464
प्रजापतिना चत्वारो वेदा असृज्यन्त ।	III/276	III/892
प्रणवादि ततो रुद्रम्....गन्धरूपे ध्रुवाहुतेः ॥	X/313	VI/3039
प्रणवेन ततः शक्तिः....तत्रैव तु विशोधयेत् ॥	V/259	IV/1609
प्रणवेन तु तत्सर्वं....त्रिंशदेकं च संख्यया ॥	I/190	II/190
प्रतिबिम्बन्ति....स्वच्छमणेरिव ।	II/27	II/379
प्रतिभातोऽप्यर्थः....प्रमातर्यविश्रान्तेः ॥	III/217	III/833
प्रतिमापूजनाद् भुक्तिः....भुक्तिमुक्तौ प्रसिद्ध्यतः ॥	III/426	III/1042
प्रतिशब्दकसंघातो नभस्येवोदितो बुधैः ।	VI/238	IV/1872
प्रतिष्ठा वापि कर्त्तव्या दग्धपिण्डे श्मशानके ।	X/360	V/3086
प्रत्यक्षतां परोक्षोऽपि....विषयः प्रतिपद्यते ॥	VII/14	V/1898
प्रत्यक्षेण यथा वृक्षो....वस्तुभावविवर्जनात् ।	I/121	II/121
प्रथमस्य तथाभावे प्रद्वेषः किंनिबन्धनः ।	VII/85	V/1969
प्रथमे मूर्तियागे....आयुरारोग्यसंपदः ॥	XI/46	VII/3152
प्रदेशो ब्रह्मणः सार्वरूप्यमनतिक्रान्तश्चातिविकल्प्यश्च ।	I/200; II/56; III/105; VII/96 (12th Āh.); XI/160	II/200, 408; III/721; V/2188; VII/3266
प्रधाने हि कृतो यत्नः फलवान् भवति ।	XII/226	VII/3516
....प्रबुध्यन्ते मन्त्रत्वाय भवाय ।	III/36	III/652
प्रभवाप्यययोरन्तरन्तः....क्रमोऽवताराख्यः ।	I/9	II/9
प्रभास्वरमिदं....तज्ज्योतिरविनश्वरम् ॥	I/64; III/33	II/64; III/649

प्रमादात्तु प्रविष्टस्य विचारं नैव कारयेत् ।	X/223	VI/2949
प्रयागो नाभिसंस्थस्तु....कोटिवर्षं तथाष्टमम् ।	IX/50	VI/2490
प्रपित्सायां समाचारं....उज्ज्वलां धियम् ॥	X/297	VI/3023
प्रलयाकलसंज्ञो....मायाभावात्स्थैर्यं न गच्छति ॥	VII/196	V/2080
प्रष्ट्री च प्रतिवक्त्री च स्वयं देवी व्यवस्थिता ।	I/268	II/268
प्रसन्ना वारुणी ज्ञेया....तदधो जगलः स्मृतः ॥	IX/39	VI/2479
प्रसार्य दक्षिणं पाणिं....मुद्रासंहारिणी प्रोक्ता ॥	X/144	VI/2870
प्रसिद्धिरागमो लोके ... ।	XII/356	VIII/3646
प्रसिद्धिरागमो लोके....तद्ग्राह्यमविशङ्कितैः ॥	I/47	II/47
....प्रहरः स्यान्नवाङ्गुलः ।	IV/56	III/1144
प्राक्तनागामिकस्यापि अधर्मक्षयकारिणी ।	IX/20	VI/2460
प्राक् संवित्प्राणे परिणता ।	II/142; III/314, 350; IX/150; X/162; XI/85, 138	II/142; III/930, 966; VI/2590, 2888; VII/3191, 3244
प्रागाशास्थे भोगदायि....संसारप्लोषभीषणम् ॥	IX/115	VI/2555
प्राणापानाश्रिते वाहे द्वात्रिंशत्तुटयः स्थिताः ।	IV/55	III/1143
प्राणायामस्तथा ध्यानं....षडङ्गो योग उच्यते ॥	III/15	III/631
प्राणायामो न कर्त्तव्यः शरीरं येन पीड्यते ।	III/97	III/713
प्राणार्कमानहठ....रक्षयेत्त्रयघट्टनज्ञः ॥	IV/89	III/1177
प्राणोऽपानः समानश्च उदानो व्यान एव च ।	III/327	III/943
प्रातिभेन महेशान....क्रियते तु शिवाध्वरे ॥	VIII/124	V/2324
प्रादुर्भूतविवेकस्य लक्षणं....मननं चावलोकनम् ।	VIII/114	V/2314
प्रायश्चित्तमकुर्वाणो....सिद्धिभ्रंशमवाप्नोति ....॥	V/31	IV/1381

प्रारब्धेकं न शोधयेत् ।	I/80; VI/103, 105	II/80; IV/1737, 1739
प्रेर्यमाणास्तु वाच्याशंभूमिं....तत्तत्फलदानसमुद्यताः ॥	VII/118	V/2002
....प्रोक्तोऽनन्तोऽसिते प्रभुः ।	V/232	IV/1582
फलभेदादारोपितभेदः पदार्थात्मा शक्तिः ॥	I/110; VI/63	II/110; IV/1697
फलाय कर्मविहितं ....एवमपूर्वमधिगम्यते ॥	VIII/8	V/2208
फाल्गुनपूर्णमास आधेय एतद्वा ऋतूनां मुखम् ।	XI/52	VII/3158
फाल्गुने द्वादशी शुक्ला....विशेषोऽन्नमहानयम् ॥	XI/20	VII/3126
....बध्नात्यात्मानमात्मना ।	VII/87	V/1971
बर्हिषि यो रजतं ददाति....रोदनं भवति ।	III/261	III/877
बर्हिषि रजतं न देयम् ।	III/261-62	III/877-878
बहिर्मुखस्य मन्त्रस्य....शक्तयः परिकीर्तिताः ॥	III/47	III/663
बहुशक्तित्वमप्यस्य तच्छक्त्यैवावियुक्तता ।	I/196; II/72, 187	II/196, 424, 539
बाह्ये गणेशवटुकौ.... ।	XI/24 (29th Āh.)	VII/3314
बिन्दुर्नादस्तथा...फलभेदेन साधकैः ॥	I/100	II/100
बिन्दुर्नादस्तथा शक्तिः....तज्ज्ञानाज्ज्ञात एव सः ॥	I/121	II/121
....बीजं स्वरा मताः ॥	II/92	II/444
बीजयोन्यात्मकात्....कादिभिश्च स्मृता योनिः ....॥	II/92	II/444
बुद्धितत्त्वं महादेवि....भोगजालसमावृतम् ।	VIII/123	V/2323
बुद्धितत्त्वे स्थिता बौद्धा....त्वव्यक्ते पाञ्चरात्रिकाः ॥	IV/131	III/1219
बुद्धितत्त्वे स्थिता बोद्धाः ....।	XII/365	VIII/3655
बुद्धिसुखदुःखेच्छा....विशेषगुणाः ।	VI/208	IV/1842

बुद्धौ प्राणे तथा देहे....संविद्रश्मिमयो भवेत् ॥	III/319	III/935
बोधिः प्रभुस्तथा योगी....कल्प्यं नामैतदन्तकम् ॥	III/296	III/912
बौद्धं च पौरुषेयं च द्विविधं....सम्यक्सारेतरविभागकृत् ।	I/85-86	II/85-86
ब्रह्मपञ्चकसंयुक्तः....शिवहस्तः प्रकीर्तितः ॥	X/32	VI/2758
ब्रह्मा तत्राधिपत्वेन....बौद्धानां परमं पदम् ॥	I/69	II/69
ब्रह्मादिकारणानां तु विग्रहं....योगी सर्वज्ञतां व्रजेत् ॥	I/102	II/102
ब्रह्माण्डमण्डपस्यान्तर्भुवनानि....अष्टावेते प्रकीर्तिताः ॥	V/15	IV/1365
ब्राह्मणस्य यथा पत्नी....ज्ञेया नित्योदिते कुले ॥	XI/64 (29th Āh.)	VII/3354
ब्राह्मणस्य रुजः कृत्या....जातिभ्रंशकरं स्मृतम् ॥	III/272	III/888
ब्रह्मणोऽण्डस्य शकलं....अन्ये तु क्रमशः स्थिताः ॥	V/16	IV/1366
ब्राह्मणो न हन्तव्यः ।	III/274	III/890
ब्राह्मणो ब्राह्मणमालभेत् ॥	III/274	III/890
ब्रह्मण्यानन्दाख्यं रूपमतो....भिन्नश्चाभेदितां समायातः।	XI/67 (29th Āh.)	VII/3357
ब्राह्मण्यं बीजशुद्ध्या....चण्डालेष्वपि धावति ॥	IX/247	VI/2687
ब्राह्मी माहेश्वरी चैव....चामुण्डा चेति मातरः ॥	I/154	II/154
भक्तिरेव परां काष्ठां प्राप्ता मोक्षोऽभिधीयते ।	VIII/137	V/2337
भगवन् मातृचक्रेश....महत् ।	XII/284	VII/3574
भगे लिङ्गे स्थितो....संघट्टान्निष्क्रमेद्रसः ॥	XI/106 (29th Āh.)	VII/3396
भट्टारकादिभूत्यन्तः....धियं वर्धयतांतराम् ॥	I/29	II/29
....भरणाद्दुरितस्थितिः ।	I/143	II/143
भस्मना रोचनाद्यैश्च अस्त्रप्राकारचिन्तनम् ।	X/222	VI/2948

भावनाबलतः स्पष्टं....तत्प्रत्यक्षमकल्पकम् ॥	VII/170	V/2054
भावा भान्तीति....भान्तीति भासते ॥	III/130	III/746
भावितः सुप्रसन्नात्मा जपहोमरतः सदा ।	III/66	III/682
भिन्नवेद्यप्रथात्रैव मायाख्यम्.... ।	I/55	II/55
भुक्तोज्झितं हि....प्राप्नुवन्त्यपि साधकाः ॥	X/353-54	VI/3079-3080
भुजङ्गकुटिलाकारा....भुजङ्गसंज्ञितम् ॥	XI/155 (29th Āh.)	VII/3445
....भुजङ्गवद्गरलसंक्रामः ।	III/234	III/850
भुवनं चिन्तयेद्यस्तु....भुवनेशत्वमाप्नोति .... ॥	I/102	II/102
भूयो भूयः परे भावे....मन्त्रात्मा जप्य ईदृशः ॥	I/135	II/135
भूयो भूयः समुद्देशलक्षणात्मपरीक्षणम् ।	I/278	II/278
भृगौ च स्मृतेर्लुप्त.... ।	V/98	IV/1448
भेदभावकमायीय....तिमिररूपधृत ॥	I/18	II/18
भेदा हि न स्वरूपं....भेदाभावादभेद्यता तेन ॥	VII/5	V/1889
भैरवरूपी कालः....भुवनाम्बिके जयसि ॥	II/224	II/576
भैरवस्य प्रियं नित्यं बहुमातृगणस्य च ।	XI/10 (29th Āh.)	VII/3300
भैरवाद् भैरवीं प्राप्तं....स्वच्छन्दाद्यैर्महाबलैः ॥	XII/383	VIII/3673
भैरवीयमहारज्जुप्रबद्धानि....सलिलावर्तगानि च ।	V/18	IV/1368
भैरवरूपी कालः....कीटान्तम् ।	III/142, 182, 198	III/758, 798, 814
भैरव्या भैरवात्प्राप्तं....मच्छन्देन महात्मना ।	I/24	II/24
भोगसाधनसंसिद्ध्यै....मायामाविश्य शक्तिभिः ॥	III/140	III/756
भोगोत्सुकता यदा प्रधानभूता....तत्रापि तारतम्यात्त्रैविध्यं ॥	VIII/152	V/2352

भ्रियात्सर्वं रवयति....सततोच्चारणाच्छिवः ॥	I/143	II/143
भ्रूमध्ये हृदये वाथ....बिन्दुभेदेन वेधयेत् ॥	XI/152 (29th Āh.)	VII/3442
मच्छाः पाशाः....मच्छन्दस्तेन कीर्तितः ॥	I/25	II/25
मत्त एवोदितमिदं....मदभिन्नमिदं च ....॥	I/29 (2nd Āh.)	II/339
मद्यमांसाधिवासेन ....प्रायश्चित्तं समाचरेत् ॥	XI/11 (29th Āh.)	VII/3301
मध्यनाडी....देवः प्रकाशते ॥	I/131	II/131
मध्यमेवात्र सदा देवि....नित्याचक्रं प्रपूजयेत् ॥	XI/51	VII/3157
मध्यशूलं त्रित्रिशूलं नवशूलं तथैव च ॥	XII/228	VII/3518
मध्ये अष्टाश्रको विष्णुः....।	V/40	IV/1390
मननं सर्ववेत्तृत्वं त्राणं संसार्यनुग्रहः ।	II/214	II/566
मनोजा गुरुवक्त्रस्था....मुद्रेयं त्रिविधा स्मृता ॥	IX/128	VI/2568
मन्त्रवादो न कर्तव्य इति कर्तृत्ववर्जनात् ।	X/196	VI/2922
मन्त्राणां च प्रलयाकलानां सतामनुगृहीतानाम् ।	VI/111	IV/1745
ममैव भैरवस्यैता विश्वभङ्ग्यो विनिर्गताः ।	II/95	II/447
मलं कर्म च....सवहेयमिति प्रोक्तं ....॥	I/61	II/61
मलः कर्मनिमित्तं तु नैमित्तिकमतः परम् ।	VI/75; VIII/34	IV/1709; V/2234
मलमज्ञानमिच्छन्ति....।	VI/60	IV/1694
मलमज्ञानमिच्छन्ति संसाराङ्कुरकारणम् ।	VI/82	IV/1716
मलयेन तु विप्राणां....शूद्राणामलिना प्रिये ॥	XI/11 (29th Āh.)	VII/3301
मलशक्तयो विभिन्नाः प्रत्यात्मानं च तद्गुणावरिकाः ।	VI/62; VIII/30	IV/1696; V/2230
मलोऽज्ञानं पशुत्वं च....पर्यायास्तत्र चोदिताः ॥	VIII/30	V/2230

महादेवो महातेजा महाज्योतिः. . . .।	V/205	IV/1555
महानवान्तरो दिव्यो. . . .पञ्चधा भिन्नलक्षणः ॥	I/282	II/282
महार्थं भैरवोक्तं. . . .तेषां प्रायश्चितानि शुद्धये ॥	VIII/186-187	V/2386-2387
महाव्योमेशलिङ्गस्य देहधूपं समर्पयेत् ॥	XII/284	VII/3574
मा किंचित्त्यज मा गृहाण. . . . ।	X/203	VI/2929
मात्रावर्गोऽप्यहंकाराद्. . . .भूतादिसंज्ञितात् ॥	VI/226	IV/1860
मात्रास्पर्शास्तु. . . .तितिक्षस्व भारत ॥	II/155	II/507
माया कलाशुद्धविद्या. . . .कञ्चुकानि मितात्मनः ॥	VI/164	IV/1798
मायारूपं भवेज्जालं. . . .कालरागयुतं चैव . . . .॥	I/26	II/26
माया-सदाशिव-शिवप्रान्तव्याप्त्री ननु क्रमात् ॥	I/217	II/217
मायासदेशपर्यन्तं. . . .चिन्मयत्वप्रकाशभाक् ॥	VI/245	IV/1879
मायासहितं. . . .इदमुक्तं ।	II/155	II/507
माया हेया शिवो. . . .मायाधर्मैः शिवः शून्यः. . . . ॥	I/116	II/116
माद्वींकं मधु विज्ञेयं. . . . ।	IX/39	VI/2479
माद्वींकः सहजस्त्वेकः. . . .पुमान् परमो विभुः ॥	XI/10 (29th Āh.)	VII/3300
मिश्रकर्मफलासक्तिं. . . .स्युघोर्राः परापराः ॥	II/86	II/438
. . . .मुक्तिश्च शिवदीक्षया ।	I/248; I/35 (2nd Āh.)	II/248, 345
मुखं वा एतत्संवत्सरस्य यत्फाल्गुनी पौर्णमासी ।	XI/52	VII/3158
मुख्यत्वं कर्तृतायास्. . . .तत्समावेशलक्षणम् ॥	I/206	II/206
. . . .मुद्राख्याः शिवशक्तयः ।	IX/128	VI/2568
मुद्रा बिम्बोदयो नाम्ना. . . . ।	XII/304	VII/3594

....मुद्रा या काचिदास्थितिः ।	III/232	III/848
मुमुक्षोर्न विशेषाय....नहि ब्रह्मणि शंसन्ति ....॥	VIII/80	V/2280
मुहूर्तादिव तत्रस्थः....प्राप्नोत्यभीप्सितम् ॥	III/14	III/630
मूले तु शाक्तः कथितो बोधनादप्रवर्तकः ।	XII/320	VII/3610
मृच्छैलधातुरत्नादिभवं....यत्र लीनं चराचरम् ॥	III/257	III/873
मेढ्स्याधः कुलो ज्ञेयो....घनव्याप्तिप्रबोधकः ।	X/188	VI/2914
मेयं साधारणं मुक्तः....पुनरत्यन्तभेदवत् ॥	III/240	III/856
मेर्वधो मलयाकारो....लक्षयोजनविस्तारः ....॥	V/49	IV/1399
मोक्षो हि नाम....स्वरूपं चात्मनः संवित् ....॥	I/302	II/302
मोचयन्ति महाघोरात्....मुद्रा हि शक्तयः ॥	XII/327	VII/3617
मौसुले कारुके चैव मायातत्त्वं प्रकीर्तितम् ॥	I/70	II/70
यः पुनः सर्वतत्त्वानि....मन्त्रवीर्यप्रकाशकः ॥	III/249	III/865
यच्चान्ते दक्षिणं....युगपद्भैरवाभिधम् ।	I/41	II/41
यजेदाध्यात्मिकं लिङ्गं बाह्यं लिङ्गं न पूजयेत् ॥	III/286	III/902
यज्जनिताभिष्वङ्गे....कश्चिद्वीतरागः स्यात् ॥	VI/163	IV/1797
यतः शिवोद्भवाः सर्वे शिवधामफलप्रदाः ।	I/48; VIII/183	II/48; V/2383
यतो नान्या क्रिया नाम.... ।	I/199	II/199
यत्करोषि यदश्नासि....तदकुरुष्व मदर्पणम् ।	VI/109	IV/1743
यत्किंचिन्मानसाह्लादि....देवमभ्यर्चयेत्सदा ॥	XI/18 (29th Āh.)	VII/3308
यत्तदक्षरमक्षोभ्यं....नित्योदितो जपः ॥	II/151; XI/110 (29th Āh.)	II/503; VII/3400
यत्तद्ब्रह्मण्डकं भाति....विश्वकर्म्मप्रसादतः ।	V/17	IV/1367

यत्ते कुर्युर्न तत्कुर्याद्यद्ब्रूयुस्तत्समाचरेत् ।	III/270	III/886
यत्र यत्र मनो याति....सर्वं शिवमयं यतः ॥	III/100	III/716
यत्र यत्र मिलिता मरीचयस्तत्र तत्र विभुरेव जृम्भते ।	III/288	III/904
यत्र रूढिः प्रजायेत....इत्याह भगवाञ्छिवः ॥	III/39	III/655
....यत्र वा रमते मनः ।	IX/57	VI/2497
यत्रापि स्यात्परिच्छेदः....सोऽर्थो नावधृतस्तथा ॥	III/90	III/706
यत्रास्ति न भयं....कालः कलयेच्च तम् ॥	I/5	II/5
यत्रोदितमिदं चित्रं....शिवशक्तिविवर्जितम् ॥	II/75; XII/373	II/427; VIII/3663
यत्रोदितमिदं चित्रं विश्वं यत्रास्तमेति च ।	II/199	II/551
यत्सृष्टिस्थितिसंहाररक्तैश्च....कालीपदं नयेत् ॥	III/191	III/807
यथाग्निर्भस्मना....भवेत्स्फुटम् ॥	VIII/111	V/2311
यथा दण्डाहतः सर्पो....गुरुणा प्रतिबोधिता ॥	III/358	III/974
यथादर्शगतां च्छायां....शिवं सर्वगतं विभुम् ॥	VIII/116	V/2316
यथान्तर्निर्मलादर्शे....विश्ववृत्तयः ॥	II/27	II/379
यथान्तोऽस्ति क्षणस्यैवम्....लोकस्य क्षणे स्थितिः ॥	IV/17 (7th Āh.)	III/1309
यथा भैरवचक्रेषु नायकः....रसेन्द्रः पारतीयकः ॥	XI/10 (29th Āh.)	VII/3300
यथा रुमायां पतिताः....तथा भावाश्चिदात्मनि ॥	I/30 (2nd Āh.)	II/340
यथालोकेन दीपस्य....तद्वच्छक्त्या शिवः प्रिये ॥	I/229; II/112	II/229, 464
यथा स्थितः....विकारनिकराञ्जहि ॥	I/29 (2nd Āh.)	II/339
यथोप्तं कालतो बीजं....प्रातिभं प्रिये ।	VIII/112	V/2312
यदसत्तदसद्युक्ता नासतः....तस्य कस्यापि शक्तितः ॥	VI/11	IV/1645

यदा जानन्ति नो तत्त्वं ....नरक गन्तुकामिनः ॥	VIII/186	V/2386
यदा तु ग्राहकावेश....तत्स्वरूपं नरात्मकम् ॥	VII/125	V/2009
यदा तु तस्य ....सेच्छायाः प्रथमा तुटिः ।	II/84	II/436
यदा त्रयाणां वक्त्राणां....शिवेनैवं निरूपिता ।	I/39	II/39
यदा देवि महान्स्थूलो....यथाभेदद्वयं प्रिये ।	VIII/119	II/2319
यदिदं हि पृथिव्यादि....आधारशक्तिः शास्त्रेषु कथ्यते ॥	IX/149	V/2589
यदि मुक्तिर्जलस्नानान्मत्स्यानां सा न किं भवेत् ।	III/120	III/736
यदि लक्षणहीना स्यात्....सर्वकर्मसु गम्यते ॥	XI/71 (29th Āh.)	VII/3361
यदीच्छेन्नरकं गन्तुं....गोषु च ब्राह्मणेषु च ॥	V/31	IV/1381
यदेतत्कामतत्त्वं....श्रृणु त्वं मृगलोचने ॥	II/168	II/520
यदैव चामरावत्या....दित्यगतागतम् ।	V/86	IV/1436
यदोल्लसति शृंगाटपीठात्कुटिलरूपिणी ।	II/104	II/456
यद्द्रव्यं लोकविद्विष्टं....वीरैराहार्यमेव तत् ॥	III/269	III/885
यद्यथा चाभिसंधत्ते तत्तत्तस्य तथा फलेत् ।	VI/88	IV/1722
यद्वेतः स भवेच्चन्द्रः.... ।	XI/105 (29th Āh.)	VII/3395
यद्वा स्वरूपपरतामपि....यथार्थमाहुः ॥	III/262	III/878
यन्निवारणम् संवित्सतत्त्वं....सा काष्ठा सा परा गतिः ॥	III/396	III/1012
यस्मान्महेश्वरः....प्रोद्धरति प्रजाः ॥	III/78	III/694
यस्मिन्काले तु गुरुणा....तदेव किल मुक्तोऽसौ .... ॥	VIII/188	V/2388
यस्मिन्यस्मिंश्चक्रवरे....पूजाविधिः स्मृतः ॥	III/210	III/826
यस्य नित्योदिता....तद्भरणे रता ।	I/9	II/9

यस्य वै स्नातमात्रस्य....न स जीवति ॥	XI/101	VII/3207
यस्य साराः पवित्रत्वे....भैरवेण भवच्छिदा ॥	XI/18 (29th Āh.)	VII/3308
यस्यां यस्यां बोधभूमौ....चातुरात्म्यं प्रपद्यते ॥	III/128	III/744
यस्यां सदा खेचरिदृष्टि....विलसत्स्पर्शोदयो जृम्भते ।	III/196	III/812
या अग्निहोत्राहुतयः....तव मार्गवित्सः ॥	IV/111	III/1199
या तूक्ता ज्ञेयकालुष्य	II/173	II/525
या तूक्ता ज्ञेयकालुष्य....वर्गयुग्मकम् ॥	II/92	II/444
यानुभूतिरजामेयानन्तात्मानन्दविग्रहा ।	II/255	II/607
यान्ति देवव्रता देवान्....यान्ति मद्याजिनोऽपि माम् ॥	I/170	II/170
याभिः संरक्षितो मन्त्री मन्त्रसिद्धिमवाप्नुयात् ॥	XII/307	VII/3597
या या संविदुदारा....तत्तद्व्यास्तवाकारः ॥	IX/85	VI/2525
यावज्जीवं सुखं....पुनरागमनं कुतः ॥	IV/16	III/1104
यावन्न वेदका एते....नास्त्यशुचिस्ततः ॥	VII/115; XI/7 (29th Āh.)	V/1999; VII/3297
यावन्न सर्वे तत्त्वज्ञास्तावद्दीपं न दर्शयेत् ।	XI/168 (29th Āh.)	VII/3458
या सा शक्तिः.... यथा गच्छति तच्छृणु ॥	I/109	II/109
या सा शक्तिर्....समवायिनी ।	I/16	II/116
युगपद्वेदनाज्ज्ञानज्ञेययोरेकरूपता ।	II/66	II/418
ये तु वर्णाश्रमाचाराः....लोकधर्मान्समाचरेत् ॥	III/277-78	III/893-894
ये त्विहागन्तवः....जपहोमप्रधानैश्च ....॥	VI/105	IV/1739
येन येन निबध्यन्ते....मुच्यन्ते भवबन्धनात् ॥	III/338	III/954
येन येन हि रूपेण....चिन्तामणिरिवेश्वरः ॥	I/157	II/157

येन सर्वमिदं बुद्धं....देवा ब्राह्मणं विदुः ॥	IX/254	VI/2694
येन येनाक्षमार्गेण....तद्गतस्तन्मयो भवेत् ॥	I/11; XI/82 (29th Āh.)	II/11; VII/3372
येनाघ्रातं श्रुतं दृष्टं....भोगमोक्षप्रदं तस्य ....॥	XI/9 (29th Āh.)	VII/3299
ये निवृत्ताधिकारास्तु....महल्लोके लयः स्मृतः ॥	V/113	IV/1463
....येनेदं तद्धि भोगतः ॥	VI/103; IX/18	IV/1737; V/2458
येषां मृतानां चर्माणि....तेऽपि रुद्रा न संशयः ॥	XI/98	VII/3204
योऽयं वह्निः परं तत्त्वं प्रमातुरिदमेव तत् ।	III/126	III/742
योक्ता संवत्सरात्सिद्धि....दर्चनं यजनं हुतम् ॥	I/32	II/32
योगमेकत्वमिच्छन्ति वस्तुनोऽन्येन वस्तुना ।	I/190	II/190
योगिनामपि मृद्बीजे....स्थिरस्वार्थक्रियाकरम् ॥	VI/33	IV/1667
योगी तथा निर्वृति....केवलमेति शान्तिम् ॥	III/34	III/650
यो जल्पः स जपः.... ।	III/227	III/843
यो यत्राभिलषेद....सिद्धिभाक् ....॥	I/101	II/101
यो यत्राभिलषेद् ....मन्त्रसामर्थ्यात् ॥	V/276	IV/1626
यो यत्राभिलषेद्भोगान् ....।	IX/20	VI/2460
यो यस्य गुर्वादेशः स तस्य मोचकः ।	III/203	III/819
यो यस्याः सन्ततेर्नाथः....ज्ञास्यन्ति च निजं कुलं ।	XI/30 (29th Āh.)	VII/3320
यो यस्मिंस्थितिसंभूतस्तस्य सा कुलदेवता ।	XI/9	VII/3115
यो यस्मिन्मन्त्रयोगेन तन्त्राचारपदे स्थितः ।	XI/52 (29th Āh.)	VII/3342
योषितश्चैव पूज्यन्ते....ज्ञात्वा शिवमवाप्नुयात् ।	XI/79 (29th Āh.)	VII/3369
यो ह वै तद्हवीरग्निषोमाभ्यां जुहोति तस्यैतदमृतीभवति ।	IX/223	VI/2663

यो हि बाधयते पापः....सर्वेषां परिकीर्तितम् ॥	III/277	III/893
यो हि यस्माद् गुणोत्कृष्टः स तस्मादूर्ध्व उच्यते ।	I/1 (2nd Āh.)	II/311
रजसा गोद्युतेनैव वायव्यं....दनुस्मृत्य परापराम् ।	IX/34	VI/2474
रसं पुर्यष्टकांशं तु अर्पयेद् विष्णवे सदा ।	X/313	VI/3039
रसायनतपोजापयोग....प्राज्ञैर्जीयतेऽनलसैर्जनैः ॥	VI/105	IV1739
रागादिकलुषं चित्तं....प्रहीनावरणैर्जिनैः ॥	I/64	II/64
रागाद्यकलुषोऽस्म्यन्तःशून्योऽहं कर्तृतोज्झितः ।	I/303	II/303
राजवर्तेन रजसा व्योमबिम्बं....शुक्ला वा व्योमरेखिका ।	XI/22 (29th Āh.)	VII/3312
राजसस्तैजसाद्वर्गः....कारणानुविधायिता ॥	VI/222	IV/1856
राज्यमिव मन्त्रिपरवशमैश्वर्यं....न रच्यते किंचित् ॥	VIII/68	V/2268
रासभ्या मूत्रकाले तु योनिः प्रस्पन्दते यथा ।	III/165	III/781
रिक्तस्य जन्तोर्जातस्य....सिद्धान्तविषमग्रहाः ॥	III/22	III/638
रुद्रशक्तिसमाविष्टः....नीयते सद्गुरुं प्रति ॥	VIII/154	V/2354
रुद्रश्च रुद्रशक्तिश्च अमनस्के लयं गतौ ।	II/75	II/427
रुद्रो रुरोद....तद्रजतमभवत् ।	III/262	III/878
रूपादिपञ्चवर्गोऽयं विश्वमेतावदेव हि ।	III/159	III/775
रेतो हराम्बु पुष्पं....द्रव्यद्वादशकं शुभम् ।	XI/16 (29th Āh.)	VII/8306
लब्धभूमेर्विरक्तस्य....भोगेन परिपूरितम् ।	III/93	III/709
लयोदयश्चित्स्वरूपस्तेन तत्कुलमुच्यते ।	XI/4 (29th Āh.)	VII/3294
लिङ्गरूपी भवेन्मेरुः.... ।	V/40	IV/1390
लिङ्गशब्देन विद्वांसः....भावानां पदमव्ययम् ॥	III/141,423	III/757, 1039

लिङ्गे परमशिवान्तां....भावयद्भिरिमैः ॥	III/285	III/901
लेशोक्तो बुद्धिबोधोऽयं....येनोत्पन्नोऽनुभूयते ॥	VI/184	IV/1818
लोकधर्मिणमारोप्य मते भुवनभर्तरि ।	IV/149	III/1237
लोकधर्मिणमारोप्य....वा मुक्तिकांक्षिणम् ।	IX/20	VI/2460
लोकपाला भवन्त्येवं....तेषां हस्तगताः पूज्या ....॥	IX/180	VI/2620
लोकानुग्रहहेत्वर्थं....तेन तद्द्रव्यमाहरेत् ॥	XI/15 (29th Āh.)	VII/3305
लोकालोकमतो देवि....व्याप्य सर्वमिदं स्थिताः ।	V/82	IV1432
लौकिके व्यवहारे हि सदृशौ बालपण्डितौ ।	XII/366	VIII/3656
लौकिकादिरहस्यान्त....वागित्थं पारमेश्वरी ॥	XII/364	VIII/3654
वक्त्राद्वक्त्रप्रयोगेण....देवतावीरसंयुतम् ॥	XI/93 (29th Āh.)	VII/3383
वक्त्रं हि नाम....योगिनीवक्त्रं ....॥	XI/89 (29th Āh.)	VII/3379
व्रतिनो जटिनो मुण्डास्....पट्टैः भूषिता भूमिपादयः ॥	III/288	III/904
व्रते पाशुपते प्रोक्तमैश्वरं परमं पदम् ।	I/70	II/70
वषडाप्यायने शस्तः.... ।	I/160	II/160
वस्तुतो हि त्रिधैवेयं....तथैवाभेदभागिना ॥	I/248	II/248
वस्तुनिर्णयशून्याभिर्....जिह्वीमस्तर्कबुद्धिभि : ॥	III/19	III/635
वस्तुभेदे प्रसिद्धस्य....वागादीनां विषाणिवत् ।	VI/43	IV1677
....वस्तुशून्यानि ।	III/20	III/636
वागेव विश्वा भुवनानि जज्ञे ।	V/221	IV/1571
वाणी पाणी भगः....गर्वो वैकारिकोऽत्र यः ॥	VI/203	IV/1837
वाममार्गाभिषिक्तोऽपि....कौले त्रिकेऽपि सः ॥	VIII/182	V/2382

वामा संसारवमनात् ....।	III/25	III/641
वामा संसारवमना स्वरूपावरणात्मिका।	VIII/131	V/2331
वामो वायं विधिः कार्यो मुक्तिमार्गावलम्बिभिः।	IX/126	VI/2566
वायुर्नाभेरुत्थित उरसि....शब्दान् अभिव्यनक्ति।	VI/215	IV/1849
वासनाभेदतः प्राप्तिः सान्ध्यमन्त्रप्रचोदिता।	IV/63	III/1151
विकल्पयुक्तचित्तस्तु....जीवन्मुक्तो न संशयः।	I/89	II/89
विकल्पयोनयः शब्दा....।	III/465	III/1081
विज्ञानमानन्दं ब्रह्म।	III/32	III/648
....वित्तशाठ्यं न कारयेत्।	IX/25, 212	VI/2465, 2652
विद्यापादार्थकुशलः....गुरुर्दीक्षां प्रकुर्वीत ....।	IX/12	VI/2452
विद्यापीठे तु पञ्चाशत्....ग्रन्थीनां मातृनायिके ॥	XI/70	VII/3176
विद्राव्य गोलकं तत्र....कुर्वीत सर्वसिद्धिफलप्रदम् ॥	XI/92 (29th Āh.)	VII/3382
विधिपूजां समाचरेत्....पवित्राण्याहरेत्पश्चात्....॥	XI/71	VII/3177
विधिवाक्यमिदं....सत्क्रियाणां फलेष्वपि ॥	III/257	III/873
विधिशक्तिरवसीदति....समुत्तभ्नाति ॥	III/256	III/872
विधेर्लक्षणमेतावद....नाज्ञातज्ञापनं विधिः ॥	I/166	II/166
विना गुरुं विना देवं....पशवस्ते न संशयः ॥	XI/67 (29th Āh.)	VII/3357
विना सर्गेण बन्धो हि....सर्गस्तस्यैव मोक्षार्थं....॥	VIII/22	V/2222
विनिवारयितुं शक्या....सात्त्वराजसवर्गयोः ॥	VI/222	IV/1856
विप्रतिषिद्धधर्मसमवाये भूयतां स्यात्सधर्मत्वम्।	VI/73	IV/1707
विभवे सति यो लोभान्न....जातुचित्परमेश्वरि ॥	IX/213	VI/2653

वेदादिभ्यः परं शैवं....कौलात्परतरं नहि ॥	I/48	II/48
वेदादिभ्यः वरं शैवम्.... ।	V/31-32	IV/1381-1382
वेद्यं वेदकतामाप्तं....तेनेदं त्वन्मयं जगत् ॥	VII/182	V/2066
वेद्यवेदकसाम्येन....योगिभिः समुदाहृतः ।	IV/75	III/1163
वेद्यो वेदकतामाप्तो....त्वन्मयं जगत् ॥	I/164	II/164
वेधदीक्षां विना....इति शाक्तस्य निश्चयः ॥	XI/131 (29th Āh.)	VII/3421
वैराग्यं नाम भोगेभ्यो वैमुख्यमुच्यते इति ।	VIII/68	V/2268
वैष्णवाः सौगताः ....जातुचित्पतिशासने ॥	VIII/189	V/2389
वौषडाप्यानने शस्तम्.... ।	X/140	V/2866
व्यवहाराः प्रतायन्ते तिरश्चामपि तद्वशात् ।	VII/53 (11th Āh.); VIII/89	V/2145, 2289
व्यापिनी पुरुषानन्त्यभोगाय....स्रोतोभिर्विश्वधामभिः ॥	VI/118	IV/1752
व्योम-विग्रह-बिन्द्वर्ण....लक्ष्यभेदः स्मृतः षोढा.... ॥	I/101	II/101
शक्तयः समयज्ञाश्च दिनान्ते क्रीडयन्ति ताः ।	XI/19	VII/3125
शक्तिगोचरगं वीर्यं तत्कुलम् विद्धि सर्वगम् ।	XI/4 (29th Āh.)	VII/3294
शक्तिश्च नाम भावस्य स्वं रूपं मातृकल्पितम् ।	I/302	II/302
शक्तिश्च शक्तिमांश्चेति....शक्तिमांस्तु महेश्वरः ॥	I/155; III/374	II/155; III/990
शक्तिस्तु मातृका ज्ञेया सा च ज्ञेया शिवात्मिका ॥	XI/60 (29th Āh.)	VII/3350
शक्तिसंस्नुतसुधारसक्रमात्....पिवति तं महामुनिः ॥	IV/97	III/1185
शक्त्यादिस्तत्त्ववर्गस्तु....विद्या रागस्तु वरवर्णिनि ।	IV/39	III/1127
शक्त्योऽस्य जगत्कृत्स्नं.... ॥	II/76, 197; V/124; VI/120; VIII/163; XI/56 (29th Āh.)	II/428, 549; IV/1474, 1754; V/2363; VII/3346

शक्तयोऽस्य जगत्कृत्स्नं शक्तिमांस्तु महेश्वरः ॥	II/108, 145, 186	II/460, 497, 538
शक्त्योऽस्य जगत्सर्वं. . . . ।	II/89	II/441
शङ्कया कुगतिं याति तस्माच्छंकां परित्यजेत् ॥	VII/106 (12th Āh.)	V/2198
. . . . शङ्कया विघ्नभाजनम् ।	III/164	III/780
शङ्काशून्योऽपि. . . . पारमेश्वरी ।	I/38 (2nd Āh.)	II/348
शनैश्वरस्य यः कालस्तं. . . . सर्वकर्मस्वसिद्धिदः ॥	IV/62	III/1150
शब्दः प्रत्यक्षत्वे. . . . स्पर्शवद्विशेषगुणः ।	VI/238	IV/1872
शब्दः स्पर्शश्च रूपं. . . . भूतादिरहंकारोऽत्र तामसः ।	VI/218	IV/1852
शब्दः स्पर्शश्च रूपं. . . . अष्टादशैवं तत्त्वानि . . . . ॥	VII/33 (11th Āh.)	V/2125
शब्दे वाचकशक्तिश्च नित्यैवाग्नाविवोष्णता ।	VII/54 (11th Āh.)	V/2146
शरीरभुवनाकारं (रो) मायीयं (यः) परिकीर्तितम् (:) ।	I/56; VI/75; VIII/34	II/56; IV/1709; V/2234
शशिभास्करसंयोगात्. . . . मुक्तये मोक्षकाङ्क्षिणः ॥	III/96	III/712
शश्वद्विश्वमनश्वरप्रकृतयो. . . . क्षीणस्थितिर्लक्ष्यते ॥	III/233	III/849
शान्तो दान्तो जितक्रोध. . . . ।	IX/253	VI/2693
शास्त्रहीने न सिद्धिः स्याद् दीक्षादौ वीरवन्दिते ।	III/48	III/664
शिखा परिमिता शक्तिः. . . . क्रियाशक्तिरिति ख्याता ॥	IV/22	III/1110
. . . . शिवं ध्यात्वा तु तन्मयः ।	I/102	II/102
शिवः प्रशस्यते नित्यं. . . . योगिनीनां प्रियो भवेत् ॥	XI/92 (29th Āh.)	VII/3382
शिव आचार्यरूपेण लोकानुग्रहकारकः ।	VIII/156	V/2356
. . . . शिव एव गृहीतपशुभावः ।	I/244, 302; VI/113	II/244, 302; IV/1747
शिवतत्त्वं कथं शून्यं तदतीतं न किंचन ॥	I/116	II/116

शिवनभसि विगलिताक्षः....अनलकोटिशतदीप्तम् ॥	III/222-223	III/838-839
शिवभावनयौषध्या....रसवच्छिवहेमता ॥	I/130	II/130
शिवशक्त्यात्मकं रूपं....कर्त्तव्यं साधकोत्तमैः ॥	I/14; XI/73 (29th Āh.)	II/14; VII/3363
शिवशक्तिसदाशिवताम्....विभक्तभावेन भासयति ॥	VI/49	IV/1683
शिवस्य परिपूर्णस्य....सम्बन्धः परिकीर्तितः ॥	I/283	II/283
शिवाम्भसास्त्रयुक्तेन....नैर्ऋताद्यावदैश्वरम् ।	IX/188	VI/2628
शिवोऽहमद्वितीयोऽहं.... ।	VIII/219	V/2419
....शिवो भूत्वा शिवं यजेत् ।	IX/184	VI/2624
शिशुना क्षिप्तमकामात्....भवेद्गणप्रान्तम् ॥	III/295	III/911
....शीधुस्त्विक्षुरसेन तु ।	IX/39	VI/2479
शुक्लमधुरशीता एव रूपरसस्पर्शाः ।	VI/237	IV/1871
शुचिर्नामाग्निरुद्भूतः संघट्टात्सोमसूर्ययोः ।	II/127; III/381; XI/106(29th Āh.)	II/479; III/997; VII/3396
शुद्धबोधात्मकत्वेऽपि....ते च विज्ञानकेवलाः ।	VI/78	IV/1712
शुद्धेऽध्वनि शिवः कर्ता.... ।	I/6	II/6
शुद्धेऽध्वनि शिवः कर्ता प्रोक्तोऽनन्तोऽसिते प्रभुः ।	V/224; VI/56; VII/155; VIII/76	IV/1574, 1690; V/2039, 2276
शूद्रोऽपि शीलसम्पन्नो....राजन्गुणाः कल्याणकारकाः ॥	IX/255	VI/2695
शून्यताऽवस्थितः....निरुपाख्यो भवत्यसौ ॥	IV/10	III/1098
शून्योद्भवो भवेद्वायुः....समायोगात् ॥	XI/78 (29th Āh.)	VII/3368
शूलानि स्युःषट् सहस्त्राण्यूनं सार्धशतद्वयात् ।	XII/246	VII/3536
शृङ्गी युवा च पूर्णाङ्ग....त्रिविधो यागसिद्धये ॥	X/29	VI/2755
शेषं कुमारिकाद्वीपे भविष्यति गृहे.... ।	XII/384	VII/3674

शेषः परमार्थत्वात् ।	I/276	II/276
शैवसिद्धो भाति....पुनरभ्येति नाधः ।	I/72	II/72
शैवादीनि रहस्यानि....त्रयम्बकादित्यनामकम् ॥	I/27-28	II/27-28
....शैवी मुखमिहोच्यते ।	I/7, 115; II/171, 188	II/7, 115, 523, 540
शौचसन्तोषतपः....नियमाः ।	III/94	III/710
श्मशानं हृत्प्रदेशः....ज्ञातव्यं योगिनीकुले ॥	XI/51 (29th Āh.)	VII/3341
श्राद्धपक्षे तु दातव्यम्.... ।	X/316	VI/3042
श्रीकण्ठ एव परया मूर्त्या कालाग्निरुच्यते ।	IV/146	III/1234
श्रीकेयूरवतीतः....षोडशैवेत्थम् ॥	III/195	III/811
श्रीक्रमसद्भावादिक ....कुलधरपूर्वासु संततिषु ॥	III/191	III/807
श्रीमत्सदाशिवपदेऽपि....हठतोऽधितिष्ठेत् ॥	III/193	III/809
श्रीभूतिराजनामापि....कालीनये गुरुता ॥	III/193	III/809
श्रीवीरनाथपादैः....कृताः शिष्याः ।	III/196	III/812
श्रोत्रं त्वक्चक्षुषी जिह्वा....तैजसश्च स सात्त्विकः ॥	VI/187	IV/1821
श्रोत्रं त्वक्चक्षुषी जिह्वा नासा चित्तं च धीव्रजः ।	VI/44	IV/1678
श्लोकगाथादि....मन्त्रत्वेनैव पश्यति ॥	III/227	III/843
षट्प्राणाश्चषकस्तेषां षष्टिर्नाली तथा तिथिः ।	IV/165	III/1253
षडङ्गुलं च सङ्क्रामो....भवेत्तच्चोत्तरायणम् ॥	IV/98	III/1186
षडेवेह स्वरा मुख्याः....विज्ञेयाः सूर्यरश्मयः ॥	II/181	II/533
....षड्विधोऽध्वा प्रकीर्तितः ।	VII/32 (11th Āh.)	V/2124
षड्विंशकं परं बीजं....वदनं चोत्तरं शुभम् ॥	XII/184-85	VII/3474-3475

षड्विंशकं तु देवेशि योगशास्त्रे परं पदम् ।	I/70	II/70
षोढा वै वेधबोधेन अध्वानं शोधयेत्प्रिये ।	XI/149 (29th Āh.)	VII/3439
संकल्पकमत्र मनः. . . . ।	I/117	II/117
संवित्तिफलभेदोऽत्र न प्रकल्प्यो मनीषिभिः ।	I/246	II/246
संविन्निष्ठा हि विषयव्यवस्थितिः (तयः) ।	III/216; XI/150	III/832; VII/3256
संसाराम्बुनिधिं यः. . . .सोऽस्मिञ्छास्त्रेऽधिकारवान् ॥	I/4 (2nd Āh.)	II/314
संसारोऽस्ति न तत्त्वतः. . . .स्वस्थो यथावस्थितः ॥	I/305	II/305
संसारोऽस्ति न तत्त्वतस्तनुभृतां बन्धस्य वार्तैव का ।	III/99	III/715
संहताङ्गुलिकौ पाणी. . . .कुम्भमुद्रा प्रकीर्तिता ॥	IX/39	VI/2479
संहितापारगस्येह सेकः कार्योऽन्यथा नहि ।	III/77	III/693
स एव प्रतिभायुक्तः. . . .पशुरेव भवार्णवात् ॥	VIII/133	V/2333
सकृद्विभातोऽयमात्मा . . . . ।	I/106; III/208; XI/55 (29th Āh.)	II/106; III/824; VI/3345
सक्रमत्वं च लौकिक्याः. . . .प्राभव्याः स्यात्प्रभोरिव ॥	II/134	II/486
स चेतनश्चिता योगात्. . . . ।	VII/34	V/1918
सजातीयप्रसिद्ध्यैव. . . .प्रसिद्धिः प्राक्तनी स्थिता ॥	XII/361	VIII/3651
सतोऽवश्यं परमसत्सच्च. . . .सदसन्मयः ॥	I/25 (2nd Āh.)	II/335
सत्यमेतन्महाप्राज्ञ प्राणायामो न कारणम् ।	III/97	III/713
सदसद्विभेदसूते. . . .जयाद्येन रूपेण ॥	III/200	III/816
सदसद्वस्तुनिर्भासी दर्पणप्रतिबिम्बवत् ॥	II/27	II/379
सदाशिवादयः. . . .शक्तीः समाक्षिपेयुः ।	I/243	II/243
सविति ब्रह्म परमम् ।	II/165	II/517

सन्तापं क्रोधने विद्या चञ्चले चपलाः श्रियः ।	X/267	VI/2993
सन्ति (न्तो) हि....प्रयुञ्जानाः ।	I/14	II/14
सन्दिग्धेऽपि पदे लोके....स्यादस्ति चेन्नास्तिको हतः ॥	IV/20	III/1108
सन्ध्याकालं विना त्रिंशत्तुटिकोऽहोरात्रः ।	IV/57	III/1145
सन्ध्या नाम सुरास्तस्मिन्वसन्ति सुखिनः सदा ।	V/113	IV/1453
सप्तेन्द्रियशिखाजालजटिले....भस्मीभावोऽग्नितर्पणम् ॥	III/233	III/849
समता सर्वभावानां वृत्तीनां....वर्णानां चैव सर्वशः ॥	III/304	III/920
समनोबुद्धिदेवानां गणे....स्वानुरूपादहंकृतः ॥	VI/222	IV/1856
समन्ताद् ब्रह्मणोऽण्डं....शतरुद्रैः समन्वितम् ॥	V/18	IV/1368
समयप्रतिभेत्तॄंस्तदनाचारांश्च घातयेत् ।	XI/163	VII/3269
....समयी राजपुत्रवत् ।	IX/16	VI/2456
समयोल्लङ्घनाद्देवि क्रव्यादत्वं शतं समाः ।	X/303	VI/3029
....समुत्थानात् क्रियादयः ।	VI/86	IV/1720
समुदायवृताः शब्दा अवयवेष्वपि वर्तन्ते ।	III/340	III/956
सम्बन्धः परमेशानि....मिश्रोऽदिव्यश्च तत्परः ॥	I/284	II/284
सर्वं खल्विदं ब्रह्म ।	II/166; III/121	II/518; III/737
सर्वं वा मय्येव स्थितम् ।	I/238	II/238
सर्वकर्तृ विभु सूक्ष्मं तत्कुलं वरवर्णिनि ।	XI/4 (29th Āh.)	VII/3294
सर्वज्ञः सर्वकर्ता च....दार्ढ्याच्छिवो भवेत् ॥	IX/203	VI/2643
सर्वत्र भैरवो भावः....परोऽस्तीत्यद्वयागमः ॥	VII/73 (11th Āh.)	V/2165
सर्वत्राभासभेदो....भातस्य नो सकृत् ॥	III/210	III/826

सर्वभावमयभावमण्डलं....विश्वमेधमययज्ञयाजिनः ॥	III/371	III/987
सर्वभावविवेकेन....प्रातिभस्य विधीयते ॥	VIII/116	V/2316
सर्वमेतत्प्रवृत्यर्थं....कल्प्यश्चेद् यथायथम् ।	I/48	II/48
सर्वलक्षणहीनोऽपि ज्ञानवान्गुरूत्तमः ।	III/67	III/683
सर्वसंहारसंहारसंहारमपि....शिवात्मिका ॥	III/221	III/837
सर्वाः शक्तीश्चेतसा....विश्वाधार एकोऽवभासि ॥	XI/128	VII/3234
सर्वाध्वनो....परं पदम् ।	I/72	II/72
सर्वार्चनं स्थण्डिले स्यान्न च तत्राधिवासनम् ।	X/222	VI/2948
सर्वालम्बनधर्मैश्च....न शून्यं परमार्थतः ॥	I/67; IV/9	II/67
सर्वासां देवतानां तु आधारः....नित्यं तत्र प्रपूजयेत् ॥	XI/15 (29th Āh.)	VII/3305
सर्वेऽनुभूता यदि....स्मृतिर्नाम न संभवेत्तत् ॥	III/451	III/1067
सर्वेशं तु कुलं देवि....तत्तेजः परमं घोरं ॥	XI/4 (29th Āh.)	VII/3294
सर्वेश्वरानधिष्ठाय श्रीकण्ठः....प्रतिनिकेतनम् ॥	V/173	IV/1523
सर्वेषामेव मन्त्राणां....सर्वमन्त्रेषु सर्वदा ॥	II/222	II/574
सर्वो ममायं विभव.... ।	III/184	III/800
सर्वो विकल्पः संसारः.... ।	I/56, 237; III/117; VIII/222; X/116	II/56, 237; III/733; V/2422; VI/2842
सर्वो विकल्पः स्मृतिः.... ।	I/134	II/134
स सिसृक्षुर्जगत्....बोधयामास पुद्गलान् ॥	VI/79	IV/1713
स हौ क्षपादिनामाना....मुक्त्वा स्वयं महत् ।	II/169	II/521
सांख्यवेदपुराणज्ञा....अमोक्षे मोक्षलिप्सया ।	III/43	III/659

साक्षं सर्वमिदं देहं....हृत्पङ्कजसमुद्गकम् ॥	III/330	III/946
साक्षात्कृतधर्मा....उपदेष्टा चाप्तः ।	I/34	II/34
सा चैका व्यापिनी....व्ययहीना च कथ्यते ॥	VI/117	IV/1751
....सा चैष्टव्येन रूषिता ।	II/173	II/525
साधकस्याधिकारार्थमक्षमालादि....पुष्पोदकसमन्वितम् ॥	X/305	VI/3031
साधनं यत्कृतम् तत्र इह जन्मनि सिद्धिदम् ।	IV/100	III/1188
सा धातोः प्रत्ययाद्....किं केन कथमित्यदः ॥	I/167	II/167
सापेक्षत्वेऽप्यपेक्षैव....नान्यत्स्यादनवस्थितेः ।	III/281	III/897
सामानाधिकरण्यं हि सद्विद्याहमिदंधियोः ॥	III/151	III/767
सार्णेनाण्डत्रयं व्याप्तं ।	II/164; III/219	II/516; III/835
सा शक्तिरापतत्याद्या....स्यात्परं नैःश्रेयसं प्रति ।	X/219	VI/2945
सिद्धयोगीश्वरीतन्त्रं....मालिनीविजयोत्तरं ।	VI/7	IV/1641
सिद्धस्याभिमुखीभावमात्रं संबोधनं विदुः ।	X/136	VI/2862
सिद्धातन्त्रमिदं देवि....योगिनीहृदिनन्दनः ॥	XII/380	VIII/3670
सिद्धानां योगिनीनां....संक्षेपोऽयं वरानने ॥	I/2 (2nd Āh.)	II/312
सिद्धानां योगिनीनां च दर्शनम् .... ।	I/34 (2nd Āh.)	II/344
सिद्धान्तके पञ्चकं सारं....त्रिकं तु भैरवे तन्त्रे ....॥	I/153	II/153
सिद्धान्तवैष्णवबौद्धा....निर्जीवा जीववर्जिताः ॥	XI/52 (29th Āh.)	VII/3342
सिद्धान्तादिषु तन्त्रेषु....सद्यः प्रत्ययकारकाः ॥	XI/3 (29th Āh.)	VII/3293
सिद्धैः संस्थापितानां तु न मानादि विचारयेत् ।	X/364	VI/3090
सुगन्धिं शीतलां दीर्घामश्नतः....सन्ति युगपत्पञ्चबुद्धयः ।	VI/220	IV/1854

सुमेरुर्हेमसंपृक्तः शरावाकृतिमस्तकः ।	V/41	IV/1391
सुरा च परमा शक्तिः. . . . भैरवेण महात्मना ॥	XI/9 (29th Āh.)	VII/3299
सुरा न पेया ।	III/278	III/894
सुराया अवघ्राणः कर्त्तव्यः ।	III/272	III/888
. . . . स्त्रुक्शक्तिस्तु स्त्रुवः शिवः ।	IX/210	VI/2650
सुव्रतं तु शुना दष्टं त्रिरात्रमुपवासयेत् ।	VIII/11	V/2211
सुसूक्ष्मो व्यापकः शुद्धः प्राणतत्त्वस्य वाचकः ॥	II/149	II/501
सूयं प्रमाणमित्याहुः. . . . ।	III/175	III/791
सूर्यादिर्मन्त्रमादाय गच्छेदस्त्रमनुस्मरन् ।	IX/34	VI/2474
सृष्टिसंहारकर्तारं. . . . प्रणतार्तिविनाशनम् ॥	I/7	II/7
सेच्छायाः प्रथमा तुटिः ।	IX/169	VI/2609
सेन्द्रियं चैव गुरुतो. . . . प्रतिभाति समं मम ॥	VIII/120	V/2320
सेयं क्रियात्मिका शक्तिः. . . . ज्ञाता सिद्ध्युपपादिका ॥	I/185	II/185
सैव शीघ्रतरोपात्त. . . . ।	II/173	II/525
सैष दाशरथी रामः. . . . ।	XII/290	VII/3580
सैषा सारतया प्रोक्ता हृदयं परमेष्ठिनः ।	I/207	II/207
सोऽरोदीद्यदरोदीत् तद्रुद्रस्य रुद्रत्वम् ।	III/261	III/877
सोऽभिषिक्तो गुरु पश्चाद्दक्षिणाभिः प्रपूजयेत् ।	XI/183	VII/3289
सोऽयमैश्वरो भावः पशोरपि ।	X/99	VI/2825
सोमं चामृतनाथं. . . . नामभिः परिकीर्तितम् ॥	II/164	II/516
सोमार्कानलदीप्तीनां. . . . व्यक्ततां नयति स्फुटम् ॥	III/128	III/744

....सोमो वर्षति चामृतम् ।	II/125	II/477
स्कन्धोऽपरः कलायास्तु....युग्मायुग्मक्रमेण तु ॥	VI/174	IV/1808
स्त्रीमुखाच्च भवेत्सिद्धिः सुसिद्धं पतासु तत्पदम् ।	XI/88 (29th Āh.)	VII/3378
स्त्रीमुखे निक्षिपेत्प्राज्ञः स्त्रीमुखाद्ग्राहयेत् पुनः प्रिये ॥	I/35; XI/88 (29th Āh.)	II/35; VII/3378
स्थित्यर्थं रमयेत्कान्तां न लौल्येन कदाचन ॥	XI/73 (29th Āh.)	VII/3363
स्नातोऽधिकारी भवति देवे पित्र्ये च कर्मणि ।	IX/41	VI/2481
स्पर्शोऽस्या अनुष्णाशीतत्वे सति पाकजः ।	VI/237	IV/1871
स्पर्शोऽस्यानुष्णाशीतत्वे सति अपाकजः ।	VI/237	IV/1871
स्फटिकस्येव....स्वरूपमनिरूप्यम् ।	II/126	II/478
स्मरणादभिलाषेण (येन) व्यवहारः प्रवर्तते ।	III/450	III/1066
स्मृताधश्छदनं मया विद्या तूत्तरमेव हि ।	IX/151	VI/2591
स्यात्परापरया साकं वामारे रतिशेखरः ।	X/6	VI/2732
स्यात्परे परया साकं वामारे संश्च भैरवः ।	X/6	VI/2732
स्रजं विमोचयेन्नाम....इतरेषां गणान्तकम् ।	III/295	III/911
....स्रोतोभेदं....स्यात्तदकीर्तनात् ॥	I/23	II/23
स्वक्रमं तु यजेन्मध्ये द्वैताचारं तु वर्जयेत् ॥	XI/52 (29th Āh.)	VII/3342
स्वातंत्र्यामुक्तमात्मानं.... ।	VI/124	IV/1758
स्वातंत्रस्याप्यबोधता ।	VI/80	IV/1714
स्वातंत्र्यहानिर्बोधस्य....स्वस्वरूपापहानितः ॥	I/55; VI/57	II/55; IV/1691
स्वदेह एवायतनं नान्यदायतनं व्रजेत् ।	XI/119 (29th Āh.)	VII/3409
स्वदेहावस्थितं द्रव्यं रसायनवरं शुभम् ।	IX/84; XI/92 (29th Āh.)	VI/2524; VI/3382

स्वधनेनापि कर्त्तव्या क्षीणवित्ते शिशावपि ।	IX/24	VI/2464
स्वनाम्ना प्रणवाद्येन. . . . विन्यसेत्कारणेश्वरे ॥	X/313	VI/3039
स्वपत्नी भगिनी माता दुहिता वा शुभा सखी ।	XI/72 (29th Āh.)	VII/3362
स्वापरामर्शमात्रं यदपराधः. . . . यद्वक्तुं नैव पार्यते ॥	VII/150	V/2034
स्वप्नेन्द्रजालवत्सर्वं. . . . ध्यायेच्छिवं विभुम् ॥	VIII/116	V/2316
स्वापेऽप्यास्ते. . . . यद्यथावस्तु जातम् ॥	I/147	II/147
स्वभावमवभासस्य. . . . स्फटिकादिजडोपमः ॥	I/27 (2nd Āh.); III/215	II/337; III/831
स्वभावे बोधममलं कुलं सर्वत्र कारणम् ।	XI/4 (29th Āh.)	VII/3294
स्वमन्त्रमक्षसूत्रं च गुरोरपि न दर्शयेत् ।	X/202; XI/179	VI/2928; VII/3285
स्वमन्त्ररक्षणं यत्नात्सर्वदा कारयेत्सुधीः ।	III/74	III/690
स्वयं गृहीतमन्त्राश्च क्लिश्यन्ते चाल्पबुद्धयः ।	III/71	III/687
स्वसिद्धान्तविरुद्धेन. . . . तत्त्वं वेद नापरः ।	III/16	III/632
स्वामिनश्चात्मसंस्थस्य. . . . तस्मादिच्छामर्शः प्रवर्तते ॥	VI/10	IV/1644
हंसो वृको वृषदंशस्ते ऐन्द्राः ।	IX/88	VI/2528
हकाररूपया शक्त्या मकारो ना हृदि स्थितः ।	II/139	II/491
हाटकेन विशुद्धेन सर्वेषां शुद्धिरिष्यते ।	V/29	IV/1379
हाहारावं घनं रुद्धं सामयं चित्रकण्टकम् ।	XII/228	VII/3518
हाहारावा महारावा. . . कन्दे षड्सलम्पटाः ॥	XII/241	VII/3531
हृदयगुहागेहगतं. . . . शिवाशयाश्मादिमश्लाघ्यम् ॥	III/286	III/902
हृदयं बोधपर्यायः. . . . ।	III/213	III/829
हृदयं शक्तिसूत्रं तु. . . . ।	I/8; XII/282	II/8; VII/3572

17. DETAILED TABLE OF CONTENTS OF THE TANTRĀLOKA IN SANSKRIT

(विषयानुक्रमणिका)

प्रथममाह्निकम्

द्वितीयमाह्निकम्

तृतीयमाह्निकम्

चतुर्थमाह्निकम्

पंचममाह्निकम्

षष्ठमाह्निकम्

सप्तममाह्निकम्

अष्टमाह्निकम्

नवमाह्निकम्

अतत्फलदायित्वम् १०५–१०६

५२ यथाभिसंधानं कर्मफलव्यवस्थानेऽपि फलानभिसंधान-
दार्ढ्यात् कर्मिणः फलसंस्कारत्यागस्ततः मायोत्तीर्णपदासादनम् १०७–१०८

५३ अनयैव परिपाट्या प्रमातुः विज्ञानाकलत्वम् १०९

५४ कर्तुरेवाभिसंधानात् कर्मफलव्यवस्थितेः दुष्कृतस्य
पराभिसंधावपि स्वाभिसंधानविरहाद् विज्ञानाकलस्य
दुष्कृतसुकृतफलभागित्वाभावः ११०–११६

५५ विज्ञानाकले क्रमेण मलस्य ध्वस्तत्वे अत्र अहंभावोदये
कार्ममलयोगाभावात् शिवावेशवशीकृतत्वस्य हेतुत्वम् ११७–११९

५६ मलस्य संसाराङ्कुरकारणत्वे श्रीपूर्वशास्त्रसंवादः १२०

५७ फलानन्तर्यभाविताया योग्यताया एव हेतुत्वात् सुखदुःखादि-
कार्यस्य हेतुतया षष्ठीतत्पुरुषगर्भं कर्मसूत्रव्याख्यानम् १२१–१२२

५८ कर्मवैचित्र्ये कार्यवैचित्र्यदर्शनादत्रैव बहुव्रीहिगर्भं
व्याख्यानान्तरम् १२३–१२४

५९ अवस्थावैचित्र्याद् अन्यदेहस्थकर्मणोऽन्यदेहस्थफल-
त्वोपपत्तौ अनुसंधानैक्यात् दोषस्याप्रसक्तिः १२५–१२६

६० फलौन्मुख्ये कर्मणः प्राच्यानुसंधिदार्ढ्यस्य अवश्यंभावित्वम्
तदनौन्मुख्ये तथात्वायोगात् तपसा ज्ञानेन च तस्य
निरोध्यत्वम् १२७–१२९

६१ अतः आरब्धकार्यस्य कर्मणोऽनिरोध्यत्वम् १३०

६२ सद्यस्ककर्मणोऽनारब्धकार्यत्वान्निरोद्धुं शक्यत्वम् १३१

६३ संस्कारदार्ढ्यनाशभङ्ग्या ज्ञानकाले मोहवशात्कृतस्य सर्वस्यापि
कर्मणः प्रदाहः १३२–१३३

६४ अत्रार्थे श्रीपरशास्त्रप्रामाण्यात् सर्वमेव संविदैकात्म्येन जानतः
देहस्थस्यापि कर्मणः दाहः १३४

६५ संविदोऽनतिरेकेण देहादिसंस्कारस्य व्यवस्थानात्
श्रीपरशास्त्रगतदेहस्थपदव्याख्यानम् १३५–१३७

६६ विज्ञानकेवलस्योपसंहारः प्रलयाकलप्रमातुरवतारश्च तत्र
तस्य आणव-कार्मद्विमलबद्धत्वं मायान्तरवस्थानं कर्मवासना-
वैचित्र्याद् यथोचितभागित्वं ब्रह्मादिस्थावरान्ते संसरणञ्च १३८–१३९

६७ न केवलमेषामधः संसरणम् अपितु ऊर्ध्वमपि, तत्र क्रमेण
मन्त्रत्वासादनम् १४०–१४१

६८ आणवमलस्यात्र ईश्वरेच्छावशात् कार्ममलसहकारित्वम् १४२–१४३

६९ चिदचिद्रूपताभासनेन अणोः भोगेच्छोदयक्रमेण पशुभावग्रहणे
ईश्वरेच्छावशादेव प्रबोधे कर्मवैचित्र्यात् तत्तत्संसाराविर्भावः १४४–१४६

९०	अणोर्निर्विकारत्वात्, समानेऽपि संसारकारणत्वे मल-माया-कर्मणां प्रतिनियतकार्यकारित्वान् मायाया एव कलोपादानकारणत्वम्	१७९–१८०
९१	अणोः किंचिज्ज्ञत्वकर्तृत्वादिसमुद्भलने ईशशक्तिसंप्रेरणात् कलाया एव हेतुत्वम्	१८१–१८२
९२	कलायाः विद्यादिवत् करणत्वाभावः पुंस्कलयोश्च प्रयोज्यप्रयोजकरूपत्वम्	१८३
९३	पुंस्कलयोर्विवेकज्ञानान्मायापुंविवेकः विज्ञानाकलत्वञ्च	१८४–१८५
९४	प्रकृतिपुरुषविवेके प्रकृत्यन्तम्, कलापुंविवेके तु मायान्तम्, कर्मक्षयात् पुंसः मायाधः संसरणाभाव इति सांख्यापेक्षया स्वमतोत्कर्षप्रदर्शनम्	१८६–१८७
९५	मायोर्ध्वं गमने प्रकृति-माया-मलविवेकत्रये सर्वत्र शक्तिपातस्य सहकारिकारणत्वं किन्तु तत्रान्त्यस्यैव मोक्षपर्यन्तवृत्तित्वम्	१८८
९६	कार्यभेदान्मायातः कलाया अन्यत्वम्	१८९
९७	कलालक्षणे स्वाभिधानस्य श्रीपूर्वशास्त्रप्रतिपादितार्थ-विरुद्धत्वपरिहारः	१९०
९८	अज्ञस्य किंचित्कर्तृत्वाभावात् किंचिज्ज्ञत्वरूपस्य विद्यातत्त्वस्योत्पत्तिनिरूपणम्	१९१
९९	पुंसस्तत्तत्प्रत्ययविशिष्टायां बुद्धौ वेद्यायां विद्यायाः करणत्वम्	१९२–१९३
१००	गुणसंकीर्णायां बुद्धौ सुखदुःखमोहादिविवेकाभावः	१९४
१०१	विषयाध्यवसाये बुद्ध्यपेक्षया विद्यायाः करणान्तरत्वम्	१९५
१०२	सर्वस्यापि विषयप्रकाशनस्य आत्मप्रकाशरूढत्वाद् व्यवहारलोपापत्तौ बुद्ध्यादिप्रतिसंक्रान्तवेद्यस्य विद्याकरण-गोचरत्वाद् बुद्ध्यादिकल्पनौचित्यम्	१९६–१९८
१०३	किञ्चित्त्वस्य प्रतिनियतवस्तुपर्यवसायित्वे निमित्तान्तरतया रागतत्त्वोपपादनम्	१९९
१०४	सामान्येन अभिष्वङ्गमात्ररूपत्वात् सांख्योक्तबुद्धिधर्मादवैराग्याद् रागतत्त्वस्य वैलक्षण्यम्	२००
१०५	कालतत्त्वस्य कार्यावच्छेदिकर्तृत्वकलनात्मकत्वम्	२०१
१०६	नियतितत्त्वस्य नियमाधायकत्वम्	२०२
१०७	विद्यादितत्त्वचतुष्टयस्य कलाकार्यत्वं भोक्तर्यवस्थानञ्च	२०३
१०८	संविदः मायादिकञ्चुकषट्कस्थितौ पशुत्वम्	२०४

दशमाह्निकम्

१७ उपचारस्य सनिमित्तकत्वाद् अर्थे ज्ञानस्याकिंचित्करत्वात् ण्यर्थे प्रकाशत्वोपचारस्य अपारमार्थिकत्वम् ४५–४६

१८ उपचारस्यापि चेतनाश्रितत्वाद् भवन्मते आत्मनः स्वतोऽचेतनत्वाद् उपचारासिद्धिः ५०–५१

१९ ज्ञानान्तरवेद्यत्वेऽपि ज्ञानस्य प्रदीपवद् अर्थप्रकाशकत्वे मुख्यामुख्यण्यर्थाऽसंगतिः ५२

२० प्रकृतार्थात् प्रदीपदृष्टान्तस्य वैषम्यम् ५३

२१ प्रकारान्तरेण वैषम्यद्रढनम् ५४

२२ अतः शिवप्रकाशार्थयोरैकात्म्याद् वेद्यतायाः पदार्थस्ववपुस्त्वं भावांशपृष्ठगामित्वञ्च ५५–५६

२३ प्रकटतासंवित्तिपक्षयोः परस्परेण संधानादत्र वेद्यतायाः भावधर्मत्वे उभयोरपि संग्रहः ५७

२४ दृष्टान्तद्वयोपादानाद् वेद्यत्वस्य अर्थक्रियाभेदोपदर्शनं ज्ञानसंवित्तित आधिक्यप्रदर्शनञ्च ५८–६०

२५ वेद्यताधर्मणः भावस्य शिवैकरूपत्वात् सर्ववेद्यत्व-रूपदोषानवकाशः ६१-६२

२६ प्रमातृप्रमेययोस्तत्त्वतो भेदेऽपि एतद्दोषानवकाशः ६३

२७ अत्रार्थे युक्तिः ६४–६५

२८ न्यायास्मन्मतयोः साम्यवैषम्यप्रदर्शनपूर्वकम् अस्मन्मते प्रमातुः तत्तदर्थावभाससंभिन्नसंविदात्मकत्वाद् वेद्यताख्यभावधर्मस्य नियतप्रमातृवेद्यत्वे पर्यनुयोगानवकाशः ६६–६७

२९ एतदवमन्यमानस्य परस्य बधिरप्रायत्वम् ६८–६९

३० एकप्रमातृवेद्यतायाः प्रमात्रन्तरसंबंधाभाववद् वेद्यतान्तरसंबंधस्यापि अनुपपत्तिः ७०–७४

३१ वेद्यतायाः स्वप्रकाशविश्रान्तौ वेद्यत्वाभावः ७५–७६

३२ प्रकाशविश्रान्तिसतत्त्वाया अपि वेद्यतायाः शिवस्वातन्त्र्याद् भेदेन भासनाद् भावधर्मत्वसिद्धिः ७७-७८

३३ एकरूपत्वेऽपि तत्तदंशांशिकाक्रमेणावभासमानाद् वेद्यत्वस्य सकलादिप्रमातृगतत्वेन चातुर्दश्यादिक्रमकल्पनाया औचित्यम् ७९–८२

३४ प्रमातृभेदाद् वेद्यताभेद इतिसमर्थनार्थम् अर्थक्रियाभेदनिरूपणम् ८३–८४

३५ तत्रापि नृत्तादौ अनेकप्रमातृवेद्यत्वात् तावत्यंशे प्रमात्रैक्यम् ८५–८६

३६ प्रमात्रैक्याच्चमत्कारानुभूतिः ८७

३७ ततः एकप्रमातृवेद्यस्य नीरसत्वम् अनेकप्रमातृवेद्यस्य सरसत्वम् ८८

३८ श्रीमालिनीविजयोत्तरप्रामाण्याल्लोकवत् शास्त्रेऽपि

वेद्यत्वस्य प्रमात्रन्तरापेक्षया विचित्रार्थकारित्वम् इति भावस्य वेद्यताधर्मोपसंहारः ८९–९१

३९ वेद्यताया अनाभासयोगे आभासस्य स्वालक्षण्यम् ९२

४० उपाध्ययोगात् घटमात्रस्य स्वरूपेण भाने स्वपरवेद्यता-संभेदपरामर्शरहितत्वम् ९३–९५

४१ शुद्धवस्तुप्रकाशने प्रकाशमानत्वाद् वेद्यत्वं न तु वेद्यत्वेन प्रकाशमानत्वम् ९६

४२ एवं सकलप्रमातारं प्रति वेद्यत्वाद् धराद्यव्यक्तान्त-पाञ्चदश्यादिकल्पनायाः वास्तवत्वम् ९७

४३ अव्यक्तान्तं सकलस्य प्रमातृत्वोक्तौ मायाकञ्चुकानाम् अनुद्रेकाद् ध्वंसाच्च प्रलय-विज्ञानाकलयोर्संग्रहः ९८–१००

४४ वेद्यप्राधान्येऽपि कञ्चुकोद्रेकात् सकलस्य प्रमातृत्वाद् अस्य पाञ्चदश्यसिद्धिः १०१

४५ प्रलयाकलप्रमातरि अस्य त्रायोदश्यम् १०२

४६ श्रीमालिनीविजयोत्तरे सकलतच्छक्त्यधिकारेण चतुर्विंशतौ तत्त्वेषु चतुर्दशधारणानामभिधानम् १०३–१०४

४७ प्रलयाकलानां प्रमातृत्वे पुंसादिकलान्ततत्त्वषट्कस्य त्रायोदश्यं विज्ञानकलानामेकादशत्वं मन्त्राणां च नवधात्वम् इति पूर्वोक्तानुवादः १०५–११२

४८ एवं मन्त्रमहेश्वरे प्रमेयतामापन्ने अप्रमेयभूतस्य शिवस्य प्रमातृत्वम् ११३

४९ अप्रकाशात्प्रकाशत्वेऽनवस्थादोषात् शिवस्य स्वप्रकाशत्वं विश्वस्य प्रमात्रधीनप्रकाशत्वम् ११४–११५

५० आदिसिद्धत्वात्तस्य प्रमाणानां तदधीनसिद्धित्वम् ११६

५१ उपदेश्यत्वेन सृष्टत्वाद् वेद्यत्वप्रसङ्गे शिवस्य मन्त्रमहेश्वरादिदशासादनम् ११७–११८

५२ तथात्वे शिवप्रत्यवमर्शाभावात् शिवभावनावैयर्थ्यापत्तिः ११९

५३ शिवात्मताऽपरित्यागात्तस्य वेद्यभावेऽपि शिवभावनावैफल्याभावः १२०

५४ श्रीपूर्वशास्त्रे शिवस्य भेदनिषेधेऽपि भूमिकान्तरप्राप्त्या न भेदाऽसङ्गतिः १२१

५५ एवं शिव-मन्त्र-महेशादीनां भेदानन्त्यम् १२२–१२३

५६ प्रलयाकलादेश्च प्रोक्ते त्रायोदश्यादिभेदे सकलवद् अकलादिके स्फुटभेदाभावाद् यथोत्तरं प्रतिप्रमातृ भेदद्वयाधिकत्व-संभावनायामपि प्रलयाकलादेः प्रलयाकलान्तरादिवेद्यत्वाभावे संख्याधिक्यानभिधानाद् भावधर्मवेद्यतामूलस्य पाञ्चदश्यस्योप-

एकादशमाह्निकम्

द्वादशमाह्निकम्

त्रयोदशमाह्निकम्

चतुर्दशमाह्निकम्

पंचदशमाह्निकम्

विश्वदिगीशत्वम् २०९

१२२ विष्णौ विधातरि च पञ्चमस्य ऊर्ध्ववक्त्रस्याभावेऽपि तत्र
षोढादिदिग्विभागस्याक्षुण्णत्वं तद्दिग्विभागस्य
पञ्चमवक्त्रोदञ्चितत्वञ्च २१०–२११

१२३ लौकिकदिग्विभागेऽपि ब्रह्माण्डमध्ये रवेः प्रकाशांशव्याप्त्या
चतसृणां दिशामुल्लासः परस्परापेक्षया तासां क्रमव्यत्ययश्च २१२–२१६

१२४ विपर्ययवैचित्र्येऽपि आसां प्रकाशमात्राधीनतया
प्रतिनियतफलप्रदत्वम् २१७

१२५ महेश्वराधिष्ठितत्वाद्धेतोर् दिग्विभागवैचित्र्यस्य सूर्याश्रितत्वम् २१८

१२६ साधकाश्रितदिग्विभागाभिधानम् २१९

१२७ सौरे इव अत्रत्येऽपि न केवलं परमेश्वरस्य अपितु
शक्रादिलोकपालवर्गस्याधिष्ठातृत्वम् २२०–२२१

१२८ लोकपालानां प्रकाशशक्त्यंशत्वप्रदर्शनम् २२२–२२४

१२९ प्रतिनियतत्वाभावात् सौर्यः दिश एव ग्राह्यतया उपदेशः २२५

१३० तत्र सर्वगानिलदृष्टान्तेन साधकाश्वाससंबोधाद् ऐन्द्र्यादिशक्तीनां
नियतदिगाधिपत्येन तदुचितफलप्रदत्वनिरूपणम् २२६–२२७

१३१ एवम् ईशानादिकारणपञ्चकाधिष्ठानादपि दिशां
तत्तत्फलप्रदत्वम् २२८

१३२ यागस्थले सर्वत्र साधकाभिप्रायेण मध्यीभूतस्य सर्वाधिष्ठातुः
शंकरस्य सूर्योदयस्य चापेक्षया पूर्वादिदिग्व्यवस्थानम् २२९–२३०

१३३ एवं मध्यनाथस्य दक्षिणपश्चिममहसः ग्रहणार्थम् उत्तरपूर्वा-
भिमुखोपवेशनेन देहशुद्ध्याचरणविधानम् २३१–२३२

१३४ तदनन्तरं देहप्राणादिशोधनोपक्रमे देहस्य बहिरन्तर्दाहनिरूपणम् २३३

१३५ दाहस्य ध्वंसत्वं देहपुर्यष्टकाहन्ताविध्वंसात मन्त्राग्नेः
ध्वंसकत्वम् २३४–२३५

१३६ एवं साधकदेहे अहन्तानास्पदीकृते देहदाहकथनौचित्यम् २३६

१३७ देहसंस्कारस्याप्यवधूननात् चिदात्मविश्रामणोपदेशः २३७

१३८ ततः साधकेन मूर्ति-प्रणव-हंमितिव्यपदिष्टाया
आद्यतरङ्गितायाः प्राप्तिः २३८

१३९ विशेषन्यासवैचित्र्योपक्रमे तत्त्वोदयकलात्मकस्य न्यासषट्-
कस्याभिधानं तत्र प्रत्येकं मुख्यतयोपास्यस्य न्यास्यत्वे प्रथमे
रतिशेखरस्य षष्ठे तु नवात्मनः न्यास्यत्वविधानम् २३९–२४३

१४० श्रीपूर्वशास्त्रे शंभुनाथनिरूपिते भैरवसद्भावन्यासविधौ
रतिशेखरवर्जनस्य न्याय्यत्वम् २४४–२४६

१४१ अत्रैव लक्ष्मणगुप्तस्याऽन्यथाव्याख्याने षड्विधशांभवन्यासा-

षोडशमाह्निकम्

सप्तदशमाह्निकम्

अष्टादशमाह्निकम्

एकान्न (? एकोन) त्रिंशमाह्निकम्

विंशतितममाह्निकम्

एकविंशतितममाह्निकम्

द्वाविंशतितममाह्निकम्

त्रयोविंशतितममाह्निकम

चतुर्विंशतितममाह्निकम्

पञ्चविंशतितममाह्निकम्

षड्विंशमाह्निकम्

सप्तविंशतितममाह्निकम्

अष्टाविंशमाह्निकम्

एकोनत्रिंशमाह्निकम्

त्रिंशमाह्निकम्

एकत्रिंशमाह्निकम्

२३ मण्डलव्याप्त्यादिविदः त्रिकशास्त्रे गुरुत्वं तस्य पादरजो-
धारणविधानम् ५०–५१
२४ त्रिशूलत्रये सृष्ट्यादित्रयस्य मध्ये च तुर्यस्य पूजनविधानम् ५२
२५ गुप्तदण्डस्य चतुस्त्रिशूलस्य यागे एतदतिदेशेन क्रमचतुष्टय-
पूजनोपदेशः ५३
२६ अत्रार्थे षडर्धहृदय-सिद्धयोगीश्वरीमतयोः अभिधानसूचनाभ्यां
प्रामाण्यम् ५४
२७ षडर्धहृदयपाठात् शूलस्य अष्टधा त्रिधा वा प्रकर्तव्यतायाः
खेचरीपुरस्य च निर्देशनम् ५५–५७
२८ अत्रार्थे श्रीसिद्धातन्त्रप्रामाण्यम् ५८–५९
२९ श्रीपूर्वादिशास्त्रान्तरैरुक्तस्य शूलाब्जविन्यासस्य
स्पष्टाभिधानोपक्रमः ६०–६१
३० प्रथमं श्रीपूर्वशास्त्रोक्तशूलविन्यासनिरूपणं तत्र चतुर्हस्तेन
अस्य त्र्यङ्गुलैः द्वात्रिंशद्धाविभाजनात् शूलसिद्धिः ६२–६३
३१ दक्षिणोत्तरपार्श्वयोश्चतुर्थेन जीवसूत्रेण पूर्वस्यां दिशि
अन्तर्मुखभ्रमद्वयानुष्ठानेन भागमानभागार्धमानं खण्डचन्द्रयोर्द्वयं
द्वयम् इति पार्श्ववर्तनाऽभिधानम् ६४–६६
३२ ततः ब्रह्मसूत्रस्याग्रे लग्नस्य सूत्रद्वयस्य विधानात् मध्यशृङ्ग-
वर्तनानिरूपणम् ६७–६८
३३ तदग्रमण्डलगतपार्श्वयोः तृतीयाज्जीवात् पूर्वोक्तगत्या षष्ठभागान्तं
सूत्रस्य नयनात् पार्श्वशृङ्गवर्तनम् ६९–७०
३४ अपरस्मिन्नपि क्षेत्रार्धे मध्यसूत्राणां प्रतिपार्श्वं भागचतुष्टयग्रहेण
दण्डवर्तनानिरूपणम् ७१–७३
३५ दण्डक्षेत्रगतभागचतुष्टयस्थितस्य पद्मस्य वर्तनाऽभिधाने
तृतीयवृत्ते षोडशदलार्धोत्पादननिरूपणम् ७४–७६
३६ तत्र एकैकदलस्थकेसरस्थानीयसूत्रतयाश्रयणेन पत्राग्रत्वसिद्धिः ७७–७८
३७ अत्रैव सितरक्तपीतकृष्णैः चतुर्भिः केसरजालकैः शृङ्गत्वं
सितरक्तपीतैस्त्रिभिः मण्डलत्वमिति रजोनियमाभिधानम् ७९–८२
३८ एतच्छेषभूतस्य द्वारस्य वैचित्र्यप्रदर्शनम् ८३–८४
३९ ततः श्रीदेव्यायामलोक्तशूलविन्यासोपन्यासः तत्र द्वादशभागमाने
क्षेत्रे मध्यस्थब्रह्मपदैकपार्श्वेन यथायथमूर्ध्वं भ्रमणात्
खण्डचक्रयुग्मत्रयवर्तनम् ८५–८७
४० ततः चतुर्थेन शृङ्गारकेणापि खण्डचक्रयुग्मयोजनम् इति
पार्श्वारवर्तनाविधिनिरूपणम् ८८

द्वात्रिंशमाह्निकम्

त्रयस्त्रिंशमाह्निकम्

चतुस्त्रिंशमाह्निकम्

पंचत्रिंशमाह्निकम्

षट्त्रिंशमाह्निकम्

सप्तत्रिंशमाह्निकम्

18. WORD-INDEX

19. CORRECTIONS

Page	*Fn., if any*	*Line*	*For*	*Read*
3		5	was therefore termed	was termed
		6	*Śaḍardhaśloka-vārtika*	*Ṣaḍardhaśloka-vārtika*
8		17	and who	who
	1	4		[Add after (SV.T.11.198)] T.A.V., V, p. 2
10	3	8	द्वयाज्ञान	द्वयज्ञान
24		14	but who also	and he also
62		9-10	*Saḍardhaśāstra, Saḍardhasāra*	*Ṣaḍarthaśāstra, Ṣaḍardhasāra*
		10	*Saḍardhahṛdaya*	*Ṣaḍardhahṛdaya*
69	3	4	X, 11. 56-57	X, pp. 56-57
78	2	1	T.A.V., XIII	T.A.V., XI
89	4	1	Verse 90	Verse 9
92	7	3	XII, p. 430	XII, p. 432
	(chart)	15	Śṛṅgāratha	Śṛṅgāraratha
93	1	3	p. 431	p. 433
94		15-16	*Tantrāloka*	*Tantrāloka-viveka*
101	2	1	IV, p. 471	IV, p. 203
120		21	one he	one hand, he
121		20-21	Tṛtīyām caturthīm	Tṛtīyām or Caturthīm
126		17	quotes but	quotes them but
129	9	2		(Add after इति) Ibid., III, p. 128
137	4	2	Ibid., IX	Ibid., XI
142		11	editrial	editorial
143	6	3	pp. 20-87	pp. 207-8
147		16	comentary	commentary
147	6	2	मदगुरु०	मद्गुरु०
150	2	2	XI, p. 19	XI, p. 19 (29th Āh.)
151		19	(Pīṭhas)	Pīṭhas)

171		5	text which	text, which
		28	all energies	all his energy
175		1	शाक्तोपायपण्डलकथन	शाक्तोपायमण्डलकथन
185	A horizontal line of demarcation across the page between 4-5th and 7-8th lines to be inserted.			
186	,,	4-5th	and after 6th ,,	
196		10-11	a collateral source of thematic organization	a Collateral Source of Thematic Organization
199	1	1	शिवात्मक	शिवात्मको
	1	3	T.A. 198-200	T.A. 10. 198-200
200		1	inform	uniform
202	2	7	T.A.V., V,	T.A.V., III,
208	4	3	T.A.V., VIII,	T.A.V., VII,
212	(fn.4 continued from p. 211)	1	भुवना नियस्यैवंविधो	भुवनानि यस्यैवंविधो
	1	5	T.A.V., II,	T.A.V., III,
215	1	3	T.A.V. VII,	T.A.V., VIII,
220	1	3	Jayaratha's	Jayaratha
	3	3	रुपात	रूपात्
224	(fn. 5 contd. from p. 223)	3	XI, p. 252	X, p. 258
227	3	2	योगोप॰	यागोप॰
236	2	1	सूयन्दु॰	सूर्येन्दु॰
241	2	3	देव्य	देव्य:
242	1	6	XII, p. 390	XII, p. 391
246		24	*M.V.T.*	*M.V.V.*
		27	*M.V.T.*	*M.V.V.*
249		25	T.A.2.12-44	T.A.3.12-14

20. TABLE OF CONVERSION OF REFERENCES APPEARING WITHIN THE *INTRODUCTION TO THE TANTRĀLOKA* FROM THE KSTS EDITION TO THE MLBD EDITION OF THE *TANTRĀLOKAVIVEKA*

Page	*Footnote*	*Line*	*Existing reference to the KSTS edition*	*Corresponding reference to the MLBD edition*
4	5	2	I, pp. 14-15	II, pp. 14-15
	6	2	I, pp. 29-30	II, pp. 29-30
5	Fn. 7 contd. from page 4	4	XII, p. 389	VIII, p. 3679
	1	2	V, p. 19	IV, p. 1369
	2	2	p. 186	p. 1536
	5	2	I, p. 35	II, p. 35
6	1	2	I, p. 31	II, p. 31
	2	4	I, p. 50	II, p. 50
7	6	5	V, p. 4	IV, p. 1354
8	21	4	V, p. 8	IV, p. 1358
	2	4	V, p. 16	IV, p. 1366
	3	7	X, p. 254	VI, p. 2980
10	1	3	I, p. 53	II, p. 53
	2	2	p. 3	p. 3
			p. 52	p. 52
	3	10	XII, p. 428	VIII, p. 3718
13	3	5	I, pp. 52-54	II, pp. 52-54
	5	4	VIII, p. 102	V, p. 2302
	6	2	,,	,,
14	3	4	IV, p. 203	III, p. 1291
15	2	2	X, p. 57	VI, p. 2783
	5	5	IX, p. 71	VI, p. 2511
16	1	3	V, p. 186	IV, p. 1356
19	4	2	I, p. 34	II, p. 34
20	1	3	I, pp. 14-15	II, pp. 14-15
21	2	5	VIII, p. 137	V, p. 2337
22	Fn. 4 contd. from page 21	4	VII, p. 44 (11th Āh.)	V, p. 2136

29	3	2	XII, p. 412	VIII, p. 3702
	5	8	XII, p. 413	VIII, p. 3703
30	5	2	I, p. 14	II, p. 14
35	2	4	I, p. 31	II, p. 31
37	Fn. 8 contd. from			
	page 36	4	VI, p. 211	IV, p. 1845
	1	3	V, p. 275	IV, p. 1625
38	1	4	III, p. 467	III, p. 1083
40	1	4	III, pp. 192-3	III, pp. 808-809
42	3	4	III, p. 194	III, p. 810
	4	4	III, p. 193	III, p. 809
43	4	1	IX, p. 122	VI, p. 2562
	5	3	,,	,,
44	1	5	XII, p. 184	VII, p. 3474
45	5	5	I, p. 34	II, p. 34
	7	2	I, p. 35	II, p. 35
46	1	4	I, p. 236	II, p. 236
	3	4	,,	,,
	4	4	,,	,,
	5	1	III, p. 192	III, p. 808
47	3	5	I, p. 32	II, p. 32
48	5	6	III, p. 356	III, p. 972
49	1	3	V, p. 283	IV, p. 1633
	3	4	VII, p. 129	V, p. 2013
50	3	5	IX, p. 122	VI, p. 2562
	4	4	IX, p. 177	VI, p. 2617
52	1	11	(29thĀh.) XI, p. 136	VII, p. 3426
55	2	5	VI, p. 249	IV, p. 1883
56	1	3	VII, p. 101 (12th Āhnika)	V, p. 2193
57	3	5	X, p. 292	VI, p. 3018
	4	3	X, pp. 56-57	VI, pp. 2782-2783
59	6	3	VII, p. 33	V, p. 1917
63	3	5	II, pp. 72-73	II, pp. 424-425
65	Fn. 1 contd. from			
	page 64	5	XI, pp. 172-174	VII, pp. 3278-3280
67	2	3	VII, p. 107	V, p. 1991
	3	3	VI, p. 175	IV, p. 1809
68	1	2	III, p. 114	III, p. 730

	2	2	V, p. 199	IV, p. 1549
	3	7	X, p. 89	VI, p. 2815
69	Fn. 4 contd. from page 68	8	III, pp. 468-469	III, pp. 1084-1085
	3	4	X, pp. 56-57	VI, pp. 2782-2783
70	2	4	V, pp. 14-19	IV, pp. 1364-1369
71	1	3	XI, p. 89	VII, p. 3195
	2	5	XII, pp. 187-188	VII, pp. 3477-3478
	4	4	V, p. 145	IV, p. 1495
72	1	1	I, p. 206	II, p. 206
	2	2	II, p. 99	II, p. 451
	3	1	II, p. 146	II, p. 498
73	1	3	V, p. 186	IV, p. 1536
	2	6	VI, p. 41	IV, p. 1675
	3	4	VII, p. 30 (11thĀh.)	V, p. 2122
74	1	3	V, pp. 122-128	IV, pp. 1472-1478
75	1	4	VIII, p. 127	V, p. 2327
	2	1	V, p. 145	IV, p. 1495
	3	2	V, p. 199	IV, p. 1549
76	1	15	III, p. 433	III, p. 1049
	2	3	I, p. 309	II, p. 309
77	1	3	XII, p. 390	VIII, p. 3680
	2	9	I, p. 84	II, p. 84
	4	1	I, p. 202	I, p. 202
	1	1	II, p. 121	II, p. 473
78	2	1	XI, p. 150	VII, p. 3440
	3	2	V, p. 186	IV, p. 1536
	4	2	I, p. 117	II, p. 117
	5	2	I, p. 130	II, p. 130
	6	6	I, p. 203	II, p. 203
79	1	2	III, p. 112	III, p. 728
	3	3	VI, p. 169	IV, p. 1803
	4	3	III, p. 124	III, p. 740
82	2	3	IX, p. 25	VI, p. 2465
	3	3	IX, p. 285	VI, p. 2725
83	2	2	XI, p. 2 (29thĀh.)	VII, p. 3292
	3	2	I, p. 74	II, p. 74
	5	2	VI, p. 250	IV, p. 1884
	6	3	IV, p. 97	III, p. 1185
84	1	3	III, p. 443	III, p. 1059

85	Fn. 5 contd. from page 84	3	IX, p. 194	VI, p. 2634
	1	2	II, pp. 94-95	II, pp. 446-447
88	1	2	XII, p. 430	VIII, p. 3720
	2	3	p. 432	p. 3722
	3	1	p. 431	p. 3721
	4	3	XII, p. 433	VIII, p. 3723
89	1	1	XII, p. 430	VIII, p. 3720
		2	XII, p. 431	VIII,p. 3721
		3	p. 432	p. 3722
	2	1	p. 430	p. 3720
	2	2	,,	,,
	2	3	p. 432	p. 3722
	3	1	p. 430	p. 3720
	3	2	,,	,,
	4	1	,,	,,
		2	p. 431	p. 3721
		3	p. 432	p. 3722
	5	1	p. 431	p. 3721
	6	1	,,	,,
		2	,,	,,
	7	1	p. 430	p. 3720
	8	2	,,	,,
	9	1	,,	,,
		,,	p. 431	p. 3721
	10	1	,,	,,
90	1	3	XII, p. 430	VIII, p. 3720
	2	5	p. 430	p. 3720
	3	5	,,	,,
	4	5	pp. 430-431	pp. 3720-3721
91	1	3	XII, p. 431	VIII, p. 3721
	2	2	p. 431	p. 3721
	3	2	p. 430	p. 3720
	4	6	p. 431	p. 3721
92	1	3	XII, p. 431	VIII, p. 3721
	2	1	p. 431	p. 3721
	3	1	p. 432	p. 3722
	6	2	I, p. 310	II, p. 310
	7	3	XII, p. 432	VIII, p. 3722
93	1	3	XII, p. 433	VIII, p. 3723

	3	3	p. 433	p. 3723
94	1	3	XII, p. 433	VIII, p. 3723
	2	3	p. 434	p. 3724
	3	6	p. 432	p. 3722
95	2	3	XII, p. 433	VIII, p. 3723
	3	3	p. 433	p. 3723
96	1	7	I, p. 11	II, p. 11
	2	3	III, p. 203	III, p. 819
97	1	2	III, p. 192	III, p. 808
		4	p. 198	p. 814
	2	3	pp. 192-193	pp. 808-809
	4	1	XII, p. 433	VIII, p. 3723
98	1	1	I, p. 310	II, p. 310
	2	5	XII, p. 433	VIII, p. 3723
	3	2	p. 434	p. 3724
	4	1	I, p. 310	II, p. 310
	5	3	XII, p. 433	VIII, p. 3723
	6	3	I, p. 2	II, p. 2
99	1	2	I, p. 2	II, p. 2
	3	5	VIII, p. 205	V, p. 2405
	4	2	IX, p. 30	VI, p. 2470
	5	4	XII, p. 198	VII, p. 3488
100	1	6	III, p. 233	III, p. 849
	2	1	III, p. 471	III, p. 1087
	3	1	X, p. 305	VI, p. 3031
	4	2	XI, p. 172 (29thĀh.)	VII, p. 3462
	5	1	I, p. 2	II, p. 2
	7	1	II, p. 264	II, p. 616
		4	IV, p. 307	III, p. 923
101	1	3	VIII, p. 205	V, p. 2405
	2	1	IV, p. 203	III, p. 1291
	3	5	XII, p. 434	VIII, p. 3724
	4	5	pp. 434-435	pp. 3724-3725
102	1	2	XII, p. 435	VIII, p. 3725
	2	2	p. 434	p. 3724
	3	3	p. 432	p. 3722
	4	5	p. 434	p. 3724
103	1	5	XII, p. 434	p. 3724
	3	2	X, p. 221	VI, p. 2947
104	1	2	I, p. 15	II, p. 15

		4	V, p. 260	IV, p. 1610
	2	3	X, pp. 91-92	VI, pp. 2817-2818
	3	4	I, p. 2	II, p. 2
	Fn. 4 contd. from Page 104	2	p. 3	p. 3
105	1	2	I, p. 42 (2nd Āh.)	II, p. 352
	3	2	IV, p. 203	III, p. 1291
	4	3	I, p. 1	II, p. 1
106	1	3	I, p. 1 (2nd Āh.)	II, p. 311
	2	1	p. 42	p. 352
	3	2	IV, p. 58 (7th Āh.)	III, p. 1350
	4	2	III, p. 471	III, p. 1087
	5	4	I, p. 1	II, p. 1
107	Fn.6 contd. from page 106	7	XII, p. 434	VIII, p. 3724
	1	3	III, p. 203	III, p. 819
	2	2	p. 179	III, p. 795
108	1	3	II, p. 5	II, p. 357
	2	6	p. 25	p. 377
	4	3	VII, pp. 64-65	V, pp. 1948-1949
109	1	2	III, p. 202	III, p. 818
	2	4	p. 162	p. 778
110	1	3	III, p. 161	p. 777
	2	6	pp. 189-191	pp. 805-807
	3	3	p. 193	p. 809
	4	1	pp. 193-202	pp. 809-818
111	1	4	III, p. 203	III, p. 819
	2	4	pp. 127-129	pp. 743-745
	3	5	pp. 133-134	pp. 749-750
112	1	1	V, pp. 15-22	IV, pp. 1365-1372
	1	9	V, pp. 20-21	IV, pp. 1370-1371
113	2	3	VII, p. 18(11th Āh.)	V, p. 2110
	3	1	p. 19	p. 2111
	4	3	p. 20	p. 2112
	5	2	p. 19	p. 2111
	6	4	VII, p. 21(11th Āh.)	V, p. 2113
114	1	4	VII, p. 26(11th Āh.)	V, p. 2118
	2	3	p. 26	p. 2118
115	2	2	V, p. 260	IV, p. 1610
117	Fn.2 contd. from			

	page 116	4	I, pp. 85-86	II, pp. 85-86
	2	2	I, p. 281	II, p. 281
	5	2	II, p. 166	II, p. 518
	7	2	III, p. 158	III, p. 774
	9	2	V, p. 275	IV, p. 1625
118	2	2	VI, p. 46	IV, p. 1680
	3	1	IX, p. 28	VI, p. 2468
119	1	1	IX, pp. 63-65	VI, pp. 2503-2505
	3	3	I, pp. 116-117	II, pp. 116-117
120	Fn.4 contd. from			
	page 119	3	I, p. 26(2nd Āh.)	II, p. 336
	1	2	I, p. 150	II, p. 150
	3	3	I, p. 40 (2nd Āh.)	II, p. 350
	6	2	III, pp. 150, 160, 165, 167, 169, 173, 178, 181,183, 185, 187, 202	III, pp. 766, 776, 781, 783, 785, 789, 794, 797, 799, 801, 803, 818
121	2	6	VI, p. 46	IV, p. 168
	3	3	IX, pp. 162-163	VI, pp. 2602-2603
122	2	3	IX, p. 162	VI, p. 2602
	3	2	p. 243	p. 2683
	5	3	XII, p. 246	VII, p. 3536
123	1	4	X, pp. 91-92	VI, pp. 2817-2818
124	1	4	IV, p. 57	III, p. 1145
	4	4	III, p. 58	III, p. 674
125	1	1	V, p. 14	IV, p. 1364
	2	8	pp. 14-19	pp. 1364-1369
126	1	4	I, p. 39-45	II, p. 39-45
127	Fn. 4 contd. from			
	page 126	1	III, p. 136	III, p. 752
		2	III, p. 190	III, p. 806
		2-3	III, pp. 166-167, 163, 173, 223	III, pp. 782-783, 779, 789, 839
	1	1	III, pp. 161, 189	III, pp. 777, 805
	2	2	IX, p. 139	VI, p. 2579
	4–5	2	IX, p. 140	VI, p. 2580
	6	3	III, p. 280	III, p. 896
	7	3	XI, p. 44	VII, p. 3150
128	1	5	XI, pp. 28-29 (29thĀh.)	VII, pp. 3318-3319

	2	2	III, p. 191	III, p. 807
129	1	1	III, p. 192	III, p. 808
	2	2	II, p. 73	II, p. 425
	3	1	III, p. 196	III, p. 812
	5	4	II, p. 219	II, p. 571
	6	1	I, p. 11	II, p. 11
	7	1	III, p. 203	III, p. 819
	8	1	p. 233	p. 849
	9	2	III, p. 128	III, p. 744
130	2	1	II, p. 202	II, p. 554
131	1	2	V, p. 102	IV, p. 1452
	2	1	p. 103	p. 1453
	5	5	V, pp. 102-3	IV, pp. 1452-1453
132	1	4	V, p. 104	IV, p. 1454
	3	5	V, p. 57	IV, p. 1407
	4	3	V, p. 57	IV, p. 1407
	6	2	V, p. 142	IV, p. 1492
133	2	8	V, p. 204	IV, p. 1554
134	1	7	V, pp. 240-241	IV, pp. 1590-1591
135	Fn. 3 contd. from page 134	4	V, pp. 243-244	IV, pp. 1593-1594
136	Fn. 3 contd. from page 135	3	IX, p. 19	VI, p. 2459
	2	3	IX, p. 231	VI, p. 2671
137	1	5	IV, p. 142	III, p. 1230
	2	2	p. 143	p. 1231
	3	2	V, p. 199	IV, p. 1549
	4	2	XI, p. 12 (29thĀh.)	VII, p. 3302
	5	2	I, p. 150	II, p. 150
138	1	3	IX, p. 39	VI, p. 2479
	3	2	VI, p. 250	IV, p. 1884
139	1	2	VI, p. 250	IV, p. 1884
	2	2	VII, p. 208	V, p. 2092
	5	3	XI, p. 6	VII, p. 3112
140	1	4	XI, p. 74 (29thĀh.)	VII, p. 3364
	2	4	III, pp. 173-174	III, pp. 789-790
	4	2	IV, p. 220	III, p. 1308
141	1	2	III, pp. 357-358	III, pp. 973-974
	4	3	III, pp. 442-443	III, pp. 1058-1059
	5	2	XI, p. 19	VII, p. 3125

142	1	2	XII, p. 184	XII, p. 3474
	3	3	XII, p. 198	VII, p. 3488
	4	2	VI, p. 119	IV, p. 1753
	5	1	p. 125	p. 1759
143	2	2	I, p. 103	II, p. 103
	4	1	I, p. 143	II, p. 143
	6	3	II, pp. 207-208	II, pp. 559-560
	7	5	VI, p. 167	IV, p. 1801
144	2	1	VIII, p. 211	V, p. 2411
	3	2	IX, p. 19	VI, p. 2459
	5	1	IX, p. 44	VI, p. 2484
145	3	2	X, p. 272	VI, p. 2998
	5	2	XII, p. 393	VIII, p. 3683
	6	2	p. 395	p. 3685
146	1	2	XII, p. 247	VII, p. 3537
	2	1	X, p, 249	VI, p. 2975
147	1	2	III, p. 443	III, p. 1059
	2	1	p. 203	III, p. 819
	3	2	IV, p. 10 (7th Āh.)	III, p. 1302
	4	2	IX, p. 19	VI, p. 2459
	5	2	pp. 162-163	pp. 2602-2603
	6	3	X, pp. 91-92	VI, pp. 2817-2818
148	1	2	I, pp. 299-300	II, pp. 299-300
	2	2	III, p. 371	III, p. 987
	2	3	III, p. 65	III, p. 681
	2	5	I, p. 33	II, p. 33
	3	2	p. 15	p. 15
	4	2	IV, p. 10	III, p. 1098
149	1	2	III, p. 135	III, p. 751
	2	2	XI, p. 168	VII, p. 3274
	3	2	III, p. 58	III, p. 674
	4	1	IX, p. 19	VI, p. 2459
	5	2	p. 197	p. 2637
	6	2	I, p. 157	II, p. 157
	6	3	p. 180	p. 180
150	Fn. 7 contd. from page 149	2	VII, p. 80	V, p. 1964
		4	XII, p. 212	VII, p. 3502
	1	2	X, pp. 91-92	VI, pp. 2817-2818
	2	2	XI, p. 19 (29thĀh.)	VII, p. 3309

	3	1	II, p. 28	II, p. 380
	4	2	II, p. 12	II, p. 364
		4	III, p. 63	III, p. 679
	5	1	II, p. 5	II, p. 357
		2	p. 25	p. 377
151	1	2	I, p. 16	II, p. 16
	2	3	IX, p. 184	VI, p. 2624
	3	3	I, p. 134	II, p. 134
152	1	3	IX, p. 48	VI, p. 2488
153	1	3	III, pp. 102-103	III, p. 718-719
	2	1	p. 15	p. 631
160	3	2	I, p. 165	II, p. 165
		4	p. 166	p. 166
		6	p. 179	p. 179
161	1	4	I, p. 40	II, p. 40
		6	III, p. 107	III, p. 723
		7	VII, p. 66	V, p. 1950
		8	VII, p. 67	V, p. 1951
		9	XI, p. 38	VII, p. 3144
	2	2	I, p. 29	II, p. 29
	3	1	I, p. 4	II, p. 4
		2	I, p. 15	II, p. 15
162	—	20	V, p. 145	IV, p. 1495
	1	2	V, p. 57	IV, p. 1407
163	—	6	III, p. 160	III, p. 776
	—	9	IV, p. 203	III, p. 1291
	—	11	VIII, p. 1	V, p. 2201
	—	13	VIII, p. 86	V, p. 2286
	—	15	IX, p. 44	VI, p. 2484
	—	17	IX, p. 48	VI, p. 2488
164	—	1	I, p. 236	II, p. 236
166	—	9	VI, p. 180	IV, p. 1814
	—	11	VI, p. 179	IV, p. 1813
	—	13	VIII, p. 80	V, p. 2280
	—	16	III, p. 443	III, p. 1059
168	4	4	III, p. 307	III, p. 923
172	2	2	I, p. 268	II, p. 268
180	5	2	XI, p. 133	VII, p. 3239
184	1	1	XI, p. 85	VII, p. 3191
187	1	3	IV, p. 5	III, p. 1093

188	3	2	VII, p. 207	V, p. 2091
189	1	1	IX, p. 245	VI, p. 2685
	3	3	IX, p. 285	VI, p. 2725
	5	1	X, p. 114	VI, p. 2840
190	2	2	X, p. 212	VI, p. 2938
	4	2	X, p. 237	VI, p. 2963
	5	2	XI, p. 47	VII, p. 3153
191	1	3	XI, p. 97	VII, p. 3203
192	Fn. 3 contd. from page 191	2	IV, p. 2	III, p. 1090
193	1	2	III, p. 469	III, p. 1085
194	1	4	VIII, p. 215	V, p. 2415
	2	3	XI, p. 114 (29th Āh.)	VII, p. 3404
	5	2	XII, p. 303	VII, p. 3593
195	2	4	X, p. 323-326	VI, p. 3049-3052
197	2	2	I, p. 196	II, p. 196
	3	3	I, p. 7	II, p. 7
	4	8	I, pp. 238-39	II, pp. 238-239
198	1	3	I, p. 303	II, p. 303
	2	6	II, p. 254	II, p. 602
	3	4	VI, p. 73	IV, p. 1707
	4	4	VII, p. 44	V, p. 1928
199	Fn. 5 contd. from page 198	3	VII, p. 86	V, p. 1970
	1	5	X, p. 76	VI, p. 2802
	2	5	XI, p. 45 (29thĀh.)	VII, p. 3335
200	1	6	XII, p. 337	VII, p. 3627
	2	6	III, p. 9	III, p. 625
	3	4	III, pp. 53-56	III, pp. 669-672
	4	3	IX, p. 136	VI, p. 2576
201	1	3	VII, p. 189	V, p. 2073
	2	4	II, p. 249	II, p. 601
	3	5	IV, p. 2 (7th Āh.)	III, p. 1294
	4	3	II, p. 59	II, p. 411
202	Fn. 5 contd. from page 201	3	II, p. 233	II, p. 585
	1	3	II, p. 247	II, p. 599
	2	7	III, pp. 373-374	III, pp. 989-990
	3	5	III, p. 409	III, p. 1025
	4	2	III, pp. 433&458	III, pp. 1049&1074

203	1	7	XII, p. 348	VII, p. 3638
	2	2	I, p. 152	II, p. 152
	3	2	II, p. 236	II, p. 588
	4	2	III, p. 336	III, p. 952
204	1	3	III, p. 48	III, p. 664
	2	5	IX, p. 11	VI, p. 2451
	3	3	VIII, p. 88	V, p. 2288
	4	5	VIII, p. 101	V, p. 2301
	5	3	III, p. 346	III, p. 962
205	1	2	III, p. 461	III, p. 1077
	2	2	VII, p. 104 (12thĀh.)	V, p. 2196
	3	3	XI, p. 63	VII, p. 3169
	4	3	IX, p. 9	VI, p. 2449
	5	3	IX, p. 90	VI, p. 2530
206	2	2	I, p. 249	II, p. 249
207	1	5	I, p. 151	II, p. 151
	2	6	III, pp. 457-458	III, pp. 1073-1074
208	1	9	II, p. 190	II, p. 542
	3	2	XII, p. 343	VII, p. 3633
	4	3	XII, p. 41 (11thĀh.)	V, p. 2133
209	2	3	VII, p. 173	V, p. 2057
	2	7	IV, p. 49 (7thĀh.)	III, p. 1341
	3	5	V, pp. 129-130	IV, pp. 1479-1480
	4	3	VIII, p. 215	V, p. 2415
	5	7	VIII, pp. 216-217	V, pp. 2416-2417
210	1	5	XI, p. 9	VII, p. 3115
	2	4	XI, p. 87	VII, p. 3193
211	1	5	V, p. 194	IV, p. 1544
	3	6	XII, p. 335	VII, p. 3625
212	Fn. 4 contd. from page 211	2	II, p. 257	II, p. 609
	1	5	III, p. 393	III, p. 1009
	2	2	IV, p. 62	III, p. 1150
	3	3	V, p. 2	IV, p. 1352
	4	2	VI, p. 179	IV, p. 1813
	5	6	VI, p. 180	IV, p. 1814
213	1	4	VII, p. 36	V, p. 1920
	2	3	IX, p. 153	VI, p. 2593
	3	3	IX, p. 154	VI, p. 2594
	4	4	XI, p. 161 (29th Āh.)	VII, p. 3451

214	1	3	I, p. 219	II, p. 219
	2	5	III, p. 37	III, p. 653
	3	4	VI, p. 95	IV, p. 1729
	4	3	VII, p. 98	V, p. 1982
215	Fn. 4 contd. from page 214	5	X, p. 169	VI, p. 2895
	1	3	VIII, p. 168	V, p. 2368
	2	3	VI, p. 130	IV, p. 1764
	3	6	VII, p. 12	V, p. 1896
	4	4	VIII, p. 37	V, p. 2237
216	1	5	VIII, p. 70	V, p. 2270
	2	3-4	VII, p. 32	V, p. 1916
	3	2	V, p. 195	IV, p. 1545
217	Fn. 4 contd. from page 216	5	VIII, p. 147	V, p. 2347
	1	7	VII, p. 97	V, p. 1981
	2	3	X, p. 352	V, p. 3078
218	1	3	I, p. 223	II, p. 223
	2	4	XI, p. 143 (29thĀh.)	VII, p. 3433
	3	4	VII, p. 83	V, p. 1967
219	1	3	III, p. 442	III, p. 1058
	2	2	V, p. 2	IV, p. 1352
	3	3	VII, p. 36	V, p. 1920
220	Fn. 4 contd. from page 219	1	X, p. 55	VI, p. 2781
	1	3	X, p. 57	VI, p. 2783
	2	4	VII, p. 41	V, p. 1925
	3	4	VII, p. 68	V, p. 1952
221	1	7	I, p. 179	II, p. 179
	2	5	III, p. 41	III, p. 657
	3	4	XI, p. 93	VII, p. 3199
222	1	5	VIII, p. 80	V, p. 2280
	2	4	I, p. 215	II, p. 215
	3	6	III, p. 51	III, p. 667
223	2	5	VIII, p. 163	V, p. 2363
	3	3	X, p. 127	VI, p. 2853
	4	3	X, p. 244	VI, p. 2970
224	Fn.5 contd. from page 223	3	X, p. 258	VI, p. 2984
	1	4	X, p. 300	VI, p. 3026

	2	1	X, p. 352	VI, p. 3078
225	1	5	VIII, p. 99	V, p. 2299
	2	3	VIII, p. 215	V, p. 2415
	3	2	I, p. 249	II, p. 249
226	1	4	X, p. 122	VI, p. 2848
	2	2	III, p. 442	III, p. 1058
	3	4	X, p. 339	VI, p. 3065
227	Fn. 4 contd. from page 226	5	X, p. 161	VI, p. 2887
	1	3	X, p. 343	VI, p. 3069
	2	3	XI, p. 128	VII, p. 3234
	3	3	IX, p. 91	VI, p. 2531
228	2	5	IX, p. 188	VI, p. 2628
	3	7	IX, p. 198	VI, p. 2638
229	1	2	III, p. 442	III, p. 1058
	2	5	IX, p. 161	VI, p. 2601
230	Fn. 3 contd. from page 229	1	X, p. 189	VI, p. 2915
	1	4	X, p. 372	VI, p. 3098
	2	2-3	XI, p. 133 (29th Āh.)	VII, p. 3423
231	1	3	IX, p. 92	VI, p. 2532
	2	9	VII, p. 68 (11th Āh.)	V, p. 2160
	3	6	VI, pp. 103-104	IV, pp. 1737-1738
233	Fn. 2 contd. from page 232	3	X, p. 307	VI, p. 3033
	1	6	XII, p. 372	VIII, p. 3662
234	Fn. 2 contd. from page 233	2	X, p. 254	VI, p. 2980
	1	6	XI, p. 118	VII, p. 3224
235	1	4	XI, p. 94 (29th Āh.)	VII, p. 3384
	2	2	IX, p. 258	VI, p. 2698
	3	3	XI, p. 171	VII, p. 3277
236	2	6	II, p. 216	II, p. 568
	3	6	III, pp. 297-298	III, pp. 913-914
237	1	5	III, p. 443	III, p. 1059
	2	4	X, p. 353	VI, p. 3079
	3	4	XI, p. 178	VII, p. 3284
238	Fn. 4 contd. from page 237	3	XI, p. 19 (29th Āh.)	VII, p. 3309
	1	4	XI, p. 114 (29th Āh.)	VII, p. 3404

239	1	2	X, p. 187	VI, p. 2913
	2	3	X, p. 192	VI, p. 2918
	3	2	X, p. 211	VI, p. 2937
	4	4	XI, p. 157	VII, p. 3263
240	1	3	XII, p. 235	VII, p. 3525
	2	3	XII, p. 281	VII, p. 3571
	3	3	X, p. 4	VI, p. 2730
	4	2	III, p. 443	III, p. 1059
241	1	3	I, p. 153	II, p. 153
	2	4	IX, p. 61	VI, p. 2501
	3	3	IV, p. 106	III, p. 1194
242	1	6	XII, p. 391	VIII, p. 3681
249	—	26	III, p. 25	III, p. 641
250	—	11-12	I, p. 70	II, p. 70
324	fn.	10	I, pp. 39-44	II, pp. 39-44